SCREAMING EAGLE GLIDERS

Contents

CHAPTER 1

Training

MAY 7, 1942, WAS A TYPICAL SPRING DAY at Camp Claiborne, Louisiana. The weather was so warm and humid from an earlier rain that the uniformed men of the 82nd Infantry Division gathered for a special assembly had to wear raincoats to keep dry. Over 14,000 soldiers were to be officially reactivated into the division. Its colors had been in storage since the post–World War I demobilization in 1919.

Loudspeakers were mounted high on towers positioned throughout the area so that every soldier could hear what was going to be said from the elevated wooden stage before them. A keynote speaker was en route. The officers were excited, for this was going to be a big day, even for their new commander, Maj. Gen. Omar Bradley.

The much-anticipated speaker who caused this stir was Medal of Honor recipient Alvin York of World War I fame. The former Tennessee sergeant of the 82nd "All American" Infantry Division had been made famous by the motion picture industry's depiction of his life and exploits in the 1941 movie *Sergeant York* starring Gary Cooper as York.

York arrived late, stepped up to the microphone, and began. His fourteen-minute speech, along with the others made that day, was being broadcast over the New Orleans radio station WWLS to the outlying areas of Louisiana. A tall, husky man who wore a dark suit and tie and sported a gray fedora, he read his speech with his right hand thrust into his coat pocket. York commanded attention from everyone present, even though there were about twenty dignitaries with him and the day was hot and humid. (Some 321st Field Artillery Battalion members remembered that the ranks thinned as men passed out while in formation, "dropping like flies." Stretcher-bearers and ambulances were kept busy

Camp Claiborne. The 321st Battalion's sign, prior to the division's split into two airborne divisions. STEPHENS/DETTORE

attending to those who fell out and transporting them to the infirmary.)

York told the troops that they would do better in battle than his 82nd Division of old had in France years earlier in World War I. He spoke of the division's glorious history, sharing a few personal anecdotes from that war. He said—in between laughter, whistling, and applause—"Freedom is not a thing you can win once and for all. We never owned freedom; we only got a lease on it." He spoke about the positive attributes of the American soldier over the lies told about them by the enemy, and said that the boys of '42 were better trained and equipped than any other army before them. Maj. Alvin York would not be disappointed by what these soldiers would accomplish.

Following the speech, General Bradley quizzed York on which rifle skills had proved to be most effective while he was overseas during the war. York replied that close-up shooting, between 25 and 50 yards, was an important skill to have. Bradley ordered that a rudimentary course of small targets be placed throughout the woods at the camp. Soldiers then walked through the woods and fired quickly at the various targets. After observing this walk-through firing session, both leaders were impressed, York with the semiautomatic Garand rifle and Bradley with the accuracy that could be achieved while on the move. (York reportedly said that if the Garand rifle had been available to him during the First World War, none of the Germans would have escaped him in the Argonne.) The results of this demonstration convinced Bradley to change what was being taught on the army rifle ranges across the country, rather than just instructing soldiers in long-range static shooting.

While at Camp Claiborne, the men of the 321st Field Artillery Battalion were trained to be soldiers. Here, they got their first patch to sew on their uniform shoulders: a factory-fresh 82nd "All American" patch. Nobody even thought of an airborne tab.

Camp Claiborne, May 1942. About fifty men and their coaches stand on part of the firing line at the rifle range. The entire line could accommodate 300 soldiers. The men at the rack are selecting rifles for the next firing order. STEPHENS/DETTORE

Camp Claiborne. Pvt. Norman Deethardt wearing the 82nd Infantry Division patch prior to the division being split in two and designated as airborne. STEPHENS/DETTORE

Camp Claiborne. Cpl. Harvey Baker in a photo studio with his tailor-applied 82nd Infantry Division patch. BAKER FAMILY

The mostly green troops learned that the whistle at 5:45 A.M. meant to fall out for roll call in exactly ten minutes. The weather changed so quickly that no one knew what to expect. At times it appeared to rain from cloudless skies. It was drill, drill, and more drill. The art of saluting was perfected, and the men learned to not forget to say "Sir" to the officers. The on-the-hour words "take a break" were most welcome.

Early on, these new soldiers had an important army philosophy to remember, one they were told over and over again: they could be easily replaced, but their hardware could not be. It appeared to these fresh recruits that their lives came in second, with equipment being more valuable.

After a few weeks, the first 5-mile hike was made to a gravel pit outside the camp. Even though an ambulance was trailing the battalion for the stragglers who couldn't make it, the men preferred the blisters. No one wanted to look weak. That night laughter could be heard for quite a distance from a party at the gravel pit. Those who were already exhausted pitched their pup tents and went to sleep instead.

The bugs were plentiful and bloodthirsty; the only way to keep them off was to bathe in kerosene. The chiggers were especially bad; they worked their way under the soldiers' canvas leggings, making it almost impossible to kill them during a hike.

Pvt. Paul Miho (HQ) from Cleveland, Ohio, was a baseball player who played in the minor leagues.

Camp Claiborne. Fresh recruits resting after a march. STEPHENS/DETTORE

Camp Claiborne. 321st soldiers entertaining themselves at the gravel pit after a long march. PERKINS

He soon found himself on "special duty," which meant his primary function was to play ball. The battalion was getting ready for a 25-mile road hike when Capt. Samuel Williams saw Miho in formation. He yelled to the noncommissioned officer in charge, "What the hell you doing with my ball players?" The order was given: "All ball players fall out." The sergeant in charge of the run told Miho, "I'll catch up to you later."

A championship game was coming up: the 319th versus the 321st. At the time, the 321st was part of the 82nd Infantry Division, and its commanding officer, Col. John Works, was an avid baseball fan. He told his team that if they won the game, they could go home that afternoon on furlough. It was a blowout. By the sixth inning, it was 19–1 in favor of the 321st. The commanding officer of the 319th came out to the field and said, "Cease fire." The game was over, and everyone in the 321st was

Camp Claiborne. Pvt. Robert Wyatt (left) and Pvt. Clyde True (right). TRUE

Camp Claiborne. The 82nd Infantry Division, 321st Field Artillery, commander Col. John Works drinking beer from a ceremonial helmet at the gravel pit. DUNLAP/DETTORE

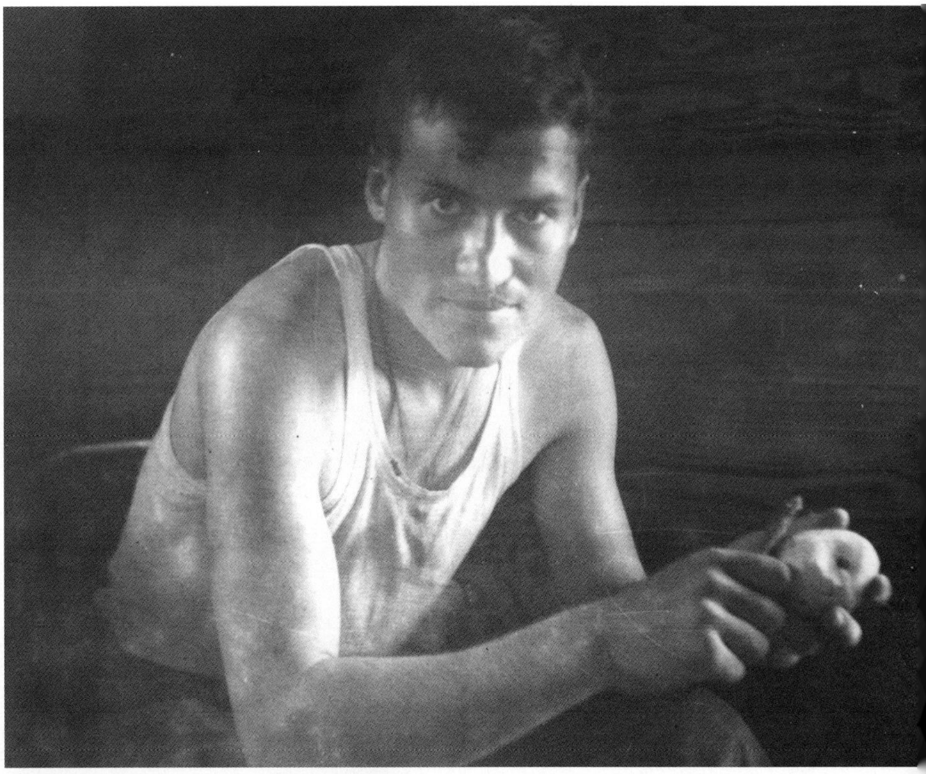

Camp Claiborne. Pvt. Burdette Wilkinson on kitchen police duty. WILKINSON FAMILY

Camp Claiborne. From left to right: Capt. Harry Dunlap, Capt. Frederic King, and Maj. John Tyler. DUNLAP/DETTORE

pleased. However, the sergeant did catch up to Miho after the furlough. Miho was assigned to kitchen police duty, guard duty, and every other unpleasant duty imaginable.

After a few months of training, artillery familiarization with the vintage French-manufactured 155mm howitzers commenced. All the intricacies of the gun were studied, including getting it into position and simulating fire. The forward observers practiced correcting fire by using a 37mm gun mounted on the 155mm barrel. It was far cheaper to fire the smaller 37mm ammunition; the 155mm was much larger and vastly more expensive, even though it was produced during the First World War.

Camp Claiborne. Several shots of 155mm French howitzers used in training. STEPHENS/DETTORE

Camp Claiborne. Private Wilkinson using a hand-powered generator. WILKINSON FAMILY

Camp Claiborne. The loading crew of a 155mm howitzer. STEPHENS/DETTORE

Camp Claiborne. An extremely dangerous 155mm unexploded projectile (dud) lying in the training area. STEPHENS/DETTORE

Camp Claiborne, June 15, 1942. Tents being changed to hutments for the men of Headquarters Battery, 321st Field Artillery. WILKINSON FAMILY

During this time, the phrase "cannoneer hop" became part of the lexicon of the artillerymen of the 321st. The idea was simple: each soldier was trained in all the preparing and firing positions for the artillery piece. In case of an emergency, the gun could be sighted, loaded, and fired by just a few men as long as everyone on the gun crew was trained for every position. While the gun was being prepared during training, an officer would pull a soldier from the crew who then pretended to be wounded. The officer would yell "Cannoneer hop!" and everyone would change positions at the gun and continue to ready for fire.

The tar-papered barracks at Camp Claiborne were better than pyramidal tents and lent themselves to a more proper inspection. Pvt. Charles Tewkesbury of Detroit, Michigan, a fresh arrival, asked Private Deethardt how to get ahead; he was one of the privates who reached for quick advancement. Deethardt advised him that proper military etiquette must be followed during the barrack inspection performed by Colonel Works and his aide. If Tewkesbury knew what to say and when to say it, the colonel would surely take notice of his military knowledge and promote him.

Inspection day arrived. Colonel Works and his orderly stepped into the barracks that morning at the appointed time. Tewkesbury was on the lookout for them. He raced from his bunk to the door inside the hut and stood perfectly erect. As soon as Works and his aide stepped inside the door, Tewkesbury barked out his prepared command in a booming voice: "At ease!" The stunned colonel stopped dead in his tracks, made an abrupt about-face, and exited the building without saying a word, his bewildered aide walking briskly behind him. When it was safe to do so, the men roared in laughter. Tewkesbury found out rather quickly just why they did so. The correct command was "attention," commonly pronounced "ten hut." However, the episode did not deter him

Camp Claiborne. The 82nd Infantry Division (not yet airborne) open-air theater. Note the massive backdrop painting of a jeep.
STEPHENS/DETTORE

Camp Claiborne or Fort Bragg. Young Abe, the 321st's American bald eagle mascot and soon-to-be 101st Airborne Division mascot. STEPHENS/DETTORE

from his goal of attaining recognition. He was later transferred to the 907th Glider Field Artillery (GFA) Battalion.

Pvt. Leo "Fritz" Corrigan (HQ) was from Cleveland, Ohio, and operated the radio at the Fire Direction and Control (FDC) while on the 155mm gun range. A forward observer requested one round to be fired. Colonel Works, resplendent in his cavalry uniform, was standing alone in back of the guns, watching the operation. (He was often referred to as "Seldom" Works by his officers and their wives.) Corrigan erroneously asked the battery to fire six guns simultaneously. The concussion knocked Works flat on his back, to Corrigan's horror. Despite the mistake, Corrigan completed his radio training and was made corporal, later becoming Capt. Samuel Skinner's radio operator and jeep driver.

Maj. Edward Carmichael, the commander of the Headquarters and Service Batteries, was presented with a mascot for the 321st while at Camp Claiborne: an American bald eagle that had been captured in Wisconsin years earlier by the Wisconsin State Game Farm. (Carmichael was a Wisconsin native, having served there in the National Guard.) The eagle was named "Young Abe" and quickly became a fixture in the division. As mascots go, this eagle was held in high regard by the men of the 321st. During a formal ceremony in November 1942 at Fort Bragg, the men decided that Young Abe was the rightful mascot of the newly formed 101st Airborne Division. The eagle was presented to Gen. William Lee in a formal presentation also broadcast over the military radio system. Men were detailed to take great care of the bird; these caretakers were carefully chosen from the ranks of the 321st.

Young Abe's cage was opposite the Divisional Artillery Headquarters (DivArty) at the upper corner of the division's drill field. In a letter written a few years after the war, Sgt. Nelson Kopacka (B Battery) of Cleveland, Ohio, wrote, "General McAuliffe after his morning tour of the area would stay and talk to

Young Abe every day. We in the 321 could see the two together every morning; we had the upper drill area. What they talked about no one knows except he and the bird."

In early July 1943, the 321st was away from Fort Bragg participating in the Tennessee maneuvers, putting their newly formed skills into action. Sergeant Kopacka was detailed to take care of Young Abe. The eagle died while in his care. Rumors circulated as to the cause of Young Abe's demise, ranging from a disgruntled soldier, poisoning because of an airborne divisional rivalry, and even old age.

Sergeant Kopacka continued in his letter:

> I know the records show the cause of death of Young Abe on July 6, 1943 as unknown. I believe now as I did then that it was a respiratory failure. When the division left Bragg for the Tennessee maneuvers I was left behind as acting First Sergeant of the casual company to pick up 101 A/B men being discharged from the base hospital and lock up replacements that were being shipped in from other outfits [who] were given the choice of volunteering for airborne training or the stockade.
>
> Along with this I inherited the care of feeding Young Abe, with the instructions that he be fed diced raw beef, diced bread and fresh water once a day. If the meat was too chunky and anything but beef, he refused to eat. [The] Post Quartermaster refused me beef rations for Abe because somebody forgot to authorize a beef ration for him before they left for Tennessee. We were eating the prevalent food of . . . every day, goat meat, and Abe refused it.
>
> For a time I scrounged beef from the 3 mess halls, and what I got must have been the private supply of the mess Sergeants, as it ran out and [I] was down to opening up C ration cans and picking out the pieces of beef.
>
> The evening previous to his death there was one helluva wind and rain storm and the next morning the sun came out hot and strong. The air was so heavy that it was almost impossible to breath. A person literally had to gasp for air. Well, Young Abe was from the cool clear climate of the Wisconsin woods and the job of attempting to breathe in the suffocating atmosphere was just too much for him—he collapsed.

When a pass was given, some of the men went to Alexandria, Louisiana, or other small towns in the area. Another place to go was just outside camp. It was called "boom town," a strip of beer joints and carnival-style concessions. Since it had girls and alcohol, this collection of rip-off joints was tolerated and much frequented by the soldiers from Camp Claiborne. Quite a few of the men returned to camp broke but happy.

Here at boom town, Private Deethardt—known as the B Battery funnyman—hatched an idea. One of the youngest soldiers, who was straight from the farm, kept complaining that he was a virgin and was

Camp Claiborne. The honky-tonk strip outside camp.
STEPHENS/DETTORE

anxious to lose that title. All he talked about was getting a girl. Deethardt knew the local prostitutes made their way to a pond situated on the camp grounds and hosted many parties, especially on payday weekends. Pay was only distributed once a month. It wasn't much for a lowly private, who received only $21 each payday. Many of the men had to have money sent to them from home. In time, the money would flow in the other direction.

Deethardt took donations from the other men in his battery to hire a certain prostitute some were familiar with and to give her to a certain well-known, shy farm boy. Five dollars was the going rate. All were expecting some tall tales after the encounter; they thought the stories would be worth every penny to hear.

The local girl took the challenge and the $5 to break in a new customer. She was delighted to learn the young soldier was a virgin, and she planned to have some fun with him because of it. The two got together at the pond in the evening, but it didn't turn out the way she thought it would. When she saw Deethardt again, she set him straight. "You told me that boy was a virgin, and if he was, so am I!" she said. She went on to tell him that the boy was no stranger to a woman and that he about wore her out to death; if Deethardt knew of any other virgins in camp, she wasn't interested. According to Deethardt, she told him, "It was the hardest I ever worked for a few dollars, and I never want that boy for a customer again!" The young soldier from the farm never said much of the encounter, to the dismay of his benefactors.

In the early days of 1942, a series of tests were given to army divisions across the country. The War Department needed airborne divisions, and the U.S. Army didn't have any. The top brass kept this desire secret from the men of the 82nd Infantry Division.

The camp was spit-polished to the maximum in anticipation of the officers from Corps headquarters. The Headquarters, A, B, and C Batteries of the

Camp Claiborne, May 9, 1942. Soldiers awaiting buses to leave camp on a Saturday afternoon. WILKINSON FAMILY

Camp Claiborne. Carrier pigeons were used early in 321st communications training but not in combat. WILKINSON FAMILY

321st, along with the rest of the 82nd, were put into testing when the officers arrived. An inspection officer asked one of the men from a firing battery a rehearsed question: What is in the recoil of your gun? "The cannonier [*sic*] gave the reply, 'Nitroglycerin, Sir.' The officer screwed up his face and wrote something down in his little book. Only then did the Sad [sack] realize that he should have said nitrogen."[1]

When the test scores were compared across the country, the 82nd scored the highest of all the Triangular Divisions in the Corps. The 321st did better than any other artillery battalion in the division, with 84.5 percent in all-around efficiency. The division average was 82.2 percent. The rookie artillerymen took pride in this due to the fact they only had seventeen weeks of training compared to other divisions who had trained for at least a year.

The 321st scored the second highest of all the battalions in Division Artillery. Official records for the 321st list the arrest rate as the second lowest in the division: three arrests out of a total of 328 for the division in a six-month period, and seven AWOLs (absent without leave) out of a division-wide total of fifty-six. (Venereal disease rate was one of the lowest in the division, at 3.5 percent.)

Capt. Edward L. Carmichael of Hudson, Wisconsin, was one of twenty-eight officers of the 82nd Infantry Division battery commanders of Group 1, 2nd Section. He had assumed command of the 321st on August 16, 1942, and was promoted to lieutenant colonel when it became part of the 101st Airborne Division.

> The day came and when we were assembled in front of Division Headquarters, General Griswold, Fifth Corps Commander, praised the division for its brilliant performance in the Corps tests. When he had finished speaking, General Matthew B. Ridgway, the Commander of the 82nd, took his position on the speakers' platform and told us, "Due to the extraordinary

Camp Claiborne, August 15, 1942. The first—and last—review of the 82nd Infantry Division prior to its being split.

demonstration of ability and efficiency in our Corps tests, I have the proud pleasure of announcing the War Department's decision that the 82nd Division has been given the signal [*sic*, single] honor of becoming the two first Airborne Divisions of the Army of the United States!" After this statement, there was a silence that could have been cut with a knife. Suddenly, its significance dawned on the men. Such a rousing cheer as the one that went up was never heard before.

All the fellows had illusions of flying everywhere they went. Even to Alexandria [Louisiana], I guess. We also gathered from the speech that we were definitely on the top side of the Army. We were destined to write the book on Airborne Training and Battle Tactics.

It was decided which Infantry Regiments and which Artillery Battalions should make up the two new Airborne Divisions—the 82nd and the 101st.[2]

Lt. Samuel Skinner wrote in an undated diary entry:

> Nothing much happened until one day in August [when] we had a Div Review. And this is the time that Gen Ridgeway [*sic*], who had just replaced Gen Bradley, told us that he had some great news for us. It happened that we had just undergone an army test and came out first, so because of this we were selected. Gen Ridgeway [*sic*] told us that we were the ones chosen for two new airborne divisions. In other words, we had all been made airborne. Everybody applauded and whistled and then the next day began thinking about it.
>
> This meant that we would have to very physically fit and be able to undergo long strenuous marches. We began to march and have been marching ever since. You would have thought we were old-time infantry men—they didn't have anything on us.

Gen. William C. Lee made his first appearance at this review; he and General Ridgway both took the salute of the troops marching by the review stand. A few days later, on August 19, 1942, Lee, a World War I veteran, spoke at another formation—this time, it was his troops. He was presented as the new commander of the 101st Airborne Division.

The 321st battalion history, *Mission Accomplished*, written just after the war ended, recorded General Lee as having said, "Men you have a destiny."[3] What he actually said, in part, as recorded in General Lee's issued General Order #5, dated August 19, 1942, was that the 101st "has no history, but it has a rendezvous with destiny."

This phrase turned out to be famous and most intuitive, but it actually originated elsewhere. Years earlier, President Franklin D. Roosevelt said it during a speech at Franklin Field, Philadelphia, on June 27, 1936. The president had just accepted his party nomination to run for a second term, and the opposition was questioning the wisdom of his Democratic party's platform of the New Deal. In front of a crowd of 100,000 people, Roosevelt said, "To some generations much is given. Of other generations much is expected. This generation of Americans has a rendezvous with destiny." Six years later, General Lee repeated in part those exact words.

Camp Claiborne. Pvt. Jesse Hopkins with his newly issued M1 carbine. STEPHENS/DETTORE

On September 1, a few weeks after the review, Gen. Anthony McAuliffe, in charge of the artillery, secured the airborne rocker tab for the newly formed airborne divisions and left Washington, D.C., for Camp Claiborne, Louisiana.

The artillerymen of the 321st had no choice: they were now glider field artillery. (The paratroopers were volunteers, quite unlike the glider riders.) At first, these soldiers believed that being in an airborne division was an easy way of getting from place to place—they would be traveling first class via airplanes. That line of thinking diminished when the 5-mile hikes of old turned into 10-mile hikes or more. No more hiking on the back of a truck—it was all done on foot. The 155mm guns were turned in, and 105mm howitzers were used instead for practice and drill.

Night marches were cross-country all over southern Louisiana through swamps and any other hazardous terrain that could be located. Day marches would finish with a 500-yard obstacle course consisting of walls to climb, ditches and a series of chest-high fences to jump, and barbed wire to navigate through. A stream with wooden poles sunk into the streambed doubled as steps to cross. Lastly came a stream of twenty feet or more that could only be crossed by swinging on a rope. That was the first half of the course. It repeated itself for the last 250 yards.

Rumor was the 101st was going to move, but to where was supposed to be a guarded secret. Just about everyone had heard one place or another, but one rumor kept surfacing: Fort Bragg, North Carolina, which seemed to be a logical conclusion because the division's cadre was from there. On September 16, 1942, a small contingent of soldiers left Camp Claiborne and flew to Fort Bragg. This advance party sorted out the details to move the rest of the 101st Division there.

Camp Claiborne. Signage displaying the split of the 82nd Infantry Division into two airborne divisions. Note the 101st does not have its iconic eagle symbol yet. STEPHENS/DETTORE

Camp Claiborne. Unknown soldiers in front of the 321st glider sign. Note the lack of an airborne-designated rocker, which would come later. STEPHENS/DETTORE

Camp Claiborne. Cpl. Harvey Baker hamming it up for the camera on the obstacle course, wearing his GI-issued suntans. BAKER FAMILY

Left: Camp Claiborne. An unknown soldier alongside a 327th Headquarters sign, pointing to the word "Glider." FULTON/DETTORE

In the waning days of September, the 321st turned in their 155s for the last time and were issued additional ¼-ton trucks (jeeps), which were loaded onto railroad flatcars. The drivers acted as guards, and for four days these men were out on the flatcars, exposed to the black cinders of the coal-powered locomotives and the elements of Mother Nature.

At Westfield, Alabama, several flatcars derailed, injuring several of the men. The cars were put back on the track, and the advance move of equipment continued. The train contained forty flatcars and nine Pullmans, which spent most of their time paused on sidings. The going was so slow, it was decided to use two locomotives to speed up the move.

A few days later, the remainder of the battalion was moved by passenger train to the still top-secret

In September 1942, outside the small town of Abingdon, Illinois, a family farm was about to suffer. The Wynkoop family farmed a 160-acre piece of land, raised crops, and owned a small herd of milking cows. The work was manual; muscles were the machines that got things done. There were no tractors; horses did the plowing and brought the crops in each fall, just as most ordinary small family farms operated throughout the country. Large families made the work easier, so the bigger the better. There were nine Wynkoop kids helping their father, William, and mother, Betsy.

The Wynkoop farm unraveled because of the war. William was not well and depended on his children to do the chores. But five of the nine children were called to serve their country; four boys and one girl put on uniforms and left the farm, their talents and physical labor becoming part of the war machine. The few siblings left behind could not keep the farm going. It was eventually lost, and the remainder of the family moved into town.

One of the sons, Dwayne Wynkoop, found himself in the 101st Airborne, assigned to the 321st Glider Field Artillery Battalion as a radio operator. He survived the war, returned home, and tried to settle in. He went to work for a company that made porcelain toilets and sinks, but the work was not for him—not now. He joined the air force, taking up and refining his old skills as a radioman. After serving in Korea, Vietnam, and (secretly) Laos, Wynkoop retired after twenty-six years as a master sergeant. Once off the farm, he never returned to that type of work. Like most soldiers of his generation, he spoke little of his time in Europe. ■

location of their new camp. All the men were strictly forbidden to talk to anyone they might encounter at any of the stops. If there were any doubts as to where they were going when the troops were loading, those doubts ceased when they started to roll down the tracks. The cadre, all former Fort Bragg men, kept mentioning what a great place Bragg was. If anyone doubted the final destination, he just wasn't listening.

The boys of the 321st were underwhelmed when they arrived at Fort Bragg, after how much their cadre had talked it up. They'd been told Bragg was a lovely place, not like the sun-drenched, muggy, dusty, and bug-infested grounds of Camp Claiborne. But all of that was a lie.

After about a week, the men received the artillery pieces they would train on: the time-tested 75mm pack howitzer. The gun looked like a toy compared to the 155s the artillerymen had been using, and the wooden-spoked wheels didn't add a look of ferocity. In time, however, the men would move beyond feeling slighted for being assigned such a small howitzer, which they called a "pea shooter."

The beauty of the 75mm pack howitzer was that it disassembled into manageable pieces for ease of transportation. It could be broken down into seven pieces for mule transport (hence the name "pack"), or divided into nine pieces, including ammunition, for parachute drops. Developed in the 1920s in the United States, it weighed 1,440 pounds, with an accurate range of 28,860 yards or approximately 5.5 miles. The barrel's life expectancy was for 20,000 rounds of ammunition fired through it.

Eventually the battalion had the opportunity to train with the 75mm pack howitzers. Initially no one could locate the manuals for the guns, but the division's can-do spirit enabled them to overcome this problem by trial and error. After it was all figured out, somebody finally found the manuals.

These guns were known to be battle-tested and accurate but, in their current configurations, not fit for modern times. Pvt. Norman Deethardt (B Battery), from Cincinnati, Ohio, observed this firsthand. A small convoy of six jeeps was towing the 75mm pack howitzers down a hard-packed road when they all came to a stop. As Deethardt approached, he noticed the occupants of the jeeps were standing out on the road and staring at the guns. The guns had wooden spoke wheels, designed to be towed by horses at naturally slow speeds. Unaware of this, the

Camp Claiborne brig. From left to right: Cpl. Nelson Kopacka, Lt. Sam Skinner, and an unidentified provost sergeant. KOPACKA FAMILY

Camp Claiborne. The 101st Division brig. KOPACKA FAMILY

newly drafted drivers had towed the howitzers at a normal jeep speed of 40 mph, causing the greased hubs of the wooden wheels to overheat and disintegrate. The end result was a long line of five of the six guns sitting on their chassis, resting on the pavement, the spokes splintered and strewn about like wooden matchsticks. Deethardt remarked it was a comical sight, though not for the jeep drivers. Pneumatic tires with steel rims were soon forthcoming out of modern necessity.

On December 11, 1942, the 321st was marched over to Pope Field at Fort Bragg in order to view a

Captain Murphy would later bring General Pratt into Normandy by glider. The CG-4A was fitted with a steel plate on its underside, making it unwieldy to fly even by the best of glider pilots. Upon landing, Pratt was killed, along with the copilot. General Taylor had promised Pratt that on the next mission he would go in by glider and Pratt could parachute in. Taylor felt no obligation to go into Holland by glider. ■

Battery Street at Fort Bragg.
STEPHENS/DETTORE

Fort Bragg. A 75mm pack howitzer with wooden spoke wheels. STEPHENS/DETTORE

Fort Bragg. A 75mm pack howitzer with newly acquired pneumatic tires. STEPHENS/DETTORE

Waco CG-4A glider in the air. It was sturdy enough for some fancy air maneuvers. The man performing the demonstration was the famous stunt flyer Capt. Mike Murphy. The men were put at ease, now knowing the capabilities of aircraft constructed of a tubular steel structure, with wings framed out of wood, and the body skinned in a stiff, thin, canvaslike fabric.

The demonstration was only a one-day affair, but that was enough to instill the confidence needed to trust their tethered gliders while being towed to the fields of war. Initially the glider riders were given parachutes during training, but the folly of that idea was soon realized, in part because it was impossible to reach the required altitude for a successful deployment of the chute.

On one of these training days, the glidermen met Hollywood actor John "Jackie" Coogan, who was now a glider pilot. As the soldiers stood around watching glider landings, one craft came down hard on the runway, damaging a wing and spinning into parked gliders. When the pilot, Coogan, got out and inspected it, he found the left wheel strut was damaged, as were a couple of the parked CG-4As. A colonel came out to view the damage, and Coogan was overheard telling the officer that he was done flying gliders. The actor was known for his dislike for most officers. (Coogan also was known for his coarse talk. When he met someone, he liked to say, "Shake the hand that shakes the cock that screwed Betty Grable." They were briefly married before she became a Hollywood sensation.) The colonel became angry and told Coogan, "You'll fly what we tell you to fly."

Flight Officer (F/O) Coogan would become an excellent pilot, flying CG-4As in Burma and India with the 1st Air Commandos. In late 1944, he was brought back to the States for a war bond drive, along with a few other pilots.

It would take until June 2, 1944, for the army to determine what made a soldier a qualified glider rider. On this date, the War Department published Circular 220, which stated that a soldier who had satisfactorily completed the course of instruction in knots and lashing, loading organizational equipment in airplanes and gliders, and safe landing principles, and had participated in at least two glider flights under tactical or simulated tactical conditions was

Glider landings during training.

therefore rated "a qualified gliderman in the Army of The United States and is entitled to wear the glider qualification badge."

While at Laurinburg–Maxton Airfield in North Carolina, the training never ceased. It would be a two-month ordeal. The first task to master was learning the tie-down knots used for securing payloads in the glider; the baker bowline and the double half-hitch were two of the most favored. The men were timed and allowed twenty minutes to fully load a glider, figure out the center of gravity, and tie down the payloads. Training demanded that the entire process be done in complete darkness and silence.

To get the men up to airborne standards, there were plenty of hikes, overnight field problems, and even mock three-day battles. The glidermen were mentally and physically fatigued.

On one of the practice glider flights, a soldier had to relieve himself. Before anyone knew what was happening, he had kicked a hole in the side of the glider. The rest of the glider riders yelled at the soldier for doing such a stupid thing, fearful that the thin-skinned glider was now going to peel off in flight. To their immense relief, it did not.

PUTTING IRON ON THE TARGET*

When the 75mm pack howitzers went into position, two aiming sticks were lined up in front of each gun. Wire was laid from each gun to a central switchboard; the battery executive had the coordinates of the gun position and direction of fire. The base piece (the third gun section for a six-gun battery) was in position at the battery center, which was located at the coordinates. The aiming circle was set in a position from which it could be seen by the crews of the pieces. The executive aligned the aiming circles in the direction of fire, sighted on the base piece, and commanded, "Number 3, aiming point this instrument." The gunner of the #3 howitzer responded, "Aiming point identified." The exec then read an angle to #3. The gunner set this angle on his sight and traversed the tube (barrel) and/or shifted the trails until the vertical crosshair of the panoramic telescope was on the eyepiece of the aiming circle. While #3 was sighting on the exec's aiming circle, the exec read an angle to each of the other howitzers. This procedure was continued until all howitzers were laid in the direction of fire.

The forward observer had several methods by which he could indicate the location of the target. He knew his location on the map and estimated the target's location on the map (not always as easy as it sounds). One method by which he could bring fire on a target was as follows:

FO: Kansas 12, this is Kansas 63, fire mission, over.

FDC: Kansas 63, this is Kansas 12, send your mission, over.

FO: Base point is 600 right, 30 below, short, three mortars firing, will adjust, over.

FDC: Base point is 600 right, 30 below, short, three mortars firing, will adjust.

Message to observer: Fuse quick, concentration 20, Baker, when ready. (The concentration number would be recorded for possible future use. If the observer had a subsequent target on or in the vicinity, the concentration number would be used to locate the target.)

FDC: On the way, over.

FO: On the way, out.

FO: 100 left, 400 short, over.

FDC: 100 left, 400 short, out.

FDC: On the way, over.

FO: 50 right, 200 over, over.

FDC: 50 right, 200 over, out.

FDC: On the way, over.

FO: On the way, out.

FO: 100 short, fire for effect, over.

FDC: Baker firing for effect, over.

FO: Baker firing for effect, out.

FO: Range correct. Repeat fire for effect, out.

FDC: Range correct, repeat fire for effect, over.

FDC: Baker firing for effect, over.

FO: Baker firing for effect, out.

FO: End of mission, mortars neutralized, over.

FDC: End of mission, mortars neutralized, over.

FO: Roger, out.

At the FDC (either battery or battalion), the target was plotted, the range and deflection were measured, and the difference in altitude between the guns and the target was determined. The fire direction officer (FDO) decided what fuse to use, what charge (and number of powder bags), and how many rounds would be fired in "fire for effect." These data were used as the basis for the fire command to the guns.

The FDC transmitted a message to the forward observer, informing him that the battery would fire fuse quick, three rounds in effect, and the concentration number.

The battery exec decided which piece (or sometimes two pieces) would be the adjusting piece and indicated that in his command, which he then sent back to the battery: "Battery adjust, one round, shell

*Written by former Sgt. William Stone, B Battery forward observer.

HE, charge 3, deflection 2910, site plus 4, elevation 267."

The howitzer section chief repeated the commands to his section. The powder man cut the charge (powder bags). The number-one man set the deflection and traversed or shifted the trail until the vertical crosshair of the sight was aligned on the aiming sticks. The gunner set the arithmetic sum of the sight and elevation on his own sight, and elevated or depressed the tube until the bubbles on his set were leveled. (The chief of section might check the quadrant—site plus elevation—with his own quadrant.) When the elevation was announced, the number-two man rammed the round into the breech and closed the breechblock. When his section was ready, the chief told the battery exec, "Number three ready." The exec then commanded, "Number three, fire."

The exec commanded the battery, "Battery three rounds, deflection 2920, elevation 259." When all pieces had reported "ready," the exec commanded, "FIRE." When all rounds had been fired, the exec reported to the FDC, "Baker rounds complete."

The phone would ring at the #3 gun back at the gun position. (At night, if the gunner corporal was going to sleep, he used the phone as a headrest so that he would be sure to hear the FDC ringing the gun section for a fire mission.) The corporal would grab the receiver, push the button, and say, "Number three." The battery executive officer or recorder would reply, "Number three adjust." Normally, the #3 gun adjusted for the battery's six guns. The operator continued, "Shell HE, charge three," meaning three bags of gunpowder charges were to be used out of the four packed in the shell casing. The four bags of gunpowder were stitched together with a cotton thread in a daisy-chain fashion. In this case, one bag was removed by cutting the cotton thread, using the edge of the shell casing as the knife.

The next command was, "Base deflection right 140, elevation 256." The gunner corporal would repeat the commands to his gun crew. If it was low-light conditions, a member would light the hooded lights (flashlights) on the aiming sticks. Another member would adjust the sights and elevation on the pack howitzer. Next, the iron trail bar would be used to shift the trail of the gun; for this fire mission, it would be about 14 inches to the right, or 1 inch for 10 mills of deflection.

After the powder bags were cut, they would be pushed into the brass shell casing and the projectile would be inserted on top of them. An adjustment would be made on the aiming light for elevation and then leveling the bubble. The 75mm round would be loaded into the breech, and the loader would say, "Ready." After the sight adjustments were completed, the loader would say, "Set."

The gunner corporal would depress the button on his handset receiver and report to the executive officer, "Number three," raising his arm. If this gun was the only one firing, the FDC would say, "Number three, fire." The corporal would repeat the order and drop his arm. The loader would yank the lanyard, firing the howitzer. At this time, the corporal would depress the button on the phone again and say, "On the way."

Fort Bragg. A partial gun crew mimicking "ready to fire" with the appropriate hand signal. STEPHENS/DETTORE

DEVELOPMENT, PRODUCTION, AND USE OF THE CG-4A GLIDER, 1941–45*

In late February 1941, Gen. Henry "Hap" Arnold instructed Wright Field engineers to develop design criteria for large gliders. By March, requests were sent to eleven companies, asking that they submit glider designs based on those criteria. There were a few caveats: Glider production was not to interfere with powered aircraft production, and thus the design and manufacture were not to use aluminum, which was prioritized for use in powered aircraft only. The glider manufacturers also were not to be currently involved in building powered aircraft. There were to be two sizes or capacities: eight-place and fifteen-place.

Of the eleven companies, only four responded with proposed designs, which were designated "cargo glider" (CG) and numbered one (CG-1) through eight (CG-8). The odd numbers were eight-place gliders, and the even numbers were fifteen-place. Two of the companies—Frankfort Sailplane Company of Missouri and Illinois and Bowlus Sailplane Company of California—were soaring glider producers, one a successful bi-wing power plane producer and the other a wooden streetcar manufacturer.

The contracts called for two flight test articles (an "article" was a contracted item) and one stress test article. Of the flight articles, designated "X" models, the XCG-1, XCG-2, and XCG-6 designs were not produced. The XCG-5 failed the stress tests, and the XCG-7 and XCG-8 were deemed as not meeting the design requirements. Waco of Troy, Ohio, delivered the only design that passed both the stress tests and flight tests: the XCG-3. Its flight tests resulted in a redesign of the cockpit and troop entry area, morphing the glider from an eight-place into a nine-place and changing its production designation to CG-3A. Only 100 CG-3A were delivered before production was canceled because the glider was deemed to not be of great enough capacity.

General Arnold had expressed a desire to have a jeep ($^1/_4$-ton truck) with wings that could carry two men and arms, land behind enemy lines, shed its wings, and drive off as a fighting unit. The XCG-4 Waco design did just that. It was large enough to carry a jeep, and the nose (cockpit) of the glider was hinged at the top and could swing up and out of the way to allow equipment to be quickly loaded and unloaded. Additionally, the jeep could be attached to a steel cable that, when the jeep was moved forward out of the glider, would raise the glider's nose; a release mechanism would disconnect the cable when the jeep had cleared the glider. This system worked only when the load had motive power. The $^3/_{32}$-inch, 5-ply, plywood floor could carry upward of 5 pounds per square inch. The strong, steel tube frame was the same construction that had been used for powered aircraft before aluminum (which, of course, was not to be used for glider production). The wings were $^3/_{32}$-inch mahogany, plywood-covered, wood-rib construction. The front spar wings and fuselage were covered with aircraft fabric (often incorrectly described as canvas). Unfortunately, the fabric and plywood provided no more protection to the troops than did the thin aluminum skin used on powered aircraft. The addition of a dorsal fin and other modifications to the XCG-4 changed its production designation to CG-4A.

The wingspan of the CG-4A was 83 feet, 8 inches; the chord was 10 feet, 6 inches, and the fuselage was 48 feet, $4^5/_8$ inches long. In addition to the cockpit/nose opening, on each side of the fuselage, aft of the nose and near the seat of the jeep, was a triangular escape hatch; at the rear of the cargo section, on each side, was a hinged door for troop entry. A quick-release opening in the top of the cargo section was experimented with but never put into production.

The original design called for two radios, one forward and one aft, both to be removed by the troops upon exiting. This was changed to one radio system known as the SCR-585, which was eliminated by the middle of 1944 and replaced by the interphone, wire-on-the-towline system. Despite attempts to

*This section written by Charles L. Day.

GLIDER LOAD WEIGHTS	
Crew, pilot, and copilot	200 pounds each (includes weapons)
Troopers	240 pounds each, 13 soldiers maximum (includes weapons and equipment)
Jeep (1/4-ton truck)	2,366 pounds
37mm antitank gun	975 pounds
75mm pack howitzer	1,355 pounds
24 rounds for 75mm pack howitzer	521 pounds
105mm narrow-carriage, short-barrel howitzer	2,500 pounds
2 HE 105mm rounds, boxed, w/ fuse	120 pounds
1/4-ton trailer	1,350 pounds, plus load
1-ton trailer	1,350 pounds, plus load
Clarkair bulldozer	4,195 pounds
5-gallon gasoline can	35 pounds (can and gasoline)
Solo motorcycle	575 pounds
Handcar	80 pounds, plus load
Bicycle	60 pounds
Flak jacket	24 pounds (without apron)

provide reliable communication between the glider and its tug, many gliders flew combat missions without any voice communication between them. Lights flashed from the tug signaled the cutoff time for the glider. Unless the tug experienced an absolute emergency, it was not to release the glider early because of the danger of the towline snapping back into the glider and damaging the flight surfaces or coming through the windscreen.

The CG-4A design's net weight was approximately 3,500 pounds, with a load capacity of just over 4,000 pounds. With variations in the type of wood used and added flight equipment, the production net weight increased to approximately 3,750 pounds. The design gross weight remained at 7,500 pounds, with a redline speed of 150 miles per hour. The glider was rated to carry an emergency load of 9,000 pounds, at which the top speed was 128 miles per hour.

Its normal landing distance was 600 to 800 feet, although some glider pilots developed their own landing techniques in order to stop in approximately 300 feet. These usually resulted in tearing off the skids and damaging the nose and floor of the glider. Although the CG-4A had the flight-control surfaces, such as a rudder, ailerons, trim tabs, and elevators, the glider did not have flaps. The upper-wing surface had spoilers that decreased the lift, causing the glider to quickly lose altitude.

In order to find the glider's gross weight for flying, the following weights were predetermined for the CG-4A pilot to estimate the total weight and balance of the cargo.

During the original XCG-4 flight testing and the ensuing use of production gliders at glider pilot training schools, a variety of major changes to the CG-4A were incorporated. These included adding a dorsal fin to the vertical stabilizer, changing the nose-open slide lock, adding a dual steering wheel for the copilot, adding a landing light, refining the towline release, making the so-called "training wheels" with brakes standard in place of the tactical dropping off the wheel carriage, adding a tail chute to help the glider get on the ground faster, fixing the bolt on the Griswold nose-protection device, and adding two different nose-skid systems. Many other minor changes were made to facilitate production by the various manufacturers.

There were sixteen prime contractors and hundreds of subcontractors for the CG-4A, from auto and refrigerator companies to fine wood furniture and piano companies. Small aircraft manufacturers, retail store fixture manufacturers, a beer brewery, and a ketchup and pickle company also were proficient subcontractors. Ford Motor Company at Iron Mountain, Michigan, became the largest producer, delivering 4,190 CG-4As at the lowest average cost. A travel trailer manufacturer in Indiana had the distinction of producing the fewest—one—at the highest cost: just over $1.7 million.

The gliders were built with the same stringent aircraft standards as powered aircraft were. The contracts were for blocks of serial numbers, which were consecutively assigned to production articles. As with powered aircraft, the serial number consisted of the contract year (not necessarily the year of production), followed by a dash and the contract article number, such as 42-54321. This number was stencil-painted as 4254321 on the vertical stabilizer and as 42-54321 on the port side immediately below the pilot's window. Similar to some fighter aircraft, the gliders were shipped overseas in large wooden crates. In order to fit inside the Liberty ships, each 3,750-pound glider was disassembled into five heavy-duty crates, totaling slightly over 20,000 pounds, with the longest crate just over 25 feet long.

The towline for the CG-4A was 11/16-inch diameter nylon and 350 feet long. For a double tow by one tug, a 75-foot length was added, making the second towline 425 feet. Although there were three fighters, four bombers, and six cargo aircraft tested and approved as tugs for the CG-4A, the C-47 became the dominant tug. The infamous C-46 was not used as a tug until March 1945 for the Varsity mission, the crossing of the Rhine River into Germany.

A system generally known as the "snatch" was developed for retrieving a stationary CG-4A glider by a C-47 in flight (see photo sequence on page 134). Over 600 gliders were retrieved using this system during World War II. In some instances, it was used to snatch gliders carrying up to twelve wounded on stretchers in Germany and in the Burma–India theater. The nylon towline for the snatch was 275 feet long and 15/16-inch diameter. In addition, the system used just over 1,000 feet of 3/8-inch-diameter steel cable on the reel inside the C-47.

Unlike the glider pilots of the British airborne, the U.S. gliders and glider pilots were assigned to troop carrier wings, groups, and squadrons, not to the airborne infantry and artillery divisions. Troop carriers were charged with transporting the airborne troops and artillery. The airborne glider infantrymen loaded the gliders under the approval of the glider pilot, who had the final say on total weight and balance.

Most glider pilots were trained in phases using single-engine L-type powered aircraft, two-place soaring gliders, three-place training gliders, and, finally, the CG-4A to receive their wings. By earning their wings, they had completed tactical flight training in the United States or England. The L-type aircraft provided what was called "dead stick" training. The pilots would fly to various altitudes, cut the engine, and glide to land within a specified distance of a predetermined point. This was done both in daylight and at night without lights. Depending on their civilian flying experience, glider pilots generally logged over 100 hours of flying time by the time they received their wings. Like power pilots, glider pilots were required to fly a minimum number of hours per month to stay proficient. They also were qualified to fly as C-47 copilots, and many of them flew hundreds of C-47 copilot hours on supply missions. Some glider pilots also were trained navigators and flew as such on combat missions in C-47s.

Although gliders were used for many small missions, there were eight combat missions considered the most significant: Burma, the Philippines, Sicily, Normandy, southern France, Holland, Bastogne, and Wesel. The Sicily glider operation was primarily carried out by British pilots, but due to the lack of availability of Horsa gliders, they used many American CG-4As. Since there was also a shortage of British glider pilots, twenty-four U.S. glider pilots volunteered to fly as copilots. Five of these U.S. pilots were killed in the action.

A 75mm pack howitzer being loaded into a CG-4A. FORD MOTOR COMPANY POSTCARD

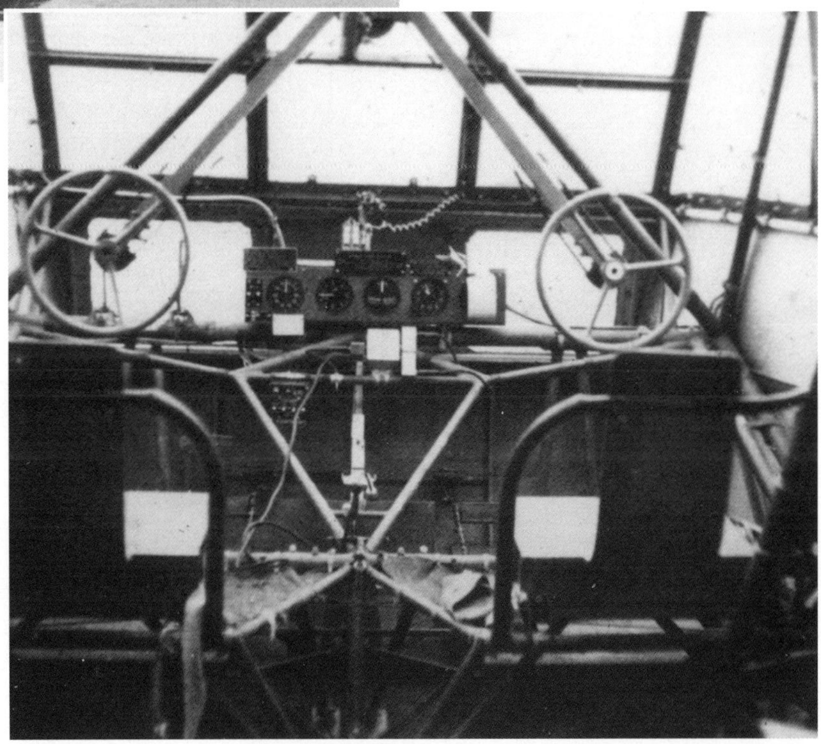

Waco CG-4A controls.
TURKAL FAMILY

In total, approximately 220 glider pilots were killed in action during the war, and nearly as many were killed in training or noncombat flying accidents. The 82nd Airborne glider infantry KIA in the CG-4A mission in Normandy was 7/10 of 1 percent. The Horsa was three times more dangerous than the CG-4A, with 2.1 percent of glider pilots KIA in the U.S.-flown Horsas. In Holland, the 82nd Airborne Division KIA in the CG-4A glider was 1/10 of 1 percent; no U.S.-flown Horsa gliders participated in this mission. Statistically speaking, these KIA numbers are minute and very much refute the general notion that gliders were extremely dangerous and deadly to the riders.

TRAINING CONTINUES

The battalion would travel back and forth many times between Fort Bragg, Laurinburg–Maxton Airfield, and other places for training. It was nonstop work getting to know their gliders and 75mm pack howitzers. It was all about speed: traveling to an airfield, loading the gliders, taking off and landing, and then putting the guns into position ready for a fire mission was always paramount. One last training session took them to Kershaw, South Carolina, along with the entire 101st Division. Here, the glidermen earned the respect of the paratroopers, something they would never lose. The troopers realized the glidermen were going in with them, instead of digging in somewhere to the rear where it was safer. The glidermen trained hard and long, sometimes alongside the troopers. Their fates were now intertwined.

Camp Claiborne. Cpl. Herman Stephens now wearing the 101st eagle patch without airborne tab. STEPHENS/DETTORE

One of the Camp Claiborne original soldiers was Cpl. Herman Woodrow ("Bud") Stephens from Greenfield, southern Ohio, an ordinary draftee for the most part who left his small-town job as a shoe factory employee to enlist. Two things made this soldier different: he wrote more than sixty letters home (not including postcards, parcels, money orders, and greeting cards), often in great detail, between March 1942 and V-J Day; and he was transferred twenty-seven times while in the U.S. Army. He would later say he was fried at Camp Claiborne, frozen in the Aleutians, and thawed out in the Philippines.

In his letters home, he critiqued movies he had seen and spoke highly of the musical "floor shows" whenever time was available to sit down and enjoy them. But he didn't like the men back in his hometown who evaded the draft because of their so-called "afflictions." Stephens knew the men and their abilities, and in his view, all were capable to be alongside him in the army. He was serving with many who appeared crippled but did their jobs efficiently and without complaint.

In the spring of 1942, Stephens wound up at Camp Claiborne in the 82nd Infantry Division and assigned to its 326th Infantry Battalion. A short time later, he was transferred to the 321st Artillery, first with C Battery and later with A Battery. Artillery of one form or another would be his home for the next twenty-seven duty stations. He didn't complain to those back home of the constant moves.

Following are summaries from his letters telling of not only army life but also life as he viewed it while on the move. Letters sent home required no stamps; soldiers instead wrote "free" in the postage area. Stephens would not send home a single V-mail, preferring stationery-type envelopes and writing paper.

March 27, 1942, Fort Thomas, Kentucky: Now in F Company waiting for special clothing that's not in army storerooms due to his abnormal size. (He stood at 5 feet, 9 inches, weighed 230 pounds, and wore a size 13 shoe). He must wait two weeks as clothing orders of this nature go to Philadelphia, PA. F Company is filled with men waiting for special clothing and shoes. Fourteen men are in his barracks; one of them is a World War I veteran. Some have been waiting over forty-four days for their army-supplied clothing.

A new group of men came into his barracks; they spent one night and then were shipped home because sixteen of the twenty-one couldn't read or write.

April 5, 1942, Camp Claiborne, Louisiana: Writes home to say the camp is filling up with soldiers and soon to be a full division. He is assigned to C Battery. The ground has been scraped clean, not a blade of grass anywhere. Spanish moss hangs from the trees. The area is filled with the stink of swamps filled with alligators and snakes. Mosquitoes and chiggers that get underneath leggings and become a constant itch that can't be scratched are everywhere. Newly promoted Maj. Alvin York of World War I fame arrives at camp for a tour.[4]

Camp Claiborne. Capt. Howard Upchurch, C Battery commander, 321st Infantry Battalion, 82nd Infantry Division, who was KIA on June 6, 1944. At that time, he was assigned to the 377th Parachute Field Artillery (PFA). STEPHENS/DETTORE

Right: A segregated sanatorium in North Carolina. STEPHENS/DETTORE

Fort Bragg. Corporal Stephens snapping a "high ball," GI slang for a salute. STEPHENS/DETTORE

April 12: First day of training, and no walking will be necessary. Trucks pull the 155mm gun, which fires a 100-pound projectile, and the soldiers ride in the bed of the trucks. The battalion commander, Colonel Works, tells the men that the idea of their training is to get them in shape quickly just in case "things get worse," but that he has no expectation the artillerymen will ever be used. The 321st Battalion consists at this time of four 155mm guns per each battery—Able, Baker, and Charlie. There are nine men per gun crew, with an additional 135 men per battery. Another fifty men assigned to the battalion perform other jobs.

May 5: 100 truckloads of Coca-Cola arrive daily, but outside the camp there is not a bottle to be had anywhere. He goes fishing on a Sunday and sells his catch of 35 pounds to a local businessman for $4.50, which is more than a week's army pay. Rumors of maneuvers all over the United States in a few weeks fill the air.

May 7: At the rifle range shooting .22-caliber rifles. Every soldier there was given thirty-five rounds of ammunition. It rained all morning. Got soaking wet and hiked back to a hillside to listen to Major York.

May 10: Kitchens, mess hall, and storage rooms are sprayed and scrubbed three times a day for cockroaches.

May 17: Training all week on 1917 (British) Enfields, but only five good rifles out of the lot. Shoots in blinding rain and electrical storm. Soon will be getting special lightweight "automatic" rifles (M1 carbines), now being manufactured. Procures an army driver's license, which rewards a soldier with promotion to private first class and an extra $6 per month in pay.

May 24: At rifle range to score for qualification and is tipped off that if anyone shoots a 180/200, they become .50-caliber machine gunners. Four machine gunners are detailed to a battery to protect

A camping sign showing 1942 rates. STEPHENS/DETTORE

Camp Claiborne. Lt. Joseph Perkins (nicknamed "P-40") wearing early 321st insignia.

Camp Clairborne. A 37mm cannon affixed to a 155mm gun barrel.
STEPHENS/DETTORE

it from low-flying aircraft, tanks, and armored vehicles. Although an expert shot, he doesn't want to score high, because that would entail having to carry the weapon on his back and memorize 200 parts, plus assemble the weapon in the dark within eight minutes. He prefers the big guns and purposely scores 179/200.

June 7: On the howitzer range shooting 37mm cannons mounted to the barrels of 155mm guns, which is cheaper ammunition but uses the same alignment instruments.

June 14: Moves from pyramidal tents to freshly built tar-papered barracks. Takes three hikes in three days at 10, 15, then 22 miles, bringing the howitzers with them. Gets lost twelve times in 10 miles and blames the new reconnaissance officers.

June 28: In one week, takes two 25-mile hikes and three 10-mile hikes at night wearing gas masks.

August 2: Fires all twelve 155s of the battalion three seconds apart and hears the explosions of impact one and a half minutes later: "sure sounds swell." Laid woven cane mats under the wheels of the guns because the ground was wet.

August 9: Was told that no one over 185 pounds or over age thirty is to be in the division. Officers ask for volunteers who want to be parachutists. The much beloved 155s are given up in exchange for 75mm pack howitzers.

August 14: Notified that the 82nd Infantry Division will be split into two airborne divisions. A practice review on Friday will be held for the big event scheduled on Saturday.

August 15: Issued new steel pot helmets. Officers ride in a car past the men and go to a review stand as the men march by. Soldiers everywhere are passing out due to the heat, keeping the medics busy. He becomes a gunner on a howitzer gun crew and is promoted to corporal. His duties are handling the gunsight and setting off deflections and elevations. Tells his parents, "When you write, leave the 82nd Division part out." Rumors rampant that the division is going to be shipped to Helena, Montana, or Fort Bragg for thirteen weeks of infantry training.

August 24: Another review. Infantry march with bayonets, but not the artillerymen. Didn't fire the 155mm due to the cost of $100 per round.

September 5: Rumors that anyone over the age of thirty-two will be transferred out of the airborne and that the division will be moving to Fort Bragg. Stephens discounts the movement rumor because he thinks it would be a well-kept secret and not a prevalent topic of loose conversation.

September 6: He is now in Able Battery. Charlie Battery was collapsed and the men sent to either Able Battery or Baker Battery. The 321st now has only two firing batteries. The men are told that they are going to be a "guinea pig outfit and [that they will be] doing all their experimenting with us." They are told that another year of training is in store for them and that all the generals who want to know anything about it will come and inspect them.

He says that three inspections later, they still don't have any of their new equipment and that the new general of the 101st (Lee) inspected them yet again, so they had to borrow the guns and equipment to display things they had never seen before and might not see again. They had three hours to borrow trucks, guns, tools, and instruments, take them out to the drill field, clean the guns, and display the equipment. Plus they had to get into uniform, line up the guns, and lay out all the equipment on the covers at the back of the guns. A group of generals walked down the line and inspected the men as they stood at attention, careful not to look at the inspecting officers or move in any way. Stephens says the officers sometimes stopped at a man and asked any kind "of crazy question that he can think of to try to get you to look at him or catch you off guard."

He further writes:

> Well, Friday General Bill Lee walked down the line and I was the only one he asked any questions in a Battery. Just to show you what kind of questions they ask, here's what he asked me. He walks down the line, steps to one side of me and reaches out and taps me on the chest (he's trying to get me to look at him). He says, "How much do you weigh? 240 pounds sir. What did

A French 155mm howitzer being used in training at Camp Claiborne.
STEPHENS/DETTORE

you say? 240 pounds sir. Have you gained or lost since you've been in the army? I've stayed just about the same sir. [Actually, he had lost 3 pounds.] What state are you from? Ohio, sir. What do you think of this airborne stuff? I don't know what to think about it sir.

Stephens continued later in the letter:

The only thing we know about the glider artillery is . . . that they will pick out a place like an airport or something of the kind. The bombers will come over and bomb it very heavily, trying to knock out everything they can. Then the parachute artillery go in and take the place using the bomb holes for cover after they have taken the place. We are towed in the gliders and take over and enlarge the place, knocking out gun emplacements, railroads and fortifications—but that's more or less a guess for anyone—don't know much more about it.

At this time, Stephens is 40 pounds over the weight limit for glider riders. Unknowingly, his fate is sealed, but whether it's from the simple fact of being overweight or the awkward chance conversation with the "Father of the Airborne," General Lee, is open to speculation. Whatever the case, he didn't see that his future life in the army was about to change course, because that same night he went to the tattoo parlor in Alexandria to get his very first tattoo, an eagle, on his arm.

October 15: Given field rations for the first time and gives them a high rating. Describes each meal's contents in minute detail, down to the manufacturer's name on each item.

October 17: Three hikes a week of 10 to 12 miles, two of which are double-time. Training also includes one hour of judo a day, running an obstacle course, climbing over an 8-foot smooth fence, jumping ditches, crawling through tunnels, climbing up a big tower and down the other side, and swinging across big water holes on ropes. Training is eight and a half hours for five days, and four and a half hours on Saturdays plus four hours at night.

November 9: The eagle mascot Young Abe is on parade. The announcer over the loudspeaker says, "Here comes the 321st, full to the gills," but meant to say "armed to the teeth."

A soldier at Fort Bragg with the newly introduced field rations.
STEPHENS/DETTORE

October 24: The battalion was taken 28 miles outside camp to simulate a glider landing inside enemy territory. Their guns were emplaced and fired; the other artillery battalions were supposed to locate and either capture or destroy them. The soldiers of the 321st were to keep that from occurring. That evening, the battalion was given a field problem: find a point on the map using only compasses, which they did by 7 A.M. the next morning during the worst storm Stephens had ever seen. Lightning was striking all around them, and the towed guns were constantly getting stuck in the mud. It took another three hours to return to the jump-off point. The battalion was then ordered to march the 28 miles back to Fort Bragg with full packs and rifles in a heavy rainstorm

The 907th GFA (sister unit of the 321st GFA), 101st Airborne, on parade at Fort Bragg in November 1942, passing in front of the 321st barracks. WILKINSON FAMILY

Camp Claiborne. A soldier holds a newly-introduced M1 carbine displayed during a field problem. STEPHENS/DETTORE

on a road turned to mud. He writes that they left on Tuesday morning and returned to camp Wednesday evening, and that the men were dead on their feet: "A few more of those walks and sleeping in the rain and I'll be twisted into a knot."

November 22: Tells his parents it's exciting to travel down a road at 40 mph in a jeep with blackout lights. (Covers with a narrow horizontal slot cut into them were placed over the headlights, allowing only a minimal amount of light to shine onto the road. These were normally used while a vehicle was being driven in combat situations.) He observed 240 8-inch howitzers in position and fired a few at a time all day and night. The guns were 2 miles away and the firing shook the barracks and rattled the windows and doors. He said if a soldier was outdoors, the muzzle blast could be felt on his face. The shells

JWO Edward Chaumont at Fort Bragg with a full pack.
WILKINSON FAMILY

could be heard as they passed over the barracks; a few minutes later a rumbling noise emanated from the exploding shells 15 miles away.

December 6: The rumor was that the division was not going to Nebraska for glider training because there was room for only a single division, the 82nd Airborne. Instead, they were going to a place 40 miles away called Laurinburg.

December 11: Battalion moves to Laurinburg–Maxton glider air base for training. Spent the prior two weeks in training, loading and unloading gliders at night on crude mock-ups. Observes Mike Murphy, a famous stunt flyer, give demonstrations on what a glider could do and is told the reasons behind using gliders in combat: "Planes weigh 31,000 pounds and carry loads of 4,900 pounds. A plane costs $50,000 and burns 90 gallons of gas an hour. A glider weighs 3,650 pounds and carries 3,750 pounds and costs two to three thousand dollars each.[5] Since no gas is used there is no fire after a crack-up."

December 19: Spends one month glider training at Laurinburg–Maxton and says it is a dump. The officers tell them that anyone over the age of twenty-five should be sent home because those who are older than that can't learn.

December 28: Informed they could fly to Miami for free, courtesy of the Air Corps, but it would cost $1 to rent a parachute.

January 3, 1943: Still at Laurinburg–Maxton. Cameras are strictly forbidden, so four rolls of film are put away for future use.[6] The initial glider flight is a half hour. Anyone in the battalion can take as many glider rides as he desires, as long as permission is granted by the battalion commander. Most of the soldiers don't think twice about going up in a glider anymore.

January 10: Writes that a 75mm pack howitzer gun crew was killed at Fort Bragg by an exploding gun. He blames the new officers for not knowing how to handle ammunition properly.

January 17: Things are going badly in training for the division, and the War Department cancels further airborne training. He writes that General Lee went to the War Department with a personal request for more time, which was granted. All soldiers must make 5 miles in fifty minutes with full packs to remain in the division.

January 24: One more flight flies a tactical load battery problem. Airborne training is almost over, and now it's back to Fort Bragg.

January 31: Receives folding-stock carbines.

February 21: Writes home to tell his parents that the United States might have to fight Britain and Russia next after "this business," and that "they will be fighting us with our own equipment."

February 28: Spends three to four days a week on the artillery range. A gunner swabbed a barrel on a 75mm pack howitzer with hot water, and the swab

Camp Claiborne. Sgt. George Hammond (right front passenger), PFC Al Wilson (driver), and Private Easton (rear passenger), all presumably from Headquarters. STEPHENS/DETTORE

A glider training flight. TURKAL FAMILY

A guesthouse at Camp Claiborne. STEPHENS/DETTORE

froze inside the tube. The entire gun had to be towed to the motor shed and thawed out.

March 5: Transferred out of the 101st Airborne Division to a field artillery battalion at Fort Eustis, Virginia. While stationed at Fort Bragg, he must turn in his army wristwatch, which was shockproof against cannon fire. His personal wristwatch stopped due to the concussion of the howitzer blasts, and he doesn't think it can be repaired.

March 28: Receives a letter from his good friend, PFC Jesse Hopkins (A Battery) from Harmony, West Virginia, which tells of a training accident that had a somewhat humorous twist.

Hopkins wrote that Gen. George Marshall, the chief of staff, and Anthony Eden, the British foreign minister, were here "one day this past week [and] we had to put on a show for them." The "show" was actually a demonstration held March 22–24, 1943, at Southern Pines, North Carolina. Two parachute infantry regiments took part: the 502nd from the 101st Airborne Division and the 504th from the 82nd Airborne Division. Both regiments were supported by their respective artillery battalions.

Wooden grandstands were erected for the military's top brass, assorted dignitaries, and guests to view the awaited spectacle. A parking lot adjacent to the grandstands was packed with various motor vehicles. A parachute drop supported by live artillery fire and capped off with a staged resupply glider landing was planned; the gliders were to be released in such a way that they seemed to appear from nowhere at the rear of the grandstands, gliding silently over the heads of the spectators and landing on the fields directly in front of them. It was to be quite the dramatic finish.

Hopkins continued: "But you know, the fellows taking part in something like that [don't] get to see much. I bet we shot up a million dollars' worth of ammo. My ears are still ringing next day." He also wrote that two parachutists were killed in the demonstration drop.

The "humorous" twist came when one of the guns in a firing battery fired a short shell—a round that lands and explodes at the wrong location, generally short of its target, and causes unintended destruction—that landed next to the crowded grandstand

and exploded. It blew up three jeeps and tore a large hole in General Marshall's car. A few soldiers were slightly injured in the mishap. An investigation was immediately conducted to determine which battery and gun were at fault. The gravity of the potential loss of life for esteemed guest General Marshall, the British foreign minister, and a host of other dignitaries drove the investigation. For several days, every gun in every battery in every battalion of both airborne divisions, plus another artillery brigade from Fort Bragg, was suspect. Finally, the results of the investigation came in: the short shell was a 75mm round fired from a gun belonging to A Battery, 319th Battalion, of the 82nd Division.

On April 27, 1943, General Lee sent out a notice with the heading: "Marking of Officers and Warrant Officers Clothing and Equipment by Command of Major General Lee." The notice instructed soldiers that all of their equipment—pistol belts, blankets, gas mask bags, canteen covers, pistol magazine and first aid pouches, shelter tents, mess kit cans, cups and utensils, musette bags, and all clothing (including suspenders)—was to be marked in accordance with the guidelines. Markings consisted of the letter "X," followed by the first letter of the soldier's last name and the last four digits of his army serial number. (This practice later assisted future historians and militaria collectors in determining the original owners of clothing and equipment.)

The grandstand at Fort Bragg, with dignitaries being presented with a show of airborne capabilities, complete with a surprise glider landing. Anthony Eden is seated in the bottom row (center, without head covering).

PFC Jesse Hopkins (A Battery).
G. J. DETTORE COLLECTION

Medic Joe Horner of Tennessee was in the 29th Infantry Division at Fort Bragg. While getting ready to go on leave, he saw another 29th Division soldier whom he didn't know being picked on by two soldiers from another outfit in downtown Fayetteville. They had picked a fight because they didn't like that the 29th Division soldier was wearing a "fancy rope" (a blue infantry cord) on his uniform.

Horner evened out the battle by jumping into the fight. The military police were called, and everyone was put under arrest and sent to the stockade. The soldier who was the object of the attack was upset that being placed under arrest rescinded his furlough; he had been in town waiting to leave, and now blamed Horner for his predicament. Horner tried to explain that he was not going to be able to go on leave either, but his fellow infantryman would have none of it.

Horner was summoned by his commanding officer a few days later. The captain said he had a report and that talk of a court-martial was bandied about. Once court-martial proceedings got underway, there would be no stopping them. But if Horner volunteered for the 101st Airborne, which was looking for volunteers to be paratroopers, his case would be closed. Horner replied, "I'm volunteering, sir." He left the office and walked directly to the 101st area, where he was told that glidermen were needed most. The 321st it would be. There was talk of extra pay, and he no longer had to wear the infantry shoulder cord on his uniform, which the soldiers of the 29th hated to wear anyway. What Horner did not know was that in less than three weeks he would be sailing to England.

While at Fort Bragg, the 321st Battalion's medical sergeant, Farris Crowe from Nashville, Tennessee, noticed Horner's name on the list of recent volunteers. Unbeknownst to Horner, Sergeant Crowe asked his officers if he could have Horner for his section. The answer was yes. Crowe's wife came from the same small town as Horner back in Tennessee, and Horner knew her parents and relatives. He had no previous medical training and would get what little was offered to him for just a few weeks in the classrooms before shipping out. Most of the time, his job was to be a jeep driver for the medics or when Capt. David Davidson, the acting surgeon in charge, needed a driver. He would have to hone his skills in the field. Horner stayed in the 321st medical section until Bastogne. He eventually transferred to the Headquarters Battery wire section.

While traveling to England by ship, British rations such as fish and oxtail soup combined with the rolling seas made Horner and almost everybody else sick. Some enterprising officer, with the help of several English sailors, was selling bacon, lettuce, and tomato sandwiches on the sly to anyone who would pay for the luxury. That enterprise didn't last very long—the soldiers were upset by their British rations, and even more so when some of the sailors tried to take advantage of them. It riled up enough men who then reported him. The officer was brought up on charges and court-martialed.

Arriving in England, their new home was to be the horse feed barn at Whatcombe Farm. The nearest fair-sized town was Oxford. Horner and John Gring (another medic from La Porte, Indiana) decided to extend their pass by two days. Horner had been promoted just one month earlier to private first class. They were enjoying themselves immensely with a couple of gals they met. When the two medics got back to camp, they were busted back down to privates. (Ranks changed frequently over the course of the war, with soldiers either being demoted for poor behavior or receiving battlefield promotions.)

The physical training for medics was the same as for the rest of the battalion. Horner didn't mind the long marches. Born in the hills of Tennessee, the only transportation he knew were his own two feet, and he walked everywhere he needed to go. At the end of a long march (sometimes 30 miles), the medics would be just as tired as the rest of the men, but their day was not over. Foot blisters and a host of other ailments had to be treated. Most of the other medics were beat from the march, so Horner took up some of their slack. He was often the last to finish treating the men of the battalion.

> One of B Battery's soldiers was infamous for finding the shortest route on a march. Pvt. Ernest White Jr. of Jonesville, Louisiana, would drop out of a march and reappear at the end. No matter what punishment was given to White for not following orders, the likeable soldier just would not adhere to them. He was eventually transferred to another unit. After a short time there, White was transferred again for circumventing his training. He eventually wound up back in the 321st, where he stayed until the end of the war. Once in combat, White rose to the rank of sergeant. ■

Glider training was mandated for the medics, and many would get their first taste of this peculiar experience in England: loading, lashing, and flying. Some of them got sick and vomited the entire time they were in the air, no matter how stable the glider ride was. Horner would take their place and forge someone else's name on the clipboard so no one would be the wiser. He did this many times, enabling the absent glider medics to receive their monthly glider flight pay bonus.

On one training flight in England, the tug pilot exceeded what was regarded as the maximum safe airspeed for its towed CG-4A, 150 mph (the accepted normal towed speed was 110–130 mph). The fully loaded glider was being towed at 170 mph, and the glider pilot grew angry. He felt the C-47 tug pilot was showing off and trying to scare the glider riders. He snapped, "That's enough of this shit," and slapped the release, cutting the glider loose from the tug.

The glider came down far from its designated landing zone into an isolated field. The astounded English farmer, finding them to be Americans, brought out beer for the glider crew, which turned the landing into a party in his barn. The glidermen

Lt. Dr. David Davidson, the 321st Battalion's assistant surgeon, administering shots. HENDERSON FAMILY

Camp Claiborne. The 321st Battalion's medics: PFC Bernard DiPasquale (rear), Sgt. Farris Crowe (center), and PFC John Gring (front). CROWE FAMILY

settled in for their delightful short stay. The glider pilot and copilot weren't worried a bit about cutting loose early due to the circumstances, knowing it was the tug pilot who was in error. The glider had to unloaded, taken apart and its wings removed, and driven back to base in a flatbed truck. Transportation was provided to return the glider riders to Whatcombe Farm.

In Normandy, Horner was a jeep driver and assigned to the medical detachment. He arrived off the coast of France with the rest of the 321st medics on the Liberty ship *John S. Mosby*, which was loaded with men and equipment. He drove the waterproofed jeep ashore on June 9. Most of the injuries treated were sprained ankles from the paratroopers' hard landings in a backward motion.

When the casualties were overwhelming, the 321st medics would be called in to help out the medics of other 101st units. The walking wounded were directed to the closest aid station or sometimes evacuated to the 321st. These aid stations would be no more than foxholes for the medics and open areas with medical supplies at the ready to treat the wounded. Each battery had its own medics, including the Headquarters Battery. Horner, as the battalion's surgeon's driver, was not assigned to a particular battery and instead floated from one battery to another depending on where he was needed at the time.

When the batteries stopped firing and the surrounding area quieted down, it was the job of the aid men to scour the fields for bodies. They would go on foot through fields and hedgerows, searching assigned areas. On one of these excursions, Horner thought he was a dead man. On a cow path leading through a hedgerow, he observed a German soldier crouching on the bank of the opposite side, with a rifle pointing directly at him. Horner was in the middle of the field and had nowhere to go. He froze, unarmed and scared, and stayed motionless, waiting to see what the German was going to do next. Even though he was an unarmed medic, he knew full well it was a case-by-case situation whether or not that fact meant anything to the enemy. He noticed the German was very still, so with arms raised Horner slowly approached and discovered that a single bullet had passed through the side of the German's helmet just above the ear, killing him instantly. This was the reason the German was so still. Horner spent some time looking at the dead enemy soldier, amazed at what he was seeing.

After this incident, Horner procured and always carried a folding-stock carbine, destroyed his medic identification card, and eventually discarded his Red Cross armband, since any medic carrying a weapon violated his status as a noncombatant. Col. Edward Carmichael, the battalion commander, eventually sent word to the other medics that if anyone in their detachment was to carry a weapon, they had better discard their medic identifications. Horner was ahead of the curve on that advice.

The Holland campaign was different. It was the 321st Battalion's first combat glider ride, and the glidermen were fully versed on the debacle of the numerous Normandy paratrooper misdrops caused by the C-47 pilots. A number of gliders had suffered the same fate.

Horner's glider departed from Aldermaston with another medic, battalion surgeon Capt. David Davidson, and two glider pilots, plus a jeep. This CG-4A glider was slightly different, as it was equipped with two-way radio communication with the tug pilot. Very few gliders had this option for the Holland mission, and it was much appreciated by all involved. A communication wire ran alongside the towrope, taped every 10 feet or so, but due to the stretching and contraction of the nylon towrope, the wire often snapped apart, rendering it useless. Horner's glider also had an experienced Normandy pilot and a newly trained copilot, F/O Louis Gonzales, possibly because one of its occupants was the battalion surgeon. The majority of the other 321st glider lifts to Holland consisted of a single glider pilot; the highest-ranking passenger would occupy the copilot seat and take orders from the pilot.

The chatter between the tug and glider pilots was constant so there would be no misunderstanding during the flight about its proper landing zone destination. The glider riders made sure the C-47 tug pilots knew this wasn't Normandy and that they should make sure they brought the glider riders to the correct landing zone, and not miles away from it.

Horner's glider started to get hit by enemy fire soon after reaching the mainland. The intensity was strongest over any patch of woods. Sounds of rounds traveling through the glider fabric made a popping sound like popcorn being popped. Sometimes the German bullets would strike the metal tubular frame of the glider and then ricochet at the most unusual angles. One of these bullets struck Horner in the back of his hand, even though he was sitting in the driver's seat of the jeep. However, what worried him the most was the jeep's gas tank underneath his seat: one luckily placed enemy bullet was all it would take to light it up into a fireball.

As they got close to their landing zone, shrapnel tore through the cockpit's plexiglass window, blowing a hole on the copilot's side in the nose of the glider. The copilot screamed, "I'm hit, I'm hit!" as blood ran down his face. Trying to calm him, Horner reassured him it was only a light flesh wound and that the blood was just a trickle, nothing serious; after all, the glider was loaded with medical personnel. After a short time, the copilot settled down to resume his duties.

The glider pilot cut loose the towrope for the glide into the landing zone, taking what seemed continuous fire from the Germans below. Upon landing, the glider riders hurriedly exited the glider, a skill impressed upon them during training. They scrambled for a nearby ditch and jumped in. Gliders were landing everywhere, some overshooting the landing zone. The glidermen had been told to rendezvous at any point where they observed orange flags being waved. The small group started down the ditch toward an orange flag, only to stop, wondering if the Germans had captured a flag and were attempting to lure them into a trap. It was decided it looked safe enough, so that was where they headed. Cautiously approaching the orange flag, they noticed it was an outpost of paratroopers who were dug in with a machine gun. For now, they had it made.

When darkness fell, it was deemed safe to return to the glider and unload its cargo. The pilot and copilot also returned to help, sitting back in their seats and yanking the front two hold-down ropes loose on the jeep. The rear lines were released by the others, and Horner started the jeep and raced forward. A steel cable was attached to the rear of the jeep's bumper, running forward to the cockpit. The pilot released a latch handle, allowing the forward motion of the jeep to pull the cable; this caused the hinged cockpit to rise, with the seated glider pilots still strapped in. The jeep continued to accelerate, raising the cockpit high enough to allow the jeep to pass underneath it and out into the field.

This sudden burst of noise alerted the Germans, and they started to drop mortar rounds near the glider. Horner heard hollering from his glider—"Hey, wait for me!"—but the area was too hot. He kept going and yelled back, "I'm not stopping. Meet me at the outpost!" He made it back to the paratroopers' area; the rest of the men also returned without any injuries.

The glider unloading training method had been updated after Normandy. The jeep drivers were now told to hook up everything from the glider, tow it all to the battalion rendezvous area, and sort it out there. Any other way, which would involve attempting to locate the correct trailer or gun for the proper gun section and matching it with the correct jeep, was now considered time-consuming and potentially dangerous. Horner's job was to locate the medical detachment trailer for his section. If he had to travel from glider to glider on a landing zone, it would take hours, especially under enemy observation and fire.

On September 26 at 0305 hours, the entire battalion was alerted for a night march south from Uden to Veghel. They would travel on what was commonly known as "Hell's Highway," the paved road between Eindhoven and Arnhem. At 0400 hours, they arrived at daybreak southeast of Veghel and almost immediately came under intense enemy mortar and artillery fire. The area had been recently occupied with foxholes and slit trenches scattered about some orchards.

Horner was driving, and his passenger was medic Pvt. John Gring. They were towing a trailer loaded with packs that some of the artillerymen had thrown in while on the march. They had just pulled in underneath the trees when an enemy round burst overhead, sending shrapnel flying. Gring was unhitching the trailer and was knocked down by a fragment that bounced off his .45-caliber pistol, ripping off the top leather flap. Other pieces of shrapnel littered the jeep

One of the more colorful medics in the detachment was Pvt. Stanley Woods from Russellville, Ohio. On November 12, while standing guard near the kitchen, a huge German shell exploded near him, throwing Woods twenty to thirty feet into the air along with a mass of earth. Miraculously, he was not killed or injured physically, but mentally the war was over for him; he would remain with the cooks from then on. The crater was so deep and wide a small house could have fit inside. It was such an oddity, even in a combat zone, that shortly after the incident occurred other 321st boys would come to see the crater and shake their heads in disbelief. ■

from the front to the rear, punching holes in the packs stored for the march. Horner rolled out of the jeep, which made Gring think he was hit, so he got up and started to run over to help. Another burst sent additional shrapnel into the jeep and struck Gring again, knocking him down for the second time and blowing out a tire on the trailer. This time, Gring was hit in the leg, but he made it over to Horner, only to find him unhurt. The firing was well aimed and so heavy that the farmhouse nearby was peppered with shrapnel, which could be seen bouncing off the walls and roof in all directions.

Another medic—Roy Hammonds from Fincastle, Ohio, nicknamed "Bear" because of his surly disposition—spotted a foxhole and jumped into it. However, the first person to make it in was Colonel Carmichael, who said there wasn't enough room for two. Hammonds replied, "Give me a minute, and I will let you know," and jumped right on top of his colonel. Another shell burst exploded overhead and struck Hammonds. The colonel survived, but Hammonds was seriously wounded.

The Headquarters Battery supply sergeant, Lawrence Benninghoff from Bellevue, Ohio, was also hit. He was wounded in the groin and was taken to a field hospital in Horner's jeep along with the other wounded. The hospital had recently moved, so finding its new location was stressful and dangerous work. Horner drove back through the town of Veghel, spooked by its deserted streets, continuing the hunt until he finally found the newly set-up field hospital and dropped off his wounded.

On October 5, 1944, a call came into the aid station that a major was killed and his body needed retrieval. The pick-up location was given. The closest aid station was a 321st one manned by Private Horner and Pvt. Stanley Matycich, of Moran, Michigan. Normally, the medics would rotate turns leaving their aid station when a call came in, whether it was to render aid, pick up a wounded soldier, or bring in a corpse. This time, it was Matycich's turn to go.

Matycich jumped into the jeep and traveled to a crossroads not far from his intended destination, but the intersection came under heavy German artillery fire. He returned to the aid station without the major's body. The battalion surgeon, Captain Davidson, was there waiting to inspect the body and asked what happened. Matycich told him about not being able to get through because of the shelling, adding, "That guy's dead, so why do I want to get killed?"

Horner had no love for the British soldier while he was in Holland. He felt they were never in a rush to do anything. On one occasion, a call came in that an aid man was needed; directions were given, and in no time Horner was on the road and lost. He passed a lone British soldier standing on the road; they glanced at each other and Horner kept going. The farther he traveled, the more lost he felt. Realizing it was best to stop and go back to his starting point, he approached the lone British Tommy again, who was still standing near the side of the road. Horner told the Brit he was lost and showed him on the map where he wanted to go.

"I was wondering where you were going, because just over there is where the Germans are," the British soldier said, pointing to the area from where Horner had just returned. Horner said he believed the sole reason the British soldier was stationed at that outpost was to stop and warn people of what was ahead, but for some reason this particular time the Brit hadn't thought it was necessary. ■

Dr. Davidson looked at Horner and asked him, "Well, would you go get him?" Horner said he would try and made his way to the crossroads. Before he reached it, he stopped short, knowing he would be under enemy observation and that artillery fire would rain down again. The Germans anticipated he would be at the intersection by the speed he was traveling and fired on an empty crossroads. When the fire stopped, Horner accelerated around the craters, eventually making it to the correct area near the Linge Canal by the railroad track embankment. He was waved down by some paratroopers who were with the body; it was Maj. Oliver Horton of the 3rd Battalion, 506th PIR.

The troopers said their major had walked up the embankment onto the railroad tracks to get a better view, despite knowing the Germans had the area under observation, and was killed. They helped Horner put the dead officer in the passenger seat, as there was no carrier on that jeep. Typically, a litter was fastened across the hood of the jeep alongside the windshield and covered with a piece of canvas. If necessary, the canvas could be rinsed off later of any blood and reused for the next casualty. The major's body was not blood-soaked, but Horner had to reach over and grab the corpse on occasion to keep the body from falling out during the ride back to the aid station.[7]

Leaving Holland by truck, the 321st Battalion made its way to camp at Mourmelon, France, on November 29, 1944. As a jeep driver, Horner had a trailer and was assigned to bring firewood from outside the camp for the stoves, which were set up in the pyramidal tents. He did this all day long, following the same route. As he entered camp with the very last load, some of the men started to bug him, saying, "You got the jeep, and they [the guards] know you and will let you out. We know where there's a dance." One persistent member of the group was Pvt. Melvin Partin (A Battery) from Barbourville, Kentucky. Reluctantly, Horner agreed, and sure enough, the guards didn't even glance at the five of them as the men passed through the gate and off the base.

Unfortunately, Horner was unaware that after his last run for wood, a road grader had come along, heaping up a ridge of dirt in the center of the twisting road. As Horner's jeep approached a narrow, single-lane concrete bridge over a river, the wheels on the passenger side straddled the high-mounded dirt, sending the jeep onto an uncontrollable course straight into the concrete edge of the bridge.

The force of the impact ejected all of its occupants and pushed the motor into the cab of the jeep. One of the soldiers wound up in the river, crying for help that he couldn't swim and was drowning. Horner had injured his leg, and the only way he could get to the drowning man was by crawling. He made it down to the river's edge, slid into the water, and grabbed the collar of the soldier's uniform. He tried to pull him to the bank, but the soldier was heavy and struggling. A civilian who happened to be walking down the road witnessed the accident and rushed to help Horner pull the soldier from the river.

Austria. Medics PFC Stanley Matycich (right) and PFC Roy Hammonds (left). DIPASQUALE/DETTORE

One of the other occupants was hurt badly enough to be sent home to the States. Another spent time in the hospital before returning to the battalion along with Horner. It was agreed that since two of the men weren't badly hurt, they would sneak back into camp in order to not be associated with the debacle. Horner feared this would most certainly lead to his being court-martialed by Colonel Carmichael, and he dreaded what was to come.

As it turned out, Carmichael had just departed on a pass, leaving Maj. John Tyler in charge. The major was a close friend of Horner's boss, good old Sgt. Farris Crowe, and he decided to conduct a trial immediately, while the colonel was away. Horner was found guilty and restricted to the camp area for two weeks. He also had to pay $500 for the totaled jeep; the fine was to come out of his pay in monthly deductions. No charges were filed against the jeep's other occupants, but they felt responsible for getting Horner into this mess and each gave him $100 toward the cost of the jeep. Months later, Colonel Carmichael came across the paperwork of the mishap and called in Horner. He was furious that Horner wasn't court-martialed and gave him a

A 155mm cannon, developed in 1938 and also called a "Long Tom," at Fort Sill, Oklahoma. WILKINSON FAMILY

Farris Crowe was an easy-going, good-natured man, and the medics loved to pester him in their own way. It started in England and carried over into Normandy. One of their jokes was to gather up the dinner K-rations and remove everything but the cheese from the box. Crowe would invariably arrive late and, not knowing he was being toyed with, would empty out the box and exclaim, "Goddamn it—all I ever get is this goddamned cheese!"

On one occasion during the morning roll call, Crowe hurried to his usual place in front of his troops and stood at attention. As the first sergeant walked down the lane in front of all the assembled troops of the battalion, the same retort came: "All accounted for and present, Sir." The first sergeant would then move to the next group, and so on until he approached Sergeant Crowe's medics last. Crowe stood tall and in a commanding voice barked out, "All accounted for and present, Sir!" The first sergeant, not skipping a beat, said, "They may be all accounted for, but you don't have anyone present." Puzzled, Crowe turned around to see not a single medic standing behind him. The formation was dismissed, and he found all twelve of them asleep in their bunks. ■

chewing out, saying he would make sure if something like this ever happened again, he would personally guarantee one.

As the 321st Battalion proceeded into the Bastogne area with the rest of the 101st Division, other soldiers were going the opposite direction in a jumbled array of various units. Many were without weapons and had no idea where their commands were. "What do you expect to do with those popguns?" was a common refrain.

Standing fast was the 969th Battalion, which was fitted with 155mm howitzers ("Long Toms") manned by black artillerymen and commanded by white officers, a surprising sight for the 321st. The artillerymen of the 969th said it was a sight to see truck after truck loaded with troopers coming in to help them. They told the new arrivals that they weren't leaving and would do whatever they could.

On January 8, 1945, the results of a division-wide drawing for a thirty-day furlough back to the States were announced. Criteria for nomination varied from unit to unit and included things such as not having any negative disciplinary action and being free of venereal diseases. One of the names written on a piece of paper and pulled from a 321st helmet was Sgt. Farris Crowe, the good friend of the battalion's second in command, executive officer Major Tyler. Coincidence or not, Crowe wanted to get out, and it was Horner's job to drive him out of Savy, which was still under enemy artillery bombardment.

"You got to get me out of here right now," Crowe said excitedly. Horner replied, "Hey, I got to get back here after I get you out, so I want you to promise me something right now. When you get to Nashville, you call my sister and tell her I'm okay." Crowe kept his promise. Crowe would not return to the 321st, mustering out in Georgia. Many years after he was mustered out, he developed heart problems due to shrapnel from a chest wound he had received in Holland. When a heart specialist looked at his X-ray, he noticed objects embedded near Crowe's heart. Crowe eventually received a partial disability from his wartime injury.

In Savy, outside Bastogne, the battalion medics were set up in various barns and small houses. Initially, Horner, Matychich, and Gring's aid station was in a barn complex on the Grandes Fontaine farm, the same farm where the 321st firing batteries were emplaced. German counterbattery fire was not uncommon, and when a shell landed near the barn, the stone building's large wooden doors would fly open from the concussion. One of the medics left a "calling card" in the area, behind B Battery. The message was burned into a tree and read: "WE IS AIRBORNE."

On another occasion, Horner was cleaning out his jeep, which he routinely did to keep it clear of loose grenades. In the course of picking up soldiers, both living and dead, it was considered safe practice to remove the grenades from the bodies before transporting them. An accidental pulled pin from a grenade still on the body of a semiconscious trooper being transported in a bouncing, sometimes erratic vehicle was a strong possibility.

Horner inspected the inside of his jeep closely for grenades, in all the nooks and crannies, and was leaning over the front seat to check the back when a lone German 88mm shell came roaring in. By now, the medic could tell if shells were coming in close or going to be over, and this one was going to be really close. He dove out of the jeep. The round hit about ten feet away, dug itself into the frozen ground, and then plowed its way back out. The 88mm shell then bounced across the snow, smoking and creating steam as it rolled through the barnyard—it was a dud. Horner later said that if it hadn't been a dud, he would have been a goner. He couldn't understand why when the Germans fired their 88s they never sent more than four rounds. Just when it started to hurt, the firing stopped; often, if they had continued, the damage inflicted could have been catastrophic.

On February 28, Pvt. Joe Horner transferred to Headquarters Battery's wire section, having decided he wanted a change from the blood and gore and the chance to see a different type of action. He spent the rest of the war with them. At the end of the war, the wire section, along with some other headquarters soldiers, discovered a hidden supply of champagne in the basement of the Platterhof Hotel in Berchtesgaden. A 6x6 truck was brought in and loaded with the bubbly, which lasted for three weeks. The cache probably would have lasted longer, but the wire section gave much of it away to selected friends of the battalion. It was kept hidden in a house nearby, and when the battalion officers found out about it, some were angry they hadn't gotten a single bottle.

Horner was a "high-point man" and in the first group to leave the 321st and ship back home. After

Headquarters medic Cpl. Bernard DiPasquale alongside the 321st aid station at Savy, N 50° 01.279, E 0050° 42.288.

DIPASQUALE/DETTORE

From left to right: PFC John Dapp, PFC Stanley Matycich, Corporal Horner, and PFC DiPasquale (seated in center) at the Savy headquarters aid station.
DIPASQUALE/DETTORE

Right: At the Savy headquarters aid station: PFC Dapp (front left), Corporal Horner (front right), PFC DiPasquale (back left), and PFC Eugene Rau (back right). DIPASQUALE/DETTORE

Lt. Davis and Sgt. Harold Dittmer locate hastily hidden bottles of champagne behind a false wall in the basement of the Platterhof Hotel in Berchtesgaden. They spread the find to other 321st artillerymen (from left to right): PFC William Joyce, Cpl. Melton Stevens, and PFC Billy Wilkins. WILKENS FAMILY

V-E Day, a point system was put in place to determine which soldiers would be shipped home first. Initially, a soldier had to have eighty-five points; this total decreased as time and events progressed. Roughly one point was given for each month of service from 1940, and one point for each month spent overseas. Five points were given for the first awarded medal, such as the Distinguished Service Cross, Silver Star, Bronze Star, and Purple Heart. A soldier received five points for each campaign star and twelve points for each child under eighteen, up to three children.

While coming in for a landing in Holland, Horner had been lightly wounded in the hand. He had planned to forget about it, but Captain Davidson had advised him, "For the Purple Heart, all it says is that you have to be wounded. It doesn't say how badly." Because Horner applied for the Purple Heart, he received the extra points that pushed him over the requirement.

CHAPTER 2

Overseas

IN JUNE 1943, the entire 101st Division knew a massive test of their honed airborne skills was near. Again, the 321st was loaded onto the train and headed to a spot approximately five miles outside Springfield, Tennessee, for a full field maneuver. By now, the men took it for granted that any train ride was going to be slowgoing with a chugging, coal-fired, old-fashioned locomotive that spewed prodigious amounts of soot and cinders. It was in the air and on their uniforms. Worse yet, waiting for them in the fields were chiggers and more mosquitoes than they could kill.

Shortages of all types of war materiel were abundant, and making the maneuver realistic proved difficult. Firecrackers were used to simulate gunfire and jeeps doubled as tanks. One jeep would pull another jeep simulating the 75mm pack howitzer; the "howitzer" jeep then was pushed into position, and the driver blew the horn to represent fire was "on the way." The gunner would read the speedometer as if he were reading deflections. It was creative warfare.

For the first phase of the maneuvers, the men were loaded onto trucks, then onto the assembly area, simulating a glider landing in enemy territory. The glider infantry came into the mock battle by glider, landing in the fields instead of on paved runways. Those countryside fields provided rough landings, and many of the gliders were damaged extensively.

At this time, Gen. Bill Lee made his first glider landing—a rough one at that, fracturing several of his ribs. "Next time I'll take a parachute," he said.[1]

A 75mm pack howitzer at Camp Claiborne. STEPHENS/DETTORE

Whatcombe Farm. From left to right: PFC Paul Miho, T/5 Merle Fulton, and S/Sgt. Victor Truesdale. WILKINSON FAMILY

The glider riders complained to anyone who would listen that their job was just as hazardous as that of paratroopers, but they were not paid likewise for it. This argument would not be laid to rest until July 1944 when hazardous duty for glidermen was formally recognized and they were compensated with an additional 20 percent of base pay instead of a flat $50 per month.

The battalion headed back to Fort Bragg after the completion of the maneuvers and spent part of August wondering if it could possibly get any hotter. After a final inspection on the drill field, the medics conducted physicals. A secret move was soon to come, and at this point, nobody was going to be labeled unfit for duty and no furloughs were given.

This was the final Saturday leave that Cpl. Burdette Wilkinson from Painesville, Ohio, and Sgt. Victor Truesdale from Westville, South Carolina, both of Headquarters Battery, were to have while in the States at Fort Bragg. They decided to go to Truesdale's home for dinner, hitchhiking all the way there. They had to be back that same night, as the airborne sector at Fort Bragg was to be locked down, allowing no one in or out. On Sunday they were all to board trains to New York for shipment overseas, destination unknown.

The 321st departed Fort Bragg for the last time on August 30, 1943, and headed for the train station, where they were met by a band playing the artillery song "The Caissons Go Rolling Along." They boarded the same type of slow, well-traveled train to Camp Shanks in New York, where the battalion settled in for a few days. Here, an intense last-minute fury of form signings took place, along with viewings of various training films. From this point on, all outgoing mail was censored by the officers of the battalion. "We have had to start censoring the outgoing mail tonight," wrote Capt. George Dunkelberg in a letter to his wife. "I read well over a hundred letters. Some are good, some bad, and some very funny. They have requested that the word 'Gliders' be left out of our address, so you might mark that down for future reference."

It was also at Camp Shanks that Pvt. John Nasea Jr. (B Battery) of Detroit, Michigan, got a sense of things to come. Lectures and army training films—including how to brush your teeth and how to render a proper salute—filled his day, but one film in particular, *Kill or Be Killed*, put everything in perspective for this young soldier. Things were about to change.

On September 4, 1943, the men, under the command of airborne officer Gen. Anthony McAuliffe, were ordered to remove their shoulder patches, and all mail sent was to have an APO address of New York. This was done for the benefit of the unseen enemy. All precautions were studied and made in preparation for the next destination. It was time to move by train again, but this time under the cover of darkness. The battalion pulled out of Camp Shanks and headed for the port of embarkation, bypassing the sights of New York City. One day later and after a short ride by truck, it was time to get on the water.

After a short ferry ride from the docks at 42nd Street, the Eaglemen went to the HMS *Samaria* in full field pack, carrying their barracks bags up the gangplank. The *Samaria*, of the Cunard line, was built in 1920 as an English passenger ship and would be scrapped in 1956. The mode of transport was officially termed a "ship," but to the soldiers, it was a cattle barge. The smell was overpowering as they slowly made their way onto the ship, loading until late in the night. As soon as they stepped foot onboard, their pay increased 20 percent, about an extra $4.20 a month for a glider rider. At 10:00 A.M., as the ship left the safe harbor of New York, the first glimpse of their voyage by those lucky enough to be topside was that of the French luxury liner *Normandie* lying on her side. The French government-subsidized vessel had been seized while in the port of New York in 1942, since France was currently occupied by the Germans. During its conversion to a troop ship, the liner caught fire and sank. Eventually it was refloated and later scrapped in 1946.

Along with the 321st Battalion were the 506th PIR, the 327th GIR, the 326th Airborne Engineer Battalion (AEB), and others, totaling approximately 5,000 men. Earlier, as a passenger ship, the *Samaria* had sailed with approximately 3,200 people. However, the glidermen could have had it much worse: the luxury liner HMS *Queen Mary* carried about 15,000 while pressed into service as a troop ship.

It didn't take long to determine that the soldiers of the 321st were deep in the hold of the *Samaria*. The smell didn't just linger in their assigned bunking area; it seemed to emanate throughout the entire ship. Pvt. Nasea, along with many others, sought better arrangements. Their idea was to string hammocks on deck and sleep outside, but that was not such a smart plan. Soon, the ship was going to cross the North Atlantic. The real problem that lay ahead was the threat of German submarines and U-boats. There was no greater target than an overloaded troopship or two.

While the men of the 321st were boarding the *Samaria*, the ever-inquisitive Pvt. Burdette Wilkinson (HQ), the battalion's radio repairman, was paying close attention to details that most missed. He noticed obvious "English" signs on the ship and what he termed a "screwy-looking fire extinguisher" with a nameplate out of Liverpool affixed to it. His guess was that Liverpool, England, was their destination. He would be correct.

Life on board was difficult. There were thousands of men—with all of their equipment—vying for limited space. Some of them resorted to sleeping on deck in the elements, preferring the cold but fresh air. The corridors were also packed with men who found them more comfortable than their assigned areas. The farther below deck, the greater the filth and the staler the air. Lack of fresh water was the norm. Showers were taken with salt water, which didn't allow the soap to lather; instead, it turned into a slimelike substance. Wearing the bulky life jackets was mandatory at all times, and they slowly acquired the stench and filth of the voyage.

The glider riders of the battalion remember most vividly the British food rations: dried fish, rotten-smelling hard-boiled eggs, stewed tomatoes, and coffee that was considered more of a foul brew. The ship was operated by British naval officers, and the stewards were Indian. Pvt. Hubert "H. C." Warren (A Battery) of Cookeville, Tennessee, encountered food he had never seen before and had no inclination to taste: kippered herrings for breakfast, along with moldy bread and orange marmalade.

Seasickness was the norm, not the exception. Rumors abounded, the favorite being sightings of German U-boats. However, none were ever seen. On at least one occasion, depth charges were fired, furthering the rumors.

Pvt. Harry Sinkutch (HQ) of Grosse Pointe, Michigan, noticed the latrine was on one side and the kitchens nearby on the other. The latrines were in a constant state of being overloaded, overflowing across the floor through the kitchen. It seemed to him the cooks were stirring the huge pots with dirty broomstick handles. Stewed tomatoes on moldy bread only made matters worse.

Private Wilkinson wrote in a letter home:

> We sailed in a convoy of many ships and one of them was Ziegler's [Marion Siegler] Battery. Somehow we found out and watched that ship. . . . The convoy always changed direction to fool the subs or something. At night in blackout and in the fog in the day and on clear days we could watch it. Sometimes it was behind ours, sometimes in front of ours, sometimes on the right. Some high-payed Navy guy must have kept that all straightened out.
>
> One foggy day you could hardly see across the ship. I was sitting up on deck reading a book the Red Cross issued to pass the time. All at once I noticed the boat wasn't rocking in the usual slow rhythm but was staying toward the left, and it seemed everybody on the boat was next to the left rail [port side] but I couldn't figure out why. Everybody started to holler so I dropped the book and went over to look, and then through the fog I dimly made out another boat—only it was coming right at us. The fog was plenty thick but the other boat got close enough to recognize men from [Siegler's] Battery next to the rail hollering and waving their arms same as our guys. They tooted the whistle and fog horns, and our boat turned and the other one turned. Everybody knew we were going to bump, and the ocean looked so cold too. But somehow we didn't bump, although a razor blade wouldn't go between. Something was wrong with the other ship and it went back.

The other ship was the HMS *Strathnaver*, loaded with men of the 101st Division, 502nd PIR, 907th GFA, 377th PFA, and many others, totaling over 5,800 troops. Because of numerous mechanical problems, the ten-day crossing for them would evolve into an experience that lasted more than forty days. The near-sinking of these two troop ships and the subsequent rescue of the personnel put almost the entire 101st Airborne Division at risk at that single moment. The fog, the cold, and the isolation surely would have taken a tremendous toll.

Wilkinson continued:

> And so we finally arrived in Liverpool. We got off near the Customs house and it was deserted, only Army and Navy men connected with getting us off the boat. We had just sailed by some bombed docks and a sunken ship showing the top of the mast at low tide. The little we saw of Liverpool was from the docks to some railway station. We passed the first bombed houses and stores. The ones still standing had broken windows boarded up [and] it all looked deserted. We saw almost no civilians in the street, dark, boarded-up stores, no lights, no cars, or street cars or taxis. It just about got dark as we got to the railway station. The bombing had occurred

Whatcombe Farm, England. Col. Edward Carmichael and the band leading the battalion to church on Thanksgiving Day, 1943.
WILLIAMS FAMILY

> long ago [and] grass grew on the places where buildings had been. At that time it gave us a desolate queer feeling to go through this "dead" town. Nobody spoke; we just stared, open mouthed.

The 321st arrived at the former Whatcombe Horse Farm on September 16, 1943, after a 200-mile train ride from Liverpool and a 6-mile GMC 6x6 truck ride from Wantage. The battalion was unimpressed with their new home. It was a recent change in use; the horse stables, now replete with bunk beds, accommodated men instead of horses. The smell of horse manure permeated the area no matter how many times the stalls were scrubbed. The mattresses were pointy-ended bags filled with straw. Lt. Samuel Skinner, now the B Battery commander, put his hand on a mattress to feel its stiffness. A rat ran out of the end of it. The place was filled with rats.

One of the men complained about the living conditions, saying that the housing conditions favored about 50 men, not 450. At other times, it was considered the muddiest place on earth, even though the walkways were shoveled every morning to remove the mud.

Gradually, the men's feelings would change because it was now their home. Their affection for the English people nearby also grew. By the time of the Normandy invasion, the men and the civilians nearby had become concerned for each other's well-being.

The officers' quarters were nearby at Fawley Manor in Berkshire, an ancient building built in 1611 and resembling a castle to the men stationed below. It was often referred to it as such. The enlisted men were given kitchen police duty at the manor, where they were used as waiters for the officers. Some considered it an easy duty, while others resented it.

Whatcombe Farm, England. Kneeling: Raymond Nagel (left) and Witcher (right). Standing, far right: Gilbert Quinn, 2nd Gun Section, B Battery. WITCHER/DETTORE

Whatcombe Farm, England. From left to right: Joseph Baumeister, Jim Haney, Leo “Fritz” Corrigan, and Dick “Moose” Moss of the A Battery gun section. Baumeister was the lucky winner of the drawing from A Battery to go home for a Christmas furlough. G. J. DETTORE COLLECTION

Whatcombe Farm, England. Cpl. Vernon Raker (left) and PFC Dick Moss (right) standing in front of their "home," horse stable #12. RAKER FAMILY

Whatcombe Farm, England. Standing (from left to right): Lloyd "Pinky" Tomblin, Dick "Moose" Moss, Ray Busch, Dizzey, Joe Weidle, and Fareman. Sitting (from left to right): Kalwei, Luther "Fat" Hasting, Gene Powers, and Allison. RAKER FAMILY

Officers' quarters at Fawley Manor. WILLIAMS FAMILY

Fawley Manor, England. Lieutenant Davis with an English child evacuated from the city.

Capt. Samuel Skinner was tasked with the responsibility of giving an orientation talk to the battalions' fresh arrivals upon reaching Whatcombe Farm. He kept a small notebook and jotted down topics to be discussed in greater detail with the men. Some of the items on his list were:

Encourage the men to visit British homes if invited.
Send money home.
Visit the Red Cross Club (you may invite British officers).
Race question.
Venereal disease.
Do not issue any passes to Marlborough.
Be careful about salutes. We will salute British soldiers.
Drivers should stay with their vehicles.
Men cannot wear the leather garrison belt.
Insignia will be taken away.
Any man writing on his field jacket will file a statement of charges.
No hot fire when going to bed.
Search before men go on pass or furlough. ■

Fawley Manor, England. Lt. Dr. David Davidson (left) and Capt. Sam Williams (right) with censored-out eagle patches. WILLIAMS FAMILY

Fawley Manor, England, February 1944. From left to right: Lt. William Nugent, Lt. Arnold Kruvant (killed in action on June 6, 1944, while with the 377th PFA), and Lt. James "Buck" Davis. DAVIS FAMILY

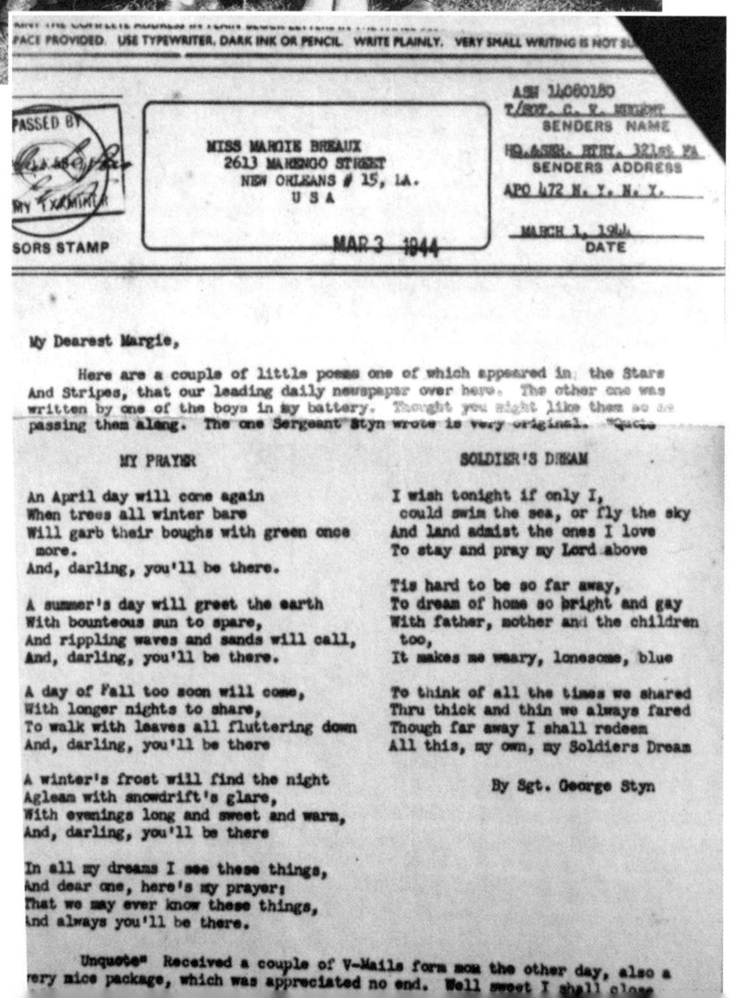

PACE PROVIDED. USE TYPEWRITER, DARK INK OR PENCIL. WRITE PLAINLY. VERY SMALL WRITING IS NOT SU

PASSED BY
BY EXAMINER
SORS STAMP

MISS MARGIE BREAUX
2613 MARENGO STREET
NEW ORLEANS # 15, LA.
U S A

MAR 3 1944

ASN 14080180
T/SGT. C. V. NUGENT
SENDERS NAME
HQ.&SER. BTRY. 321st FA
SENDERS ADDRESS
APO 472 N. Y. N. Y.
MARCH 1, 1944
DATE

My Dearest Margie,

Here are a couple of little poems one of which appeared in the Stars And Stripes, that our leading daily newspaper over here. The other one was written by one of the boys in my battery. Thought you might like them so am passing them along. The one Sergeant Styn wrote is very original. "Quote

MY PRAYER

An April day will come again
When trees all winter bare
Will garb their boughs with green once more.
And, darling, you'll be there.

A summer's day will greet the earth
With bounteous sun to spare,
And rippling waves and sands will call,
And, darling, you'll be there.

A day of Fall too soon will come,
With longer nights to share,
To walk with leaves all fluttering down
And, darling, you'll be there

A winter's frost will find the night
Agleam with snowdrift's glare,
With evenings long and sweet and warm,
And, darling, you'll be there

In all my dreams I see these things,
And dear one, here's my prayer;
That we may ever know these things,
And always you'll be there.

SOLDIER'S DREAM

I wish tonight if only I,
could swim the sea, or fly the sky
And land admist the ones I love
To stay and pray my Lord above

Tis hard to be so far away,
To dream of home so bright and gay
With father, mother and the children too,
It makes me weary, lonesome, blue

To think of all the times we shared
Thru thick and thin we always fared
Though far away I shall redeem
All this, my own, my Soldiers Dream

By Sgt. George Styn

Unquote" Received a couple of V-Mails form mom the other day, also a very nice package, which was appreciated no end. Well sweet I shall close

Fawley Manor, England. Owners of the farm with 321st officers. Front row (from left to right): Mrs. Peggy Jeffs, Lt. Carroll Holland, Miss Phylis Beasley, Mrs. Barrett, and Lt. Fitzpatrick. Back row (from left to right): Maj. Thomas Henderson, Frank Barrett, Capt. Dr. Davidson, Stanley, Lt. Johnny Jordan, Mrs. Jordan, and Lt. Henry Kowalczyk.

Whatcombe Farm, England. Sgt. Charlie Nugent sends his future wife a V-mail letter containing a poem, "Soldiers Dream," published in the *Stars and Stripes* military newspaper and written by 321st Sgt. George Styn.

NUGENT FAMILY

The word was out in A Battery that Pvt. Jess Harmon of Handley, West Virginia, standing six feet tall and with blue eyes, was bad news. He told anyone who would listen how good he was with a knife. Or about the time he burned down a cabin with his wife inside. Each time he retold a story, it would become more gruesome, especially if he was drinking—so much so that the men of A Battery started to doubt them all. A few of the braver lads would say, "You tell 'em horseshit; you've been on the road."

Pvt. Charles Cosner from Bayard, West Virginia, was also in A Battery. Cosner was perhaps the smallest soldier in the entire battalion at five feet one inch tall—certainly the shortest in his battery. His facial features resembled a Kewpie doll and shaving was unnecessary. When the artillerymen went into the town pub for drinks, his buddies had to vouch that Cosner was a soldier with their unit and not their village mascot. If the bartender made a quip about how young-looking he was, an acidic reply was quick to follow—Cosner swore like a drunken sailor.

One night at Whatcombe Farm, Harmon was passed out in the sleeping quarters, his snoring so loud it disturbed all the other men around him. Cosner pulled out a wad of Beech-Nut chewing tobacco from a pouch he carried, jumped on Harmon's chest, and stuffed the tobacco into his open mouth. Harmon awakened from his drunken slumber, spat out the tobacco, and looked around. Cosner took off running, then stopped and said, "Go ahead and hit me—you're big enough. What are you afraid of?" A little more taunting from Cosner ensued, but Harmon simply went back to sleep. ■

In early February, the army found a way to ease their complaints about the censorship of their mail by the officers. Twice a month, a soldier could write home and place his letter in a regulation blue envelope stamped SOLDIER'S LETTER. This meant the letter within could not be censored by a company, battalion, or regimental officer. It would, however, still be censored by the chief military censor. The intention was to give a soldier the ability to address highly personal family matters in a letter home without fearing it would be discussed by his peers. All other rules of censorship remained in place.

A massive parachute drop was planned for the benefit of British prime minister Winston Churchill and Gen. Dwight D. Eisenhower on March 3, 1944, when they were going to make an inspection of the troops. PFC Harry Sinkutch (HQ) was near enough to their vehicle to hear Eisenhower and Churchill's conversation. Churchill said to Eisenhower, "I thought these paratroopers were going to be big, but they look small to me." Eisenhower hesitated, and then replied, "They may look small, but they're mighty."

One of the local children, an eleven-year-old boy named W. Brian Marsh, made friends with 1st Sgt. Wellington Troutman (HQ) from Mascot, Tennessee. The youngster and some friends would come into camp and shine shoes in exchange for spare candy left over from the K rations. A treat for the soldiers was fresh bread, which was not rationed. It was brought into the camp by the kids and shared with the soldiers. The soldiers would smear it with fresh butter, a treat for the children. Peanut butter was their second choice, something not found in the English diet.

The chalk pits doubled as a firing range. There, the young boys were taught how to fire the carbine—big stuff indeed! Some of the boys were allowed to drive jeeps on the grounds at Whatcombe or were taken for a tour of the Waco CG-4A glider fuselage used for training purposes. The lads were put in the pilot seat and given an explanation on how the instruments and controls operated. During Thanksgiving and Christmas, the big 6x6 trucks would show up after school and take them to holiday parties given at the farm.

As would be expected, many love stories swirled around the battalion, particularly during their time in England. PFC Joseph Januskevitz (A Battery) from Plains, Pennsylvania, met an English gal, and they got engaged. But there was at least one problem: the

England. Prime Minister Winston Churchill speaking at the airfield. PERKINS FAMILY

England. Soldiers from the 101st perform a demonstration jump for Churchill. DAVIS FAMILY

Whatcombe Farm, England. Standing (from left to right): Dick Moss, Kalwei, Stanley Van Pelt, Lloyd "Pinky" Tomblin, Joe Baumeister, Everett "Nick" Nichols, unidentified soldier, Jess "Stout" Harmon, "Big Steve" Stevens, Leo "Butch" ("Fritz") Corrigan, and Joe. Kneeling (from left to right): Jim Haney, Vernon Raker, and Irish. RAKER FAMILY

Right: Holland. Standing (from left to right): Bernard Katz, Donald Rogers, and Vernon Raker. Sitting (from left to right): Oare, Miller, and Charles Cosner. RAKER FAMILY

Whatcombe Farm, England. A Christmas party for the neighborhood children, who were always after the glidermen's candy rations. PFC H. C. Warren is at the far right rear, wearing glasses. NUGENT/DETTORE

Whatcombe Farm, England. More of the village children: Nealy, baby Lizabeth, Mike Knezevic, and little Gilbert. TURKAL FAMILY

Whatcombe Farm, England. The farm owners hold a dance for 321st officers at the manor. From left to right: General McAuliffe, Capt. Frederic King, Mr. George Dowser, and Maj. Thomas Henderson. WILLIAMS FAMILY

Whatcombe Farm, England. From left to right: Capt. John Fuller, Capt. George Dunkelberg, and Col. Edward Carmichael. WILLIAMS FAMILY

Whatcombe Farm, England. A disciplinary infraction march was ordered by Colonel Carmichael. Notice the smiling faces and the English officer in the mix. This method was used to build cohesion among the officers. WILLIAMS FAMILY

Officers' quarters at Fawley Manor, England. NUGENT/DETTORE

mother of the soon-to-be bride didn't want her daughter to leave England, so she devised a plan to keep her at home.

The battalion left their base at Whatcombe Farm for the last time in September 1944. If all went well, Januskevitz would marry his fiancée whenever he got a chance to return. They promised to correspond until that day arrived, but the mother of the fiancée interfered with that. Every letter Januskevitz sent to his intended bride was interdicted by her mother. Most likely, every letter the daughter left in the care of her mother was never posted. The mother would tell her daughter that the soldier had forgotten about her and had no intentions of ever coming back to marry. After all, why wasn't he writing to her? The daughter relented and after the war married an Englishman.[2]

Another love story of a different sort involved a young daughter of an employee who lived and worked at Whatcombe Farm. The daughter became pregnant, though it's unclear if the baby's father was in the 321st or not. The father held the Americans responsible for his daughter's situation and was aghast that the soldier denied responsibility. Word was put out, asking if anyone in the battalion would marry the girl. Many in the 321st were aware of her presence on the farm. One soldier stepped forward, PFC Jesse Loop (A Battery), and wed the gal. He told his buddies, "I'm going to get killed, so I might as well get married."

While at Whatcombe Farm, men could occasionally secure a "Walking Pass" for a day, which would allow them to be away from their camp and go anywhere they could walk to and return by evening. The closest village was about eight miles away. Once a week, trucks would take the men to Oxford for one day and bring them back at night. Those who caught a venereal disease would be treated by the battalion surgeon and demoted one rank. This happened to some of the men two or three times.

M/Sgt. Albert Bender of Bellevue, Ohio, knew how to get things done by begging, borrowing, or stealing—but mostly by stealing. If something was needed and couldn't be found, it was, "Go see Sergeant Bender." On more than one occasion, the roads became a mess from all the traffic, resembling a plowed field more than a road. Somehow, during the night a road grader arrived, and by the morning light, Bender had the roads at Whatcombe Farm scraped and leveled. He was the oldest man in the battalion, born in 1895; a short, wiry man, his deep-lined face made him look twenty years older than he was. Those who walked into Bender's room at Whatcombe Farm in the morning were guaranteed to see two things: his teeth in a cup and a bottle of whiskey under the bunk. Bender's daughter had married the 321st Headquarters supply sergeant, Lawrence Benninghoff from Bellevue, Ohio.

Bender's reputation as a barterer was legendary. While the battalion was in Normandy, he and a small group who all acted as rear echelon stayed behind.

M/Sgt. Albert Bender (looking at camera) at Whatcombe Farm. LINZ FAMILY

Whatcombe Farm, England. Colonel Carmichael leading the battalion to church services celebrating Armistice Day, November 11, 1943. WILLIAMS FAMILY

Lumber was needed. At the nearby lumberyard outside of Whatcombe Farm, Bender noticed a broken-handled hammer lying on a stack of boards. It didn't take long for the yardman to be talked out of the hammer, but not until a new handle was installed.

Word came down from command that twins could not serve in the same section. B Battery had a set: Pvts. Lynn and Lyle Strouse of Kingston, Illinois. They were not only in the same battery, but also in the same gun section. Lt. James Davis gave them the news that they had to be split up and that there was nothing he could do about it. The Strouse twins had a reputation for fighting between themselves—knock-down, drag-out fights. They always made up, so no one ever said anything about it. On one occasion, they threw 75mm rounds at each other at the gun pit. Everybody just got out of the way until both of them cooled down. They got along with everybody but each other and were well liked.

Just as Davis was leaving with one of the twins in his jeep to take him to another battery, an officer ran up, waving a piece of paper, and said, "Stop, you can't take him." Davis, known as a no-nonsense officer, responded, "Like hell I can't." He was given the pink piece of paper to read. When he finished, Davis asked Strouse why he hadn't said anything about the note's contents. Strouse was perplexed and asked

Twin brothers T/5s Lynne (left) and Lyle Strouse of B Battery.

him what he meant. It turned out when the twins were drafted, their mother sent a letter to Mrs. Eleanor Roosevelt, requesting that she ask the Draft Board and the War Department to keep her boys together all the way through. A mother herself, Mrs. Roosevelt approved and relayed the request, written on her pink stationery, along to those who could honor it. The twins stayed in the same gun section throughout the war and rode the same glider into Holland. Although one sustained a hand injury, they made it home together.

In March, the battalion commander of B Battery, Capt. Samuel Skinner, wrote in his diary:

> Later on in March the Col. got all excited about the invasion and sent Fuller [A Battery commander], Dunkelberg [HQ Battery commander] and myself to [the] vicinity of Dartmouth to act as observers for the 44 Field Art. of the 4th Div. He thought we would be with them on the invasion. We rode an LST out in

Right: England, March 1944. Capt. Samuel Williams leans against a Devon earth fence built of stone and soil, several hundred years old and similar to the Normandy hedgerows. A significant intelligence failure was that the glider pilots who did land in Normandy were told that the hedgerows were only going to be a few feet tall. However, this photo was taken while on a four-day invasion practice with 4th Division, evidence that at least one infantry division was aware of the unusual Normandy terrain, which contradicts the commonly held belief that it was a complete surprise. WILLIAMS FAMILY

Whatcombe Farm, England. Jim Haney, Dick Moss, old Sgt. Hartley, Doc Christian, and Allison (kneeling). RAKER FAMILY

the Channel for 3 or 4 days around the last of March and landed with them on a beach on the coast of England. That was quite some show.

Sometime in March, 1st Sgt. Timothy Shea (B Battery) from Worchester, Massachusetts, was sent out, along with others, to recruit for the 101st. Pvt. Bernard Simmons of Marion, Indiana, was in a replacement unit referred to as a "repple depot." He heard that someone was going to give a talk in a building near his quarters. He quickly found out it was a colonel in the 101st Airborne Division and that the unit wanted volunteers for a glider outfit. The colonel was talking up his division, saying how good they were. Then he handed the meeting over to Shea, who told the group that those who wanted to join should stay behind and the rest could leave. Simmons, in the back of the group, moved forward with a bunch of other men to better hear what the sergeant was saying. Shea was taking down names. He looked at Simmons and asked him what his name was. He instinctively replied, "Simmons." Shea wrote it down in in his book. Simmons quickly said, "Sergeant, I don't want to go in that outfit." Shea said he told everybody to leave who didn't want to be in the outfit, and Simmons hadn't left, so he was in it. Simmons protested, but his fate was sealed. He was now in the 321st. He was loaded onto a truck and sent off to Whatcombe Farm, arriving at night.

The training never ceased, and not just the physical conditioning held in the complete darkness of morning, when it was so dark that some of the men would stray to the rear of the formation and hide. The first combat training exercise occurred on October 2–9 in the Aldbourne–Ramsbury area with the 506th PIR. The 321st participated in division-wide field problems, Horsa glider training, and field artillery ranges. In all, there were fourteen different training exercises, the last one held on April 13–14, 1944.

There were two fuselages of a CG-4A on the grounds at the farm for training purposes. Many a

First Sgt. Timothy Shea of B Battery.

jeep and trailer was loaded and unloaded in that glider—so many that the cable attached to the rear of the jeep that allowed the nose of the glider to rise as the jeep drove out had to be replaced multiple times. The fix was simple enough in training: lift up the nose of the glider manually and hold it up with a 2x4 piece of lumber.

Glider training at the airfields had its moments, from sheer panic to unbridled laughter, and sometimes both almost simultaneously. Cpl. Woodrow Stephens (A Battery) from Champaign, Illinois, had logged some civilian flight time back home. The glider pilots took full advantage of this, with the help of Stephens, and prepared an orchestrated joke on the glider riders. The glider pilot would loudly go on and on about how tired he was from being out all night drinking. While in the air, Stephens, in the copilot's seat, would secretly pull a pin overhead that allowed the steering yoke to shift over from the pilot to the copilot. Stephens would act surprised as the pilot feigned sleep. Then, Stephens would pretend to wake the glider pilot, saying the glider was falling apart. The pilot would take back the controls, and Stephens would look back and laugh at those glider

The firing range at Imber, England, with 75mm pack howitzers. WILLIAMS FAMILY

England. Capt. Sam Williams shaving. Helmets were useful for this task. DAVIS/DETTORE

The Imber firing range. B Battery Sgt. Norman Deethardt is at the far left. DAVIS FAMILY

riders behind him. This trick worked only if the Waco CG-4A had been manufactured before mid-1943; specifications after that date changed so that there were dual controls for the pilot and copilot. The joke was replayed on a few additional flights until the trick was well known throughout the battalion.

Early in April, the battalion spent the first week in live-fire training for their 75mm pack howitzers at the artillery range in Tilshead. On one of those fire missions, someone down the line made a mistake. A fire mission was put out and relayed, and the guns were fired, but one of the rounds hit a wooden water tower, rendering it useless. Somebody was going to get reimbursed, courtesy of the United States government.

A 101st Division–wide program was initiated on April 8, 1944: a two-week exchange. Soldiers of the 321st and artillerymen of the 53rd Worcester Yeomanry Airlanding Light (A/L) Regiment, 6th British Airborne, traded places. Ten Brits came into the battalion and ten 321st men from different batteries made a temporary departure into the British airborne. Among the chosen were Sgt. William Plummer, PFC Howard Krivos, PFC Edmund Florkowksi, and PFC Lemuel Slayter of B Battery, and Cpl. Vernon Raker of A Battery.

Raker wrote:

> The first morning, when a figure entered the barracks, blowing a whistle, summoning men to revile [*sic*], I was the only one who got up. The Limey's were screaming, "Stow that bloody whistle and get the hell out of here." When I was nearly dressed and was heading out with my shaving kit, one of the boys raised up and said, "Hey Jock, it's your turn to fetch the tea." One of the lads slipped into his shoes, gathered up about a dozen tin cups, and still in underwear, headed for the kitchen to fetch tea. I was the only one from the barracks to stand formation.
>
> The Sergeant-Major, replete in his hob-nailed boots, cut quite a figure as he made a very correct about-face when the officer of

England. From left to right: Maj. Thomas Henderson, Lt. Dr. David Davidson, Capt. Joseph Perkins, and Capt. Samuel Williams.

England, Imber firing range. Standing (left to right): Major Henderson, Captain Perkins, and an unknown soldier. WILLIAMS FAMILY

A B Battery 75mm pack howitzer positioned in beechnut trees during a training exercise at the Imber firing range, April 1944. WILLIAMS FAMILY

the day appeared. With a snappy salute, he reported, "All men present and accounted for, SIR!" The officer glanced briefly at the dozen men assembled, and said, "I say sergeant, it appears there are a few men missing." "It is possible you may be right sir." "I ask you sergeant, do you know where they might possibly be?" "Perhaps at the Naffi sir, having a cup of tea." "Yes, what an excellent idea, dismiss your men, and let's join them."

One day, a class was given on how to load a British Horsa glider. A mock-up was on hand, and it was time to load a jeep and a 105mm howitzer and lash them down. About ten British soldiers took part, with the rest of the battalion resting under the wings and smoking.

An officer reading from a chart would inquire where a particular tie-down should go. He then explained to those paying attention its proper location. This went on until all the tie-down positions were explained for the jeep and gun.

Raker recounted: "The men present would nod they understood. The entire morning was consumed on saying how things were to be done, but not one tie-down was effected, and only about a half dozen men had any conception of what was to be done. What the hell kind of an army was this anyhow?"

Another class given was on aircraft identification. Only one airman in the group could tell the difference between a Spitfire and a German Me 109: Raker. He remarked to one of the noncoms that he thought it was vital to know the difference between enemy and friendly aircraft. The British soldier disagreed, saying that while he was at Dunkirk after being shelled ceaselessly, "troops were overjoyed to see an English spotter plane circle over them putting out a billow of smoke like a skywriter." Next came a squadron of German bombers that dumped their loads through the circle of smoke and onto the beach packed with retreating British and Allied forces. His point was simple: it didn't make any difference what the make of the

England. A group of 321st officers with a British officer, photographed prior to D-Day. HENDERSON FAMILY

England. PFC Anthony Ludwig (bottom row, left) of B Battery on detail with fellow 321st soldiers and British counterparts during the exchange program. LUDWIG FAMILY

airplane was; the most important question was who was flying it. "I learned in Bastogne that he had a valid point," Raker wrote.

The last training exercise occurred near the end of April at a civilian-evacuated seacoast area in Torquay, England, which resembled the Normandy coast with 3 miles of beaches. The battalion was billeted in various hotels and summer resorts. Training took an unusual twist: the 321st's part of the exercise was the invasion of the "Westwall," which included landing craft and other amphibious equipment. Umpires tagged key individuals as wounded in order to ascertain the efficiency of the battalion without them. Exercise Tiger took place April 22–30 and used live fire from naval and artillery pieces. The landings lasted two days, April 27 and 28, but ended in disaster when the "Germans" sank amphibious landing crafts participating in this mock invasion of Normandy. All participants were forbidden to talk about Exercise Tiger, also called Slapton Sands, under threat of a court-martial. During this exercise, 946 men died (none from the 101st); it was kept secret for forty years.

Capt. Frederic King (HQ) was injured in a jeep accident while participating in Exercise Tiger and sent to the 316th Station Hospital. While there, he received a letter from Brig. Gen. Maxwell Taylor, dated May 3, 1944. The letter reads: "Dear King: I was very sorry to learn of your accident during Exercise Tiger but I am glad to learn that it was not too serious. It is particularly disastrous to lose 33 1/3% of the Division squash-playing strength. Best wishes for a speedy recovery. Sincerely yours."

Three officers transferred out of the 321st prior to D-Day. Second Lt. Irving Levick was a former acrobat who was in prime physical shape and displayed his abilities to the men in the battalion, teaching jujitsu while at Whatcombe Farm. Levick had taken jump school training in England and said his job was to direct naval fire on D-Day, but his mission "never materialized."

Research has proven that statement incorrect. The 321st Battalion history states: "We had sent a Forward Observer Team to jump in with the 506th Parachutists. Their job was to direct Naval and Self-propelled 105[mm] fire until we got in. This proved to be the only support the infantry had for the first few days, due to our being held up in getting ashore."[3]

While on a pass to visit his soon-to-be bride who lived nearby, Levick missed the return truck ride back to camp. Apparently the driver of the truck left earlier than the normal appointed time of departure. Levick found a couple of military police and told them of his plight. The police said they would drive him back to camp, but somebody had stolen their jeep.

Colonel Carmichael was notified that Levick didn't return to camp and was now AWOL. When Levick returned the next day, he was confined to his quarters by order of the colonel. Carmichael made it clear that the lieutenant was not wanted in the 321st.

Shortly thereafter, Levick transferred out to DivArty as an assistant to the communications officer, missing all combat missions of the division. When asked why the colonel disliked him so, he replied "because of my physical abilities. . . . he was jealous of that."

First Lt. Arnold Kruvant of New Jersey was a Camp Claiborne original. He transferred to the 377th Parachute Artillery Battalion and became the S-3, jumping into Normandy even though he had never had jump training. Kruvant carried in with him the funds for the battalion, $500 in U.S. currency. He is listed as KIA and MIA on June 6. He was twenty-six years old.

Kruvant's widow was well known and well liked by the men of the 321st. They decided at the time that she would not be told of her husband's gruesome

The closed area at Torquay, England. The local population was moved due to secret training exercises. From left to right: 321st soldiers Corporal Schofield, Doc Brady (the dentist), and James "Buck" Davis pull maintenance on a jeep at an abandoned gas station. The designation on the bumper was scratched off by a censor. NUGENT/DETTORE

From left to right: Ken Charles, Atwood, and George Turkal in Paignton, England, April 1944. TURKAL FAMILY

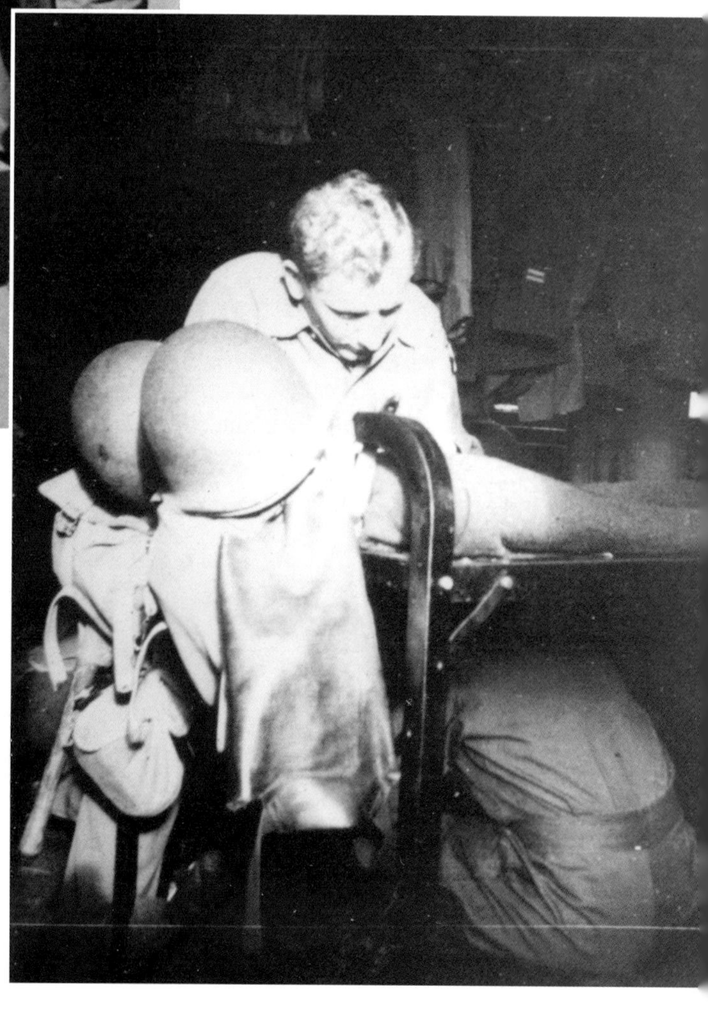

England. Corporal Turkal writes home from Airborne Naval Shore Fire Control school. TURKAL FAMILY

death. Several 321st officers recalled that Kruvant was bayoneted to death while hung up in his parachute harness, dangling from a tree just off the ground. Why his body was never positively identified remains a mystery to this day.

Capt. Howard Upchurch from Montgomery, Alabama, also transferred to the 377th PFA. He is listed as KIA on June 6. He was thirty-three years old, married with a young son. Upchurch is buried in Montgomery County, Alabama.

The navy and the army worked out a plan that provided an innovative solution used during the first days of the Normandy invasion. In late March 1943, a naval school was set up near the coast of England, called Airborne Naval Shore Fire Control, Third Army, to train airborne troopers on the methods used in firing their big guns. Quite a number of these soldiers were from army field artillery battalions, but were temporarily assigned to the 101st. These artillerymen were to be placed on various warships off the coast of Normandy: cruisers, destroyers, and battleships at their disposal. The purpose was to give the lightly armed paratroopers and other units big-gun capabilities until their artillery was ashore and firing. The schooling would allow these thirty or so soldiers to receive fire missions from those on Normandy soil. The fire missions were to be radioed in to the warships off the Normandy coast. The transmitted map coordinates were converted by those soldiers on the ships to naval firing standards.

The 321st had one soldier assigned for this duty: Cpl. George Turkal (HQ) of Massillon, Ohio. He was excellent in mathematics and already trained on radio.[4] His ship assignment was the USS *Nevada*, a battleship of World War I vintage that had been refitted several times and had been at Pearl Harbor on December 7, 1941. It was now armed with sixteen 5-inch guns, along with an assortment of other weapons.

Conversely, the navy sent Lt. J. G. Francis Galbraith to the 321st Headquarters to assist in fire missions. He stayed with the battalion until June 24, 1944, then transferred back to the navy.

Cpl. George Turkal of Headquarters Battery. TURKAL FAMILY

CHAPTER 3

Normandy

AFTER TRAINING FOR OVER TWO YEARS and being classified as a glider artillery battalion, it was assumed the 321st would glide into combat. The men had been drilled tirelessly on loading, lashing down, and unloading equipment in their CG-4As at breakneck speeds, mostly in the dark and total silence. How wrong they were! Since April 1944, aerial photography showed that the landing zones to be used in Normandy were currently being planted with obstacles—mainly Rommel's "Asparagus" wooden poles, some of which were topped with mines, placed in flooded fields. It was part of General Field Marshal Rommel's plan to thwart just such a use of those fields by gliders.

It was also believed that not enough Waco CG-4As were on hand to make such a landing, even though they were being uncrated and assembled twenty-four hours a day in England, coupled with a limited availability of tugs to tow them there. C-47s would be making multiple round-trips as it was. The 321st would go in by sea. That information was conveyed to the executive officers early in May 1944.

When the invasion plan was still being worked out in March, it was proposed the 101st would go in one day and the 82nd the next.[1] This way, there would be enough C-47s available to tow in the glider personnel. Roughly three gliders would be assigned for every tug. However, this plan was scrubbed.

England. Brig. Gen. Anthony McAuliffe, commander of 101st Airborne Division Artillery, and his staff check situation maps while on maneuvers in May 1944. Brig. Gen. Gerald J. Higgins, assistant division commander, looks on. KOPACKA FAMILY

The following report was signed by Lt. Colonel Edward Carmichael.

CONFIDENTIAL
Normandy After Action Report

TO: Commanding General,
101st Airborne Division

July 28, 1944

The 321st Glider Field Artillery Battalion, with a full complement of men and officers, left its home station 15 May 1944 under the command of Lt. Col. EDWARD L. CARMICHAEL, and proceeded to a marshaling area [Camp 87] in South Wales. The unit remained at the above camp until its embarkation at Cardiff, Wales, 4 June 1944 and sailed for France 5 June 1944. The Battalion sailed on two different ships with personnel sailing on the "U.S.S. Susan B. Anthony" and organizational equipment on the "S.S. John S. Mosby." D-Day was announced to men on both ships while at sea and all personnel were briefed on the unit's mission.

At 0800 hours 7 June 1944 the "U.S.S. Susan B. Anthony" struck a mine and sank. [This is erroneous; the *Susan B. Anthony* struck two mines.] The 321st Glider Field Artillery Battalion did not suffer any casualties and all officers and men were transferred to other craft, from whence they were transferred to landing craft. Personnel from sunken ship began arriving on the beach at 1500 hours 7 June 1944 and upon organizing, moved to assembly area. Personnel and equipment from "S.S. John S. Mosby" arrived at assembly area 9 June 1944 after suffering from numerous casualties from spent anti-aircraft fire aboard landing craft, which was firing at enemy aircraft. Nine of these men were evacuated and six returned to the unit at a later date.

The Battalion occupied its first active position on 10 June 1944 at 1015 hours in direct support of the 327 Glider Infantry Regiment with one Battalion of the 401st Glider Infantry Regiment attached. Contact was made with the 327th Glider Infantry Regiment rear Command Post at 1000 hours. Liaison and Forward Observer parties were sent out and contact was made with the forward Command Post two thousand yards East of Carentan. On 11 June 1944 the 327th Glider Infantry Regiment attacked Carentan from the North and East and close support was given to the 401st GIR in its assault down Bassin à Flot, North of the town. A rolling barrage was laid down to cover the advance and the 401st GIR met little resistance during its advance. However, when said barrage was lifted, resistance stiffened greatly and it was at this time that the 401st suffered many casualties.

On 12 June 1944 the 327th GIR was relieved by the 501st Parachute Infantry Regiment in Carentan and was given the mission of securing the Canal de Vire et Tou line South East of Carentan. The 321st Glider Field Artillery Battalion took up a position 2,500 yards East of Carentan in the vicinity of the town of Catz.

The forward observers of this Battalion fired numerous missions during the attack launched by the 327th GIR attacking astride the road to St. Lo. This fire was partly responsible for the supported Infantry reaching its objective. It was necessary to withdraw across the railroad on the following day to straighten the line and organize for a threatened Panzer attack.

During this action many of the Divisional units were surrounded, particularly the 377th Parachute Field Artillery Battalion Command Post, and some missions were actually fired behind enemy lines. One Infantry Battalion was cut off for thirty-six hours. The 321st Glider Field Artillery Battalion suffered five casualties during said activity, these being enlisted men wounded while operating in front lines with liaison parties.

In addition to the supporting fires, the Battalion fired harassing fire almost continuously until 15 June 1944 when the Battalion, with the rest of the Division, took up a defensive position Southwest of Carentan. This position was held until 27 June 1944. At this time a position was occupied in the vicinity of St. Sauveur le Vicomte and the unit remained there until 29 June 1944.

When the Divisional defensive position was vacated, the Battalion moved North toward Cherburg and established a camp prior to being shipped back to England. During the period from 29 June to 9 July 1944, motor patrols were assigned and dispatched regularly in accordance with a Division Artillery order and assigned areas policed. The Battalion returned to its initial landing beach and sailed from France for England on 11 July 1944 and arrived in South Hampton [*sic*], England, 12 July 1944. . . . Home station was reached the same day.[2]

After the battalion left Whatcombe Farm on May 15, it was bumped from one marshaling area to another, finally ending up in South Wales. Waterproofing jeeps, guns, and other types of essential equipment removed any doubts of being involved in a glider-borne operation. This was done at Camp 87 near the port of Cardiff, Wales, where the battalion stayed until May 28. The 90th Infantry Division was also getting prepared there. The word from the officers was that the higher-ups were constantly making changes on what the men would take with them and how they were to do things.

After three or four days, things slowed down and passes were given out for visits to the town of Abergavenny (nicknamed "aggravated Annie" by the soldiers of the battalion due to its strange-sounding name). It didn't take long for fights to break out between some black troops and some glidermen from the 90th and 321st. A 321st soldier was leaving a building where a fight had broken out and was stabbed in the back with an ice pick. He recovered and made the landing into Normandy. After this incident, black troops went into town one day, and white troops the next. The 321st machine guns were placed on the sides of the road by Capt. Samuel Skinner (HQ) of Jacksonville, Florida.

While at camp, Gen. Anthony McAuliffe and Colonel Carmichael walked among the 321st boys. McAuliffe would engage in small talk with the soldiers and ask how things were going, then move on. This went on until he met Cpl. Leo Weaver (B Battery) from Watson, West Virginia. McAuliffe asked him how things were going. Weaver replied, "Not so good, sir." McAuliffe asked what was wrong, and Weaver told him there was no hot water for the showers. Carmichael turned pale, and the next day hot showers were available.

Baseball games were played constantly, so much so that Capt. Frederic King (HQ Battery and the battalion's S-2, later commander of B Battery on July 1, 1944) mentioned them when he wrote home. In a letter sent to his parents on July 3, 1944, he wrote: "Our average day consisted mainly of playing baseball until we wondered whether the Germans would have a team."

On May 29, the battalion loaded onto two ships, and moved out into the bay the next day. The battalion embarked from Cardiff on June 4 and finally sailed for France on the fifth. The men were not told of their destination until they were at sea on June 5. Everyone received the invasion leaflet from the Allied Supreme Commander, Gen. Dwight Eisenhower.

Merle Fulton (T/4) was a farmboy from Lucas, Ohio. Assigned to headquarters, one of his jobs was to keep the gasoline-powered generators functioning properly. These generators were needed to power the radios, the lifeblood of communication between the firing batteries and the FDC.

Fulton left Whatcombe Farm on May 18 for Camp #87 in Wales. He spent the first week getting ready for the invasion. For almost another week, Fulton and the other 321st boys played sports, went to shows, or rested.

On Friday, June 2, Fulton traveled to Cardiff and boarded the Liberty ship *John S. Mosby*. On June 3, the packed ship left port to join the rest of the invasion fleet. The *Mosby* was so overloaded that many of the men, including Fulton, slept on the steel deck of the ship.

On the morning of June 5, personnel were informed that the next day was D-Day, at which time the Eisenhower invasion leaflets were to be handed out. The plan was to unload both cargo and men on June 7 at Utah Beach and to meet up with the rest of the battalion from the *Susan B. Anthony*, which was to be unloaded first. That didn't go as planned as the *Susan* was sunk on June 7 and the *Mosby* couldn't be found while off the coast of Normandy.

Every evening, from June 6 (Tuesday) until the *Mosby* was unloaded late on June 9 (Friday), the ship was under bombardment from the Luftwaffe. Luckily no hits were scored on the *Mosby*. This was not the first time Fulton was caught in the sights of the Luftwaffe. While on furlough earlier in the year, he was returning from Salisbury, England, in January and just made it into London when the air raid sirens went off. He spent the next three hours hunkered down in the Underground while the city was under attack.

"Late Friday evening just as the first LCT left for the beach, several enemy planes came over and strafed us [and] several of the men on the LCT were lost [wounded, not killed]," Fulton wrote. "Five of the planes were shot down in less than ten minutes. Finally at 0130 hrs. Saturday morning we started for the beach with the equipment. We landed around 0230 hrs. and walked about a mile to our assembly area."

By Saturday, June 10, the 321st was in position and had its first fire mission. It was to be a light day for fire missions: sixty rounds of M54 and five rounds of smoke fired in total by the battalion.

One of the 321st transport ships was named the USS *Susan B. Anthony*, a converted passenger steam liner built in March 1930. She was originally put to sea with the name of SS *Santa Clara*, but was acquired by the navy on September 7, 1942.

She left the port in Wales overloaded and carrying approximately 3,000 soldiers and 400 sailors. A

Whatcombe Farm, England. From left to right: T/5 Merle Fulton, Cpl. Paul Miho, T/5 Wilkinson, and S/Sgt. Victor Truesdale of Headquarters Battery.

Reoutfitted USS (AP-72) *Susan B. Anthony.*

USS *Susan B. Anthony* being assisted by a destroyer in unloading troops after striking two German mines off the Normandy coast. This series of photographs was taken by a sailor on a ship standing by to render assistance. Later in the war, he discovered that his brother, also a sailor, was on the *Susan* at the time of her sinking. The photographs were given to his brother after the war, but the identity of those sailors has been lost to time.

The *Susan B. Anthony* sinking.

decision was made to split the battalion into two groups. The smaller group boarded the USS *John S. Mosby*, a Liberty ship that held their guns and other equipment. Personnel consisted of the jeep drivers, chiefs of sections, and two men from each gun section. The remainder would sail on the *Susie*, which had the capacity to hold more men. This way, it would be assured that the loss of one ship at sea would not completely wipe out a highly trained and motivated artillery battalion.

The *Susan B. Anthony* (AP-72) arrived off the coast of Normandy on June 6. The ship's armaments included one 5-inch gun and four 3-inch guns. During the night of the sixth, several alerts followed by "all-clear" signals occurred. On June 7, she proceeded to her destination: Utah Beach. The plan was to unload the men just before noon. Practice rope ladders (scramble nets) were in the middle of the ship for training purposes to instruct the men on how to disembark to landing crafts. Early that morning, at exactly 0800 hours, while breakfast was being served below deck, she struck a mine from a previously swept channel and lost all power.[3]

Some eyewitnesses reported the blast was so powerful it lifted the ship out of the water. With the ship rapidly taking on water and listing to starboard, the commander, Capt. T. L. Gray, ordered the soldiers to the port side. This was a temporary fix, as the engine room soon caught fire, expediting the sinking.

The radioman on the ship had just received information that a German sub was in the immediate vicinity. He was typing up that information to give to the captain when the explosion occurred. He never got a chance to finish the message, which went to the bottom still sitting in the typewriter.

Commander Gray declared that the ship was lost and had to be abandoned due to the accelerated rate it was taking on water. An orderly evacuation began, starting with the soldiers, when the tug USS *Pinto* (AT-90) and two British destroyer escorts, the HMS *Narborough* and the HMS *Rupert*, pulled alongside.

The soldiers were told to inflate their Mae Wests (CO_2 cartridge–activated life preservers) and discard their packs and leggings. The crew attempted to lower the lifeboats, but the ropes were jammed. Not one boat could be freed. The destroyers came to assist, one lashed to each side of the *Susan B. Anthony*, which was accomplished with great difficulty.

At 0822 hours, the *Pinto* pulled alongside. Over the *Susan B. Anthony*'s loud-hailer, it was requested she be towed into shore for beaching. A few minutes later came the reply from the *Pinto*: "The task force commander denied your request for beaching." Her fate was sealed.

Forty-five men received non-life-threatening injuries, many of which occurred when the explosion caused the men on the top bunks to hit their heads on overhead steel beams. Heavy wooden timbers that held the hatches in place were dislocated and fell into the hold, causing additional injuries. Orders were given to break open the gun lockers, and anyone could take what he wanted. The sailors went in first, taking the highly prized semiautomatic .45-caliber pistols. A naval lieutenant ordered the destruction of the navigational equipment. Sailors grabbed axes and swung them at compasses and any other precision instruments that would have value to the enemy. It was an act of necessary vandalism that sailors grudgingly performed. The *Susan B. Anthony* was their home and a ship they loved.

The soldiers were told to leave their packs below in case they had to jump overboard and to keep only their helmets. There would be plenty of discarded gear on the beach. Because of the loss of power, searching below decks in complete darkness would only lead to chaos and eventual casualties. However, some managed to grab a few essential items just after the explosion before they ran up on deck.

Two new destroyers arrived and lashed themselves to the ones already fastened to the *Susan B. Anthony*. Lt. Samuel Skinner, commander of B Battery, was the last man of the 321st to leave the sinking ship. He made it to the first destroyer, which was already crowded, and started to cross over to the next via rope ladders, but the ropes snapped. He climbed back to the first ship. Since the destroyers were British, all the rescued men were served tea. The destroyers became their home for a couple of hours. The sea was so rough many of the men became seasick.

Skinner wrote:

> Finally we crawled over the net again onto a landing craft; there must have been about 60 of

> us. That little skipper asked us which way to go. All we knew was Utah beach and where it was was another problem. He had never been in to shore as yet. That was really a rough baby, and we rode it for at least an hour and a half or maybe two; finally we beached and waded in waist-deep. The beach was quiet and nobody was shooting at us. We fell in two ranks and marched off in a column of 2's. . . . the first man we saw was Col. Harper who was in charge of the beach from our division. All the way to our assembly area he was giving us the latest poop from our paratroopers. We marched about a mile to assembly area and dispersed and dug in. The Germans really gave us a break there. They waited until we got dug in and then strafed us. No harm was done and the digging business took on new life.

Waiting for the 75mm pack howitzers of the battalion to be brought in was a problem. "In the meantime our paratroopers were crying for artillery. We could do nothing about it," Skinner continued. "The channel was rough and landing operations were behind schedule. We really felt bad about it and they got mad as hell when they saw us there as they marched prisoners back to the beach. These were trying days; we had visions of being pushed into the sea and artillery was falling on us all the time." Skinner said the forward observers "could never see any further than the next hedgerow."

Cpl. John Christener (HQ) of Silver Lake, Indiana, was reading *Stars and Stripes* on the top bunk at the time of the explosion, which bounced him off onto the floor. He heard orders to leave everything behind but the gas masks. The men were just starting to leave the sinking ship via rope nets onto the English destroyers when he saw a high-ranking officer tell Colonel Carmichael to step back from the net. He was told to be the last of his men to leave the ship.

When Christener made it to the beach, he saw two small, orange, toylike German tanks loaded with explosives. He also noticed two 6x6 GMCs stacked with dead GIs, waiting to be driven up to the edge of the road near the beach. The trucks were filled to the sideboards with bodies. German fighter planes appeared and strafed them. In the distance, he could see dead paratroopers hanging from the trees. He recalled that days later, when the battalion moved inland with motor transportation, they would take friendly small-arms fire from nearby fields. Many times guys were heard yelling to the nervous GIs to hold their fire.

Pvt. Bernard Simmons (B Battery) was below deck when the explosion rocked the ship and the lights went off. He started to grab his pack, but was ordered to leave them behind, remove his leggings, and get on deck. After leaving the Landing Craft, Infantry (LCI), he realized this was not a maneuver in the English countryside. Dead bodies were everywhere, and German fighter planes were strafing the beach. He quickly dug a foxhole and got in. A chunk of metal whizzed by and landed in the hole. It just missed him. With so much firing going on, it was impossible to say where it came from.

Another soldier from the *Susan B. Anthony* was Pvt. H. C. Warren (A Battery) of Cookville, Tennessee. He grabbed a pair of binoculars hanging off a bunk and scurried up the stairs into the sunlight. On deck, the captain of the *Susie* could be heard over his bullhorn conversing with the other ship captains nearby. He was giving them details as to the condition of the crippled ship. It was no simple task to board one of the ships alongside. The cargo net ladder was moving with the waves, and the rescue ship was bobbing up and down. The soldiers had to time their jump from the net to the rescue ship in order not to fall into the Channel.

The English ship Warren was on traveled up and down the coast for an hour and a half. Its rescued soldiers were given corned beef sandwiches and rum. They watched the activities onshore and the massive firepower being unleashed farther inland in amazement.

As their LCI unloaded its men, other 321st soldiers could be seen up and down the beach, assembling in small groups after being unloaded. Smoke was drifting from farther inland toward the beach and small-arms fire could be heard. Sgt. Marlin Davis (A Battery) from Shelby, Ohio, approached Warren and asked him where he got the binoculars, knowing he wasn't issued them. Warren said he found them somewhere on the beach. Davis opened the case and found his own name written on the inside. Warren lost the binoculars. Sgt. Charles Simmons (A Battery) from Evans, Louisiana, was standing nearby and said, "Warren, I'm telling you something. My binoculars are going to be hanging outside my pup tent tonight." Private Warren took the hint and acquired those binoculars. He retained them for the rest of the war until they were accidentally left behind in a 40/8 railroad car.

That evening, Warren spotted an unused foxhole and enlarged it with the help of T/5 Everett Nichols (A Battery) from New Meadows, Idaho. They scrounged up discarded lifebelts from the beach, inflated them, and placed them on the bottom of the hole.

By 0905 hours, the main deck of the *Susan B. Anthony* was underwater at the stern. Navy personnel were the last to abandon the ship, and most left by 1000 hours. They jumped into the water, followed by Captain Gray. They were rescued shortly thereafter. By 1010 hours, the *Susie* had slipped beneath the water. Her sailors would later say she was a true lady for not taking anyone with her to the bottom.

During the sinking, the essence of Col. Edward E. Carmichael came into full view. It was not a pretty picture.

Capt. Orwin Talbot, the 90th Infantry Division, 359th Rifle Company commander, left the assault bridge area, located across from the captain's quarters, immediately after the blast and descended below to check on the situation. He wanted to instill calm and confidence in his men that everything was under control. He was proud to see his presence was not needed. The scramble nets were lowered, and in an orderly fashion the soldiers slowly made their way down to the waiting destroyer. Mingled in was Colonel Carmichael, even though his men had not yet started their evacuation.

The colonel was told that he was not to leave the ship before all of his men had done so. Only a short time had passed when again Carmichael attempted to make his way into a group readying themselves for transfer to one of the rescue ships. This time, the *Susie*'s Captain Gray grabbed the colonel's arm, stating, "You will not leave this ship before your men do, and I'm not going to tell you again." Captain Talbot observed the incident and was stunned by the behavior of a United States officer. (In 1969, Talbot, then a lieutenant general, was the commanding general at Fort Benning, Georgia. It was his decision to try Lt. William Calley for the My Lai massacre that occurred on March 16, 1968, in South Vietnam.) This incident was also observed by several 321st glidermen, including Pvt. Bascom Baker (A Battery) of Marshville, North Carolina, and Cpl. Vernon Raker, gunner for A Battery, who remembered: "Rope ladders were flung over the side as a small British vessel pulled alongside and eager hands grabbed the bottom rungs of the rope netting to bind the two vessels together. When a sailor ordered us over the side, the first man to hoist a leg was our Colonel. The sailor grabbed the Colonel roughly and threw him back against the bulkhead exclaiming, 'Enlisted men first, officers go last.'"

By late afternoon, those who had transferred to the destroyer escorts were now being sent ashore. The original destination for the 321st was the 4th Division sector of Utah Beach, named "Tare Green." However, they were now headed for Omaha Beach, the 1st Division zone and approximately ten miles from their assembly area. Corporal Raker wrote:

> As the LCI headed for the beach [the] sounds of war got closer and closer. We were told to stay low and pray if we knew how. I was comforted to discover a buddy huddled next to me, Ed Lytle from gun #4. Ed immediately engaged in a conversation that had me in stitches before we hit the beach; it went something like this. "Rake, I done been in this man's army for nearly three years. I've been awarded sharpshooters medals for the M-1 rifle, the 30 caliber carbine, and the 45 pistol. I am a gunner on the 155, 105 and 75 howitzer. I've been a model soldier, I'm trained to kill, but here I am on D-Day, landing on Omaha Beach, and the only thing I've got to fight with is this little ole jackknife." He opened his hand and displayed a folded-up knife that was best suited to cleaning finger nails. I offered Ed my carbine, warning him that the damn thing didn't shoot straight

> anyhow. Ed declined but went on to say, "Rake, if you don't mind I'm going to stay close by you. If you should 'get it' then I'll just take your carbine until I can find something better." Moments later, the LCI dropped the front gate, and we waded ashore in water up to our hips.

The LCI trip took one hour from leaving the destroyers to arrive at the beach. The second and final landing craft departed the destroyers at 2100 hours and reached the beach at 2225. These 321st boys gathered on the beach but had one pressing question: Where was the rest of the battalion and its guns? It would take an hour and fifteen minutes of marching to reach the assembly area.

Pvt. Harry Sinkutch (HQ) was loaded into an LCI headed for the beach. A large enemy shell hit alongside the craft, spraying everyone with water. Captain Dunkelberg (HQ) was the first off the ramp when they neared the beach. Sinkutch thought the Germans would aim for the front of the LCI and wait to fire until the ramp was dropped; something unorthodox was needed. The ramp was dropped. Instead of following Dunkelberg, Sinkutch jumped off the side of the ramp, lost his balance, and dropped into water chest-deep. Dunkelberg reached over and grabbed him.

Sinkutch recovered his balance but was now about five men back as they walked toward Utah Beach. He thought to himself, if he was going to die, let it happen now. He moved quickly through the water to the front position, next to Dunkelberg. The captain noticed the move and said, "Are you ready, Sinkutch?" The reply was, "Yes, sir."

On the beach were two German tanks that looked like toys. Sinkutch wondered what they were and how they worked. Nearby, he glanced to a spot just off the beach where medics were busy treating the wounded. He also observed a German prisoner-of-war cage with about fifteen to twenty Germans inside the wire cage.

Sgt. Hubert Jauquet (HQ) from Green Bay, Wisconsin, made it to the beach after wading through water up to his armpits. He looked up to see a German fighter pass overhead, so close that he could clearly see the pilot's deathly-white face. The airplane was on fire and smoking. The pilot was obviously dead, but still at the controls. It traveled about another hundred yards inland and exploded.

PFC Hugh Worthy (B Battery wire section) of Brookhaven, Georgia, came ashore and noticed shell craters throughout the area and Germans being held prisoner in barbed-wire pens. The next instant, a German fighter plane dropped from the sky and made a strafing pass of the beach. Worthy made good use of one crater, diving in headfirst.

Corporal George "Cokie" Crim (B Battery) was from Gerrardstown, West Virginia. As he stepped off the landing craft into chest-deep water, he noticed a fellow soldier struggling. Pvt. Earnest Smith (B Battery) had stepped in an underwater shell hole and inflated his Mae West life preserver to keep from

Whatcombe Farm, England. Capt. Sam Williams (left) and Lt. James "Buck" Davis (HQ). Williams broke his ankle wrestling not long before D-Day. They took off his cast and sent him on his way. DAVIS FAMILY

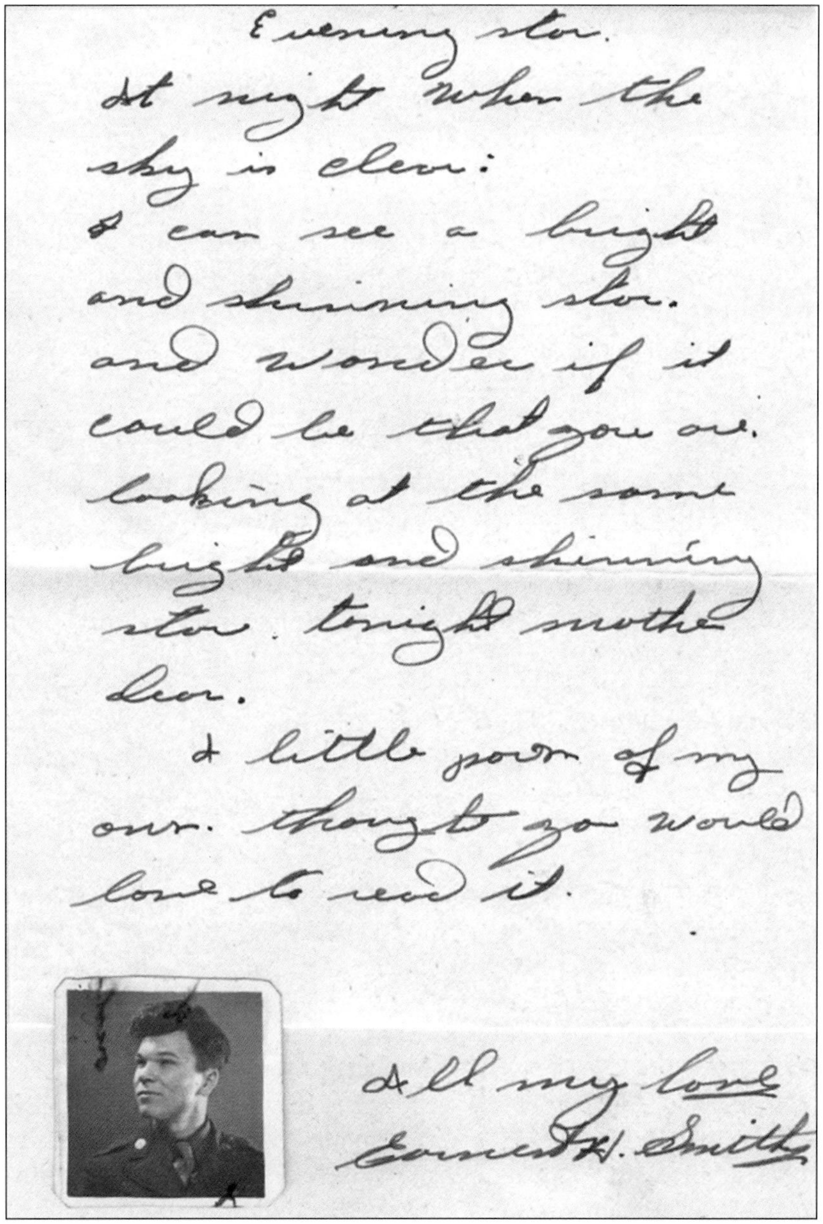

Evening star.
At night when the
sky is clear:
I can see a bright
and shining star.
and wonder if it
could be that you are.
looking at the same
bright and shining
star. tonight mother
dear.
A little poem of my
own. thought you would
love to read it.

All my love
Earnest H. Smith

This water-damaged photo of PFC Earnest Smith (B Battery), was intended for his mother. It was soaked during Smith's walk from the landing craft to Utah Beach, when he was almost swept out into the Channel. His mother would eventually receive the photo under the most unfortunate circumstances in September 1944. RICKY LONG FAMILY

drowning. However, Smith's new problem was that he was floating out to sea. Crim rushed over and grabbed him, pulling Smith to shallower water.

Corporal Crim thought his landing on Omaha Beach would be much different. What he saw that day never left him for the rest of his life. Some of the landing crafts strayed off course while dodging partially sunken obstacles and disembarked their loads onto the wrong beach. This was most likely the case for Crim's experience that day.

While searching his landing area for weapons and any other serviceable equipment, Crim spotted a Red Cross tent. Thinking it would be an ideal place to scavenge some needed goods, he made his way there. This area had been assaulted on June 6 by the 29th Division; the first wave was the 116th Infantry Regiment, A Company, which suffered a two-thirds casualty rate at their sector: "Dog Green," the bloodiest beach landing of the entire Normandy invasion.

As Crim neared the tent, he observed stacks of corpses covered with GI blankets. They were stacked like cordwood, most with their boots protruding from underneath the olive-drab wool blankets. All except one. Instead of a pair of boots, Crim could see a shock of red hair, which he recognized immediately as belonging to his friend and neighbor, Herman "Junior" Dunham. He did not inquire any further as to the identity nor attempt a closer look. He just knew it was Junior. Cokie would later say that if there was ever a man who was too kind to be in the army, it was Junior. It just wasn't in his nature to harm a fly.

Crim hadn't known his friend was in the 29th Division. When interviewed by the author just weeks before he died, Crim said he never knew for sure if it was Junior's corpse piled among the dead on Omaha Beach that day. Even though Junior's body was eventually buried near Crim's hometown, Crim refused to visit the grave. The headstone verifies Junior's death as June 6, 1944. For Crim, it was a wound that would not heal.

Cpl. Paul Miho (HQ) was ordered by Colonel Carmichael to locate the 506th PIR command post. He was to relay the message that the 321st was on the beach but had no artillery. When the 75mm pack howitzers finally arrived, Miho would act as part of a forward observer team with Lt. Francis Canham (B Battery) from Barker, New York. Miho carried the SCR-610 radio. While performing the forward observer work, Miho was well aware that if he was spotted, the Germans would send an 88mm artillery round at him. At first, being in a forward observer team was exhilarating, spotting targets and raining artillery fire upon the Germans. But after a few experiences, it became just another job.

He soon learned that it wasn't just the 88s that were out to get him. On another occasion, a sniper aimed a bit too high and knocked off leaves from a tree just above his head. When they realized what was happening, the team changed locations quickly.

The early morning of June 8, about 0200 hours, the Germans began shelling the rear of their area with the dreaded 88s for the first time. Later, at 1700 hours, three German Me 109s came down, firing away just 500 feet off the beach. It seemed like every Allied weapon available, from the beach to the offshore naval armada, opened up on those German airplanes. Two American P-38s suddenly appeared from high above, diving down and firing on the middle Me 109, causing it to trail smoke. It flipped upside down; a body hurtled out and a parachute partially deployed. The downed Luftwaffe pilot disappeared from view. The second Me 109 was also hit and trailed smoke. By now, all the German aircraft had disappeared from sight as the third was fired on by one of the P-38s.

A short time later, A Battery gun crewmember in Corporal Raker's gun section, Pvt. Albert Di Masi from Brooklyn, New York, emerged with a German pilot. Di Masi was moving the pilot forward by poking him with his carbine. His prisoner limped with an obvious injury to his left foot. Upon closer observation, the pilot's eyebrows and hair were singed, and his skin was badly burned. Raker couldn't help but notice that Di Masi considered himself a number-one war hero for having captured an enemy officer. He "crowed for days about his brave deed of capturing a guy that practically fell into his lap," Raker recounted.[4] A 327th GIR soldier was marching some German POWs down to the beach and took the pilot with them.

A few of the men now ashore were watching groups of German prisoners being marched to the POW pens. The military police had this duty down pat. The POWs were normally marched to the beach by the capturing soldiers, who were then relieved of their prisoners by the military police. A member of one of the gun crews asked how the 101st was doing. The military policeman replied, "THEY were doing good. THEY don't take prisoners." Another told Raker that one trooper had brought three prisoners to his captain's makeshift headquarters to turn them in. He was directed to take the prisoners down to the beach a few miles away. The trooper protested, but his orders were firm—take them to the POW cages. The trooper herded his prisoners behind a hedgerow, fired three shots, and reappeared. "The bastards tried to run away, so I had to shoot them," he stated.

Di Masi had the first combat souvenir of the battalion: a pistol taken from the downed pilot. Unfortunately for him, it was confiscated by a 321st officer, Capt. James Davis (A Battery). Davis sent as many quality weapons as he could acquire back home throughout the war, including an MP 40 German submachine gun.

The men dug in at the beach for the night. Many substituted their helmets for entrenching tools. Although wet, cold, and hungry, they had survived the landing in Normandy. They were now at war, even though they didn't have their packs or rifles. It was time to scour the area for weapons and essential equipment.

PFC Sinkutch dug in just off a road on his third night in Normandy. He heard some movement in his foxhole and shot at what he thought was a snake. It turned out to be a candy bar that had fallen out of its wrapper. First Sgt. Wellington Troutman (HQ) was nearby. He got out of his foxhole and yelled, "Did you hear that Sinkutch, did you hear that? A Kraut sniper just took a shot at me!" Sinkutch, not realizing it was the shot from his carbine that Troutman was talking about, said he hadn't heard it. After Sinkutch crawled back into his hole, it dawned on him what happened, and he told Troutman about the candy bar. It wasn't long before the first sergeant became the joke of Headquarters Battery. Troutman later transferred out by his own request.

On the morning of June 9, three men of A Battery were ordered back to the beach from their assembly area. The hope was to make contact with the remainder of the battalion unloading its guns. Artillerymen Cpl. Vernon Raker, Pvt. H. C. Warren, and Pvt. Lloyd "Pinky" Tomblin were traveling on an elevated road with a marsh on both sides. A single aircraft, flying from the Channel on a course inland, swept in low. The soldiers dropped to their bellies on the steeply banked road. They could see it was a British-marked Spitfire, but the navy and every other gunner on land did not. The plane, trailing smoke, banked to the right and made a wheels-up flop into the marsh about sixty yards away. The canopy flew open, and the pilot started to climb out. Tomblin and Warren had their rifles ready, drawing a bead on the airman as Raker approached the downed aircraft. They weren't sure if the pilot was going to be a German in a captured Spitfire or an unlucky Brit. The pilot saw Raker and exclaimed in an English accent, "You're a Yank, aren't you?" The pilot made his way through the marsh in a rush, saying there were armed rockets under the wings; all it would take was a little heat to set them off.

The soggy pilot then met the other two artillerymen on the roadside nearby. "Bloody hell," he said. "Since when did you Yanks declare war on England?" After the pilot calmed down, he went on to say he knew it was against orders to fly over the beach, but being curious, he just had to take a look anyway. Curiosity cost him an airplane, which didn't seem to be of any great concern to him. The pilot got his wish: a close-up view of the beach, only now at ground level. He hitched a ride to the beach for a seaborne trip back to England.

Since the morning of June 6, the howitzers, jeeps, trailers, most of the 321st supplies, and the other half of the battalion's soldiers were on the Liberty ship USS *John S. Mosby*. It was the lead ship of the convoy and was now anchored somewhere off Utah Beach, anxiously waiting to be unloaded. Among his duties, the 101st beach master, Col. Joseph "Bud" Harper (shortly to become commander of the 327th Glider Infantry Regiment on June 10), was actively attempting to locate the *Mosby* and get the much-needed artillery into the fight. Exactly where it was, nobody knew.

The passengers of the *John S. Mosby* observed the sinking of a ship but did not know it was the *Susan B. Anthony*. The *Mosby* was scheduled to unload its cargo and crew on June 7, but somehow the vessel was missed and anchored offshore waiting to be unloaded. For three nights, she stayed put while German night-bombers and night-fighters kept the area hot. A German fighter engaged in aerial combat was so loud it could be heard below decks. One of the bullets pierced the ship's hull and continued into one of the sleeping holds. A blood-curdling scream reverberated throughout the bunk area; S/Sgt. Theodore Thibodeau (B Battery) of Ishpeming, Michigan, was hit in the ankle. He was in charge of the third gun.

T/5 Merle Fulton (HQ) wrote of his experiences on the *John S. Mosby* in a letter to his wife. "We had to sleep on the steel deck of the ship because of the large amount of equipment we had. On the night of

June 6th, we were bombed for the first time. We were supposed to land on Wednesday [June 7] morning but for some reason they did not get to us until Friday. During the time from Tuesday [June 6] until we were unloaded we were bombed every night. . . . Most rode on a jeep or trailer through the water from the LCT to the beach. Those who were not lucky enough to get a ride had to walk in water up to their waist to get ashore. We landed about 2:30 and walked about a mile to our assembly area where we spent the rest of the night."

The morning of June 9 was rainy. A navy officer pulled alongside the *Mosby* and asked its captain what the ship was carrying. The captain replied, "Kansas Airborne Artillery." This was the 101st unit code designation for the 321st GFA Battalion, used in radio communication and certain written documents for security purposes for the duration of the war. The conversation ended abruptly with the words, "We have been looking for you for two days. Prepare to unload at once." Almost immediately, Landing Craft, Tanks (LCTs), came alongside for that task. By 2100 hours, the first of two LCTs was fully loaded and headed for its destination of Utah Beach with jeeps, howitzers, and men of the 321st.

As the LCT made its way toward shore, the Luftwaffe arrived—five Me 109s. The Germans started to strafe the area, and British Spitfires went after them. All guns on the beach and on the water were brought to bear on the 109s and fired ferociously. Within ten minutes, all the enemy planes were knocked down. It was still daylight. Many of the soldiers said the intense racket of so many different sounds of gunfire melding together overloaded their senses. Spent rounds in the air were now coming down everywhere. Most missed their targets and landed among friendly forces both on land and in the water.

The steel deck of an LCT became the unintentional target of some of the spent rounds. Ricocheting sounds of 20mm projectiles could be heard throughout the packed naval craft. The projectiles knocked down soldiers and blew out pneumatic tires on badly needed equipment. The deck was awash with blood. The tally was fifteen wounded; nine had to be evacuated to England, and six were treated on

Normandy. An LCT leaves the *John S. Mosby* and heads for Utah Beach loaded with 321st jeeps. A few minutes after this photograph was taken, it was hit by friendly fire, causing numerous casualties. The soldier lighting a cigarette (foreground) is Sgt. Harvey Baker. Behind the steering wheel of the lead jeep (left) and wearing goggles on his helmet is PFC Elmo Smiley. Both soldiers are from the same gun section in B Battery. Note the dark-colored flag at the stern, possibly green to mark for the section of beach, named "Tare Green," that was the unloading point for the 321st. *MISSION ACCOMPLISHED*

shore and stayed with their battalion. All of the wounded sent to England survived, and most eventually returned to the battalion.

PFC Leo Corrigan (HQ) was hit in the leg. He wanted some sulfa powder to put on his wound but wasn't carrying any. He noticed a soldier next to him had some in a pouch on his belt. He asked for it, but the other soldier said he didn't have any. Corrigan pointed to it on his belt saying, "Yeah you do, it's right there." The piece of shrapnel was never removed from Corrigan's leg.

Pvt. Wendell Byrnes, B Battery, from Chicago, Illinois, was about to enter the shooting war. He felt he was predestined for the Medal of Honor. When he entered the LST, he found himself at the rear of the craft alongside the naval pilot operating the craft. He could not see over the side and was curious what lay ahead. Pulling himself up to the top edge of the LST, he observed the battleship *Texas* fire a salvo from its guns inland at unseen targets. After each one, a series of tugs would push the great battleship to its former position in the water to prepare for another target. This realignment kept the massive rounds on target. If the ship was not properly sited, the fire would be inaccurate, even with forward observers inland to direct the fire. The computations needed to be exact to minimize the friendly fire fatalities that often occurred in the heat of battle.

As Byrnes slid back down to the metal decking of the LST, he was awed by the destructive forces at work. He stared forward and wondered what he would experience when he went ashore. That time was nearly at hand. He barely noticed the enemy aircraft flying above, partly because of the massive explosions from the firing battleship. An orange flash appeared directly in front of him. It was noiseless, but suddenly Byrnes was bleeding from his stomach and his feet. He was hit, along with fourteen other 321st troopers.

Byrnes was grabbed by two 321st soldiers, one at each arm. They dragged him onto Utah Beach from the LST and left him there. He could not use his legs and was bleeding heavily from the stomach area. He passed out and awoke hours later to find himself some distance from the beach aid station. Fearing he would die soon, Byrnes crawled down Utah Beach across the remnants of a battle-scarred terrain until he was spotted by some medics.

The private was taken into a surgeon's tent and operated on, then placed face up in a slit trench a short distance away. He lay there for over a day, watching the ever-present Luftwaffe do its best to diminish the impact of the Normandy invasion. The 321st private felt that if he went to sleep, he would never awaken. He jabbed his fingers painfully into his eye sockets every time drowsiness approached and managed to stay awake until he was moved aboard ship to receive further medical attention. He could not help but think of all those jump boots protruding from underneath the olive-drab GI blankets stacked next to the surgeon's tent. The dead troopers never had the opportunity to be placed in a protective slit trench, then carried by stretcher and placed carefully onto the England-bound LST.

Byrnes would not be awarded the Medal of Honor and receive a hero's welcome back in Illinois. He now realized the price was too high for such an award. It was a boy's dream that was left on the blood-drenched LST. He was now a veteran whose dreams and aspirations had irrevocably changed. But the young private had not lost his will to fight. He spent the next three months recuperating in a hospital, then in September entered his next battle by way of a glider.

Arriving on the beach from the *Mosby* was Capt. Frederic King (HQ Battery), a graduate of Princeton University, Class of 1938. He wrote in a letter home that he landed just east of St. Mere Englise. "You may find it on a map (you'll have a harder time finding it on the ground now)." He also mentioned how he waded ashore in chest-deep water, ruining his last watch.

He continued:

> This war is worse for some than it is for others, but as soon as that first bullet whistles by it becomes real. You don't have to tell anybody you are scared & no one asks you; he knows it. Most of the time you are fighting mad over the fact that someone got you mixed up in this thing, & I am afraid that not once did a principle such as Democracy enter my mind.

Whatever they're fighting for, the American soldier is as good as any have ever been.

King also wrote of the German soldiers and the German fortifications on the Normandy beaches: "They're tough and the defense of their westwall was brilliant, but they won't win. France is paying a terrific price—every town I've seen is a shambles, and most worse than that."

The lead jeep, towing a 75mm pack howitzer, was driven by PFC Elmo Lincoln Smiley (B Battery) of New Harmony, Indiana, the jeep driver for the 6th Gun Section. Before the war, Smiley had worked the Mississippi and Ohio Rivers as an oiler for tugboats and attained a coveted oiler's license, which enabled him to work in the engine rooms of tugs and ships. When the war broke out he volunteered for the selective service. Upon being asked what he would like to do, he informed the official about his license and his desire to be in the navy using these learned trade skills. However, his abilities appeared to lend themselves more to glider field artillery. Not long after, he was glider bound. He was assigned to a gun section as a driver and towed the 75mm pack howitzer throughout Europe.

The jeeps were "waterproofed" while in Wales, modified so that they could be driven in water that was over the hoods. A breather tube (snorkel) was attached to the intake, allowing the engine to "breathe" even though it was underwater. Sometimes jeep drivers forgot to remove a can placed on the breather snorkel or to extract rags stuffed inside the snorkel. The result was a stalled jeep sitting in the water as soon as it left the LCT. The fan belts were also removed and had to be reinstalled upon reaching land. The entire waterproofing job was done to ensure that when a jeep left the LCT, it would race to the beach and not disrupt the unloading process.

In Smiley's drive to the beach, he hit a few underwater shell craters that were deep enough for the water to come up to his neck. At one point, the only way he could see above the water was to partly stand while driving ashore. He would remark later that nothing tasted as bad as cigarettes that were dried out after having been soaked in water. His gas-impregnated uniform fabric didn't "breathe," and the trapped moisture did not evaporate in a timely manner.

> The motor vehicles that were given names were required to have the first initial match their battery. For instance, an A Battery jeep might be named *Alice*. Smiley's B Battery named his jeep *Bangtail*. A jeep from HQ Battery was painted with the name *Hilda*. However, this rule was not strictly enforced. ■

There were more qualified jumpers in the 321st than spots for them to fill. Aircraft space was limited for the jump into Normandy. Lt. Carroll Holland (HQ) from Minneapolis, Minnesota, and Lt. John Jordan (HQ) of Portsmouth, Virginia, flipped a coin while at Whatcombe Farm. Both officers wanted to go, but Holland called the toss and won. The disappointed Jordan was fond of saying that if he went, the Germans would never see him; since he was tall and skinny, all he had to do was turn sideways. Much later, outside Bastogne, he would discover otherwise.

One liaison team jumped into Normandy with the 506th PIR on June 6. The team consisted of Lt. Carroll Holland from Minneapolis, Minnesota; Pvt. Max Helms (HQ) of Marshville, North Carolina; radioman PFC Earl Patchin (HQ) of Joplin, Missouri; and Cpl. Lawrence Wilkinson (HQ) of El Paso, Texas.

Patchin jumped in at 0114 hours with a British leg bag and a case of batteries for the SCR-610 radio. He was under intense antiaircraft fire and deployed his leg bag after his chute opened. Enemy ground fire severed the rope on his leg bag and perforated his map case and map of the drop zone. After landing in the middle of a hedgerow, the clouds broke and he observed movement at the edge of the hedgerow in the moonlight. He thought his number was up, but discovered it wasn't Germans, only sheep. He landed on the assembly area, not on the landing zone. He got out of his harness by cutting the suspension lines from the main chute and tucked them away in the pocket of his jumpsuit. Patchin then crawled out of

Cpl. Lawrence Wilkinson (HQ). WILKINSON/DETTORE

the hedgerow and clicked his cricket (a device paratroopers used to signal each other in the dark) once. He heard a two-click reply. It was Pvt. Martin Majewsky of the 506th PIR. Patchin could read his white cloth nametag on the jumpsuit. They were ordered not to fire their weapons in the dark for fear they would shoot other paratroopers. Patchin went on to Coleville to meet the rest of his team at the 506th command post, set up in a barn. Their mission was to direct naval and self-propelled 105mm guns until the 321st came ashore.

A few days later, Patchin spotted a German submachine gun at the edge of a wooded area close to the road. When he went to pick it up, a sniper fired a shot at him and missed just as he bent over. That ended Patchin's desire for German souvenirs for the duration of the war.

Early in the morning of June 9, Colonel Carmichael and his battery commanders traveled to the village of Le Groseiller on reconnaissance. The next day, the 321st went into position to support the 327th GIR.

The battalion finally assembled near the landing beaches on June 10 and headed to their first firing position. After a march of just over two hours, they arrived at 1015 hours and dug in near the village of Le Groseiller. The S-2 Journal entry for the night of June 10 at 2300 hours reads: "Bombed by enemy aircraft. No casualties." It sounds simple enough, but there was more to the events of this entry. Corporal Raker wrote in detail about the bombing:

> Our weapons finally arrived and we headed toward the front to give artillery support to our beleaguered infantry [near the village of Le

NORMANDY CAMPAIGN FIRING POSITIONS

Village of Le Groseiller June 10, 1015 hours	
A Battery	41.8–90.9
B Battery	41.8–90.9
Command Post	41.9–90.9
Village of Catz June 12, 1525 hours	
A Battery	44.0–85.9
B Battery	44.2–86.0
Command post	43.8–85.8
1,500 yards west of Carentan June 15, 2240 hours	
A Battery	37.5–84.3
B Battery	37.8–84.3
Command Post	37.8–84.3
West of St. Sauveur Vicomte June 27, 2115 hours	
A Battery	17.36–94.34
B Battery	17.81–93.99
Command Post	17.3

> Groseiller]. We were positioned just inside a hedgerow and told to dig in. Like all the fields in Normandy, this five acre patch was surrounded by hedges and small trees. We dug in the gun, got the camouflage net up, readied some ammo, then set about digging foxholes for ourselves along the hedge directly behind us. It was 11:00 pm, but with "double daylight savings time" in effect, the sky was still grey above and we could still make out shapes. We became aware of a plane, which by its curious drone certainly couldn't be Allied. The lad on the .50-cal. machine-gun mount spotted the plane, and opened up on it. The bad thing was, he had the weapon set on single-shot, and he was shooting tracers. He got off three rounds before the low-flying bomber disappeared. The plane made a lazy circle and came back to lay its eggs about where the tracers had come from. The bombs didn't land close to the machine-gunner, but one of them landed in the back of a truck loaded with ammunition. The ammo went sky-high and the air was filled with burning powder bags. The captain was so pissed it's a wonder he didn't court-martial the idiot who gave our position away . . . but blame[d] it on opening jitters.

PFC Smiley wondered how the Germans could fly at night but Allied protective fighters could not. A lead German plane would come in to draw fire while the second aircraft hung back and took notice of the origin of the antiaircraft fire. Then the second plane, having spotted the truck's mounted .50-caliber machine guns, would come in and drop its load of bombs. On this occasion, the bombs hit a nearby truck loaded with ammunition and caused an immense explosion. The machine gunners were warned in no uncertain terms that if they opened up at any more planes, they would be the ones shot.

By 0500 hours the next morning, all twelve guns were registered and in direct support of the 327th GIR Liaison, and forward observer parties were out and ready to make their presence felt by the enemy.

At 0900 hours on the eleventh, the rear echelon met up with the battalion. The seaborne element, led by WO (Junior Grade) Edward Chaumont of Ozone Park, New York, consisted of 6x6 trucks, supplies, cooks, clerks, and whatever else was needed to make the battalion whole.

Truck driver Cpl. Woodrow Stephens (A Battery) was assigned to pick up the remainder of the battalion's loaded trucks, which were sitting on the docks in England, and ferry them to Normandy. He did this three times, getting to England by air transport. On one of those trips, he observed unattended cases of coffee and put them on his truck without the proper requisitions forms. When he made it back to the A Battery cooks, they told him their kitchen took a hit and the stoves were ruined. They took the remaining good parts to make one workable stove. The coffee was also lost, and the cooks were beside themselves. Stephens took them to the back of the truck and showed them the cases of coffee he had midnight requisitioned. This elated the cooks.

Liaison Section 2 of Headquarters Battery consisted of Lieutenant Perkins; Cpl. Max Helms, B Battery's radioman, from Marshville, North Carolina; Pvt. Joe Trouba, from Omaha, Nebraska; and Sgt. Everett Hughes, from Pennington Gap, Virginia, all of whom were working with the 327th GIR. This team, along with several other officers from the 327th, was standing underneath a tree 5 feet away from their command post east of Carentan at Saint-Hilare-Petitville, map coordinates 40.6-84.3, when a German 81mm mortar exploded just above them. The tree burst killed several of them and wounded Hughes, Trouba, and Helms. All of the wounded were seriously injured and did not return to the 321st. Perkins escaped unscathed and upright while the rest of his team lay strewn around him in the dirt. The radio was peppered with shrapnel, now useless. It was 1100 hours.

A piece of shrapnel pierced Helms's helmet and entered his brain. He was evacuated to safety, but because of the seriousness of his wound it appeared to be a hopeless endeavor. Cpl. Irving John from Toledo, Ohio, took over his position. Helms did survive his wounds, but suffered from convulsions.

The first B Battery forward observers to be sent out were Lt. John Jordan, Cpl. Paul Galant, and T/5 Howard Krivos. Galant and Krivos were wounded and evacuated the next day and replaced by Pvt.

Normandy. Lt. James Wicker, executive of A Battery, laying an aiming circle. This was used to emplace the six guns parallel on any desired compass direction. WILLIAMS FAMILY

William Stone. Stone remembered being driven up the road in a jeep and seeing 327th GIR soldiers crouched in the ditches on both sides. It gave him an uneasy feeling. When he found Jordan, the officer was all business. Stone said to him, "Take it easy, Lieutenant. There are plenty of others who would like to get a piece of the German Army. Save some of it for them."

At about the same time, 2,000 yards east of Carentan, a forward observer team led by A Battery's Sgt. Donald Roy from Cleveland, Ohio, and radioman Cpl. Walter Mitchell, of Wolcott, New York, met up with the 327th GIR at their command post. This team was assigned to the 401st GIR and was on the move to its objective. The plan was to attack Carentan from the northeast side of the town down Bassins à Flot, a mile-long, tree-lined canal that stretched from the Douve River into Carentan itself. It was man-made and could handle barges and small watercraft. Additional troops were to attack from the west and northwest. The task force was commanded by 101st Brigadier General McAuliffe. "The plan was to burn up the town and blast it into submission with all available fire from the Division and attached units, including naval guns."[5]

This would be the first fire mission conducted by Sergeant Roy and Corporal Mitchell. After they made it to the canal, they set up their observation

Normandy. Cpl. Paul Galant of B Battery (with curly hair and seen here lying on a stretcher) being transported back to England aboard a hospital ship. *RENDEZVOUS WITH DESTINY*, 246

post and laid down a rarely used rolling barrage to cover the advance. Up and down several times into the trees the 75mm rounds landed among the enemy. Roy later remarked how perfect the barrage looked. He appreciated the mathematical skill and knowledge it took to make such a show of force possible and gained a whole new respect for the 321st FDC section of his own battalion. The battle-hardened Germans had learned their trade and were well dug in. The barrage stopped with the 401st GIR advancing. It was met with fierce resistance and suffered heavy casualties. The terrain favored the Germans and bogged down any further advance for the day.

In Normandy, Roy learned valuable lessons that could only be learned in combat. First, he waited until his forward observer team found an excellent observation post that would be used for some time before calling for wire to be laid up to him. Until then, communication was through battery-operated walkie-talkies. He also learned that when wire was laid to the observation point, in the dark it was safer to get back by grabbing the communication wire and following it to friendly territory.

While working with Lt. Carroll Holland (B Battery) in a forward observer party, two enlisted men were seriously wounded. They were Pvt. Howard Krivos (HQ Battery) from Cleveland, Ohio, and Pvt. Joseph Kujawa (B Battery) of St. Paul, Minnesota. Their work contributed in knocking out a German 88 near Carentan. (Krivos would be wounded again in Holland doing forward observer work. He returned, but this time was assigned to FDC.)

Normandy. Pvt. Frank Barys (left, with his fingers in his ears) and Pvt. James Calabro of B Battery, 2nd Gun Section, with a 75mm pack howitzer in full recoil.

Normandy. Another shot of the howitzer in partial recoil.

Normandy. Cpl. Lyle Wood (left) and PFC Everett Nichols. H. C. WARREN FAMILY

Altogether, the battalion expended 847 rounds and 39 smoke shells on June 11. A single entry in the 321st journal at 2100 hours reads: "Firing ceased. Town in flames."

At 1330 hours on June 12, the battalion received new orders to close station march. They were to move their guns to a place called Catz, 2,500 yards east of Carentan. It would take nearly two hours to reach this small village, crossing the Douve River over a pontoon bridge constructed by the engineers. By 2200 hours, the twelve 75mm pack howitzers were registered and prepared to support the 327th GIR.

Capt. Joseph Perkins, assigned to the 327th as a liaison officer, was looking for the command post just moved near the town of Pellerin. It was 2200 hours. He was met by Captain Klein, the 327th Headquarters Company commander. Klein had just discovered some German activity nearby, and upon reaching the command post excitedly told Harper, "Colonel, there is a whole company of Krauts over here a short way, all lined up with mess kits for chow." Harper replied, "Get our artillery liaison officer and fire on them." Perkins, Klein, and six others headed out to locate the target, which took less than a half hour.

"It was twilight and we could see very little," Perkins recalled in a letter to Harper dated March 6, 1983. "We ran across a field crouched down. I found our coordinates on the map and opened the net [radio communication]. The first thing I heard was a German talking. What the hell do I do now? I thought. We were overriding his signal. Can you hear me, I asked? Loud and clear, came the answer from our man further up the line. But the German heard us too; he could have only been 100 yards away. He knew we were close, and was quite upset."

The battalion fired one round on Perkins's map coordinates. It landed 30 yards behind the small group of Eaglemen, luckily in a hedgerow, which

Perkins credited for saving their lives. They retreated back into an irrigation ditch. Perkins adjusted the guns and gave the order over the radio, "Fire for effect." Six guns belonging to one battery of the 321st fired four rounds each and all came down on target. Both batteries fired a total of thirty-eight rounds on various targets on June 12.

Later, it was learned that thirty dead Germans were found at the former chow line, which helped clear the way for the 327th GIR to Montmartin. Perkins freely admitted after the war that he was not a very good forward observer. Colonel Harper disagreed and wrote, "You did a fine job that day."

That night, Perkins and his team found themselves in a barn not far from the command post. They had been living on D-rations for a week, and nothing but candy bars for four days. Suddenly a half-track arrived with cans of bacon. Perkins's driver, Cpl. Neal Batchelor of Oswego, New York, took the jeep about four hundred yards up the road and raided a farmer's field of potatoes. Perkins wrote later, "I've eaten in the best restaurants in the world, but that meal, potatoes and bacon, was the best meal I've ever eaten!"

The first forward observers to enter Carentan on June 12 were Sergeant Roy and Corporal Mitchell. It was determined that a German counterattack was imminent. However, this did not occur until the next day. The town itself was lightly held by a rear guard of approximately 200 enemy soldiers who provided cover for their retreating forces. The Germans attempted to retake the high ground on which Carentan stood—they wanted the terrain more than the town itself—but were not successful.

Just after midnight on June 13, enemy artillery fire landed among the firing batteries but did not cause any casualties. At 1000 hours, a different type of

Normandy. PFC H. C. Warren (at left, smiling), with his A Battery gun section. Pvt. Robert Bunyard is at the extreme right.

H. C. WARREN FAMILY

danger presented itself. A sniper had infiltrated the area and was taking shots at the red-leggers. Previous patrols had been sent out but were unable to locate the sniper. A few days later, another patrol was sent out. One sniper was located and killed. His firing position was an unlikely spot, but a sharp-eyed trooper figured it out. In a field of dead cows, the sniper had slipped into a blown-up carcass. However, the dead animal's movements negated the advantage he sought. His adversaries couldn't help but admire his ingenuity, but scoffed at the location of his death.

While here, Pvt. William Stone (B Battery) was riding shotgun with Colonel Carmichael. They were traveling down a road and slowed to make a left turn. Stone heard a woman screaming as they turned the corner and saw a small boy running toward them with something in his hand. The child raised his arm to throw the object at them. Before the occupants of the jeep could react, he had tossed a flower into the jeep. "My heart still beats fast when I think of what could have happened," Stone said years later, recalling the incident.

The battalion fired 636 rounds of 75mm ammunition with an additional 32 rounds of smoke in support of airborne troopers fighting countless battles in the areas around Carentan during these two days. A couple of the howitzers were fired so heavily that the rifling came out in chunks from the barrel. The artillerymen stopped firing when the damage was noticed. Ordnance had to be called in to change the barrels.

The 321st "Confidential" journal titled "Action Against Enemy, Report After/Action Report" states that in this time frame:

> The forward observers of this Battalion fired numerous missions during the attack launched by the 327th attacking astride the road to St. Lo. This fire was partly responsible for the supported Infantry reaching its objective. It was necessary to withdraw across the railroad on the following day to straighten the line and organize for a threatened Panzer attack.
>
> During this action many of the Divisional units were surrounded, particularly the 377th Parachute Field Artillery Battalion Command Post, and some missions were actually fired behind enemy lines. One Infantry Battalion was cut off for thirty-six hours. The 321st Glider Field Artillery Battalion suffered five casualties during said activity. These being enlisted men wounded while operating in front lines with liaison parties.

Complete records of casualties for the 321st in Normandy have not been located. Likewise, records of the infantry battalion that was cut off for thirty-six hours are elusive. The battalion was possibly a unit from the 83rd Infantry Division, but that is conjecture.

Many 321st soldiers told of two ammo trucks that blew up the night they moved into their first gun position; the blast was so powerful it shook the ground they were on. They thought the entire invasion stockpile had blown up. The plume of smoke that followed seemed to confirm their initial thought. Not everyone knew what had just transpired. The debris from the trucks blocked the road for part of a day.

While in this position, war souvenirs were free for the taking. Dead Germans and their weapons littered the area near the gun positions. Past lectures of booby traps attached to weapons and bodies gave pause to anxious souvenir hounds.

Pvt. Luther "Fats" Hasting (A Battery) of Meridianville, Alabama, spotted a German machine pistol and a German grenade nicknamed a "potato masher." They lay close to the sixth gun position of A Battery. Raker took charge by looping a rope into a noose to lasso the items and pull them clear. It was a precaution that was adhered to early in the war but soon abandoned. There were no explosions, and the booty was kept.

Around 0200 hours, Hasting and Pvt. Gene Powers (A Battery) of Paragould, Arkansas, were on guard duty. They awakened Raker and told him something was moving in the field to their left. They had hollered, "Halt," but the movement continued, so both of them had emptied their carbines into the direction of the noise. They wanted to know what they should do now. Both were told to go back. Raker put them at ease by telling them that whatever was trying to get them was probably dead. When morning broke, they scoured the area for the dead

Normandy. From left to right: An unidentified soldier, PFC Joseph Weidle (KIA February 8, 1945), Sgt. Marlin Davis, and Cpl. Everett Nichols, gun section members of A Battery, pose with captured German weapons. HENDERSON FAMILY

Normandy. B Battery's 4th Gun Section (from left to right): PFC Lemuel Slayter, PFC Wilson Mullins, Pvt. Raleigh Nealey, PFC Robert Palm, PFC Witcher, PFC Frank Kanspik, and PFC Gilbert Quinn. KOPACKA FAMILY

Germans. Both Powers and Hasting were red-eyed, unable to sleep after being relieved from guard duty. The A Battery boys located the dead menace after a short search: one thoroughly dead, shot-up cow, a victim of one of the many mistaken-identity shootings or firefights that took place during the initial days of the Normandy campaign.

At twilight, 2135 hours, on June 15, the battalion was again on the move to a new location. This type of night move had been practiced many times during training. It would take one hour and fifteen minutes to reach the new location, 1,500 yards west of Carentan near a village called Douville. The 101st Division offensive mission was completed, and they were now on the defensive. The Germans were fighting hard to break through the Allied lines to link up with their beleaguered comrades. The plan was to push the invasion force back into the sea, if the Germans could gather enough forces.

On one of the many fire missions during this time, the A Battery commander, Capt. James Davis, was dead on his feet from exhaustion and nearly made a tragic mistake. The six guns were about to fire when truck driver Cpl. Woodrow Stephens yelled, "Third gun out!" The guns did not fire. Captain Davis chewed Stephens out for stopping the fire mission. Stephens replied that the guns were pointed in the wrong direction; they were aimed toward Utah Beach, now teeming with Americans and fresh supplies. Davis thanked the truck driver for his quick thinking.

The battalion arrived at an apple orchard on June 15 to occupy their new position. The A Battery's six 75m pack howitzers were placed without any problems, but B Battery encountered a most unusual situation.

First Sgt. Timothy Shea (B Battery) uncharacteristically stopped his cannoneers from emplacing their six 75mm guns near the orchard, not far from a farm complex. He had spotted two dead Germans close to the area where his guns were to be placed. Ordinarily, something like that would be of no concern, but these two corpses created a serious problem. The bodies were no more than six feet away from each other, and both were impaled with 75mm projectiles that were duds. One man had died standing with his back against an apple tree. His head tilted downward with his helmet still on. One of the dud projectiles had gone into his upper chest and nailed him against the tree. The second German was lying on his back, looking straight up. The other projectile had entered his chest, staking him to the ground. Both bodies appeared to be recent kills, perhaps victims of the battle that occurred earlier in the area with soldiers from 4th Division, supported by tanks from the 70th Tank Battalion.

Shea ordered Smiley to get a rope and pull the corpses out of the immediate area. Smiley wrapped a 25-foot length of rope around the feet of the German impaled to the ground. As he started to drive away to pull the slack out of the rope, he thought maybe it should be longer in case the projectile exploded. But he pulled forward anyway. The bones cracked and snapped as the body was dragged about thirty yards away, but no explosion. He returned to the second German, tied the rope to his feet, and drove off. The cracking bones could be clearly heard as if branches were being yanked off a tree, but again, no explosion. It was now safe to emplace the guns.

It was nearly dark when one of the three machine gunners assigned to protect B Battery opened up on a target approximately 150 yards away. A German could be seen sitting on the side of an elevated railroad embankment. However, this enemy soldier didn't react, befuddling the machine gunners. They waited and watched for any movement, trying to determine his intentions. Did he want to surrender? They didn't wait any longer and fired another burst. This time, they were sure they got him. The next morning, the crew slowly made their way to the embankment. The German still sat there. As they got closer, they could see his face was black; his head bent forward from his torso at an angle that had caused blood to pool in the face area. He had obviously been killed days earlier. The dead soldier was lying more on his side than sitting, but the angle plus the distance gave the machine gunners the illusion of a threatening enemy.

The defensive mode of the battalion didn't translate to quiet days. On June 17, the pack howitzers fired 1,958 rounds of 75mm ammunition. The enemy attempted to silence the guns by shelling

B Battery's 2nd Gun Section near the village of Douville. From left to right: Sgt. Harvey Baker, PFC Victor Viscio, Cpl. Arthur Robinson, PFC Raymond Nagell, PFC Woodrow Bowser, PFC Virgil Teaford, and PFC "Pop" Deskins (extreme right in shadow). Note the white stenciled name *Bambi* on the howitzer's barrel. BAKER FAMILY

Normandy. The center of this photo taken near the apple orchard shows the area where the two German soldiers were impaled. BANDO COLLECTION

the batteries, but did not draw blood. The guns of the 321st worked throughout the night, harassing the enemy until daybreak.

In charge of the battalion ammunition was Sgt. Harold Dittmer (HQ) from Elmwood Park, Illinois. He recalled that a week after the invasion, as the war settled down for the night, crickets could be heard chirping on a beautiful June evening. Then the noise of war would pick up again, starting with a burp gun, then machine guns, then mortars lobbed back and forth. His battery would start firing, then the 105mm guns, and then the 16-inch guns, sounding like an express train going overhead. Forty minutes later, it stopped. Crickets could be heard once again. It was as if nothing happened.

Every morning, Dittmer called the firing batteries. They told him how many rounds of ammunition each had. He would then go to the beach and pick up fresh 75mm rounds. Normally, there were approximately forty rounds at each gun. His ammo runs occurred each day while in Normandy.

The battalion stayed at the defensive gun position near the apple orchard for thirteen days, expecting a German counterattack. They were allotted 600 rounds of 75mm ammunition per day, which equaled 300 rounds per battery. During this time, the battalion was in direct support of the 327th GIR and several missions with the 502nd PIR. Approximately 9,440 rounds of M48, the standard ammunition used for the 75mm pack howitzer in Normandy, was expended during that time. These rounds were fitted with M54 fuses that had two actions: timed and super-quick. The timed, or "airburst," allowed for a twenty-five-second delay and was the most feared by enemy infantry. The super-quick rounds detonated upon impact.

On June 19, Maj. Thomas Henderson, S-3 Headquarters Battery, from Tucson, Arizona, wrote a

Normandy. An unidentified 321st A Battery gun section. HENDERSON FAMILY

Normandy. B Battery's 5th Gun Section (from left to right): PFC Samuel Simpson, PFC Adolph Bonath, and Cpl. Leo Weaver.
KOPACKA FAMILY

typical entry for the period in the "SECRET S-3 Report No. 1." The unit remained in direct support of the 327th Glider Infantry throughout the period covered by this report. One liaison officer operated with the 1st Battalion, 401st Division, and the 1st Battalion, 327th Division. Two forward observers operated with each liaison officer. Between 1800 and 2300 hours, fire was placed on strongpoints, mortar positions, fortified houses, and small troop concentrations, but there were no night fire missions. The weather was rainy. (All of these daily secret reports included the weather for the day.) The last entry reported that "Due to poor ground observation, it is difficult to determine the exact results of missions fired; however, Infantry Commanders report our fires effective."

It was not out of the ordinary in this campaign for the 321st engage in "harassing" fire missions. The battery fired these missions unobserved, without a forward observer to direct and adjust the fire. The FDC of the 321st knew where the rounds would impact, but their effectiveness was unknown. The purpose was to keep the enemy on edge and without sleep. Sometimes the Germans would fire counter-battery rounds at the cannoneers for the same reason. No serious casualties resulted from this type of fire while in Normandy. Credit for this bit of luck was given to the excellent way the men were dug in.

On June 23, it was noted in the 321st logs that at 1230 hours, ten German planes strafed their area. Two of those trailed smoke, a sign of being hit. No casualties were suffered on the ground. Small-arms fire could be heard during the night, but its whereabouts could not be located.

By this time, the cannoneers had acquired the skill of determining whose guns were fired by the sounds they made. It was a skill that could only be honed during combat. In some cases, the sounds of gunfire and its duration gave the men at the guns an idea of who held the field that day.

This type of fire would continue without respite until June 24. Times of the harassing fire would vary. Sometimes, it started late in the afternoon, around 1900 hours. Other times, it started at 0130 hours. Targets such as mortar positions and various strongpoints were often unobserved but considered to be effective per the infantry commanders. For instance, on June 18, 1,494 shells and 65 rounds of smoke were fired during such times.

On the twentieth, the weather was cloudy and windy. Most forward observers and liaison officers remained in direct support of the 327th GIR with one exception. One forward observer team was sent to the 502nd's 1st Battalion and stayed with them until the twenty-fifth, at which time forward observers from the 377th took their place.

The 101st used small airplanes, two-seater Piper Cubs called L-4s by the military and nicknamed "Grasshoppers." The "L" stood for "liaison," and the nickname came from the plane's ability to jump from one field to another, using them as landing strips. This aircraft was powered by a 65-horsepower engine and used primarily for spotting targets for the artillery in front of the main line of resistance. They were also used to adjust fire for the artillery and to perform reconnaissance for division artillery. The KIA rate for liaison pilots in the 101st Division during the war was 41 percent.

Liaison pilot Lt. Richard Fort of Fort Meade, Florida, one of the two pilots assigned to the 321st from Normandy to Berchtesgaden, reported that most of the pilots flew by themselves, approximately 60 percent of the time. (At the Army Air Force training school in Pittsburg, Kansas, their uniform patch motto was "Artillerymen with Wings.") The other 40 percent of the time, an artillery battalion officer or air observer accompanied the pilot. The speeds normally flown were 65–70mph. A large number was painted on the side of the fuselage for identification purposes, big enough that it could be observed from the ground. The number assigned to

Normandy. B Battery's 1st Gun Section (from left to right): PFC Carl Gustafson, PFC Henry "Dutch" Ira, PFC Lawrence Ferrone, Cpl. George Crim, PFC Elbert Douglas, Pvt. Roy Rosberg, and PFC John Nasea Jr. IRA FAMILY

Normandy. PFC George Shepard (A Battery) washing clothes in a gasoline-fired inversion water heater. TURKAL FAMILY

the 101st Division was 58. Near the end of the war, some pilots painted the first letter of their last name on the tail of their aircraft, indicating who the pilot was. Most L-4s were designated with large letters that corresponded to specific pilots. For instance, Lieutenant Fort's L-4 had the letter "C" painted on the skin of the aircraft. Maj. Shannon Powers from Ohio, commanding officer of the Air Observer Pilot Section, had the letter "A" on his Stinson.

Lieutenant Fort came to England along with another sixty other air liaison pilots prior to the Normandy invasion. On D+6 (June 12), the pilots came into Normandy on a Landing Ship, Infantry (LSI). Nearly all of the pilots were assigned to different divisions fighting there. Fort was attached to the 321st and sent directly to the Air Liaison Section's observation post. The section was set up in a field with several quite-used Horsa gliders strewn about, acting as their headquarters. Major Powers, previously a captain in North Africa, was in charge of the section.

There were initially ten pilots in the section, but the number was then upped to twelve. A crew of fifty additional soldiers, including mechanics, cooks, and jeep drivers, kept the pilots in the air. The pilots shared nine L-4 aircraft and one Stinson L-5. The latter was not used for combat missions since it was a faster airplane, instead normally reserved for shuttling high-ranking officers from the division. Each artillery battalion was assigned two pilots equipped with flak jackets, parachutes, and a .45-caliber semiautomatic pistol on every flight. The flak jackets doubled as seat cushions to protect the pilots from ground fire. Their parachutes were useless at low altitudes. Depending on the flight conditions, the level of flight during combat was between 400 and 1,500 feet.

Pilots spent approximately one hour in the air, then landed, refueled, and switched pilots. A pilot might fly three different missions in a day, depending on need. The most dangerous campaign for these fliers was Holland, not only because of the time

Lt. Richard Fort at Normandy. Note the number 58 on the fuselage, denoting the 101st Airborne Division. FORT FAMILY

Normandy. L-4 pilots around a British Horsa glider. From left to right: an unidentified soldier, Lt. William McRae, Lt. Dick Fort, Lieutenant Cherry, and Lt. William Hebenstreit. Note the 101st stenciled helmet inside the glider. FORT FAMILY

Horsa gliders in a field at Normandy on June 27, 1944, photographed by Lieutenant Fort. Note the L-4 using the Horsa wing as cover from observation at far left. FORT FAMILY

Carentan, Normandy, photographed on June 27, 1944, by Lieutenant Fort. FORT FAMILY

More Horsa gliders at Normandy. FORT FAMILY

Normandy. Note the concentration of bullet holes near the bottom of this Horsa glider's fuselage. ROBINETTE FAMILY

Normandy. Another shot of the same Horsa glider. Note the aircraft's skin is made out of wood and what appears to be an upside-down, sheared-off windshield frame previously belonging to a jeep named *Boogie Woogie*. ROBINETTE FAMILY

spent there, but also because the Germans were on both sides of the area known as "Hell's Highway."

Bastogne was the second-most dangerous campaign due to the snow-covered landing fields. "Taking off in the snow was difficult and in general it was [hard] just to circle the area to get altitude to look for targets and find out just how far from Bastogne forces were from relieving our division at Bastogne," Lieutenant Fort wrote.

Pilot Lt. Carl "Doc" Dillard, the other air liaison pilot for the 321st, was from Saltillo, Mississippi, and was attached to the battalion on January 12, 1944. He and another pilot departed from Welford Air Base near Newberry, England, on D+2 (June 8). Each flew an L-4 airplane. They were instructed to fly into Normandy on a narrow air path to avoid being shot down by friendly troops.

Throughout the war, the two pilots were designated to fly for the 321st. However, any liaison pilot could step in and perform the duties for another battalion. On June 22, Maj. Shannon "Chief" Powers was in charge of the liaison pilots who flew for the 101st. He was about to take off with a passenger, Lt. George Jones of the 377th PFA, when General McAuliffe, the artillery commander of the 101st, arrived at the landing strip and stated he needed Powers to come with him. The twenty-nine-year-old Lieutenant Dillard was ready and willing to take

Normandy. FORT FAMILY

Powers's place. He would be the single fatality of the battalion during this campaign.

The first mention in the records of the 321st of an observation airplane was dated June 22. The weather had limited the effectiveness of these slow-moving airplanes, and on that cloudy day, the S-3 report noted "observation is limited." Nevertheless, Lieutenant Dillard was up in the air scouting for targets, with a 377th PFA lieutenant as his air observer, twenty-six-year-old George R. Jones from Wilkes-Barre, Pennsylvania. The crew could have been spotting for the 2nd Battalion of the 327th GIR, the 1st Battalion of the 401st GIR, or the 1st Battalion of the 502nd PIR. What is certain is that the daylight fire missions of the 321st were directed at German mortar positions and a truck convoy.

The fabric-covered L-4 was unarmed. It appeared suddenly and came in unusually low, right over the gun sections dug in at the edge of an apple orchard south of a railroad track, 1,500 yards west of Carentan. It was not unusual to spot the Piper Cub just overhead of the battalion. The men marveled at the bravery of the pilot whom they knew was directing their fires from the air. The routine was dangerous. Cpl. Vernon Raker recalled in his postwar memoir that Lieutenant Dillard would often fly over suspected enemy positions, throttle back into the sea breeze, and become almost stationary. This action drew enemy ground fire, which he would plot on his map. Then he would make a steep dive away from the action. The coordinates would be relayed by radio to the 321st FDC, requesting fire missions on specific targets.

Pvt. H. C. Warren (A Battery) remembered that on June 22, an Me 109 dropped down, fired on, and chased the L-4. Dillard tried to blend into the treetops in the hope that the fast-flying fighter would lose sight of his target after he overflew him. The artillerymen on the ground jeered the fighter pilot, while others yelled in support for their airmen. The fight didn't last long as both airplanes disappeared from view. The fighter's guns went silent, but his engine could be heard growing fainter.

Lieutenant Dillard and Lieutenant Jones's airplane crashed near St. Georges-de-Bohon, approximately six miles due south from the 321st gun pits outside Douville. The crash-site territory was occupied by the Germans, and no one but the enemy knew that this was the location of the wrecked aircraft. Dillard was listed as MIA on July 4, 1944. That date would be the first in a series of errors confounding the families of the lost airmen. Dillard's mother, Virginia, never knew for certain how her son died or on what day.

Major Powers was grief-stricken when he learned that Lt. "Doc" Dillard's aircraft didn't return and was most likely shot down. He was not only his commanding officer but also, more importantly, his best friend in the service. Immediately after gathering all the information available at the time, the liaison pilots started an air search for the two men. It was a dangerous mission, flying slowly over enemy territory and peering into areas that may hide a downed, crumpled-up airplane. The pilots tried their best, but never succeeded in locating the wreck.

After the initial notification, Virginia Dillard's dilemma continued. She received another notice from the War Department that Carl Dillard was killed in action on August 22, 1944. That was then changed again to list July 4 as his date of death, then yet again to April 16, 1945. She wondered if it was all one big mistake. When she found an error in the government's listing of her son's serial number on one of the reports sent to her, she wrote to the War Department, exasperated, on April 20, 1946:

> Dear Sirs,
>
> I received your letter recently about burial places of my son who was classified as killed (on April 16, 1945). This terrible news being sent to me in different forms since he was first reported to have missing in action on July 4, 1944.
>
> There has been some great mistake about it all, yet we realize if he is yet alive we are unable to learn anything through any source of his whereabouts.

She corresponded with the War Department until 1950, trying to determine how her son had died, but without success. She did eventually receive her son's belongings, which were stored in a footlocker and in cardboard boxes. Hundreds of pounds of effects were sent from the camp at Whatcombe Farm to her house in Saltillo, Mississippi, and stacked in an upstairs closet. Everyone knew the closet was not to be opened by anyone except Virginia; no one ever saw her do so.

The Germans came across the downed aircraft and buried both Lieutenant Dillard and Lieutenant Jones in a single grave. The American Graves Registration was alerted of the location and exhumed both bodies on April 11, 1945. Dillard had suffered a skull fracture and many other broken bones. He was badly decomposed and had no personal effects on his body. Both were positively identified by their dog tags. Even though Dillard and Jones went down in the same aircraft, Jones's family was notified that he was killed in action on June 22, 1944. He was later buried at the American cemetery St. Laurent in Normandy, France. Carl "Doc" Dillard had four burials: three in Normandy and one outside Saltillo, where he was finally laid to rest in the family plot.

June 22 brought restrictions to the firing batteries. The 101st Division Artillery deemed it necessary to limit the sectors that fire could be directed upon. The order essentially reduced the number of fire missions. No unobserved firing was allowed unless called for by Division Artillery. This order lasted until the end of the Normandy campaign.

Division Artillery requested an average of eight unobserved fire missions per night. During the period of June 22–27, an average of 568 rounds of 75mm ammunition and approximately 26 rounds of smoke were fired per day.

Around this time, a visitor arrived looking for his friend from A Battery, Cpl. Vernon Raker. The visitor, PFC La Vern A. Selland (B Battery) of the 377th PFA, was also from South Dakota. Known to his family as "Arne," he stood 6-feet-4-inches tall and was all muscle. The men knew each other from childhood and had met once again at Fort Bragg. Selland was glad to see his pal and wanted to tell him what he had just experienced. He had been in

Lt. Carl Dillard, 321st L-4 pilot, photographed in England just prior to D-Day. FORT FAMILY

the thick of things since he came into Normandy, and it had taken him twenty-one days to get back to his battalion. So "Stuts," as he was called by Raker because of his stuttering disorder, began his tale.

He started off by saying that his parachute drop into Normandy was the easiest night jump he had ever made. The 80 pounds of gear didn't seem to hinder him, but strapping his M1 to his leg was not a good idea. The rifle slipped away below his feet and impacted the ground with such force that it shattered the butt stock and rendered it useless. Selland landed in a tree, which saved his life. Others dropped into flooded areas nearby. As he dangled from the tree, he saw his fellow soldiers drown but could do nothing to save them.

His stick had been given air sickness pills, which made him drowsy, making his initial time on the ground unsettling. During that time, it was essential to find a weapon, and he did. He spotted an equipment bundle that contained a bazooka and rockets. There were three rockets to a canvas bag, so he grabbed a couple of those. He loaded the bazooka and went looking for his section.

Walking alone, he came across a captain who had a few men with him. This group had traveled just a short distance down a road when a German convoy appeared from the opposite direction. The paratroopers were ordered into the roadside ditch and stayed out of sight to allow the convoy to approach. When the truck convoy was nearly abreast of the hidden troopers, the captain jumped from the ditch and ordered the lead truck to halt. The sudden stop caused the entire convoy to jam bumper-to-bumper. The driver of the lead truck got out and laced his hands behind his helmet in surrender.

Stuts said this sight unnerved him. He jumped from the ditch, pointed the bazooka at the driver, and fired a rocket into him. The rocket passed through the driver and into the bed of the truck, which was carrying ammunition. The truck exploded like it was the 4th of July, Stuts said. The captain wanted to shoot him for taking the action he did, but it was more important for the troopers to scramble away from the convoy and back behind the hedgerows.

Stuts was sent out alone just prior to daybreak the next day to reconnoiter. He unexpectedly found himself in the middle of a plowed farmer's field. In front of him was a concealed battery of German 88s. It was now light out, and he feared the enemy would see him if he tried to go back. He could hear their voices as he slowly buried himself in one of the furrows using his trench knife and helmet. Staying motionless for the entire day, he heard the firing of the 88s and the chatter of Germans. At nightfall, he was able to crawl back across the field to safety. This would haunt him for years to come.

(The event would haunt him for years to come. For the rest of his life, he would become sullen and disappear for part of the day on June 6 every year. It was a secret he tried to keep to himself, but those close to him knew. After the war, he returned home and became a successful farmer. One June 6 evening, while returning home from a dance with his wife, he suddenly pulled his car over and got out. His wife, Florence, followed him and asked what the problem was. Crying, he said, "It can't be right to have killed so many people." Attempting to console her husband, Florence said, "But that was your duty." It was the only time she ever saw the tough, hard-working family man cry. For the next twenty years, he was awakened during the night by nightmares of his combat experiences, some of which he shared with his wife. Selland died of cancer at the age of fifty-one.)

PFC Laverne "Stuts" Selland of the 377th PFA.

While Selland was telling his stories to Raker, A Battery fired all six guns simultaneously for a fire mission. Stuts nearly disintegrated emotionally, talking in gibberish. The war had played a sick joke on this sandy-haired lad. Regaining his composure, Stuts continued. He cursed the pilots who misdropped him and the other troopers in Normandy. They had ignored the proper drop zones and scattered the 377th all over the Cotentin Peninsula. They were briefed not to fire their weapons on the first night, but to use their crickets to locate their own men. The "crickets" were small, rectangular brass devices with a base plate made of spring steel; when the spring base plate was depressed and released, it made a distinct sharp sound, mimicking a cricket's noise. These were issued to the paratroopers to signal others in the dark and hidden in the fields. When a German was killed, his pockets were searched. Crickets were often found in their pockets, taken from other 101st troopers.

June 27 was a cloudy, rainy day. The men did not know at the time, but this would be the last day the 321st would send out rounds from their guns in Normandy. Nearly 300 rounds were fired by midafternoon and then silence fell. It was time for another move.

The battalion was relieved at 1700 hours and preparations were made for a new position. By 1900 hours, the 321st was on the move, and the battalion reached its destination west of St.-Sauveur-le-Vicomte at 2200 hours. Here they were to prepare to reinforce the fires of their sister battalion, the 907th GFA, which was operating in direct support of the 501st PIR.

By now, the rain had stopped and the weather had turned to fair. The 321st guns were laid using the base point of the 907th, but registering them was not allowed. If the howitzers were called upon to fire, they would be registered at that time using the base point of the 907th and adjusted if necessary.

Capt. Samuel Skinner, commanding officer of B Battery, wrote home to his father on July 3, 1944. "They tell me that we can mention anything that is history, so here goes," he began.

> I didn't come in by glider, thank the Lord for that. I guess you are surprised at that, but I am very thankful, cause I believe that is what saved the day. . . . I've only got one gun left that has a good tube. Oh yes, the other five will still shoot but they are bad for wear. . . . When our guns came we went into position and then began the battle of Carentan. I believe we helped to set it on fire because it blazed up right after we let loose about 70 or 80 rounds. We had to destroy the town before we could take it. Then we changed positions and [were] almost overrun by a counter attack. We were lucky some tank destroyers had landed to ward off a tank attack.

Skinner closed the letter with, "I think I'll take another bath from my helmet."

While at St.-Sauveur-le-Vicomte, Lt. James Davis tried to satisfy his taste for some fresh meat. The soldiers weren't allowed to wander into a farmer's field and slaughter his cattle; if they wanted fresh beef, they had to be creative. Davis spotted a herd of cattle. He grabbed a piece of stiff wire and tied a grenade around a cow's neck. The idea was to make it look like the animal was hit by an explosion of some sort. He grabbed another piece of thick wire and fashioned the end into an L shape to act as a handle. He attached the other end of this wire to the pin of the grenade so he could pull it and run.

The cow took off running with the wire still attached. The animal snagged the wire on a fence and pulled the pin off the grenade. This startled the cow, and it turned and started to chase Davis. He dove to the ground and the grenade exploded. Waiting in the wings were those he called his "West Virginia Mafia boys," whose job was to butcher the animal and take a section of it for themselves. Not in the plan was Gen. Maxwell Taylor, commanding general of the 101st Airborne Division, approaching them on foot. He was going down the road and heard the explosion. The area had been quiet for some time, and he was curious what caused the noise. "Those damn German land mines are sure killing a lot of animals around here," he remarked. Davis got the hint and told him that some steaks would be coming to his command post shortly. Everybody got their cut, and the matter was closed.

At 1000 hours on June 29, a close station march order was given. It was time to head for the rear area to set up camp near Cherbourg. The battalion would stay in this area and perform motorized patrols and police the area until July 9.

At this camp, everyone was kept busy doing something. Sgt. Earl Patchin of Joplin, Missouri, was detailed along with others to "tag and bag" dead American and German soldiers. The Americans were placed into mattress covers. A number of dead Germans were in bunkers and had to be dragged out. Patchin accomplished this unpleasant task by using the suspension lines he saved from his parachute. He tied one end around the corpse and the other end around his waist and pulled. He had not forgotten how the Germans had a habit of booby-trapping just about everything, so he thought this would be the safest way to complete the task. The 6x6 trucks were loaded with dead; Americans were taken to the

---

Capt. James Davis (HQ) gave jeep driver Cpl. Neal Batchelor a Luger pistol and told him to clean it. After thinking about it, Batchelor decided he didn't want to and asked his buddy, Cpl. John Christener, for advice. Christener told him not to do it—since it wasn't an American weapon, the captain couldn't order him to clean it. Batchelor didn't want to get into trouble for refusing and didn't know what to do. He asked Christener what he would do. Christener pointed to a hedgerow: "Face east, and go over there and toss it over." Batchelor did just that. When Davis asked for his gun, he was told someone had swiped it. ■

Normandy. B Battery's 3rd Gun Section: Tommy Davis, Norman Deethardt, Arnold Baker, Eugene Weber, Cecil Croft, Charles Smith, and Harold "Willie" Turner. KOPACKA FAMILY

Normandy. From left to right: Lt. Carroll Holland, Lt. James Wicker, and Capt. Jack Fuller, B Battery commander.
N. PERRY JACOBS COLLECTION

PFC Eugene Weber (B Battery), from Bolger, Texas, had always heard that the first dead soldier seen is never forgotten. He was about to put this to the test. Weber was both a motor-pool mechanic and jeep driver for his battery; if needed, he could fill in on a gun crew, too. While in the Cherbourg area, he spotted a dead German, recently killed. He looked at the soldier carefully, not seeing any obvious wounds. About six feet away from the corpse lay his helmet. It was upside down and had the name "Weber" painted in white letters on the back. He left the helmet where it sat. Seventy years after observing that dead soldier, PFC Weber still remembered it well. ■

cemetery at Sainte-Mère-Église, and the Germans were taken to the cemetery across the road.

Pvt. George Adams, a machine gunner in A Battery from Dysart, Pennsylvania, had little need for the three .50-caliber machine guns he manned in Normandy—they never had any enemy soldiers as targets while in France. Each battery had three machine guns: one placed to the left of the firing battery, one to the right, and one in front. Later, .30-caliber guns were carried into combat along with the .50-calibers. Each gun had radio communication with their battery.

At 2215 hours on July 9, the battalion arrived at an orchard, their bivouac point to prepare for their embarkation at Utah Beach—the same beach where most of the 321st had landed at the start of the hostilities. The battalion arrived on the beach on July 10 after a two-hour march. The boat ride back to England started with LST transports at 2130 hours that same day. On July 11 at 1100 hours, their ship finally left the waters of France.

The men of the 321st reached Southampton, England, at 1015 hours on July 12. An additional three-hour train ride to Newbury brought them almost home. The last few miles were covered on the backs of 6x6 trucks. They finally arrived at Whatcombe Farm at 1745 hours.

The battalion history, *Mission Accomplished*, recounted how the soldiers felt as they departed France:

> We were thrilled that morning when we got the order [to] pack and get ready to leave. We had been promised a furlough as soon as we got back and we were in a hurry to go. Everyone had a lovely picture in his mind about what he was going to do on that seven days. The only thing now was to get started.
>
> With our packs and rolls on our backs we started for the trucks that had been parked over in "B" Battery's area. Soon we were rolling along. The happy French people of Normandy tossed us bottles of wine, cider and calvados. They were very thankful for their liberation and they knew that the 101st had played a major role in this invasion of their homeland that had driven the Germans out.
>
> The trucks moved rapidly along the roads that had been partially cleared of the debris. Places that had once been peaceful little villages were now only heaps of rubble. Still the people were happy. About six or seven o'clock in the evening we pulled into an orchard near Utah Beach. We were told that we would spend the night here. The men paired off and pitched pup-tents and made themselves as comfortable as possible for the night, all the while thinking how much difference there was that night to the one of June 9th [this writer obviously was on the *Mosby*, not the *Susan B. Anthony*] when they had been here only a short month ago. Daylight came soon as the Normandy nights are very short in summer. We struck our tents and shouldered our rolls and packs for the walk to the beach.
>
> We had walked very little during the past thirty days and that, combined with the "Cs," "Ks" and ten-in-ones that we had eaten, didn't put us in a walking condition, but the knowledge that we were going away from all this kept us moving, even though the pace was a

Cpl. Neal Batchelor (HQ Battery) in Holland.

Normandy. From left to right: PFC Lawrence Rasler, PFC Harold Hazelbaker, an unidentified soldier, and Pvt. Butler Marks, all of the A Battery machine-gun section. HENDERSON FAMILY

Normandy. A German gun emplacement near the beach. WILLIAMS FAMILY

England. Wounded from the Normandy campaign being unloaded. DOUBEK FAMILY

A disguised bunker in Normandy. WILLIAMS FAMILY

slow one. At last we made it. Then, as usual, we had to sit around waiting for the LST's, which seemed like long enough for them to be made, I think.

Here for the first time we were aware of the vast stream of supplies and men that were pouring onto the beach that we had done so much to take and hold. During the weeks that we had been blasting away at the Krauts with everything we had, the men that had stayed behind at the beach had not been idle. This place no longer looked like the one on which we had dashed across under strafing ME 109's. The multitude of barrage balloons was still there but the sounds were gone. There was no intense Ack-ack and you could only faintly hear the boom of the big guns, far beyond Carentan.

Finally, after everyone was completely disgusted, tired and hungry, we were told to fall in line to load. This was [a]bout nine o'clock in the evening. We filed aboard, expecting to leave almost immediately, but instead we pulled out only a little way and waited until three in the morning before actually getting started. All the remainder of the night and the next day we traveled very slowly, for some unknown reason. Late the next evening we docked at Southampton but still we had to remain on board until about ten o'clock next day. Here we saw our first buzz-bombs as they traveled overhead on their way into Southampton. In the distance they gave off a faint boom.

At last we disembarked and struggled up one of the town's streets to a park not too far from the docks. Had it been very far no one would have made it with all those souvenirs in their packs and rolls.

In the park we deposited our belongings on the grass and went back to a kitchen that had been set up to feed troops either coming in or going out. The food was excellent and if you didn't mind sweating out the line there was plenty of seconds. It sure tasted good after so many days of that other stuff we had eaten.

Some hours later we marched to the station and the waiting train that would take us to Newbury. There trucks were to meet us to haul us the other few miles to the Farm, our English home. All the people around this little home seemed glad to see us and happy that we were back. It was almost like a real homecoming and we were the happiest of the lot.[6]

Throughout the fields of Normandy lie approximately 900 abandoned gliders. They were not forgotten by those who kept track of military hardware, but very few power pilots were trained in the art of retrieving the Waco CG-4As from their landing zones for future combat missions. Initially, hopes were high about the number of gliders to be "snatched" and returned to England. The reality of combat soon set in when it was discovered that soldiers were stripping the fabric off the gliders and using it to cover foxholes as a shield from rain. Farmers also cannibalized glider parts for farm use.

The process of "snatching" gliders began on June 23, 1944. However, only one glider, located southeast of Sainte-Mère-Église, was located and deemed flyable on that date. That lone glider successfully made it back to England, thanks to the skill of Lt. Gerald "Bud" Berry of the 91st Troop Carrier Squadron, 439th Troop Carrier Group. The hunt for flyable gliders continued, but the Normandy retrieval process eventually ceased after all repairable CG-4As were found and put in airworthy status. Eventually, approximately twenty-six gliders made it back to England. None of the English-made Horsa gliders were recovered for future use.

After Normandy, it was common knowledge who could be counted on in battle and who couldn't, whether it was the lowest-ranking enlisted man or the top-ranking officer of the battalion. Word traveled fast, even though each battery was a small

A D-Day memorial service was held at Whatcombe Farm, possibly performed by Father McGettigan with altar boys Lt. Tony Linz (left) and Lt. Francis Canham (right). WILLIAMS FAMILY

Pvt. John O'Dea (B Battery) from Cleveland, Ohio, enjoyed two things: alcohol and reciting poetry that he tailored for any occasion on the spot. He was called upon to be the master of ceremonies whenever a dance was held while they were in England, and he had a reputation for possessing a rapier wit. During combat, when things got hot he would say, "Narrow the battlefield till the smoke cleared the way; lay the body of the great John O'Dea."

Once, he came across Norman Deethardt at his gun position and engaged him in conversation. Without any hint of reciting poetry, he said: "When I was born, so I was told, I was a month and three days old. There in the hospital upon the charts show the birth of the great Deethardt!"

In October 1944, O'Dea was on guard duty in Holland at the battalion command post, which was set up on the side of a road. A German shell landed nearby, so close the concussion rolled him like a ball, thirty to fifty feet toward a barn. He was uninjured, but after the incident he was never quite the same. ■

world unto itself and the gun crews rarely mingled. One way for a soldier to make his name known throughout the battalion was to have a reputation as a slacker. Some slackers would engage in antics that were humorous, so the label didn't do much harm. Others, however, didn't do their jobs and blamed everything but themselves for their failure in combat. The numbers were few in this last category and did not represent any battery as a whole.

One such slacker was Sgt. Gerald Shade from Warren, Ohio, who claimed he was "sicker than hell" for the entire time in Normandy with a case of the "GIs"—a gastrointestinal illness spread through food, water, and human contact that produced diarrhea, nausea, stomach pain, fever, and vomiting—that just would not quit. The excuse did not go over well. Shade was reported to never have pulled duty as chief of section during any of the 321st campaigns, always coming down with the GIs. PFC Lloyd Tomblin ran the gun crew instead.

One by one, the veterans of Normandy made their way to ask for replacements at their respective battery's supply. Shoes and socks were the most common request. Cpl. Max Raglin (HQ) from Ionia, Michigan, filled out the forms and sent them up to battalion; they in turn were bumped up to division. One of the men had lost his folding-stock carbine in France and came to settle up with the U.S. Army. The cost was $54; it became a payroll deduction from his monthly check until it was paid in full.

The battalion's casualties in Normandy were expected to be high, but that was not the case, with one KIA and approximately twenty-five wounded. Approximately fifty replacements were already en route to Whatcombe Farm while the battalion was still in Wales at the embarkation point. One of those soldiers was 1st Sgt. James Dundon from Fayetteville, North Carolina. He and the others were not allowed to sleep in the vacant horse stalls. Instead, tents were erected at the farm until the battalion returned and sleeping quarters could be permanently arranged.

M/Sgt. Albert Bender had stayed behind at Whatcombe Farm. Upon meeting him, Dundon told him there was little to do since both the men and equipment were gone. However, there were two things to learn: one was that English beer was served warm, and the second was how to "live with the smell of horse shit in the stables." Dundon was issued his 101st eagle patches and jump boots. He now felt he was in a true fighting unit.

Another recently assigned sergeant from the replacement depot ("repple depple") was Mark Sullivan from Albany, New York. He was cadre at Fort Bragg, in charge of eighty men for thirteen weeks of training, at which point he moved on to a new class of recruits. After months of begging for a combat unit, he got his wish. He was off to England to the repple depple. He was sent to Whatcombe Farm, where tents were erected and training started almost immediately. At night, lying in his cot, Sullivan could hear the transport planes flying overhead for two straight days. He wanted to be in the fight, but this was the closest he could get, and it bothered him. It wasn't long before he was assigned to the #2 gun, taking over for Sgt. Theodore Thibodeau, from Ishpeming, Michigan, who would go to lead the #3 Gun Section.

Another recent arrival was 2nd Lt. Tony Linz from Cincinnati, Ohio, who came to Liverpool from the States and was in charge of 300 soldiers. Linz was assigned to the 8th Replacement Battalion Southwest England. After his men had boarded their train, he had time to check his own orders to see that his assignment was the 101st Airborne Division. It was unexpected. The two-hour train trip took them to Newbury, where the men were divided into various 101st units. It was now June 2, 1944.

None of these men would take part in the Normandy invasion, which was still the most important secret the Allies had up to this time, but some of them would stay in the 101st, settling in and becoming troopers. For most of the who arrived on June 2, Holland would be their first combat mission, as it was for Lieutenant Linz.

Prior to leaving Whatcombe Farm for combat, it was strongly suggested that any man who had cash on hand turn it in to JWO Henry Sulecki for safekeeping. The program was called "Spearhead." The monies were turned over to Sulecki, who in turn handed them over for deposit by the division finance officer. Sulecki, from Cleveland, Ohio, was also in charge of making arrangements for soldiers to send money home and purchase war bonds. He would sign a receipt as proof of deposit when cash was turned in. There was never a hint of scandal, and Sulecki was trusted by everyone in the battalion. They did not know that his fondness for betting on the dog races was going to become their problem as well as his.

Word got back to the remaining soldiers at Whatcombe Farm that the 321st was lost at sea when their ship was sunk off the coast of Normandy. Not knowing the information was erroneous, Sulecki took the money, bet it, and lost it all. It would be safe to say he was quite surprised to find out later that not a man was lost in the sinking. When the men returned from Normandy, they soon discovered the theft. Upon learning this, Sulecki went AWOL for a week, July 17–24. He returned voluntarily to Whatcombe Farm, but said nothing of the embezzled funds.

On August 13, Sulecki was arraigned at Fawley Manor. The thirty-nine-year-old officer was tried

This series of four photographs shows a glider being snatched by a C-47. SIGNAL CORPS FOOTAGE

Left: The snatch rope being set up. Center: The snatching rope strung out in front of the glider. Right: The nylon rope snapped and flew backward into the cockpit of the CG-4A. SIGNAL CORPS FOOTAGE

Austria. A Battery's 1st Gun Section (from left to right): PFC Lester Miller, PFC Ray Busch, PFC Charles Taylor, Cpl. Vernon Raker, PFC Adolf D'Arcangelo, PFC Bernard Katz, PFC John Dzienius, PFC Bernard Allison, PFC Martin Zbick, and Pvt. William Baker with a guidon.

A Battery's 2nd Gun Section in Austria (from left to right): Sgt. Gerald Shade, Pvt. Jess Harmon, PFC Bernard Tutas, PFC George Shepard, PFC Lloyd Tomblin, Cpl. Dick Moss, Cpl. Everett Nichols, PFC George Wilson, and PFC Delray Harrington.

DUNDON/DETTORE

T/5 Tom Morrison (left) and PFC Max Raglin of Headquarters Battery.

First Sgt. James Dundon of A Battery in France. DUNDON/DETTORE

and convicted for being away without leave, embezzling $880 from twenty-four soldiers (eighteen of whom were from B Battery), and not turning in another $75 for a purchased war bond. He was sentenced to ten years' hard labor and confined to the 2912th Disciplinary Training Center, Shepton Mallet, Somerset, England. At the end of the war, he applied for clemency. The disposition for that request is unknown; however, many former soldiers convicted of various crimes were let out at this time,

Whatcombe Farm. The horse stables, converted into barracks, are on the left. The mess kit laundry is on the right, and farther down is part of the barn theater. NUGENT/DETTORE

and since his crime was not a vicious one, his prison sentence might have been commuted.

The victims of Sulecki's embezzlement were not reimbursed by the government. Colonel Carmichael was the only one called to take the stand as a defense witness. He testified about the high ratings given to Sulecki and said that other than his drinking and being late in returning from his passes, he was an efficient soldier.

In late July, upon returning from Normandy, furloughs were assigned. Lists of the men and the locations they were going were posted on the bulletin boards. Furloughs were for ten days, to places such as London, Wales, and Edinburgh.

Capt. Joe Perkins and Supply Sgt. Charlie Nugent of New Orleans, Louisiana, both of Headquarters Battery, happened to share a ride on a transport plane back to Whatcombe after their foray into Scottish culture in Edinburgh. The very last passenger to board seemed to be just another soldier at first glance, but he was not. It was a reporter, Ted Malone, who broadcast regularly on the Blue Network radio stations. (Sponsored by Westinghouse, the Blue Network would later become ABC. At the time, it was considered a second-rate network, competing against the Red Network duo of NBC and CBS.) Malone beamed his reports over to the States via shortwave radio. Those reports were cut onto records and sent along to other radio stations throughout the country for rebroadcasting.

During the flight back to England, Malone chatted with the passengers, a mixture of newly minted 101st combat veterans. They bragged not of their combat experiences, but of their good times in Scotland with the ladies and such. As a combat correspondent, Malone had learned to talk to soldiers without them feeling like they were being interviewed. Amid the laughter and the drone of the engines from the C-47, Malone kept both mental and written notes for his next broadcast.

Among the returning passengers were two troopers of the 502nd PIR, Ray Cready of Pittsburgh, Pennsylvania, and Robert Bryant of Detroit,

Michigan. They had written a poem called "Purple Heart Lane" and showed it to the reporter, who read it and asked if he could keep it. The poem was written on a crumpled piece of brown paper. The troopers said the newspapers had turned it down, saying it wasn't polished so it must not be any good. The reporter knew he had a story.

While on furlough, Captain Skinner (HQ Battery) took it upon himself to redesign the telephone system used by the field artillery. Called a thirty-line PBX, the system ran wires from the firing batteries to the FDC. Its console took two soldiers to move it. It was also underpowered and overloaded with lines not used in combat.

Skinner dissected the PBX unit, added more batteries for power, and eliminated twenty-two lines, leaving plenty available as backups in case some were cut by the enemy. The entire system could now fit in a backpack, which sped up the process of takedown and setup, something field artillery units were always doing. The army eventually adopted the unit Skinner refined, keeping it in service until the late 1980s.

Lt. William Nugent is pictured with a "marvelous" German MP40 submachine gun. He and his father were avid gun collectors prior to the war. NUGENT/DETTORE

Left: Mourmelon, France. Lt. James Davis with his captured German MP40 submachine gun pistol. Cpl. Leslie Sellers is loading the magazines. NUGENT/DETTORE

Some 321st soldiers fire assorted captured German weapons at Whatcombe Farm. Glidermen from B Battery who were sleeping nearby were awakened by the gunfire and initially thought the Germans had landed in their camp.

From left to right: Sgt. Donald Roy, Cpl. Louis Ivers, and Cpl. Lyle Wood of A Battery at Edinburgh Castle while on furlough in Scotland.

American warplanes parked underneath the Eiffel Tower in Paris. TURKAL FAMILY

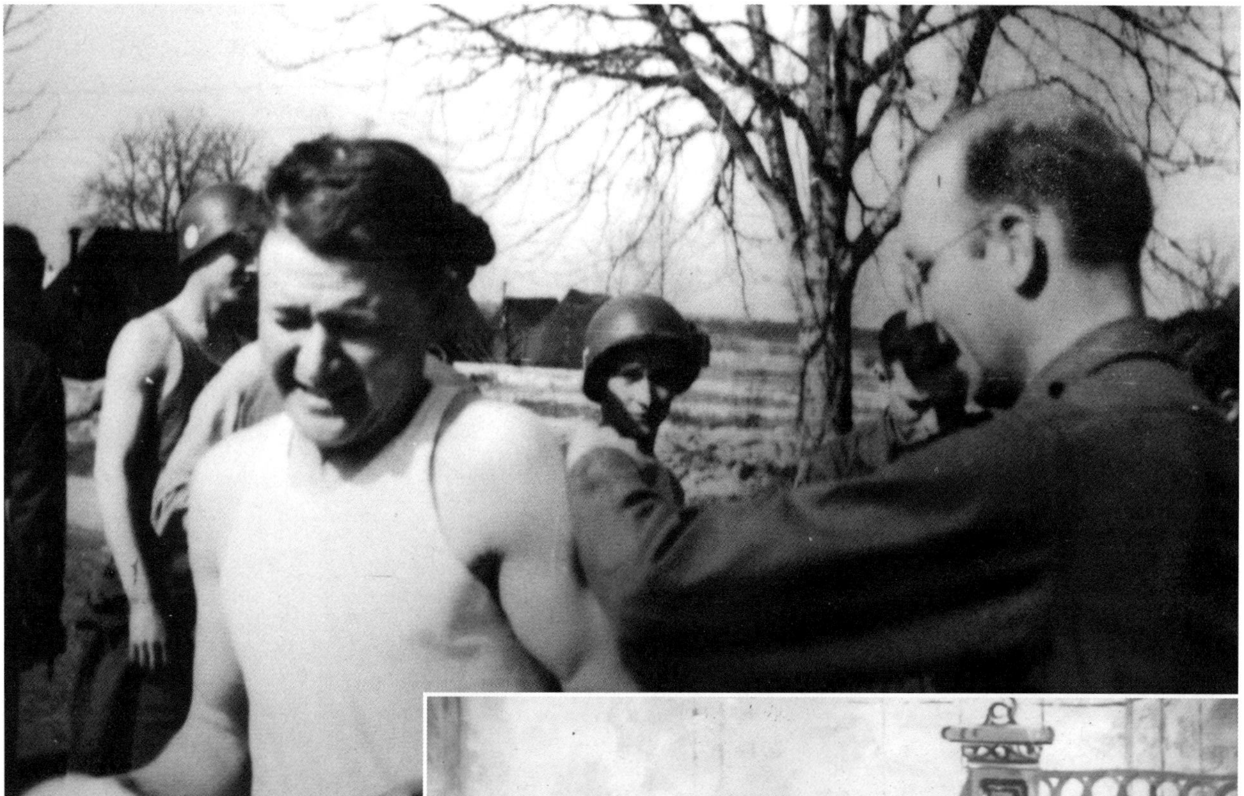

Mourmelon, France. Captain Skinner receives a shot from Lt. Dr. Davidson.
WILLIAMS FAMILY

Right: Camp Claiborne. Pvt. Harvey Baker (left) and Cpl. Bill Plummer (right).
BAKER FAMILY

CHAPTER 4

Market Garden and Beyond

ON AUGUST 14, 1944, the division was on the move again and the glidermen well understood their duties. One of the soldiers recalled the battalion's first dry runs.

> Nearly all the fellows remember the dry runs we had prior to Holland, but very few will remember the effect that the first one had on the rear or seaborne echelon. After all the men of the Battalion who were going to fly in had gone to the departure airport, Lt Chaumont took charge of the seaborne element, and after loading all the necessary equipment onto trucks they left to join other seaborne elements of the Division. In Portland, England, a small town on the Channel coast, all the men of the Division assembled. These men would go by LST [Landing Ship, Tank].
>
> Lt. Colonel [Howard] Rich, of Division QM [quartermaster], who was to be in command of the entire party, told the men all he knew about what they were going to do. They were supposed to go to France by boat and take over an area west of Paris and wait for further orders as to when the Division wanted them to join the outfit [the 321st].
>
> As soon as everything was in order to leave, the men were issued motion sickness pills and life preservers. Neither was needed. The trip over the Channel was lovely. Landing at Omaha Beach where the 1st Infantry Division had such a bloody battle on D-Day, there was a wait until the tide was right and then everything was unloaded. From there they went to a temporary assembly area. That area became a permanent one. The men waited anxiously for

> the formations of C-47s and Gliders to come over. Since none ever came they decided that the Airborne Invasion had taken place elsewhere. The weather was fine, warm and clear. They just knew that the operation had occurred.
>
> When they were finally informed that it had been a dry run, no one would believe it. "What Latrine did you get that rumor from" was the only answer one got when he told the men to pack up to go back to England.
>
> This should go down in history as the Biggest Dry Run ever. There was even the suggestion that these men get a Citation for going on this mission, the first that the Rear Echelons ever made without the aid of Combat Troops.[1]

The rear echelon did indeed eventually receive something extra for their trip. At the end of the war, points were assessed for service time and awards and then tallied up. The higher the number, the quicker a soldier got on the boat for the final trip home. The cooks and clerks who participated in that first extended "dry run" received additional points that the others in the battalion did not. It was considered another invasion, which entitled those men to beat the cannoneers in the race for home. The five extra points and one additional battle star got soldiers home one month earlier when the war ended. The men who sat it out at the airfields with their loaded gliders received nothing.

PFC Elmo Smiley was impressed by all the details the glider riders were given for the mission. The intelligence was so voluminous that they were even told that the landing zones used would have enemy guard dogs in the immediate area. The men asked, "What does that really mean for us?" The reply was, "Just be aware of the vicious dogs!"

"We went to the airport and loaded our glider for the expected landing at Charles, France," T/5 Merle Fulton (Headquarters Battery) wrote home. "After postponing it twice the mission was finally called off and we went back to our base camp."

Pvt. Woodrow Kinnear, of Pawnee, Oklahoma, and Hubert Warren, both of A Battery, sat in their loaded glider during a rainstorm. They heard the mission was called off, so they waited in the glider to be picked up. It grew later and later, so the two walked into Air Corps mess hall. Everybody wanted to know what they were still doing there. Having little choice, they spent the night at the hangar and were provided with some mattresses to sleep on. Nobody ever came back from the battalion looking for them. Later the next day, part of the battalion returned to unload the gliders and drive back to Whatcombe Farm, and Kinnear and Warren did, too. Not a word was said to them about being at the airbase for a day.

Corporal Raker had a sure method for determining whether or not the mission was going to take place. "I was broke as usual so I drew partial pay and promptly got involved in a poker game at the airfield barracks," he wrote. "I pocketed over $150 after that session and predicted the mission would be canceled because I never went anywhere with money. I sent the winnings home." Raker's premonition was correct.

On September 2, the battalion was again alerted for a glider assault. Gen. Maxwell Taylor told the troops, "We will stay here at the departure airfield until we have a mission."

Fulton wrote, "We took off again for the airport. This time we were to land at Soueneau [*sic*, Tournai], Belgium. After staying at the field for three days it was called off and we went back to again to camp."

Before the troops went back to their respective camps, General Taylor gave an impromptu speech. He said he could see the disappointment in their eyes about the canceled mission and promised them another one in the near future. The reaction to this pledge was immediate: a loud groan. Capt. Thomas White, Taylor's former aide-de-camp, was in the crowd. He said, "I don't know whose eyes he was looking in but I felt embarrassed for the general on how the men reacted to his speech." White recalled that Taylor had a difficult time in connecting with the common soldier and often misread their point of view on a situation at hand—such as believing the men groaned because they were disappointed about not going into battle.

The glidermen were paid in foreign currency in anticipation of a successful "go" for each mission. Raker's routine remained the same. "I drew another partial pay, played poker, made $100, and predictably the mission was canceled," he wrote. Both

England. From left to right: Lt. Nicholas Petrella, Lt. James Wicker, and an unknown soldier before the last dry run to Belgium. Note the standing water. LINZ FAMILY

times he paid back the partial pays when the troopers returned to Whatcombe Farm. His luck during the first dry run created a much-desired problem: a billfold jammed with so much foreign paper currency that he couldn't sleep with it in his back pocket. He threw it under the lower bunk.

The next morning, he got up and went to breakfast, forgetting the billfold. "When I returned, my chief of section, Sgt. Shade, asked me where the money was that I had won the night before," Raker wrote. "I said it was under the lower bunk, and he told me to get it. I could tell by his actions that he had found the money, so I gave a quick look and said the money was gone. Shade then began lecturing me on being more responsible, so I told him to keep my money if it made him feel any better. At first he denied having it, so I told him to just forget it. At long last, he did hand over the bulging billfold and he was still expounding when I walked away."

Capt. Tom White, former aide-de-camp to Gen. Maxwell Taylor.

To prepare the 101st Airborne Division for Operation Market Garden, General Taylor believed he had to get his division on the ground fast. Many things needed to be in place before the Germans mounted an effective counterattack, which they were famous for doing. German armor seemed to be in abundance, and the lightly equipped paratroopers needed artillery to counteract this. Mortars were the heaviest weapon at the paratroopers' disposal but just couldn't get the job done.

Taylor shifted his tactics by procuring additional gliders from the 82nd Airborne Division. The 101st would have double the number of gliders originally allotted for D+2. Coming in on September 19 along with the 321st would be the 907th GFA and the 377th PFA.

> A combination of reasons had led to exclusive emphasis upon infantry in the flights of the 17th and 18th of the first two days. With Division objectives so scattered, and the Division itself broken up into small perimeter defenses, General Taylor had felt that no matter where it was placed, artillery could not cover the entire area. . . . between allotting space not only for guns, but for transport and ammunition, or giving it to infantry, General Taylor chose infantry. Then, too, there had been the thought that 101st artillery observers who came in on D-day [September 17] could direct the fire of British guns. This plan had not worked because the distances involved were too great for the radios.[2]

In a letter dated February 26, 1975, Capt. Samuel Skinner (HQ) recalled being summoned to division headquarters on September 13, 1944, with two corporals who were radio operators.

> We were briefed given radio instructions frequencies etc. and 14 Sep were flown to Brussels and then taken in the dark of night to the Guards Armored Division. Here we briefed again on our duties. Mainly we were to ride on armored cars and sometimes tanks with the British Guards Armored Div near the front of the column, and our job was to establish communication with the 101-82 and British 1st Airborne as we got into range to direct artillery fire from airborne Batteries to clear the road out in front.
>
> Very little cooperation was given by Guards Armored; they seemed to think they had much more fire power than the airborne. Our maps were to be supplied by Guards which we never saw. We never directed any airborne fire and were completely useless.
>
> Each afternoon we were stopped and told to make tea. I thought we would never get over the bridge at Son and at Nijmegen. We did not know what was happening or what was wrong. We just were not going anywhere.
>
> Finally I got to shoot at an airplane in the bridgehead at Nijmegen. I did not shoot it down, but later decided I could do much more good if I returned to [the] 101st, so after getting permission and borrowing a jeep [I] set out for Veghel but the road was closed at Uden so [I] sent [the] jeep back and stayed with Col. Sink's 506th until the next day and reported in. Spent [the night] in a schoolhouse.

The battalion was alerted for a combat mission on September 14 at 2000 hours and arrangements to leave Whatcombe Farm for Berkshire, England, were made. On the sixteenth, the 321st left for their departure airfields at 0805 hours. B Battery, along with thirty-two men of Headquarters Battery, headed for Greenham Common. A Battery and the remainder of Headquarters Battery departed for Aldermaston.

The glidermen did not know their destination—Holland—until September 17, when all the enlisted men were briefed at their respective airfields at 1330 hours. They were told the landing zone would be easy to recognize because it was close to a large red barn. (The few who did look for it never located it.) The officers of the 321st had their briefing three and a half hours earlier at both of their airfields. All gliders were loaded and lashed, ready for their first combat glider mission, by 1700 hours.

Flight Officer (F/O) Sven Berg was born in Norway. His parents immigrated to United States when he was a child. He was an intelligent and introspective young man turned flier. Berg sent many letters

Leaving England on September 19, 1944. General Taylor told the men, "Good hunting." LINZ FAMILY

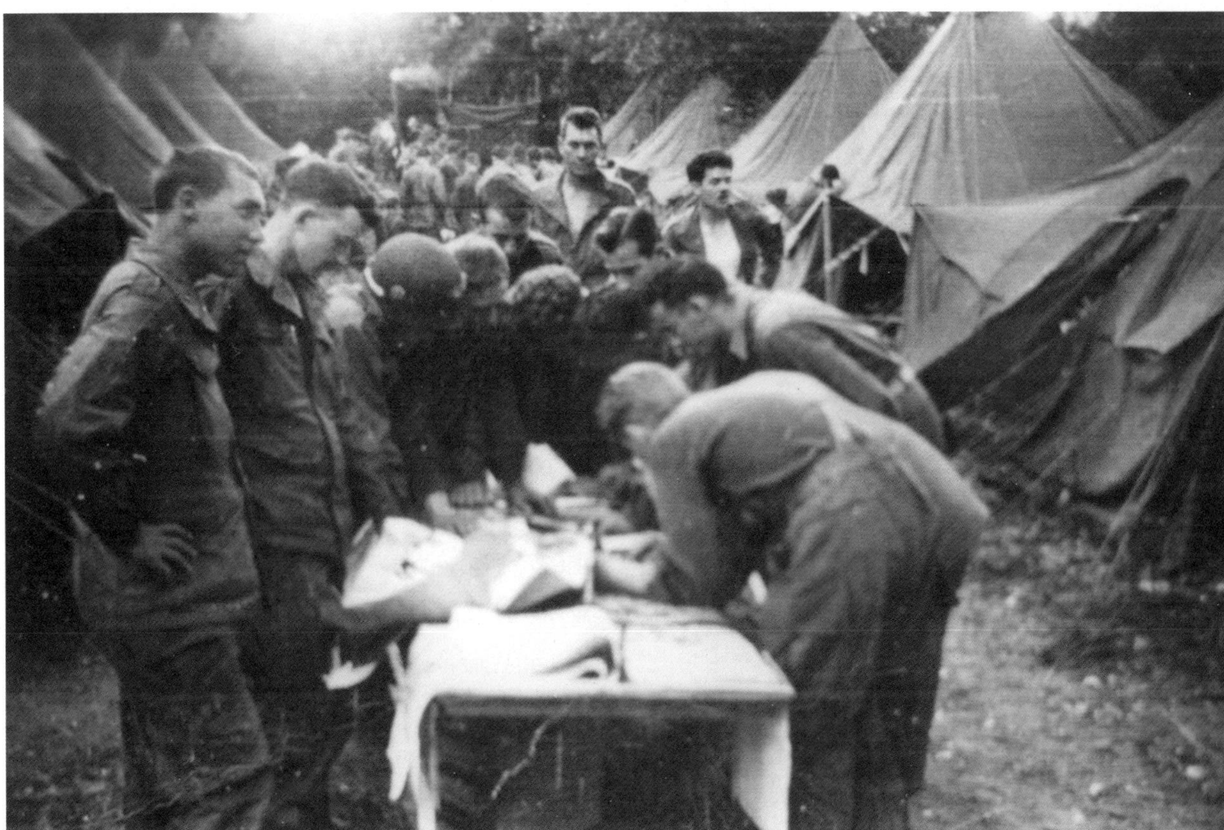

Lt. Tony Linz (foreground) receives landing zone information before takeoff from England. LINZ FAMILY

COORDINATES OF THE BATTALION'S GUN EMPLACEMENTS IN HOLLAND

Date	Command Post	A Battery	B Battery	Notes
September 19	418.272	417.267	412.268	
September 21		434.267	430.272	
September 22	4685.3625	469.362	469.361	100 yards behind the main line of resistance
September 24	521.415	519.416	520.419	Command post moved 300 yards east
September 25	492.385	494.381	491.381	
September 26				Command post moved to 4930.3818 at 1000 hours
September 27	5405.4355	5420.4230	5370.4230	
October 2	7395.5605	7346.5969	7344.5981	Nijmegen area
October 3				602.725 for the entire battalion, then changed to 604.724 at an unknown date—Zetten
October 28	6636.7035	67033.70569	67534.70576	500 yards northeast of Valburg
October 30				B Battery moved to 67506.70537 for extended range
November 15				A Battery moved to 680.704 due to heavy counterbattery fire
November 25				Battalion moved to Mourmelon, France

KEY OFFICERS: SEPTEMBER 17, 1944

Battalion Commander	Lt. Col. Edward L. Carmichael
Executive	Maj. John Tyler
S-2	Capt. Joseph Perkins
Assistant S-2	1st Lt. John Jordan
S-3	Capt. Carroll Holland
S-4	Capt. Roe Wilkins
Assistant S-4	Capt. Sam Williams
Liaison Officer	Capt. John Greenis
Headquarters Communications Officer	Capt. George Dunkelberg
A Battery Commanding Officer	Capt. John Fuller
B Battery Commanding Officer	Capt. Fred King

A glider at the ready in England, September 18, 1944. VERBEKE FAMILY

Vehicles lined up at Aldermaston, England, ready for takeoff. LINZ FAMILY

Aldermaston. General McAuliffe (front center) wears an A-2 leather jacket. Lt. Vincent Vicari is at the far left. Back row (from left to right): Col. Clarence Nelson, 907th GFA; Colonel Carmichael, 321st GFA; and Colonel Kennedy. NUGENT/DETTORE

Tug and glider pilots confer prior to takeoff from Aldermaston. LINZ FAMILY

home to his parents explaining his training and philosophy; apparently, being stateside, censorship was either lax or nonexistent.

"We have been given ground coordination tests to aid in ascertaining flight classification," he wrote in February 1942. "We were given brain wave tests (don't know what [that] is all about) and physical coordination tests. I passed these tests very credibly and will, according to the tabular classification system, be placed in a pursuit fighter and interceptor class. That suits me to the letter."

In March, Berg wrote:

> The army very recently decided to extend the aircorps into a new and little-tried field-gliding [school]. Overnight, practically, it was resolved that a number of large glider schools should be organized throughout the country. They need a large number of men with flying time and officers training in their first classes. They are offering a six-week training period during which the trainee is given a staff sergeant rating with $180 pay [monthly, including flying pay], and immediately following that, an [officer's] commission.
>
> I had long had my eye on gliding since I heard first proposals for its organization while at Cimmaron [Field, Oklahoma City]. I had already resolved then that I would snap at the first opportunity to get in on the ground floor of this new organization. Now my chance has come. I have just enough flying hours to qualify for the commission, and see a future ahead which promises much if I can come through with what it takes. Pursuit is the only alternative I would have by going on to advanced. Pursuit pilots are not wanted by airlines because they are considered to be too reckless and are untrained in the handling of larger ships.[3] My prediction is that the future holds everything in store for a commissioned glider pilot who seeks his fortune with the airlines after the war.

By July 1942, Berg's training was slightly relaxed.

> The commission—if Washington doesn't welch on this promise as it has on others—will come shortly after my schooling is completed. Promises I have learned are no good until they are in writing with signatures that have authority behind them. The prospects in this field are really inviting to commissioned officers who complete this training.
>
> This type of flying is somewhat more hazardous than motor flying and the army is finding difficulty in recruiting qualified men with flying time to handle this big job. To be early in the field as a second lieutenant is to earn quick promotions, for everything about this program is in the formative stage. They have not completed construction of any of the 10,000 gliders which are to be constructed within the next four months. Each of these gliders will carry 15 paratroopers or commandos with material.

In a November 16, 1942, letter home, Berg wrote:

> A major sent from Washington D.C. endeavored to cheer us up with the heartening news that the glider construction bottleneck has been broken. He read to us a personal letter from General "Hap" Arnold stating that our commissions would be accorded us immediately the hour we finish training on the big gliders. He said further that they have worked most of the "bugs" out of our present first line gliders and we should be flying regularly again. For the last few weeks we have been flying all kinds of motor planes. Since the successful demonstration use of gliders on recent maneuvers [General Arnold and other dignitaries attended this demonstration, held on March 28, 1942, which also involved paratroopers and artillery], the army staff in Washington has been pushing this program ahead and fast as the highest priorities for construction.

In a letter home dated March 3, 1944, from Laurinburg–Maxton Army Air Base, Berg described how training had taken a different approach to glider landings, including practice with landing on small fields with artificial fences (proof that the Allied invasion force was not entirely unprepared to find these).

I am flying gliders every day and the work is becoming more exacting and difficult. At present we are landing gliders with close and intricate formation patterns into small fields. First we practice hitting short landing areas between artificial barriers. Then we make individual approaches into strange fields which are 500–700 feet in length. These fields are surrounded by trees and stumps which leave few alternatives open to the pilot who misjudges. When the individual approach is mastered, then twenty and thirty gliders are cut loose in formation and they are all expected to scramble into a 500-ft. landing area. They are further expected to make a perfect parking dispersal [and] bring tip to wing tip in two or three rows across the field.

Needless to say, we tear up gliders. On some days our group of 200 pilots smashes up as many as 25 gliders. We are lucky usually because most of the boys are cool. They don't scare easily and when the pinch comes they think quickly. These fellows all have a lot of time on gliders and when the invasion comes you will probably hear a good deal about their work.

Berg was on flying status, which allowed him to fly as a copilot on a C-47. He could also "check out" a single-engine airplane or glider whenever he chose to do so. He was still thinking ahead to the end of the war and how gliders would play into that. "What I have in the back of my mind is to utilize the valuable training the army is giving me for the great future that gliding will have with commercial airlines at the cessation of this war. But that is a long way ahead to look." In the meantime, he told his parents that learning to fly gliders took real skill and was "great fun."

F/O Berg flew gliders into Normandy, Holland, and Germany. He brought a group of 321st troopers

England. A glider pilot with a camouflage-painted helmet and flak vest.

PFC George Verbeke of A Battery, one of the glidermen Lieutenant Berg brought into Holland. VERBEKE FAMILY

from A Battery into Holland and wrote home soon after: "Don't worry about my ability to survive future missions. My guardian angel has amply demonstrated to me that this is a period of trial for me and nothing worse. If this were not so, I can assure you that I would not be here now."

What he didn't tell his parents was what catastrophe his "guardian angel" had kept him from during his last mission: a water landing, or "ditch," in the English Channel. All the 321st artillerymen survived and were eventually picked up by a naval ship and taken back to England. Berg made it back to his base by September 26, and the glidermen returned to Whatcombe Farm on October 1. Sgt. Wayne Kuenzli got word to his unit in Holland that his gun section was alive. That bit of news was received at 321st HQ on October 3, and the men were quickly back in the action.

After the war, Sven Berg attended the University of California under the GI Bill, studying philosophy. During the Vietnam war, he joined the Merchant Marines, who took supplies up and down the Mekong Delta. He continued to work with the Merchant Marines into his seventies. One of his last jobs was ferrying tourists from San Francisco to the closed Alcatraz prison.

On September 18, Corporal Raker engaged himself in another poker game after drawing another partial pay. He went broke in three hands and dutifully notified everyone that this was not going to be another dry run.

The battalion was split into two groups, one flying from Aldermaston Airbase and the other from Greenham Common Airbase, within miles of each other. A total of 410 men (24 officers and 386 enlisted men) loaded into 71 Waco CG-4A gliders. The intended Landing Zone W was near the city of Zon. All 321st

Lt. Sven Berg. BERG FAMILY

gliders began their first combat glider assault at 1230 hours on September 19. Their glider training of more than two years would now be put to good use. The men would more than earn their extra $50 (approximately) of flight pay a month. (Officers received an additional $100.)

The Greenham Common–based C-47 tug pilots who were towing the CG-4As came from the 438th Troop Carrier Group, Squadron 88. The Aldermaston tug pilots were from the 434th Troop Carrier Group, Squadron 74. The glider pilots (flight officers) were from the same groups. Since they were short on glider pilots, additional glider pilots from the 435th Troop Carrier Group were temporarily assigned to assist with the lift.

Fifty-five of the seventy-one gliders that left England landed at the intended landing zone. Three ditched in the English Channel: two from B Battery and one from A Battery. Two carried a 75mm pack howitzer and the other carried 75mm ammunition. One of the two gliders from B Battery was also transporting passengers Sgt. Haig Pauley, Pvt. Charles Stange, PFC Raymond Arnold, Pvt. Antonio Hinojosa, PFC Adolph Bonath, and Pvt. Harold Riley. The 75mm pack howitzer broke loose on impact and injured Riley's leg. (When he applied for compensation from the government, he was denied because he never reported the injury to his command.) The glider pilot was most likely F/O Robert J. Kile of Wilkes-Barre, Pennsylvania, from the 438th Troop Carrier Group, Squadron 89. Kile drowned, and his body was never recovered.

Another glider from B Battery, also carrying a 75mm pack howitzer and troopers, was towed back to England and landed near the shoreline. The twelve remaining gliders were forced down or crashed in Holland or Belgium. (Note: Holland is not a country, but rather one of many provinces in The Netherlands. However, throughout the research of this book, veteran interviews, labeled photographs, written correspondence, and official records compiled during the war mistakenly refer to Holland as a country.)

Four days later, the final 321st glider left England carrying a jeep and three soldiers and landed safely in Holland. The unaccounted gliders for this lift carried seventy-one enlisted men and two officers. One gliderman was killed in the landing. The losses for the battalion were 18 percent on this day, September 23.

Fifty-five gliders reported they landed on the landing zone without incident. Of the thirty-six jeeps loaded onto the gliders, thirty-one landed safely while the other five were damaged upon landing. Twenty-one trailers were loaded onto the gliders in England; eighteen made it safely to the landing zone, and the other three were damaged in landing. The seaborne element consisting of a field kitchen, 6x6 trucks, and other supplies caught up via land route, arriving at the 321st command post northeast of Veghel with one warrant officer and fifty enlisted men on September 24.

The writers of *Mission Accomplished* remembered the landings (although the date is incorrect):

> On September 16, '44 we were again alerted. [Where were] we going this time? Was it just another dry run? These were part of the many questions that were uppermost in our minds. Rumors flew thick and fast, flared up, became strong and died. None of us knew anything for sure. The Army has a way of taking care of its vital secrets.
>
> Then came the morning, the whistle. The day of going to the departure airfield had arrived. Everything was in readiness. Guns and jeeps were on the line, seemingly eager to be on their way. A few good-byes to heartbroken buddies. FO and Liaison parties, and the 321 moved from Whatcombe Farm. It was a happy and adventurous crew that ruled the highways that Sept. morning. A twinkling eye for the pretty girls, a warning smile to the elderly. We were on our way and glad to be on the move.
>
> Though we had experienced it many times, our first sight of the field with its rows upon rows of C-47's and gliders again brought to us the realization of the importance of our Division. There they stood, Winged Power! And we were the men to make them so.
>
> We were assigned to billets of pyramidal tents. Each section [was] as closely associated with itself as possible. Clean new blankets, showers, entertainment, the best of food.

Everything to make our last hours under normal conditions as enjoyable as possible.

But we still had work to do. Gliders had to be loaded and lashed. Loaded to fly and if necessary, to crash-land under the most adverse conditions. Arduous months of training had equipped us with the knowledge to do this job with the minimum of confusion and delay. Briefing, the job of telling what, where and when to do a thing. The sand-table became our classroom. The position of every hedge, road or river must be instilled in our minds. It was here that the question of Where was answered with the naming of Holland as the destination. All was in readiness now. Though a certain degree of "sweating it out" prevailed, the men as a whole were confident, sure of themselves and ready to go.

Volley and baseball teams were hastily organized. The Red Cross now became a gathering place. The food being excellent, many was the man who stood in line for seconds. Though no time had been set for "Lights Out," darkness usually found the men bedded down, clean healthful fun having retired them to a heavy sleep.

On the morning of the 17th at the hour of 10:20 a tenseness filled the camp. Coming from the northwest could be seen hundreds of transports and gliders and we knew that our Paratroopers and Division Artillery were on their way. They circled the field, jockeyed for position and flew due east. We waved and wished them the best. We had confidence in them; they were our friends.

We knew that a large part of the initial success depended on them. With eager ears we awaited the news-broadcast heralding their progress. It wasn't long in coming. "ALLIED PARACHUTE AND GLIDER TROOPS HAVE INVADED HOLLAND."

They were there and the mission was under way. In about six hours the drone of engines told of the return of the carriers. We counted them. Yes, some were missing. That was to be expected. Then came the red flares denoting that some of the planes had injured persons aboard. That, too, was expected. We gathered around the pilots and co-pilots. What was it like? Was there much flak? This was the trend of the dozens of questions shot at the men who had been there.

On the morning of the 19th we were awakened by the throaty roar of the mighty transports as they warmed up prior to taxiing onto the runways. This was the day, this was IT.

Men tumbled from their bunks and hastily began preparation for leaving the area. A thorough check of the quarters were made by the officers and after a hearty breakfast we made our way to the waiting gliders. There were naturally a lot of last-minute details to be taken care of between the troops and pilots. These were handled in the usual Air Corps manner and at 12:35 the first glider took the air. At 45-second intervals one glider after another rolled from the line. The 321st was Airborne. What was before us, only God in his Heaven knew.

Over the greens of England flew the armada. As far as the eye could see stretched the chain of fighting men. Below us we could see the coast line, the channel with its treacherous currents and now Belgium.

Flying in close formation, the ships encountered heavy fog banks. Visibility was so reduced that at times only the first few feet of the tow-line could be seen.

Tug ships changed their course without the Glider knowing it. Some of them were flopped over and had to cut loose. Then came the flak and heavy machine-gun fire. We could see the black smoke and dirt and knew that we were nearing the landing zone. We felt naked up there knowing that thousands of faces, both friendly and enemy, were upturned to see us pass. With the spit of a thousand devils the fire surrounded us. T[h]rough the tail assembly, the floor, the very men themselves it penetrated. Ships and Gliders went down but the huge formation never faltered.[4]

The following excerpt was penned by S-2 Capt. Joseph Perkins and titled "Unit History for the Invasion of Holland." It was submitted to the G-2 of the

Holland. A crashed and burned glider. WILLIAMS FAMILY

101st Airborne Division on December 11, 1944. It reads in part:

> After a successful take off and flying in a close formation, the flight encountered a dense fog bank extending from the middle of the Channel to beyond the landing zone in Holland. Visibility was reduced so that at times it was impossible to see more than a foot of the tow rope, and the formation was broken up. Tug ships changed their courses without the glider pilots knowing it and some were flipped over and forced to cut loose. Fifty-seven of the seventy-one gliders eventually reached the landing zone after being subjected to heavy small arms and anti-aircraft fire the entire time they were over enemy territory. [It was actually fifty-five gliders.] Three howitzer loads were lost in the Channel and eleven were forced or shot down in Belgium and Holland. Three of [the] tug ships were shot down in flames. The enemy had the western edge of the landing field covered by mortar and small arms fire, and gliders landing in that area were immediately brought under fire, making it necessary, in some cases,

England. Getting ready for Holland. STEARNS/DETTORE

Holland. Capt. Joseph Perkins (looking at camera) and Colonel Carmichael in the command post. WILLIAMS FAMILY

to unload under cover of darkness. Losses for the day were seventy-one enlisted men and two officers missing in the fourteen gliders, one man killed in [a] landing crash, and eighteen men and two officers injured. The loss represented approximately eighteen percent of the total battalion strength.

In spite of all difficulties encountered the battalion was assembled by 1640, and at 1845 all installations were in and battalion ready to fire, in support of the 502nd Parachute Infantry Regiment in the attack on Best.

On 22 September the Battalion moved to position southwest of Veghel to support the 501st Parachute Infantry in repelling vigorous enemy counter attacks aimed at cutting the supply route in that area. The batteries went forward with two-men skeleton crews and in [the] face of enemy small arms fire organized the positions. Shortly after getting positions organized they were called on to take anti-tank positions at the bridge southwest of Veghel under direct observation and small arms fire, remaining there for several hours until ordered to displace to new positions along the St. Oedenrode–Veghel road. The battalion fired continuously in support of the Infantry in repelling numerous enemy counter attacks.

On 24–25 September when the battalion was in position on the northeast side of Veghel,

Gliders being loaded in Holland. Note the invasion stripes, only painted under the wings and the fuselage for Holland.

Right: Holland. Sgt. Nelson Kopacka of B Battery's machine-gun section scowls at the camera after being ordered to carry the communication wire spools.

it was cut off from most units of the Division when the Germans succeeded in cutting the road for a period of two days. The battalion continued to support the 506th Parachute Infantry Regiment in clearing the road and maintain[ing] their own protection by use of all available manpower in the battalion as machine gunners, bazooka teams, and riflemen. One position was heavily shelled, causing several casualties in the Command Post. The battalion proved that it could operate aggressively and efficiently under trying conditions and deliver accurate fire whenever called for.

After the Veghel battle the battalion moved to Uden, Holland and took up a defensive position, remaining five days before moving to

Holland. Sgt. Mark Sullivan's B Battery gun section stripped glider fabric and laced it into howitzer netting for camouflage.
SULLIVAN FAMILY

Europe. Note the glider wing stuck in the tree. BERG FAMILY

Holland. Retrieving equipment from gliders with the help of Dutch farmers' equipment. Note the 327th Headquarters staff sergeant in the foreground. SULLIVAN FAMILY

A B Battery gun emplacement in Holland. SULLIVAN FAMILY

The 321st command post dugout in Holland. PERKINS FAMILY

the Nijmegen area on October 2nd. Here the battalion was placed in general support of the 82nd Airborne Division, and fired the first round from a 101st Airborne Division gun to fall in Germany. During this move and the next move the battalion was ordered to use their "dim out lights" only.

On 3 October the battalion moved to [a] position north of the Waal Canal in direct support of the 506th Parachute Infantry Regiment, with a front of 14,000 yards to cover. The Infantry line was thinly held due to heavy casualties sustained earlier in the campaign, and artillery was going to have to play a major part in holding the lines. On 4 October a German Regiment of the 363rd Infantry Division launched a counter attack at Opheusden against the 3rd Battalion. Over 1,700 rounds of time and percussion shells were fired during the attack and played a vital part in repelling the attack. Prisoner of War reports later revealed that this regiment was practically destroyed. The following day the enemy again attacked with a fresh regiment. After fierce fighting, during which the enemy succeeded in making a penetration of our lines, they were finally driven back and our line restored. During this attack artillery fire was accurately placed on enemy troop concentrations and defensive fires put down to less than 100 yards in front of our troops without a single round landing on our own troops. Over 2,600 rounds were fired to repel the attack. On the morning of 7 October the enemy again attacked and succeeded in breaking through, getting to within a thousand yards of the artillery positions. Accurate fire was a vital factor in finally beating off this attack in which over 2,600 rounds were fired. During one critical period 1,200 rounds were fired by the battalion in

Holland. Sgt. Harry Stearns (right), B Battery Detail Section, with unidentified 321st soldiers. STEARNS/DETTORE

Stateside. A jeep with spools of communication wire for liaison officers and forward observer parties.

forty-five minutes. Prisoner of War reports revealed that in the three-day battle the German 363rd Infantry Division had been reduced to about 30% effective strength, due, in a large part, to the effectiveness of the artillery fire.

During this period the battalion had three Liaison and five Forward Observer parties on the line, and the calls for fire missions were continuous. So numerous and urgent were many of the missions that a Battery took over a battalion mission, firing twice the amount it would normally. Wire communications were established with all Forward Observers and Liaison details, in addition to radio, and were serviced constantly under extremely difficult and hazardous conditions. The battalion fired a total of 25,308 rounds to date without a single round reported falling on our own troops, in 906 separate fire missions.

28 October the battalion, still supporting the 506th, moved to new positions at Valburg, Holland. The 506th relieved one Brigade of the British 50th Division in the sector nearest Arnhem.

The battalion remained in this position until the 506th Combat Team was relieved by units of a Scottish Division. The guns received March Order for operation "Market" at 0345, 26 November 1944.

The battalion moved on 26 November by motor vehicles to Camp Mourmelon, near Reims, France, for resting, reequipping and training.

On September 17, 1944, four officers and fourteen enlisted men from the battalion jumped into Holland with the 506th PIR. This was the first combat jump for many of these artillerymen. All of them knew of the problems with mis-drops in the Normandy jump and hoped this would be quite different. At least this jump was during daylight, but that could pose its own problems.

Capt. Thomas White of Cambridge, Massachusetts, was recently assigned to the 321st headquarters. He had been Gen. Maxwell Taylor's

Holland. Capt. Thomas White, Headquarters Battery, at the 321st command post. PERKINS FAMILY

aide-de-camp since the Sicily campaign until a disagreement with General Taylor caused his transfer. White's new position was liaison officer to the 506th regimental headquarters.

Jumping in with him were Sgt. Earl Patchin of Joplin, Missouri, and Cpl. Lawrence Wilkinson Jr. of El Paso, Texas, both from Headquarters Battery. Patchin was the radio operator for his group and would have to wait for two days until their jeep-mounted SCR-610 radio came into Holland via 321st gliders. Wilkinson's assignment was jeep driver for the team.

Patchin's C-47 took plenty of enemy fire en route to the Zon drop zone. One of the engines was knocked out ten to fifteen minutes away from the drop zone and caught fire. The plane was losing altitude rapidly and the "green light" illuminated; the pilot kept on a straight flight path because it was time to jump. Patchin was second from last in his stick to leave the burning aircraft. He could feel the intense heat from the floor being so hot. His jump boots started to scorch his feet. He jumped clear of the falling, burning airplane, and his chute opened just as he hit the ground. The crippled C-47 came down for a belly landing; Patchin later heard the crew survived, but this could not be verified at the time. Out of the 424 C-47s that dropped the 101st Division into Holland that day, 16 were shot down. "The drop zone was a beehive of activity," Patchin said. "The Dutch people with their orange armbands and anything orange came to help us at the DZ; carts and horses helped us to clear the area."

Lt. Eugene "Gene" Brooks of Richmond, Virginia, was a forward observer assigned to 1st Battalion, 506th PIR. His radioman was Pvt. Joe Karasevic of Lorain, Ohio. Rounding out the A Battery team were Pvt. Robert Doyle of Los Angeles, California, and Pvt. Donald Falls from Coos Bay, Oregon. Unforeseen events would make this jump a lucky one for Private Falls.

Lieutenant Brooks discovered that one of the men assigned to him had refused to make the upcoming combat jump, no longer wanting to be part of a forward observer party. A replacement was needed quickly, and Falls was the man. He was jump-qualified from Fort Benning, Georgia, and had made eleven practice jumps. Brooks asked him if he had any forward observer training. Falls said, "Yes, lieutenant, I have." It was a bold-faced lie, and Falls remarked later that he would have said anything "to keep from going in on one of those shit awful gliders." His job was to jump into combat with plenty of extra batteries for the radio.

Falls had come into the 321st shortly before the Holland campaign and was asked by PFC Francis Watson (A Battery) of High Point, North Carolina, to join his machine-gun section. This was his assignment for the two dry runs prior to Holland, and he was scheduled to go in by glider on September 19 prior to Brooks's intervention. The glider that brought in PFC Watson's A Battery machine-gun section (now minus Falls) on the nineteenth with the rest of the 321st didn't make it to the landing zone. The entire glider load of men was captured and they spent the rest of the war as POWs.

This would be Private Falls's first combat jump, but not his first time under enemy fire. In April 1942, Falls was in the Oregon National Guard, stationed at Fort Stevens, located at the mouth of the Columbia River. The fort was to protect the West Coast, and Falls's unit manned the 10-inch disappearing guns there. On April 18, a Japanese Imperial Navy submarine zeroed in and fired nine shots from its deck gun at the fortifications, causing little damage. Return fire was denied by the commanding officer in order to keep the enemy from knowing what defenses were there. The damage done was insignificant. The men in Falls's unit placed a sign over their gun: "9 shots fired, 9 shots missed—to hell with Hirohito." Apparently this was a retaliatory strike for the B-25 Doolittle raid on Japan a few months earlier.

This would be Falls's twelfth jump. He looked around. Everyone in his stick was part of the 506th, but they were strangers. That would change on the ground. His face was also unfamiliar in combat, but the cannonball stenciled on the 321st helmets meant artillery was near, and they would soon ask his forward observer party for support. In a short time, the forward observer teams of the 321st would be strangers to no one at the main line of resistance in Holland.

Falls was the last man in his stick. As he stood up, he heard a strange noise that seemed to be coming from one of the C-47's engines. He wondered if it had been hit from all the flak exploding everywhere. Curiosity got the best of him, and he crouched to peer out a window. When he stood up, he was surprised to find the green jump light was lit. Most of the other paratroopers had already left the plane, and Falls had to run fast to catch up and jump out the door in hopes of hitting the drop zone. He did.

Getting out of his harness and making it to the assembly area was the priority. While running along a small wooded area, he glanced up to see a glider coming down in a picture-perfect landing. Unfortunately, another glider was circling above, no doubt looking for a landing spot of its own. It did not notice the CG-4A and broadsided it. Jeeps broke loose from their lashings and tumbled through the gliders, crushing their riders. Jumbled heaps of war materiel, canvas, and twisted airframes fell from the air less than fifty feet from him, but he kept running.

Brooks's weapon of choice for the drop into Holland was the M3 "grease gun," a .45-caliber submachine gun. Most of his team preferred the .30-caliber folding-stock carbine, but Brooks said he couldn't hit anything with the gun, and only once did he observe someone get shot by one. Other paratroopers came in with weapons at the ready, not wanting to repeat the Normandy debacle of having to assemble their rifles under fire after landing. This caused many casualties because the assembled weapons whipped around during the opening shock of the parachutes, knocking out teeth and causing other injuries.

After Brooks jumped clear of the C-47, he noticed a paratrooper below him holding a .45-caliber semiautomatic pistol in his hand. Every time the trooper pulled on his risers with that hand, he fired a shot in the direction of the descending paratroopers. Brooks yelled down to the soldier to stop firing, but the shots continued until the man hit the ground, got out of his chute, and disappeared in the mass of running men.

Maj. James LaPrade, the 506th Battalion commanding officer, was the jumpmaster for Brooks's stick. Within forty-five minutes of landing, his battalion was organized enough to move toward Zon and assist in securing the bridge over the Wilhelmina Canal. As the troopers started to move out, Brooks noticed a large German shepherd running around. It had obviously jumped in with somebody. He observed the dog taking commands from Lt. Pete Baranowski, a Headquarters/506th Battalion lieutenant. The dog would wander around but dutifully stayed close when called. Brooks commented to a soldier in his forward observer party, "I don't think that dog's going to last long here." He never saw the dog after that first day.

The team was ready to move south, but Karasevic was unable to locate his radio. He eventually found it and caught up to his party as they rested for the night at a house. The group tried repeatedly to reach the British XXX Corps without success. The next day, Brooks had the radio taken up to the loft of a windmill in the hope of increasing its reception. Much later, they learned the British XXX Corps operator wasn't familiar with the signals he was getting. Operation Market Garden had only one week to get organized, creating problems such as this. The forward observer party felt useless. It frustrated them to see excellent German targets for fire missions without having communication to the firing battery: the problems of Normandy in Holland.

One of the four forward observer teams that jumped into Holland consisted of B Battery members Lt. Francis Canham of Barker, New York; Pvt. John Braswell of Bartow, Florida; Pvt. William "Jay" Stone of Teaneck, New Jersey; and Cpl. Paul Galant of Pittsburgh, Pennsylvania. Canham's original plan was to split his men into two groups, each on a separate C-47, putting the most experienced troopers together and pairing the least experienced. First out the door would be the battalion commander of the 3rd Battalion, 506th PIR. The second person out was 3rd Battalion S-2 Capt. John Kiley. Canham jumped third and Private Stone fourth. This would be Stone's first combat jump. "I was kind of nervous," he recalled. "This was the first time I was in an aircraft that was being fired on. When I heard this stuff coming up, I said 'What's that?' to the guy next to me. He says, 'That's machine guns; they're shooting at us.' The S-2 was standing up and he must have seen me and I must have looked worried. The guy gave me a nice smile and a little nod and a wink, a real compassionate guy. He was a captain. Two days

Austria. A Battery Lt. Gene Brooks stands at the far right.

later on the road into Eindhoven he [was] lying on the sidewalk with a bullet through his jugular."[5]

Private Stone continued to describe his first jump experience. The red light near the door was supposed to go on fifteen minutes before they jumped, he said. At this point, the battalion commander stood up, hooked up, and checked the equipment. They were ready to go. Eighteen minutes later, the crew chief came back and told the battalion commander it was fifteen minutes now. Finally, the green light went on, and the battalion commander kicked some equipment out the door and then jumped. "The rest of us just piled out of that airplane as fast as we could go," Stone said. "Nobody wanted to be in that thing anymore."

He got on the ground, landing close to Canham. Their radio had been in the bomb racks in a pack, and Stone quickly retrieved it. He started to untie the padded canvas pack with the radio in it, but couldn't do it. Instead, he took out his trench knife and cut the pack open. He put the radio on his back and carried the batteries against his chest. The men then followed the blue smoke grenade to the 3rd Battalion assembly area without incident.

"The mission we had as forward observers was to direct fire for the British XXX Corps artillery, which was coming up from the south slowly, way behind schedule," Stone recalled. "Once we got to the assembly area, I tried to check in with divisional artillery [XXX Corps]. Nothing." They were 15 miles away. Stone and the others figured there was something wrong with the radio. He went over to division artillery and tried to get them to repair the radio, but they didn't have the capability. Stone left and caught up with Canham and the others on the road to Zon.

The forward observer team moved with paratroopers and crossed the rickety bridge the 326th Engineer Battalion had hastily constructed over the recently blown-up bridge that had spanned the Wilhelmina Canal. The entire 506th PIR crossed over a few men at a time, not finishing until midnight.

The 321st forward observer team had been up since 0400 hours; it was now 2200. The useless 50-pound radio and batteries had taken their toll on Stone. "Whenever we stopped . . . I would rest the radio on the window sills, taking the load off my shoulders," Stone said. "I could hear the radios the Dutch people had tuned to the BBC. The BBC [was] telling them about the operation, that the Americans [were] moving down to Eindhoven. We couldn't get to Eindhoven for another day or so. A few times I was so tired I would fall asleep while I was walking down the road and then wake up."

His team finally got across the Wilhelmina Canal around 2300 hours. It was now time to bed down, so the troopers crawled into a ditch. They laid their waterproof gas capes down for ground sheets and went to sleep. No blankets were to be had for this chilly September night.

Glider #1 consisted of a glider pilot and trained copilot. The VIP passenger was Colonel Carmichael. With him were S-2 Lt. Joseph Perkins, a radio operator, a corporal trained as a radio repairman, and a jeep driver. Equipment included a jeep with an SCR-610 truck-mounted radio and an aiming circle. Binoculars, flashlights, message books, and other supplies were packed in the jeep.

Somewhere close by down the line was Maj. John Tyler (HQ), sitting in the copilot seat of his glider. Along for the ride were PFC Leo Corrigan and a few others. Tyler had affection for the tommy gun and had carried one while in Normandy. After his glider landed, he jumped out and accidentally fired the gun, putting numerous holes into the wing.

The pilot of the glider *Miss Windy City* was Lt. Frank Doubek, a Chicago native. He was with the 438th Troop Carrier Group, 88th Squadron. This was his second combat glider flight, the first being Normandy. In his glider as copilot was Maj. Thomas Henderson (HQ). As Henderson prepared for his flight, his mind was on his father and adopted aunt: they were in the Philippines, their fate unknown.

Major Henderson's father, also named Thomas, was retired army with thirty years of service and a veteran of the Spanish-American War. Seeing an opportunity, he opened a shoe manufacturing business in Manila. On December 6, 1941, the Japanese overran the Philippines and interned the seventy-year-old in Santo Tomas. It would take three years of waiting before the family learned he was alive. His adopted sister, Flora, was Filipino and therefore not interned. She smuggled food into the camp to her brother by bribing the Japanese guards. It was risky—at any time a guard could have turned her in, with an execution soon to follow. Major Henderson had learned nothing more of his father's fate since the notification from the government on December 6, 1944, of his internment.

On February 25, 1945, word of the camp's liberation was publicized. The news was slow in coming; the actual date was February 5. Approximately 3,700 internees inhabited the camp on the grounds of the University of Santo Tomas in Manila. Although suffering from malnutrition and beriberi, "Dad" Henderson was in good health thanks to the efforts of Flora. Major Henderson received the good news that his father was alive via telegram from the Red Cross. Two days later, he received another that his father was dead, killed by the Japanese a day after liberation "as [a] result of enemy action" on the island of Luzon.

Cpl. William "Jay" Stone. STONE FAMILY

But Major Henderson did not know any of this on September 19. He had to focus on preparing himself and his glidermen for their first combat glider invasion.

The glider load consisted of a loaded jeep trailer plus eight soldiers and the pilot. All but one of the battalion was from headquarters; the other man was from B Battery and assigned to a gun section. His job was to cut the powder bags and set the fuses. PFC Joseph Carey from Indianapolis, Indiana, a former paratrooper, was now an unwilling gliderman. He transferred into the 321st from a jumper regiment

Lt. Frank Doubek was interviewed by *Yank*, the Army's weekly magazine, for the July 2, 1944, issue soon after his Normandy experiences. An excerpt from the article reads:

> One of the worst spots was where a glider pilot came down. That boy went through hell. They landed in a field and they were under fire all the way down and . . . never had a chance to get out of the glider. His pal, the other pilot in the glider, had been wounded before the glider hit the ground, and when it touched down, the first thing he said was, "Get me out of here." The glider pilot went to his pal's assistance and just then the Germans opened up with their machine guns again. The men in that glider fell wounded and dead under the wings before they had a chance to get away. The Germans came right up to the glider and killed two wounded men under the wing. One pilot [Everett Creasy] played dead and they didn't touch him. Different units of Germans passing by kept throwing machine-gun and mortar fire at the glider for twelve hours. The pilot lay there among the dead. He was soaked in the blood of dead guys and lying under bodies. Several times he wanted to commit suicide. He lay there until noon the next day when our paratroopers took over the field.

Creasy was listed as MIA and presumed dead until he later showed up back in England at his base. He was not recognized at first because his hair had turned white from his ordeal in Normandy. Doubek returned home and died at the age of forty-six, leaving behind a wife and eight children. ■

after a squabble. Although it was against orders for anyone to wear a M42 suit (the tan paratrooper jacket and pants) into Holland, Carey wore his. Pinned to his jumpsuit were his wings and on his feet were jump boots. This was to be his first taste of battle.

The glider flight into Holland took place without mishap. The landing was rough, bad enough to cause the lashed-down trailer to shift. The tongue of the trailer bounced up and pinned Carey's leg. He couldn't move, and the glider was under fire. He thought he was going to die in that position. Bullets hitting the glider made a noise like a stick poked through cardboard. Everyone bailed out, part of their training. Someone returned—Carey thought it was either Major Henderson or F/O Doubek—and freed him. Both men ran 50 feet across a field toward the woods where everybody else was going. As Carey ran, he looked down at the ground and saw a dead German, about forty years old. He couldn't help but wonder what an old guy like that had been doing in combat.

Eventually Carey made it to his gun section. While there, an incident fostered a dislike for the Brits. The guns of B Battery were emplaced, and three or four tanks pulled in behind them. They were Sherman tanks, manned by British troops. The tanks lined up and fired some rounds at targets into a field far away, then sped off. It didn't take long for the Germans to return the favor by shelling the battery.

Carey was later rated corporal by Captain King and made part of a forward observer party at Bastogne led by Lt. Marvin Mikles.

Air sickness pills were handed out to the officers and glider riders who needed them. They came in small cardboard boxes containing six tablets. The side effects varied, from induced drowsiness to a heightened sense of nervousness. Instructions on the box were: "Take one 30 minutes before and one at the time of embarking. Then take one not more often than every four hours. Do not continue taking longer than necessary. Caution: These tablets contain a sedative and cause drowsiness if taken to excess."

Lt. James "Buck" Davis knew that Pvt. George "Cokie" Crim became ill just looking at a glider, so he gave him a box of pills and told him to take one. Davis said he had to check on something and would be back shortly. Crim misunderstood his lieutenant's directions and swallowed all six pills. Davis returned

England. A 321st glider en route to the landing zone in Holland. WILLIAMS FAMILY

England. Lead ship 74 of the 434th Troop Carrier Squadron, with the squadron's group commander, Colonel Whitacre, on board, in September 1944. LINZ FAMILY

Left: England. Lt. Everett Creasy. DOUBEK FAMILY

Holland. An unidentified soldier wearing the M42 jacket alongside a knocked-out German armored vehicle.

and asked for the box back because he too wanted to take a pill before they went up. Crim said he didn't have any; he swallowed them all like he was told. Davis admonished Crim, saying he told him to "take one *pill*, not one *box*!"

In the air, Crim could see the Germans firing up at the gliders and their tugs. It was time to fight fair, and an idea came to his drug-induced mind. He had already yanked the doors off the glider and discarded them into the English Channel. A trailer was lashed down, and somewhere under the tarp were a bazooka and rockets. He grabbed the bazooka and loaded it by himself, aiming out the door and down into the fields below. Davis yelled at him just in time and said not to fire: the flames from the rocket blast would catch the glider on fire. Davis was bewildered why nobody else in the glider tried to stop Crim. Everybody on board would have been killed.

Once on the ground in Holland, Crim was unable to function for several days due to the overdose. He

England. Sgt. William Plummer with a B Battery glider, *Miss Babe Peters*, named after his girlfriend.

Holland. A destroyed German 88.
WILLIAMS FAMILY

would say of those first few days on the pills, "I could jump over the moon."

Sgt. Gerald Braden (B Battery) of Kewanee, Illinois, received a ten-minute copilot lesson from his glider pilot. (These unenviable copilots believed the training was given for a "just-in-case scenario," but getting them in the copilot seat also made for a much simpler weight balance.) Then it was time to head down the runway, pulled by the carefully laid-out white nylon rope. The sergeant was in charge of the 1st Gun Section of Battery B and his men: PFC B. L. Witcher of Saint Vrain, New Mexico; PFC William "Moon" Mullins (nicknamed after the comic strip) of Blakeley, West Virginia; PFC Frank Kanspik of Chicago, Illinois; Pvt. Robert Palm of Milltown, New Jersey; and Pvt. Gilbert Quinn of Watertown, South Dakota.

The loading manifest listed twenty-four rounds of 75mm ammunition, but the true number was thirty-three. More importantly, the 75mm pack howitzer was also lashed to the plywood floor of the glider, along with essential gear such as radios, aiming stake lights, and a tool chest.

Takeoff was uneventful, but trouble was soon to follow for these Normandy veterans. The fog that plagued many other 321st gliders that day also struck theirs over the English Channel.

Chalk 56-B's tug disappeared into the fog bank along with its towrope. The glider pilot needed to have visual contact with that line to make corrections if necessary. He was now flying blind, and the longer it continued, the more dangerous it became. The towrope gathered slack until a movement from the C-47 snapped it taut again, jerking the troopers and their flimsy craft forward.

A few seconds of visibility now and then showed the flight officer and his 321st copilot that the rope had gathered slack, wrapping itself around the wheels of the glider. It would then loop off and catch around the wing or the nose of the cockpit. Each time this happened, the fog would appear again, masking the problem and causing great concern for the glider riders. If that rope was pulled taut when wrapped around the wing, it would snap it in one quick action. All of them would tumble to their deaths.

It was time to make a choice between what seemed like certain death or cutting loose not knowing their location. No intercom was available for this gun section. The towline was released. The glider, free of its tug, glided gently down through the fog while the glidermen hoped they would not strike another glider in their path. What they observed, as the fog cleared, was both frightening and soothing at the same time. They were over the English Channel with land in sight. But could the seven men get to it before losing altitude?

It was up to the glider pilot to use all his skill to coax every second of flight time in the quest for needed range. The Waco CG-4A was approaching a landmass. The men were told to expect a water landing while the pilot prepared for the worst. The motorless aircraft touched down on the beach, just edging into a pasture near Ramsgate in Kent, England. It had been said many times before that any glider landing that could be walked away from was a good landing. This was better than that.

The 321st troopers put a guard on the glider and its essential load until the air corps relieved them. Trucks were summoned, and the equipment was reloaded into a C-47 and flown back to their starting point at Greenham Common Airbase. Five days later, it was attempted again.

The same tug pilot hooked onto the fresh glider with its familiar glider riders, the only 321st crew to fly twice. This time, the formation of gliders was from the 907th sister battalion of the 321st, and the ride began anew. Landing Zone W and the flak guns of the Germans were by now set for the altitude of the approaching gliders. Their glider was peppered, but luck was with them again as all made it in without injury. However, in less than two months, PFC Frank Kanspik would be dead, killed by German artillery fire.

Word spread throughout the Boston Hospital wards in England: paratroopers were needed for an upcoming mission. PFC Wendell Byrnes was recovering from his wounds suffered during the Normandy invasion. In the back of his mind, he knew he would make it back to his division somehow, and this was his chance.

Byrnes, still heavily bandaged, volunteered to go back, but his doctors needed convincing that he was ready. An obstacle course would be the determining factor for Byrnes and others who fell into his

England. Two members of the B Battery Detail Section: Sgt. Harry Stearns (left) and an unidentified soldier with their "Berlin-bound" glider, *Miss Marty Burkhart*, named for Stearns's girlfriend back home. STEARNS FAMILY

category. After one look at that course, Byrnes understood it wasn't possible for him to complete it. Sergeant Flannigan, a paratrooper cadre, was running the course, and Byrnes begged the sergeant to pass him.

Flannigan said he couldn't do that outright, but told him how to pass the obstacle course. Flannigan said that when Byrnes ran up to the fence, he should get someone to push him over. Doctors and officers were present but would not be at that point in the obstacle course. Once on the other side, he was to wait until all the others came back to that initial obstacle. He would get a signal that the group was coming back and should prepare himself for a push back to the other side of the high fence.

The sergeant gave the signal to Byrnes that the group was running back to the fence. This time it took two soldiers to push him over the fence, and he then ran to the starting point. Flannigan said to Byrnes in a loud voice, "I see that you made it."

The battalion was still at Whatcombe Farm, preparing to leave for the mission. First Sgt. Timothy Shea (B Battery) was surprised to see Byrnes, and so was B Battery commander Captain Skinner. Both made sure Byrnes was given light duties until he fully recovered.

The glider loading manifests had already been typed up before Byrnes was back on duty. His name was penciled in at the bottom. Going into Holland with him was the battery's set of twins, Privates Lynne and Lyle Strouse. As he was loading, preparing for a combat glide into Holland, another thought occurred: "I must be nuts."

During the glide, the enemy ground fire was so intense Byrnes didn't know if he should sit on his helmet or wear it. Their glider landed in a field with haystacks, but no other gliders were to be seen. Byrnes *did* see German uniforms, and everybody in the glider took off in different directions. "I'm not going to give these guys another opportunity to pop me—it might be the final pop," Byrnes recalled thinking. He burrowed deep into a haystack and waited. After a while, he peered out to see two Dutchmen walking around. They spotted him and in fluent English said to stay put until dark; someone would take him where he was supposed to be. That evening they returned and guided him back to the 101st lines.

There was another last-minute change to B Battery's glider load as two men switched places: PFC J. T. George from Charleston, Texas, and Pvt. John Nasea of Detroit, Michigan. It was a lucky switch for George, but not for Nasea.

Nasea wanted to be the first one out the door of his glider when it landed. The initial glider ride was

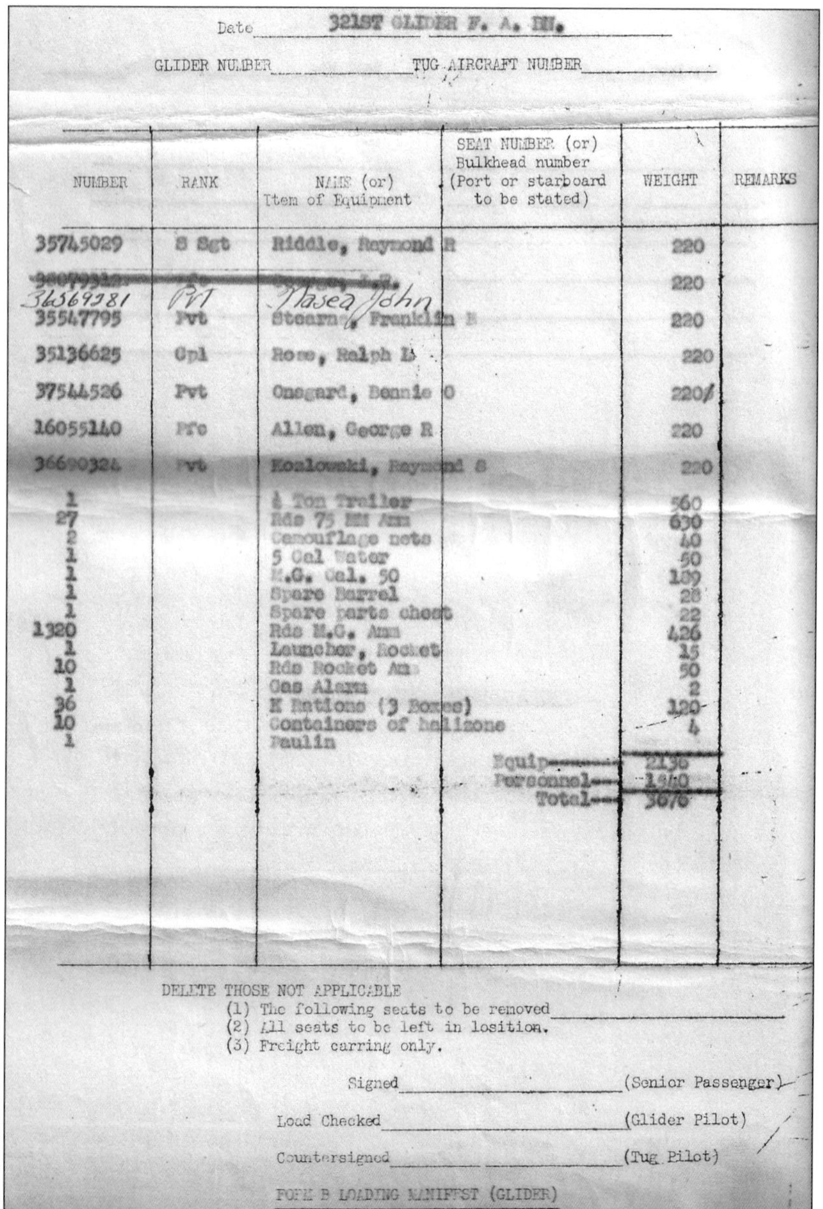

Date 321ST GLIDER F. A. BN.

GLIDER NUMBER ______ TUG AIRCRAFT NUMBER ______

NUMBER	RANK	NAME (or) Item of Equipment	SEAT NUMBER (or) Bulkhead number (Port or starboard to be stated)	WEIGHT	REMARKS
35745029	S Sgt	Riddle, Raymond R		220	
~~[illegible]~~	~~[illegible]~~	~~[illegible]~~		220	
36569381	Pvt	Nasea John			
35547795	Pvt	Stearns, Franklin B		220	
35136625	Cpl	Rose, Ralph L		220	
37544526	Pvt	Onsgard, Bennie O		220/	
16055140	Pfc	Allen, George R		220	
36690324	Pvt	Kozlowski, Raymond S		220	
1		¼ Ton Trailer		560	
27		Rds 75 MM Amm		630	
2		Camouflage nets		40	
1		5 Gal Water		50	
1		M.G. Cal. 50		139	
1		Spare Barrel		28	
1		Spare parts chest		22	
1320		Rds M.G. Amm		426	
1		Launcher, Rocket		15	
10		Rds Rocket Amm		50	
1		Gas Alarm		2	
36		K Rations (3 Boxes)		120	
10		Containers of halizone		4	
1		Paulin			
			Equip———	2136	
			Personnel———	1540	
			Total———	3676	

DELETE THOSE NOT APPLICABLE
(1) The following seats to be removed ______
(2) All seats to be left in losition.
(3) Freight carring only.

Signed ______ (Senior Passenger)

Load Checked ______ (Glider Pilot)

Countersigned ______ (Tug Pilot)

FORM B LOADING MANIFEST (GLIDER)

The 321st GFA loading manifest for Holland, showing Nasea's name penciled in. G.J. DETTORE COLLECTION

Holland. Gliders on the ground at Landing Zone W, September 19.
LINZ FAMILY

Holland. 321st gliders coming into Landing Zone W. SULLIVAN FAMILY

nothing special until they came under fire while over the continent. Nasea was reading a pocket Bible given to him at the Detroit train station when he left home. He heard the glider pilot say they were getting close to the landing zone and was reaching for the towrope release button when somebody yelled, "Is anybody hurt?" Someone on the opposite side of the glider nodded his head toward him. Nasea put both hands under his pants and felt a warm liquid: blood. A bullet fired from someone on the ground had pierced the floor of the glider as the craft came in for a landing. It ricocheted off one of the steel frame tubes and fragmented into two pieces. Traveling sideways, the pieces caused two puncture wounds under Nasea's right thigh that proved nearly fatal. S/Sgt. Raymond Riddle from Hollidays Cove, West Virginia, stuck him with a syrette of morphine.

The glider was now on the ground. Nasea looked out the window and saw 321st troopers with their carbines at a position ready to fire. He was placed on a stretcher made from a GI blanket and 2x4 boards that had been used to prop up the nose of the glider. He was placed on top of the loaded trailer and sped across a plowed field. Nasea told the jeep driver "to take it easy," but his words seemed to go unnoticed.

He was taken to a farmhouse, where he saw a hospital-style gurney and someone holding up a bottle of plasma. Women there were wearing big floppy hats. Later, he realized he was taken to the Helena Hova farm, designated as an aid station by the 326th Medical Battalion. The women with the big floppy hats were nurses.

Nasea was put in a cast from his waist down. He was paralyzed and his femur was broken. He was transferred from hospital to hospital and given varying treatments until he was finally put on a C-47 bound for England. The orderly on the plane asked him for his jump boots. Upon hearing that request, he thought to himself that if he did have them (he didn't), they would probably be taken to London and sold to the highest bidder.

He was eventually transported to Staten Island on a hospital ship. He was placed on a stretcher and put into an ambulance, still immobilized by a body cast. Here, Nasea got the news that the 101st was surrounded and felt he should be back with them. After a short trip in the ambulance, it stopped to unload. He heard German voices. The back doors opened, and he was startled to see Germans wearing enemy uniforms. He feared the worst for a split second, and was relieved to discover it was German POWs.

Cpl. Vernon Raker flew into Holland as the copilot of a glider carrying a jeep. With him were fellow A Battery glidermen PFC Lloyd "Pinky" Tomblin from Verdunville, West Virginia, the jeep driver; and Pvt. Junior Kuhl of Copen, West Virginia, who was sitting in the driver's seat of the jeep.

The C-47 that pulled their glider opted to fly just above the water. Occasionally a face would appear in a plexiglass bubble on top of the tug ship. A gliderman would give hand signals to the face in the bubble to pull up for more altitude, but all he would receive was a hand wave back.

The glider pilot pulled back on the controls to rise above a church spire and tall trees. Farmers in the fields waved at them, and instinctively the men waved back. Raker looked through the windscreen of the Waco CG-4A and watched as a German with a machine pistol seemed to fire directly at him. Smoke could be seen coming from the gun. He thought he was a dead man, but no one was hit.

At the landing zone, the fields were littered with gliders pointing in all directions. This made it difficult to find an open area. The pilot released the towrope and began turning right, then left, looking for a spot. Raker saw a stone barn straight ahead, and the pilot hollered, "Flaps!" Both of them pulled back levers and the glider dropped like a rock. Both wheels came off as they hit the ground hard, crisscrossing and spinning ahead of them off into the fields. The glider's floor broke apart; chunks of plywood and dust filled the cockpit and nearly blinded them. Raker punched a hole in the glider fabric and jumped out while the others exited the normal way.

Tomblin reentered the glider, jumped in the jeep, and started it. He revved the engine and roared forward. The steel cable attached to the rear of the jeep did its job by raising the nose of the glider. Driving out into the Dutch countryside, Tomblin received a bushel of dirt over his head as the glider's nose released the soil embedded in it.

Holland. A burned-up glider with a medic standing by. TURKAL FAMILY

Holland. A glider crash at Landing Zone W. WILLIAMS FAMILY

Holland, Landing Zone W. A trooper from 2nd Battalion, 506th, stands in the foreground. WILLIAMS FAMILY

The pilot of the glider jumped into the jeep. As they were about to leave, he yelled, "Wait, I forgot something." He carried an incendiary grenade in his pocket. He pulled it out and removed the pin. The grenade was tossed into the glider and ignited. He said, "Well there's one of those son-a-bitches I won't have to fly again."

This was Alfred Stumpo's first combat mission. Stumpo was from West Manayunk, Pennsylvania, and had learned his artillery skills at Fort Sill. He was assigned to A Battery, 321st Battalion, from the replacement depot. Coming into Holland, his glider was hit by enemy fire, perforating its thin skin.

It was a short landing, causing the tie-down ropes to snap. The glider's load of ninety-six rounds of 75mm ammunition shifted and pinned the legs of Stumpo and another glider rider next to him. They couldn't free themselves. The Germans were lobbing in mortar fire, and it seemed small-arms fire was coming from every direction. Two other men grabbed axes and chopped the plywood floor away to free the glidermen. All of them took off running for the woods, where they joined up with the rest of the gun section. The ammunition was retrieved later in the day.

S/Sgt. Thomas Roberson of Blackshear, Georgia; Capt. Frank J. Barys of Chicago, Illinois; PFC Leonard DeChant; Pvt. Woodrow Bowser; and B Battery members PFC Orville Goins from Hamilton, Ohio; Pvt. Alden Stacey from Columbia, Tennessee; Pvt. Rosario DeSantis from Port Reading, New Jersey; Pvt. Howard Killibrew (medic) from Winchester, Illinois; and Pvt. Earl Mishler from Goshen, Indiana, ran into some trouble coming into Holland.

First Lt. John Jordan (HQ), the assistant S-2 from Portsmouth, Virginia, filled out a brief report on their exploits. "The glider was hit several times by flack and the controls stuck about 10 or 15 minutes before landing, which was made under small arms fire," he recorded. "I personally think the glider pilot did a wonderful job of landing. We had to crawl back to our infantry front line in a ditch—lost [the] complete glider load. We landed at the extreme Northwest edge of the LZW under enemy fire."

Another report states they "landed in [a] pasture in Gent, Belgium, about 1515 hours, 80 air miles from designated landing zone. Had to release glider on account of tow rope ripping strip holding glass [plastic] in nose of glider and tow plane taking evasive action. Could only see 10 feet of tow rope in fog at time of release. At time of release speed was about 170. I guess pilot did a very good job all the way through. Was very glad we had a good [glider] pilot and want to say thanks to him again." Reading between the lines, it's apparent the tug pilot was less than adequate for pulling a glider into combat. The redline of a glider was 150 mph; speeds above that could cause the craft to vibrate apart.

F/O George Buckley from Milford, Connecticut, picked up a piece of chalk. For this invasion, his second, he would name his Waco glider. He christened her *Jeanne Belle 2*, after his girlfriend. If things went well and he survived this war, Jeanne would become his wife. It was a lucky name for his glider. Buckley was the youngest American glider pilot known to have served in World War II. He lied about his age by changing the date on his birth certificate. Although it was obvious to the recruiter, he chose not to say anything to the sixteen-year-old and passed him.

In the vanguard of the Normandy invasion, Buckley had brought in troopers of the 82nd Airborne Division. The sights that greeted him as he entered Normandy were a connection to back home and safer times when a sky filled with reds, blues, and yellow meant a 4th of July celebration, not an invasion.

Before the glider departed, the flight mechanics had checked the 350 feet of nylon towrope to make sure it still had some elasticity. The rope was designed to stretch 10 feet for every 100 and had a limited lifespan. A new rope would give a little, but an old one would snap when stressed, causing an unscheduled release. If this happened at takeoff, it could result in a serious crash. Finding themselves without a tug over enemy territory or water was equally unappealing.

Holland. Unidentified 321st soldiers with Dutch civilians.

Buckley decided to repeat another Normandy tradition. While in England, he came across a paratrooper who admired his brown leather A-2 jacket. He stated that he would like to get one for himself. It just so happened Buckley had an extra A-2 and was willing to trade it—for a canvas-reinforced M42 jumpsuit. He was the only glider pilot ever known to wear one into combat while flying gliders. He would wear it one more time while flying his later glider, *Jeanne Belle 3*.

The loading manifest for F/O Buckley's glider shows that his glider number was 20B. Along with the troopers of the 321st, it carried the following:

.30-caliber machine gun and ammo	150 pounds
1/4-ton truck (jeep)	2,550 pounds
3 rounds of 75mm ammo	75 pounds
Launcher rocket	15 pounds
10 rounds of rocket ammo	50 pounds
5 gallons of water	50 pounds
Camouflage net	25 pounds
Panel set AP50	9 pounds
4 rounds rocket ammo	20 pounds
SCR-610 radio	115 pounds
Pick	7 pounds
Shovel	5 pounds
Cooking outfit	5 pounds
5 quarts of oil	20 pounds
16 sandbags	5 pounds
Equipment	3,101 pounds
Personnel	600 pounds
Total	3,701 pounds

Second Lt. Anthony Linz was appointed executive officer of A Battery and was notified on September 15 that a move was going to be made the next day. The enlisted men of the 321st were alerted and left Whatcombe Farm on the sixteenth. They headed for their airfields.

Linz recalled that upon arriving at the airfield, it "was very evident right from there that this was going to happen, no dry run." Money was changed, men adjusted grenades and sharpened knives, and double guards were put on. "General Eisenhower and General Taylor visited us telling us what to expect and what we were expected to do."

Linz was to leave Aldermaston as a copilot of a CG-4A along with two A Battery glider riders: PFC Hubert "H. C." Warren and Pvt. Fred Miller. F/O George Buckley piloted their glider.

F/O Buckley wrote the following letter concerning his flight into Holland with the 321st:

> Early on the morning of the 19th, I reported to the flight line to check over my CG-4A, which was loaded and ready to go. Our objective was Landing Zone W between Zon and St. Oedenrode, on the main road of this airborne corridor leading to the Rhine. Due to the shortage of Glider Pilots, one of the three 101st Glider men in my glider was to sit in the right seat as my co-pilot. Lt. Tony Linz of the 321st Glider Field Artillery Battalion, being the ranking member on board, was chosen. He did not show too much enthusiasm, possibly because he had no flying experience.
>
> I was able to give him about ten minutes instruction on the basics of flying, and I'm certain that his main concern was the possibility that I would get hit and he would have to take over and get us down in one piece. I must admit, I gave this a great deal of thought throughout the flight.
>
> Take off was uneventful and the whole group formation took off for the continent. Shortly after crossing the English Coast and a quarter of the way across the channel, the entire Group of four squadrons (39 gliders and tugs) flew straight into a heavy fog bank. If there's one thing in this world that really upsets a Glider Pilot, it's flying into a fog bank in tight formation, with eighty or ninety other tow planes and gliders. You have no way of knowing who's going to go where, when or how, and the possibility of a mid-air collision or accidental release is enough to make your hair stand on end. We flew blind for what seemed like an eternity and when we emerged on the other side there was not another plane or glider in sight in any direction; it was the damnedest vanishing act I have ever seen. We had been briefed before takeoff that things were not going too well in the landing areas, and the men and supplies we carried must get through. My tow pilot, Capt. Bill Miller, being aware of

this, continued on towards the continent as if nothing had gone wrong. I had no intercom on this trip, so I didn't know what his intentions were. What most Glider Pilots usually say in a case like this is, "Where he goes, I go," as long as the rope stays hooked.

After crossing the coast we took a heading into Belgium which would take us to the Holland border, and into enemy territory beyond. Captain Miller started to circle at this time, waiting to see if any other 434th planes would show up so we could go together. He did not realize it, but his 360-degree turn to the left kept getting tighter and tighter and it was all I could do to stay on tow behind him. By then we had been on tow almost three hours and with no co-pilot to spell me, my hands and arms were tightening up and beginning to cramp and fall asleep. I shouted over to Lt. Linz that I thought the tow ship was lost and did he want to cut loose here and make our way to the landing zone by land. He shook his head in the negative, so we hung on. I don't think he knew how tired I was.

The tow ship at this moment took off on a beeline for the Holland border. Captain Miller had gotten the word by radio to go in. As soon as I realized that this was the last leg of our flight, I began to wonder what kind of reception the Germans would have for one lone C-47 with glider in tow. In about fifteen minutes we received the answer. Our course brought us into the landing zone between the town of Best and Eindhoven, which was less than one minute away from our objective on the outskirts of Zon. At Best, a battle was raging between the Germans and our paratroopers for control of a key railroad bridge, and as we flew past Best, at roughly 600 ft, a mobile flak wagon which I could see on my left out of the corner of my eye opened up on our tow plane. We watched, fascinated, as shells went up on through the left wing and into the left side of the fuselage and exited out the top right side where the radio compartment is located. Small bits of aluminum from the plane and spent pieces of flak flew back and peppered the front of the glider. Just when I thought the enemy fire would move back along the rope and knock the hell out of us, it stopped. Throughout the whole time we were under fire, our tow ship never wavered or took evasive action. I found out later from Captain Miller that on the way back out (minus the glider) their plane was hit quite badly again in the tail section, but managed to get back to England safely.

In a matter of seconds the landing zone appeared directly in front of us, strewn with hundreds of parachutes and gliders and the burning wreckage of two C-47s that had been shot down earlier. I cut loose and made a straight-in approach well into the center of the area, just in case the Germans were around the edges waiting for us. After we touched down, we came to an abrupt stop in the soft dirt of a potato field, which partially buried the nose of the glider. After about fifteen minutes of digging, we managed to get the front of section of the glider opened and the jeep and equipment unloaded. Not knowing exactly where we were located, Lt. Linz and the other two men in our glider, Pfc. Miller and Pfc. Warren, took off in the direction of Best where the firing seemed to be the heaviest. I took off alone on foot to find the road to Eindhoven.

"We hit the English Channel and [in] tremendous fog got to the other side, and not another plane in sight," Lieutenant Linz recalled. "I was made co-pilot of the glider because I had eight hours in on a Piper Cub. I had never landed one, but the only thing I could be sure of is that we would come down if I were the one trying to bring that thing down if the pilot were hit. We finally got up to around about Brussels and couldn't tell if the pilot of the plane [tug] was lost 'cause we circled there twice [and] finally saw a plane coming back pretty well shot up. He headed back in that direction."

They cut loose from the tug. During practice runs, the gliders wound up at airfields and came down in nice landings, Linz said, but "This was no airport. This was a field." They went through two barbed-wire fences and wound up with the glider's nose dug into a pile of potatoes.

Holland. From left to right: Capt. James Wicker, Lt. Tony Linz, and Lt. Richard Smith. Note the incorrect 321st stenciled tic applied to Smith's helmet. LINZ FAMILY

Holland. A 321st glider about to land on Landing Zone W in Holland. Due to air superiority, only invasion stripes that would be observed from the ground were necessary. The glider pilots were responsible for painting them on their gliders. TRUE FAMILY

The first thing Lieutenant Linz tried to do was start the jeep. The front section of the cockpit could not swing up because the nose was buried deep in the Dutch potatoes.

Enemy fire was coming in, and since the jeep couldn't be retrieved at that moment, it was time to get out quickly. Linz reached for his M3 trench knife, which was strapped to his right leg paratrooper-style, and cut the thin, canvaslike material. He squeezed out the side of the bogged-down glider and got all his men out.

Every motor vehicle was needed, and an airborne division carried few as it was, always coming in light. The rear echelon would follow with the remainder of the division's allotted transportation, but they would arrive much later. Linz knew this. Not only did the battalion need all its thirty-six jeeps, but this one carried a much-needed SCR-610 radio. He had to get it out.

Another jeep was located with a chain, and a plan was devised. The chain was wrapped around the flimsy plexiglass nose of the glider and back to the operational jeep's bumper. The driver accelerated, pulled the slack out of the chain, and not letting up on the gas pedal, tugged the glider nose out of the farmer's potato patch. The force of the chain's snap yanked the nose completely off the glider. The jeep pulled the front section of the glider through the field.

As they retrieved the jeep, the crew of the noseless glider looked up to see two gliders collide in midair; they had turned into each other and plummeted to the ground. Off to the right, paratroopers jumped clear of their C-47 as one of its engines was hit by ground fire and burst into flames. The flames trailed back from the engine to the jumpers. Their parachutes caught on fire, causing them to freefall to their deaths. The 321st glidermen felt helpless; all they could do was watch.

The jeep was finally driven out of *Jeanne Bell 2*, and glider pilot Buckley tossed his Thompson submachine gun to Linz, saying, "Well, I got you in. Now you get me out." That was the last time those two saw each other.

Lone glider 69B of the 321st crashed in Belgium, killing all onboard. It was the only glider crash that killed its entire crew. The glider and tug left Greenham Common and were near the end of the glider lift. Killed were glider pilot Capt. Robert Brown and his 321st passengers from B Battery: Cpl. James Szur from Lockport, New York; Cpl. Carroll Simmons from Columbus, Ohio; PFC Jon Vetter from Freeport, New York; Pvt. William Sowell from Carters Creek, Tennessee; Pvt. Earnest "Howard" Smith from Jackson, Tennessee; and Pvt. Arthur Hutchins from Clearwater, Florida. Their glider load consisted of ninety-three rounds of 75mm ammunition, a .30-caliber machine gun, and a 5-gallon can of water.

The circumstances of the crash were recorded by the C-47 tug pilot, Capt. Robert Prisou.

> On 19th September 1944, I was pilot of C-47A aircraft number 42-100756, and towing a CG-4A glider number 42-79442. I was leading an element of four ships and gliders to our drop zone. We all had instrument conditions over the Channel. This caused one of my ships to leave the formation. I continued on course with my three ships at 100 feet. At this altitude we began to break through the overcast; as we broke through we were about two miles in from the coast, in the vicinity of Blankeberghe [*sic*, Blankenberge], Belgium. As soon as we broke through the overcast I felt the glider cut. I told my Radio Operator to look out the dome so he could follow the glider. He said he pulled off to the right and struck the tow rope of the number two ship in the formation; in doing this he lost part of his wing tip and spun in. I notified my other ships that my glider had cut, and that they could continue on course. I circled down, released my rope and spotted the glider. It was a complete wreck. There was no sign of life at the scene of the wreckage. We were able to identify the glider by [the] number on the rudder.

An unknown witness on the ground remembered "how the wing of one glider was hit by the tow rope of another. The one hit got out of control and crashed. The glider crashed in a field between Scharebrug and the Blauwe Duivenkeet farm.

England. From left to right: Cpl. John Jordan, F/O Everett Banto, Pvt. Vernise Hilst, Capt. Samuel Williams, and PFC Frederic Sheppard. WILLIAMS FAMILY

Holland. A C-47 belonging to 436th Troop Carrier Group, 82nd Squadron, crashed alongside a glider in Holland. WILLIAMS FAMILY

Remnants of a C-47 in Holland. NICHOLS FAMILY

Canadian soldiers arrived at the scene and the local fire-fighters helped to recover the bodies. Through a small trail the bodies were taken to the road. Six were recovered. A seventh victim was found later underneath the wrecked glider."[6]

Following notification of her son William Sowell's death in the crash, Edna Sowell requested his body be disinterred from the American cemetery at Neuville-en-Condroz, Belgium. She received a response dated August 22, 1946, signed Major Prenn for the Quartermaster General. In part, it informed her, "As you probably know, the supply of steel for the manufacture of caskets is at present uncertain. Without this essential item, the movement of remains cannot properly be initiated."

Holland. PFC Anthony Stempien (left) and an unidentified soldier with a bazooka. LELONEK/DETTORE

Pvt. Arthur Hutchins was nineteen years old and married to Marion Lucile Hutchins. In October 1944, she was notified of her husband's death in combat. Hutchins is buried at the Ardennes American Cemetery in Neupré, Belgium, Plot B, Row 35, Grave 38.

Pvt. Earnest "Howard" Smith was twenty years old. He stood 5-feet-7$^1/_2$-inches tall and weighed 150 pounds. Everybody liked him; he was shy and displayed boyish mannerisms that endeared him to his comrades. He wrote home to his mother often and she to him. His father was deceased.

The last letter he ever wrote was to his mother on September 14, 1944. "I know God has answered my prayers for you," he wrote. "You never fear about me mother because he has well look[ed] over me and taken good care of me."

Mrs. Johnnie Smith penned a letter to her son on September 19, the day he was killed. She told him, "I'm glad you are getting my letters. I think of you last thing at night, and first thing when I awake." The letter wound its way through the postal system and onto the desk of WO (JG) Samuel Meyers of the 321st. He wrote "Deceased" on the envelope and sent it back stamped "Return to Sender." It would take quite some time for Smith's mother to receive it.

On September 21, two days after her son was killed, Earnest's mother wrote again to him: "My dear dear Son—I wonder where my darling man is this morning. Airborne gliders are landing in Germany. . . . But of course, I don't know that you are over there anyway. I just pray for the Lord to be with you, and guide and guard you all the way. . . . Hope to get a letter from you soon. Lots of love. Mother."

On October 13, 1944, Western Union sent a telegram to Mrs. Johnnie May Smith of 218 Belmont Avenue. It stated: "The Secretary of War desires me to express his deep regret that your son Private Earnest H. Smith was killed in action on nineteen September in Belgium." Private Smith's body was sent home for final burial on June 5, 1949.

Pvt. James Murphy—along with fellow B Battery troopers Pvt. Michael Kelley of Queens, New York; Cpl. Anthony Ludwig of Cleveland, Ohio; T/5 Lucian Clark of Vesuvius, Virginia; Pvt. Billy Wilkins of Van Buren, Arkansas; and Pvt. Dale Colley of McDermott, Ohio—had a true baptism for their first combat glider ride. They were part of a gun firing section and left from the airbase at Greenham Common, one of the last B Battery glider loads to depart England. The glider had its human cargo and, more importantly, its payload: ninety-three rounds of 75mm ammunition that weighed over 2,000 pounds, plus a 5-gallon can of water.

An hour or so into the flight, the glider hit the wall of fog that foiled many other 321st aircraft.

United States. Civilian Earnest "Howard" Smith just prior to entering the army. RICKY LONG FAMILY

With no intercom, the tug pilot and the glider pilot were flying by "the angle of the dangle," a glider pilot term used when he couldn't see the tug due to decreased visibility and when only a foot or so of the towrope could be observed. If the rope was angled up, the glider pilot knew that was where the tug was flying, and that wasn't good. The glider pilot needed to be above the C-47 for proper flying. Nor did he want to see the rope angled right or left.

The fog caused major uncertainty as to the whereabouts of the other flights of tugs and gliders. The danger was too great, and the decision was made to cut loose, only to find out that beneath the fog was something worse: open water.

The landing was about to take place in the middle of the English Channel with no land in sight. As soon as the glider hit the choppy seas, it bounced off the waves, slowly coming to a dead stop. Some of the glidermen inflated their life vests prior to stopping. When it was time to kick out the exit door and jump into the water, it was an awkward and difficult job to abandon their craft. With its heavy payload, the glider quickly filled with water. Waves hit the craft, producing sounds more likely to be heard coming from a boat than a glider. The men climbed out of the channel and onto the 83-foot wingspan. At least this would get them out of the cold English Channel, and perhaps they could see if help was near. One of the 321st artillerymen discovered that his cherished gloves, sent to him from back home, were still inside the nearly submerged glider. He started to slide off the wing, but Private Murphy stopped him.

It was a three-and-a-half-hour wait until an English watercraft was spotted. The watercraft, patrolling in case of an event such as this, came by and rendered assistance. Only the top of the wing and the tip of the tail marked their location. Prior to leaving the wreck, the English sailors told the crew that they had orders to destroy anything that may be a water-lane hazard. They opened up with .50-caliber machine guns, riddling the wings but being careful not to fire into the fuselage with its payload. The American-made CG-4A glider slowly disappeared into the English Channel.

Once inside the patrol boat, the men were told to disrobe and were given blankets, tea, and some rum. The glider riders were taken to Portsmouth, England,

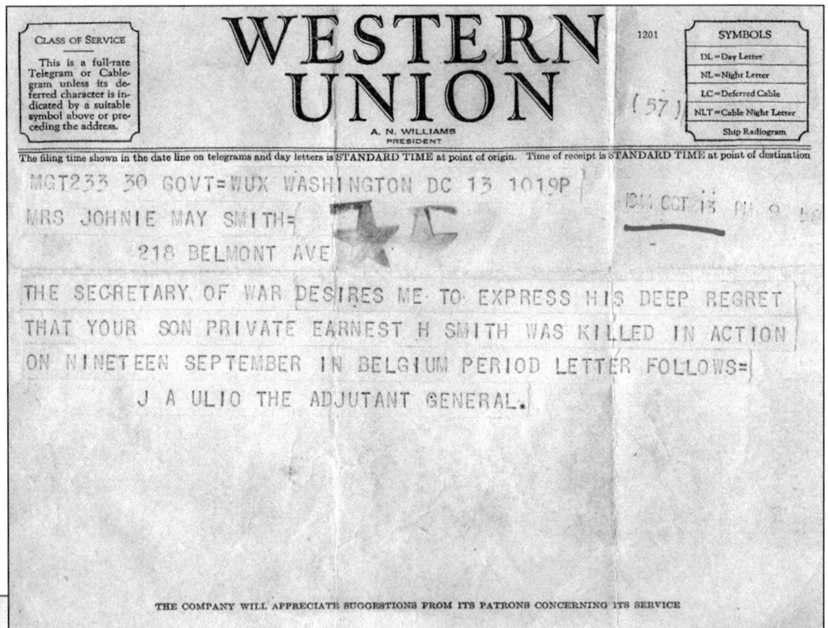

CLASS OF SERVICE

This is a full-rate Telegram or Cablegram unless its deferred character is indicated by a suitable symbol above or preceding the address.

WESTERN UNION

A. N. WILLIAMS PRESIDENT

1201

SYMBOLS
DL=Day Letter
NL=Night Letter
LC=Deferred Cable
NLT=Cable Night Letter
Ship Radiogram

(57)

The filing time shown in the date line on telegrams and day letters is STANDARD TIME at point of origin. Time of receipt is STANDARD TIME at point of destination

MGT233 30 GOVT=WUX WASHINGTON DC 13 1019P

MRS JOHNIE MAY SMITH=

218 BELMONT AVE

THE SECRETARY OF WAR DESIRES ME TO EXPRESS HIS DEEP REGRET THAT YOUR SON PRIVATE EARNEST H SMITH WAS KILLED IN ACTION ON NINETEEN SEPTEMBER IN BELGIUM PERIOD LETTER FOLLOWS=

J A ULIO THE ADJUTANT GENERAL.

THE COMPANY WILL APPRECIATE SUGGESTIONS FROM ITS PATRONS CONCERNING ITS SERVICE

Pvt. Earnest Smith's KIA telegram, dated October 13, 1944.
RICKY LONG FAMILY

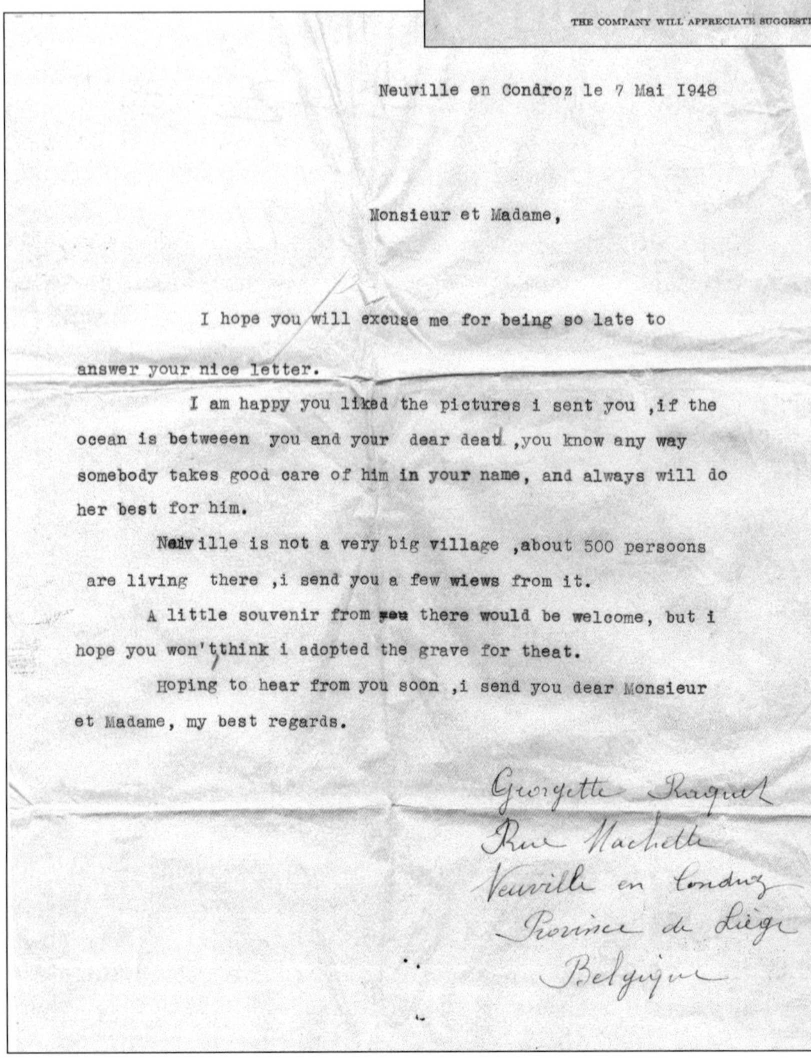

Neuville en Condroz le 7 Mai 1948

Monsieur et Madame,

I hope you will excuse me for being so late to answer your nice letter.

I am happy you liked the pictures i sent you ,if the ocean is betweeen you and your dear deat ,you know any way somebody takes good care of him in your name, and always will do her best for him.

Neuville is not a very big village ,about 500 persoons are living there ,i send you a few wiews from it.

A little souvenir from you there would be welcome, but i hope you won't think i adopted the grave for theat.

Hoping to hear from you soon ,i send you dear Monsieur et Madame, my best regards.

Georgette Ruquet
Rue Nachelle
Neuville en Condroz
Province de Liège
Belgique

Letters to Smith's mother, dated May 1948, regarding his grave.
RICKY LONG FAMILY

and debarked the rescue ship with dry, freshly pressed American uniforms courtesy of the English navy. It was several days until they would be back with their beloved battalion.

One year and three months after graduating from flight school, F/O Harold Axelson, from Dixon, California, was promoted to second lieutenant. His designation as flight officer had been a wartime rank, between an enlisted man and an officer. However, his promotion brought no increase in pay.

Axelson had flown an English Horsa glider—which he considered a "miserable beast to fly"—into Normandy with 101st troopers and his pal F/O John Devlin as his copilot. Both men were now assigned to the 434th Carrier Group, 74th Squadron, flying out of Aldermaston. It was two weeks prior to Operation Market Garden and something was in the air.

The 101st troopers were stationed in tents along the flight line. The flight crews were sealed off in their barracks area. The men marched in formation to and from the mess hall. Antiaircraft guns were set up along the airfield. Briefings were numerous, and at one point an Air Corps major from Intelligence stood up and gave a speech to the pilots. He reminded the air crews that this was a daytime operation and the greatest invasion by gliders in history. He envied the pilots who had the *opportunity* to participate in such an event. It was a pep talk that fell on deaf ears, for these pilots had been to Normandy and back. They snickered between themselves, "So, that's Intelligence?"

As in most cases, the senior-ranking 321st artilleryman in each glider became the copilot for the Holland invasion. Sgt. Charles "Alvin" Simmons of Evans, Louisiana, in charge of his A Battery gun section, got the job. What he needed now were flying lessons. The approximately forty-minute lesson was given just prior to departure while he waited on the runway. It was kept simple. The spoiler lever, attached to the floor, was positioned at the right of the copilot's seat. The pilot also had one on his left, the fuselage side. Flaps would rise from the wing if either of these levers was pulled. This destroyed the lift of airflow over the wings and resulted in a dramatic drop in speed. When the time came and landing the CG-4A was imminent, the order would be "Spoilers!" It would be Simmons's job to pull the lever—hard—while calling out the airspeed.

It was time to strap themselves in and take a quick glance back at the 75mm pack howitzer lashed to the floor and the 321st troopers aboard. Their chalk number was 56, meaning their glider would be the fifty-sixth to leave the airfield. Axelson's good friend, Devlin, would be chalk number 57, flying to his immediate right. Devlin's glider held the remainder of Sgt. Simmons's gun section and the jeep to tow the howitzer. In theory, the gliders were lined up this way so that upon landing they would come down in the same order they took off, reuniting the gun sections quickly and bringing artillery to bear down on the enemy. The 321st trained hard and long on this.

Not long after takeoff, the unnamed glider of newly promoted 2nd Lieutenant Axelson and Sergeant Simmons ran into dense clouds. Moments earlier, the entire formation, approximately 150 aircraft, was in plain sight. Now, the only visible proof of flight was a few feet of towrope. Axelson guessed the power pilot would attempt to get above the clouds, so he eased back on the control column. The glider rose steadily and popped out of the clouds at approximately 3,500 feet. He had guessed right. It was beautifully clear, but absent of any aircraft whatsoever. Suddenly, on his right, chalk number 57 popped out of the clouds along with its tug. These two flights of soldiers, all veterans of Normandy, would go into combat alone.

The clouds thinned and an occasional glimpse of the terrain below was visible. The C-47s were completely lost and continued to circle in an effort to verify a landmark. The only way Axelson could carry on a conversation with his copilot was by hollering; that was always the case in CG-4As. It was now 1500 hours. The tugs decided to drop down. A British convoy was observed on the road below and a canal came into view, the British on its south side. What the glidermen did not know was that the Germans were on the north side. Unwittingly, the glider riders were at the front lines and heading straight into the area of German control as they continued their circling.

It was too late to change course. It was now 1515 hours. The gliders were at 300–400 feet, and the

England. Glidermen of the 321st loading.

Germans let loose with everything they had, both flak and machine-gun fire.

It was obvious these gliders and C-47s were the first flights the Germans had in their gunsights that day. The enemy failed to lead their targets. Instead of firing just ahead of the moving targets, they fired directly into them. The effect was that most of the damage occurred near the tail of the glider, not in its payload area or nose section. Axelson was turning when the rudder cables were shot away almost immediately. The rudder pedal flopped to the floor; the glider could not turn left or right. The towrope was released, as no other option was available. Upon seeing his good friend release, F/O Devlin did the same. They would go in together and hope for the best.

A mere fifteen minutes had passed, and disaster was just seconds away. Unless the Waco could be turned, this part of the gun section was going to fall into enemy territory.

Early in flight training, glider pilots were taught how to do an aileron turn. It was a tricky maneuver that involved gently tilting the glider in the direction in which it was to fly. Banking too sharply would cause a fatal spin. Axelson had to complete this type of turn south toward the British lines without rudder controls. The glider lost altitude quickly and needed a landing zone. A clear field was required, but unfortunately what lay ahead was a stand of trees. The desired landing area was on the other side. He coaxed his glider just barely over the trees, landing in a hayfield and breaking through a fence before settling in another soft field planted with potatoes.

Axelson knew what happened to his close friend, 2nd Lt. Thomas Ahmad, a fellow glider pilot who had been captured. The Germans had executed him along with a number of paratroopers in Normandy near the village of Graignes. The intended landing zone had been Heisville, many miles away from Graignes.

Cpl. Richard W. Moss, the copilot of F/O Devlin's glider, most likely was aware that the other essential members of his gun section (including Sergeant Simmons) were now on the ground. His glider was about to land with a jeep and the rest of the gun crew. It was imperative to link up immediately to make them an effective, destructive artillery unit.

"F/O Devlin did a marvelous job of landing the glider under the circumstances," Moss wrote. "Many fields were trapped and he landed in a very small field, ending up crosswise on a main highway, completely destroying the glider. Unloading was done under mortar fire with [the] help of a Canadian Armored Reconnaissance Patrol."

Devlin's glider came to rest approximately one mile from the other A Battery Waco of Sergeant Simmons, but no one knew it then. The Germans had attempted to slow down the British armor by felling trees across the road. This was dangerous for Corporal Moss and his crew because the jagged stumps were two to three feet from the ground. The glider struck these stumps on the right side of the cargo section, a fact not mentioned in Moss's synopsis of the landing. The destructive force of the impact not only demolished the glider but also injured several glidermen inside. Moss himself suffered a back injury during landing that would plague him the rest of his life. A portion of the Waco was peeled back, exposing its jumbled, precious cargo. The Canadian reconnaissance patrol, which was attached to the British unit, took care of the wounded. No one was killed, and the jeep was still operational. At least the crew had transportation. Corporal Moss's group loaded the jeep and located the other half of their gun section in less than an hour. It was a brief but joyous occasion; all had survived.

Sergeant Simmons's gun section consisted of Cpl. Richard Moss, Pvt. Nicholas Marino of New Orleans, Louisiana; Pvt. J. W. Mathis of Milan, Tennessee; PFC Joseph Baumeister of Jersey City, New Jersey; Pvt. James Foreman from Paulding, Ohio; PFC Furman Kinard of Prosperity, South Carolina; Pvt. James Haliford of Big Spring, Texas; and Pvt. Jess Harmon of Handley, West Virginia. Reunited, they decided to find a place to sleep for the night. A barn was spotted nearby and the soldiers used its floor as their sleeping quarters. The next day, they would try to find out where the 321st Battalion was to join them.

The following day, September 20, Sergeant Simmons headed for the Canadian 4th Division headquarters in Louvain, Belgium. Both glider pilots and a driver went along. Close to the German lines, they had their tommy guns at the ready. Blown bridges met them at several crossings, causing the group to stop several times. They had to back up and seek alternate routes, which created many anxious moments. The howitzer was in tow, as it was too valuable to leave behind. Many scenarios came to mind while making the journey into Louvain, but what happened en route was totally unexpected, though quite common stateside: a flat tire. This flat tire was on the howitzer; no spare or repair kit was available, and they had no other options. The group slowed their jeep to a crawl, hoping to keep the flat tire on its rim. If it slipped off the wheel, the gun couldn't be towed, as it would only slide from one side of the road to the other.

They had to get assistance somewhere, so now the destination was the old city of Ghent. It was a very slow ride, which the children of Ghent approved of. When the group entered town, the youngsters jumped on the moving gun as if it were an amusement ride, laughing, cheering, and dangling from the barrel. The British garrison was located, and they agreed to take care of the gun. Simmons's group moved on toward Louvain.

Upon arriving in Louvain sans howitzer, a British lieutenant was located who could speak fluent French. This officer was close friends with the mayor, who provided quarters for the glider riders that night. While in town, Simmons made arrangements for trucks to pick up the repaired howitzer. These truck drivers were instructed to proceed to where the glider had landed near Maldegem, locate the rest of the 321st gun section, and transport them to their battalion headquarters.

British rations were given out and reluctantly accepted by the 321st troopers. All together again, they proceeded to Bourg-Leopold and contacted the 321st rear echelon (seaborne) unit under the command of Lt. Edward Chaumont. Then it was on to Veghel to catch up with the rest of the 321st Battalion. A mile south of that city, they dug in their 75mm pack howitzer near the other A Battery guns. It was September 21, 1944.

Sergeant Simmons received a Certificate of Merit from Gen. Maxwell Taylor for his work. It read: "During the campaign in Holland he displayed outstanding courage and devotion to duty in leading his men one hundred and fifty miles under adverse

Belgium. A drawing of F/O William Donkin's impaled glider by F/O Harold Axelson.

conditions after the glider in which he was riding was forced down near enemy lines."

The glider pilots Axelson and Devlin had been listed as MIA. They hitched a ride into Brussels and made their way to the airport. A British C-47 was going back to England, so the glider pilots hopped on board for home.

The paratroopers needed their artillerymen. The troopers of the 321st wished to fulfill that need. One of the last gliders in the serial to leave Greenham Common had six B Battery boys in it, plus the standard ninety-three rounds of pack 75mm ammunition. Along with the glider pilot were T/4 Walter Mitchell Jr. from Gallagher, West Virginia; Pvt. Nathaniel Meyers from Decatur, Illinois; Pvt. Stanley Strapakas from Athol, Massachusetts; PFC Raleigh Nealy from Shreveport, Louisiana; PFC Thomas Davis from Cortland, New York; and Pvt. John Patterson from Anderson, South Carolina.

They left their air base on September 19, but didn't arrive with the battalion until the next day. Problems arose from the appointed landing zone. The 321st S-2 reported that the glider was forced down behind enemy lines. The men received aid from Dutch Underground forces, who led them to

Belgium. More drawings by F/O Axelson.

British lines. They reported to the command post at 1800 hours.

These Eaglemen made it back to their battalion without injury, but not all of them would leave Holland alive. Exactly sixty days later, Pvt. John Patterson, serial number 34658723, perished from wounds he received on November 18. German artillery made their mark on that day, taking the lives of other 321st troopers as well.

T/4 Walter Mitchell Jr., a former West Virginia coal miner turned radio operator courtesy of the United States Army, was one of the Camp Claiborne "originals." Prior to takeoff, he cut a page from a magazine that wrote about glidermen and their commitment to do battle against the enemy. Mitchell decided to tape the article to the outside of his glider using black friction tape. He thought it would make a great souvenir to send home, removing it after they landed.

The glider ride carried the group into the fog and flak that many of the 321st encountered. The tug separated from the group and was hit, causing it to lose speed, then altitude. The towrope was released. Nobody knew where they were. No other C-47s were in the air and no Wacos were on the ground.

The landing was textbook, using a farmer's field near Eersel. Still completely lost, the glidermen were uncertain in which direction to head. Luckily, nobody was injured by all of the enemy fire the group was exposed to. A Dutchman came upon them and told the crew that the territory in which they landed was occupied by the Germans, so they must leave immediately. The farmer promised he would come back with a member of the Dutch Underground who would help them return to Allied-controlled territory. Mitchell went back to the glider to remove his battle-baptized sheet of paper. However, it didn't fare as well as its living counterpart; there was no trace of it.

The promised Dutchmen appeared and laid out the route the group would have to take. It was risky, but no one believed that the enemy had somehow missed seeing their glider release in the midst of occupied territory.

F/O David C. Little, the glider pilot, could not keep up with the Airborne, who were used to 25-mile marches in full field packs. He decided on another route. Since it seemed more feasible that a lone soldier could avoid detection, Little was given the names and addresses of all the Eaglemen whose families he was to write to and tell them what had transpired on the flight into Holland.

The Dutch Underground man stayed with the group part of the way, helping as much as he could. The Americans moved slowly during the day and marched on the roads all night. They never slept because they were afraid to stop. Some fell asleep

Whatcombe Farm, England. PFC Richard Moss returning from Normandy.

Holland. "Hell's Highway." LINZ FAMILY

while marching, then woke and stumbled back in line.

It was now daylight on September 20 and, remarkably, the enemy had not been seen. The group, armed with their folding-stock carbines and a Thompson submachine gun, vowed to kill as many Germans they could; they were not going to be captured alive. They were dead on their feet and hungry, but activity was observed ahead. What a sight! It was British soldiers. The group had to convince the Brits that they were Americans marching down a German-controlled road. After a few tense moments, all was well. The British trucked the six 321st boys to the doorsteps of their own command post. They were a day late, and it was time to get busy.

Trooper Mitchell always wondered what happened to the glider pilot. The promised letters notifying families of the artillerymen's glider ride into Holland never arrived. In fact, F/O Little did survive, making it back to Allied lines along with his shot-down tug pilot, 1st Lt. Robert Cobb of the 88th Troop Carrier Squadron.

First Lt. Cobb's C-47, the tug that brought in T/4 Mitchell, also landed in unfriendly territory. Cobb wrote:

> Although anti-aircraft fire was intense on the route in from Geel to the LZ, we experienced no difficulty until our flight path took us over a patch of woods south of Eersel. At that point, a burst of Flak hit our right auxiliary gas tank. Upon impact the tank caught fire, causing the gas to spread along the entire right side of the ship from radio operator's compartment to tail.
>
> My crew made immediate attempts to bring the fire under control through the use of fire extinguishers and blankets. The effect of the fluid making contact with the gas was one of a choking nature, something like phosgene gas. I was compelled to knock out the windshield and jettison the escape hatch, and both my co-pilot and myself were forced to fly with our head[s] out of the window.
>
> Although the ship was still under control the crew found it impossible to control the flames and I accordingly gave order to prepare for a crash landing. Lt. White radios [*sic*] Major Gates to this effect. The message was acknowledged.
>
> I had hoped that we could tow our glider to the LZ, for just prior to the outburst of flame, the crew chief had given the glider the red light signal indicating that we were five minutes from the LZ.
>
> At 1,000 feet the glider pilot, realizing my intention to crash land, released from my ship. I immediately cut the rope loose, picked an open pasture and came in for a normal gear-up landing.

Holland. From left to right: Lt. Charles LePors, unidentified soldier, Lt. Carroll Holland, Lt. James Wicker, Lt. William Nugent, and CWO Edward Chaumont. PERKINS FAMILY

A rut in the field caused the right engine to be severed from the wing. Immediately upon hitting, the entire plane with the exception of the pilot's compartment was ablaze. The crew chief and radio operator escaped through the window escape hatch, and I followed the co-pilot through the pilot's compartment escape hatch.

We were forced to stomach crawl away from the plane. Three or four minutes later, four British light tanks came up and picked us up.[7]

PFC Dallas Stratton (A Battery) from Mount Pulaski, Illinois, remembered his glider also hitting fog. With him were Pvt. William Dukes (A Battery) from Shorter, Alabama; Pvt. Robert McKenzie (HQ machine gunner) from Minneapolis, Minnesota; and three others, including the pilot, plus the important 75mm pack howitzer. In the fog, the tug plane suddenly dropped altitude, presumably to get better oriented, and naturally pulled the glider with it. The glider pilot released the towrope, fearing that the descending C-47's sharp turn would cause the glider to spiral out of control. Making matters worse, another glider was dead ahead.

Things looked worse upon coming out of the fog than the uncertainty of flying in it had. The English Channel came into view, and a water landing was imminent. The pilot skillfully put the tail down into the water first as Stratton kicked out the emergency door panel under the wing. He inflated his Mae West life preserver and jumped into the water. He bobbed back up near the tail section and pulled himself up on it. The copilot, Private Dukes, exited out the top of the glider and lay on the wing. (After the war, Dukes would suffer from nightmares, sometimes grabbing his German Luger and firing it into the night in anguish. His children understood why.)

A rescue plane circled above, and crewmembers waved at the downed glider crew. They waved back. A small British boat picked them up and gave them dry clothes. Before leaving the partially submerged glider, the Brits opened fire on the wings, causing it to sink.

Later that day, a larger British ship threw a rope ladder net over its side, and the glidermen climbed

Belgium. A drawing by F/O Harold Axelson. AXELSON FAMILY

Sgt. Lawrence Weinberg reported that he landed in Bruges, Belgium, and arranged transportation for nine men and ninety-three rounds of ammunition through Major de Graves of the Civil Affairs detachment. "A guard of six men was placed on [the] glider at my request, and I was told they would remain there until further word from me. Instruments on glider panel were removed. Arrived in Brussels following day. Contacted Town Major and we were billeted in hospital St. Jean. Transportation provided by Transportation unit at hospital through Lt. Jordan [321st Headquarters Battery]. Arrived at LZW following day. Serial A-70, Chalk 66-B." NETHERLANDS LOCAL HISTORY SOCIETY

aboard. Back to Reading, England, they went. They were without any money other than their Dutch invasion paper currency. It took them a few days to get back to Whatcombe Farm and finally to Holland and the battalion.

Another glider landed in Holland without much of a problem but was now under German machine-gun fire. The Dutch Underground came up to the glider while firing into the building occupied by the German machine-gun team. They helped lift the nose and unload the 75mm pack howitzer. It was obvious they wanted the artillerymen to use the gun on the building. The problem was, the only rounds available were smoke. The glider's floor had been punctured by flak, spilling all but the smoke rounds across the countryside. It was difficult to convey this problem to the Dutchmen because of the language barrier. (Double-sided pieces of paper given to the gun section sergeants before departure listed helpful phrases in Dutch, but the categories pertained to asking for help, directions, and information about the enemy or civilian suspects.) Just then, a jeep pulled up, hooked up to the gun, and they were off to war.

Cpl. John Christener's glider carried spools of communication wire. Ground fire was hitting the wings, and the men could hear the popping sound. Instinctively, they leaned forward while still buckled in to try to shield their bodies by using the rolls of wire lashed to the floor.

The glider landed and buried its nose in a ditch. They couldn't unload due to sniper fire. One bullet put a hole in Christener's pant leg, but not his leg. Some paratroopers came to help them, spotted the sniper in a tree, and shot him. A guard was put on the glider until it could be unloaded. He thought he heard some noises from inside it. He found Christener and a few others to check it out. He was advised to throw a grenade into it, so he yelled, "You better come out." No one did, so he tossed in the grenade. The explosion blew a huge hole in the glider. The Waco was empty. Apparently, the guard just had the jitters.

T/4 Burdette Wilkinson (HQ) was the copilot for his combat glider ride into Holland. The other two 321st glidermen were Pvt. Neal "Pudgie" Batchelor of Oswego, New York, and Pvt. Francis Madden of Buffalo, New York. The rest of the glider load consisted of a jeep packed with equipment.

Wilkinson had been with the 321st since Camp Claiborne and had plenty of glider experience, but not as a copilot. During all flight training with gliders, a pilot's copilot was a pilot-in-training. However, this was no training flight: it was combat. Wilkinson was told at the airfield that the "Holland mission was strictly a pushover [and] wouldn't even rate a half combat mission."

The glider pilot gave a brief synopsis of what to expect on the mission. He explained to the artillerymen that the 327th GIR had landed before them and that the fields may be congested with emptied Waco gliders. Those coming in last would have the tightest landing zone. For every spot large enough to land, there would be three or four gliders trying to land on it. Pilots had to land on a spot one-half to one-third the size of a normal landing area if some other glider landed in the chosen spot first. There was no going back up for a second approach.

Years of training taught Wilkinson that this glider was at the "maximum safe" load. The jeep with its cargo of reels of telephone wire, telephones, a radio with extra batteries, water cans filled with water, food rations, and machine gun with boxes of ammunition made the glider less maneuverable and harder to fly.

After the war, Wilkinson wrote down his story of the Holland invasion, using letters sent home to his parents to recall certain details.

> In our discussion, the pilot calmly explained that because of anticipated crowded conditions on the landing field and the difficulties of maneuvering our overloaded glider, he needed my help. During the tow, [the] pilot would fly and I would do nothing. Upon landing, as soon as the pilot released the tow rope he would call out "spoiler." I was then to pull back on the spoiler lever, lowering the wing flaps [and] causing the glider to descend rapidly. At the last moment if it looked like a crash, or near crash landing, I was to unlock the nose [by pulling another lever].

The ground crew attached the towrope, Wilkinson continued, and they were pulled slowly to the end of the secondary runway and out to the end of the take-off runway. The glider became airborne first while the C-47 tug was still rolling down the runway. This enabled the glider pilot to trim the wing tabs to compensate for peculiar loads and to get the feel of the craft while the tug plane was still on the runway. Then the glider pilot and tug pilot exchanged hand signals, the tug increased speed, and away they went. The glider pilot tried at all times to fly higher than the tug, in part to stay above the "prop wash," or air turbulence caused by the tug.

Wilkinson's glider was one of the last of the 321st loads to leave England. At takeoff, the weather was overcast, but the clouds were so far up in the atmosphere that they posed no problems. Inland, the visibility was good, and the green, quiltlike patches of the landscape lay beneath them. As far ahead as the troopers could see was a seemingly endless air parade of C-47s towing gliders. This caused a great deal of air turbulence for those who were farther down the line. Some wondered (correctly) if there was an unbroken chain of gliders between them and those now landing on Landing Zone W.

What they could not possibly have known was that their sister battalion, the 907th GFA, was supposed to follow them but had turned back. The code word for turning back, "Pennsylvania," caused all but sixteen of the eighty-nine 907th tugs to return to their base in England. The few that didn't get the message hit fog that caused much trouble. The commanding officer of the 907th, Lt. Col. Clarence Nelson, was one of the glidermen who was unaware of the turnaround and landed in Holland. When his battalion never showed, he believed they were wiped out by the Germans. The rest of his battalion was grounded in England by poor weather until September 21. The 321st was called upon to fill the void.

Wilkinson wrote:

> The tug plane went into another cloud and again the tow rope went "through the hole in the wall." We were in a "gray fog"; the glider pilot had to depend on the "feel" of the craft and tension of [the] tug rope for his piloting.
>
> We seemed to be progressing satisfactory [*sic*] in this cloud when suddenly, we came out into the clear. Where was the tug? Over there, to the left, flying at almost a right angle to our direction. [The] tug plane had swerved suddenly left to avoid a collision. We followed.
>
> Below us was blue; we were over the channel. Into another cloud went the tug. The time in the clouds was becoming longer, and the time in the clear between clouds was becoming shorter. Air turbulence was increasing. Glider ups and downs plus pitching about [were] becoming greater.
>
> We were in another cloud. The tow rope became slack, a loop laid back on the transparent nose of the glider, then the tow rope pulled "tight as a violin string" and we lunged forward even faster, then the rope became slack again. Believe me, the glider pilot was earning his pay. The loop of slack tow cable laying on the glider nose was becoming longer. [The] glider pilot maneuvered to fly higher to reduce the slack, but the loop seemed to grow longer, disappearing below the glider. Were we ahead of the tug? I peered straight ahead: nothing but gray fog. I peered to the right, and to the left, looking for other gliders. But another glider or two would have collided before I could see it. Would we ever come out of the cloud?
>
> Our pilot raised his right hand in position to strike the release lever. If he hit the lever, the tug cable would be released, and down we would go. But he did not.
>
> We came out of the cloud. Again we were not going in the same direction as the tug. Down below was a glider and below the glider, blue. That pilot had used the cable release. I hoped they did not have a jeep nor an overload, which would sink the glider before the men could get out. While I was looking at the glider going down toward the channel, we went into another cloud.
>
> Once more before the clouds thinned our pilot had his hand ready to release the tow. Releasing would be the last resort because of the weather or to avoid a collision. We were getting out of the clouds more quickly now and

there were longer intervals in the clear between clouds. At least we were going to reach the continental shore.

Wilkinson's thoughts turned to the approach that their glider was going to make over enemy territory. He knew the paratroopers had made the same run on the seventeenth and glider-borne infantrymen on the eighteenth. The Germans must surely be waiting patiently below for other waves of planes to follow that same air corridor. He would not have too long to wait.

Twice the glider shuddered. Thinking we had either a near miss or fragments hitting, I took [a] further look to the rear. Controls of a glider are wire cables and pulleys; as long as neither the pilot nor these critical lines were hit we had control. Other hits would make more holes but wouldn't matter then. I told myself I better quit looking for holes in the glider fabric. I should study the landscape below so that I would be oriented upon landing.

There was the sound of anti-aircraft fire and machine guns. Pvt. Neal "Pudgie" Batchelor, a jeep driver, asked "what's that?" Pvt. Madden sitting next to him replied, "They're shooting at us." Pvt. Batchelor took off his helmet and tried to sit on it.

Wilkinson's roommate back in garrison was Sgt. Victor Truesdale. They had known each other since training back in the States. Wilkinson noticed that the glider on the right ahead of him bore Truesdale's chalk number. One of the qualities that Sergeant Truesdale possessed was a perfect sense of direction, as if he had a built-in compass. Just viewing his glider put Wilkinson at ease, until black smoke started to come from the right engine of the tug pulling Truesdale's glider. It did not change its flight

England. A Holland-bound glider attempts to return to the airfield. Note its invasion stripes. G. J. DETTORE COLLECTION

path, but it did alert the Germans below of its crippled status. The antiaircraft fire intensified, pouring into the smoking C-47. Ironically, the enemy had suddenly quit firing at Wilkinson's glider, sparing those inside. He saw the towrope disengage from the falling tug and had only one thought: whether or not the glider that took the brunt of the German fire indeed contained his good friend Truesdale. He hoped it didn't.

Wilkinson knew he had problems of his own that needed his attention. He had to get oriented from the air quickly, searching the landscape for Eindhoven and the Wilhelmina Canal. That was not to be. He spotted woods and a large field with gliders facing in all directions, bunched up on the ground. "Spoilers," the pilot yelled, and released the towrope. The field was covered with gliders. There was no place to land.

> Automatically, I pulled the spoiler lever. We banked sharply left, sinking fast. Ahead was a small open area, too small. Was this the place the pilot had chosen?
>
> From nowhere, two gliders appeared below us and dived into "our place." . . . We were sinking fast and almost on the ground. Ahead was a tiny piece of ground surrounded by gliders. This was it! In the middle of this little area and crossways to our path was a deep ditch and [on] our side of the ditch a wire fence. We were going about 90 mph. I raised my feet; we took the wire fence like a piece of sewing thread. I hit the lever to unlock the nose. We "touched" ground, breaking off both wheels. . . . [The] body of [the] glider settled into a ditch as the skid runners dug into the bank on the far side. The glider stopped, but the jeep (behind me) kept going. All ropes and lashings broke and tore off their moorings.

The sudden stop of the glider, coupled with the unlocking of the nose while still in flight, caused the jeep to hurl itself forward, with Private Batchelor riding in its front seat. It raised the cockpit section of the glider still containing the seat-belted glider pilot and copilot Wilkinson.

The jeep was well out ahead of the landed glider, dragging its cables and moorings. Batchelor yelled, "Where's Wilkie?" He did not see him still back in the nose section locked in the upright position. The quickest way to extricate themselves from this awkward position was to unlock the seat belts, fall to the ground, and roll out of the glider into the Dutch mud. Wilkinson replied, "Never mind Wilkie. You can't go any further until you get this jeep started."

In the distance was a wooded area. Other 101st troopers were running toward it. Not knowing their location, it seemed best to follow the lead of the men ahead.

Wilkinson pointed out to Private Batchelor, "Ours was such a good landing, we didn't even have to get out of the glider." Private Madden agreed.

Gun crew Sgt. Harvey Baker (B Battery) from Blue Island, Illinois, was the copilot of his CG-4A. The landing was a rough one—the glider struck a stone fence that sent the howitzer careening forward, snapping the mooring ropes fastened to the wooden floor. Pvt. James Calabro (B Battery) from White Plains, New York, was killed instantly when the trail of the howitzer broke loose, crushing his head. The howitzer smashed its way through the nose of the glider and landed outside in the Holland field. The force ripped Baker out of his seat-belt harness, the gun knocking him senseless as he was catapulted out.

As he lay in the field, an army reporter asked him his name, hometown, and if he had a girlfriend. Still stunned and lying on his back, the sergeant must have answered all the questions correctly. He later found out his girlfriend read about him in the newspaper back home.

Cpl. Anthony Tabone (A Battery) of Galesburg, Illinois, was a replacement who came into the 321st while the battalion was in Normandy. At the airfield, he was given fifteen minutes of training about the glider by the pilot, who was hungover from the night before and drenched in sweat.

During the glider flight into Holland, Tabone got out of the copilot's seat to find water for the hungover, dehydrated pilot. A sudden movement of the glider caused him to fall forward. His outstretched hand hit close to the overhead towrope release button. They were over the English Channel. There was enough cussing to go around, and the fetching of the water ceased.

This glider carried a jeep with John Voytek (A Battery) of Larksville, Pennsylvania, riding along in the passenger side. They came down in a plowed field littered with previously discarded parachutes. One of those chutes got churned up, along with its risers, and wrapped itself around the nose of the CG-4A. Immediately the occupants came under German small-arms and machine-gun fire. They hastily exited the glider and headed for the nearby ditch to organize themselves and plan what to do next. Becoming infantry, they attacked the machine-gun nest, killing all of the Germans. Returning to the glider, they used their trench knives to slice away at the parachute and riser lines in order to lift up the nose.

The jeep was driven out, and the glider pilot was taken to a 506th command post for his eventual trip back to England. The next step was to get back to the landing zone and locate their gun section's 75mm pack howitzer along with its crew, but they were nowhere to be found. Training dictated that if their gun couldn't be located in short order, the next best thing was to find another gun and hook it up. Everyone was briefed on their rendezvous location. All men and equipment were to head there for the jeeps, guns, men, and trailers to be sorted.

The guns of the 321st Battalion were first registered on Dutch soil on September 20 at 1245 hours. Division artillery spotted a company of Germans at 1323 hours and requested two volleys of smoke from B Battery. The results were recorded as "good" and the coordinates of that fire mission logged as concentration #1.

Col. Joseph Harper of the 327th GIR had a liaison officer working out of his 2nd Battalion. It was Lt. Bernardo Hoff Knight (HQ) of the 321st from Philadelphia, Pennsylvania. The colonel requested a fire mission just east of the town of Best at the same coordinates used on a prior concentration number. It was now three hours later, and the crossroads had become busy with German soldiers and equipment. Because this was a repeat of an earlier fire mission, the B Battery gunners automatically zeroed in their guns and fired three volleys for effect. This type of firing took the enemy by surprise and was highly effective. No bracketing of the target was necessary.

Lt. Eugene Brooks's first fire mission was unique and never repeated. It started off with Capt. Tom White (HQ) picking him up in a jeep that then ran into a deep shell crater in the road. A wooden post lying in the crater kept the jeep from flipping over. They eventually maneuvered it out and made it to the 506th Regiment command post. An officer pointed to a building off in the distance and said a machine-gun nest was placed at the edge of it. Brooks called in a fire mission; three rounds were fired, with the fourth hitting dead center. The nest was blown into oblivion. This was the only time he actually saw how effective a fire mission could be.

Brooks and his A Battery forward observer team, consisting of Donald Falls, Joe Karasevic, and Robert Doyle, were engaged in putting down needed

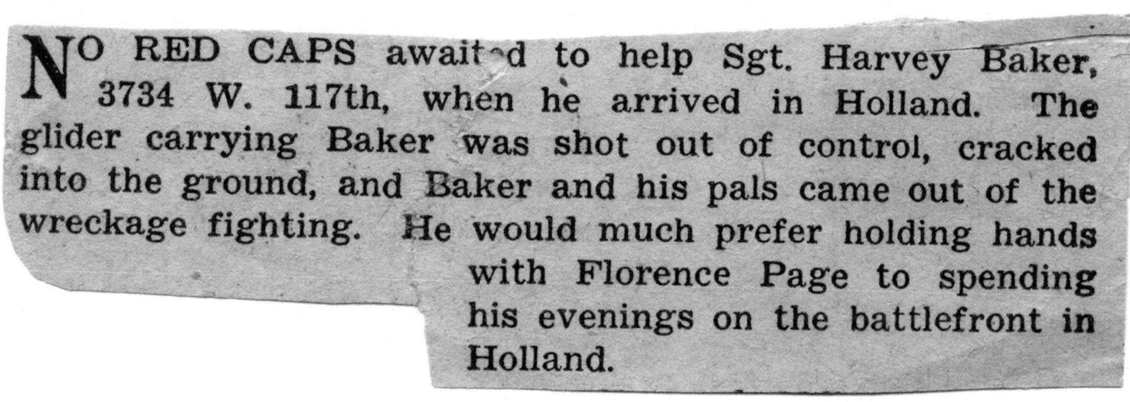
NO RED CAPS awaited to help Sgt. Harvey Baker, 3734 W. 117th, when he arrived in Holland. The glider carrying Baker was shot out of control, cracked into the ground, and Baker and his pals came out of the wreckage fighting. He would much prefer holding hands with Florence Page to spending his evenings on the battlefront in Holland.

The newspaper clipping Sgt. Harvey Baker's girlfriend read about him. BAKER FAMILY

fire between 1450 and 1506 hours for the 3rd Battalion of the 502nd PIR in Best. The enemy was in good spirits, and the team had poor visibility. Effectively timed fire threw the enemy into a state of confused retreat. The team, with the help of the 321st howitzers, followed the retreating Germans and inflicted many casualties. The action earned Brooks and his section a Commendable Action.

Lt. Francis Canham, along with the rest of his B Battery forward observer team—William Stone, Paul Galant, and John Braswell—also received Commendable Actions for their work adjusting British artillery in support of the 1st Battalion of the 327th GIR.

Lt. Bernard Zeppenfield—who had replaced Dillard as the 321st's second assigned air observer pilot after Normandy—was flying a Piper Cub two-seater, or L-4, a fabric-covered aircraft that carried 12 gallons of fuel. It weighed approximately 700 pounds and used a four-cylinder engine that produced 80 horsepower, with a fly time of two and a half hours depending on the winds. Lieutenant Zeppenfield even had his Cub custom-rigged for combat. Underneath the seat was a round cast-iron plate, previously used as a stove top for a barracks tent.

The 101st had thirteen pilots with L-4s assigned to them for the Holland campaign. Keeping the men in the air required forty-five support personnel and nine vehicles. Zeppenfield's L-4 could fly low and slow and had two-way radio communication. "Kangaroo" was the 101st Division's radio designation, and throughout his Holland stay, Zeppenfield's code over the radio was "Kangaroo 14," or "K-14."

This was to be his first combat duty. The other pilots had gained their combat experience from the hedgerow hopping in Normandy and the deserts of Africa. Zeppenfield's first mission was to get his airplane to Holland. His route took him from England to France, crossing the English Channel. He went in a flight of three aircraft and three pilots who kept in-flight contact over their SCR-610 radios. Contact with anyone else was impossible. The three pilots could easily identify each other even if they chose to stay off their radio by the large letter painted on the fuselage. A particular letter was assigned and shared

Holland. 321st soldiers in a farmer's field. KOPACKA FAMILY

Holland. A glider damaged on Landing Zone W. WILLIAMS FAMILY

by several pilots who flew that aircraft. On rare occasions, although not standard practice, a pilot would affix the first letter of his last name to the plane.

For its prolonged flight—especially over the English Channel and in anticipation of encountering a headwind—the L-4's standard fuel load was augmented with a converted heavy-bomber oxygen container. It was square-shaped with domed ends, held 9 gallons of gasoline, and was jerry-rigged with a one-way petcock. The fuel line wound its way through the cockpit and into the L-4's gas tank, which was in front of the pilot, outside the windshield. This was very much like an early 1930s Model A Ford. The extra fuel tank was mounted like a hanging sausage behind the pilot. Switching tanks improperly was fatal.

The L-4 had a rod instead of a fuel gauge. This rod would protrude out of the fuel cap mounted over the tank. When the tank was full, the rod was in a vertical position, about 12 inches high, and as fuel was consumed, the rod dropped. When the rod wasn't visible, there was no fuel left. When there was approximately 3 gallons of the 80 percent octane gas (standard truck gas), or 3 inches of rod showing, the auxiliary fuel tank petcock was turned to the open position; once open, it could not be shut off. If the pilot misjudged, the excess fuel would overflow the regular tank and spill onto the hot engine, causing an explosion.

Pilots were briefed that they had to fly in a 10-mile-wide air corridor when crossing the Channel, or the British would assume they were the enemy. Word was the Germans had captured some L-4s and were using them for reconnaissance in hopes of getting into Allied areas without being challenged. The British air-sea rescue was also alerted in case any of the planes had to ditch in the channel. (PBYs were used for this on days Dumbos were grounded due to low fog.) Each L-4 pilot carried not only his personal gear, which filled the small cockpit, but also an inflatable one-man life raft and a harness-type parachute.

The first stop on their trip was a small airstrip near the town of Le Tréport, France. The fliers had only a Michelin road map and a handheld compass for navigation. A former barnstormer, Zeppenfield and his other air liaison pilots dropped down to treetop level and followed the railroad tracks to a train station. There they could read the sign to determine which town they were near and orient themselves.

The second town, Ore, was located and was in British hands. Unbeknownst to the flyers, the runway was mined. They came in and started to land. The British soldiers were all waving furiously; to the three Americans, they seemed a very friendly lot of soldiers. Touching down without incident, they quickly learned that a de-mining team had not yet finished its job. The pilots fueled up and left the minefield behind without mishap.

Hopscotching through France, Belgium, and then finally into Holland, their final destination was Eindhoven. The crews landed and were met by the other air observer pilots who were already there. The crews stayed together and moved with the division command post, which also held DivArty. It was October 4. This was to be their routine throughout the Holland campaign.

The airfield, a farmer's onion field near a village called Slijk-Ewijk, slowly turned to mud. Taking off in the L-4s was nearly impossible because of the stickiness of the mud. Straw was then placed in the area used for the runway and chicken wire on top of that.

Almost their entire time in Holland the air observer pilots lived here. At first they erected pup tents over foxholes, placing cots inside. As the water tables rose, it was time to vacate. It only took one incident of rolling out of the cot in the morning and placing their feet into 8 inches of cold water to change locations. A hospital-style tent was located and erected, two pyramidal tents attached to each other. All the observer pilots and members of their section slept there.

It wasn't unusual to receive German artillery fire at this location. It would churn up the field but caused no real casualties—not even an airplane. Someone noticed that the bombing followed a set routine. The farmer, whose field they were in, would

Lt. Bernard Zeppenfield, a 321st L-4 pilot.

Pvt. Henry "Dutch" Ira (B Battery) from Windsor, Missouri, and Cpl. George "Cokie" Crim (B Battery) got along well. Ira was one of the older men in the battery. Both had left their gun when an enemy bombardment began but were ordered back to it. They found a hole and dove in. In the hole, they waited for the shelling to stop, knowing that the rest of the section would then show up and get the gun out of there. But the incoming rounds continued to fall.

Ira was struck in the head; a shell fragment pierced his helmet and blood ran down his neck. Crim tried to pull him out of the foxhole, but Ira wouldn't budge. Ira said, "Look at my head."

Crim asked Ira, "Should I sing, or do you want a smoke?"

Ira replied, "Leave me alone. Shut up, you shell-shocked son-of-a-bitch, I'm talking to a higher power!" Ira's head was tilted back and his eyes were closed. He was praying and wouldn't put his head down until he was finished. He later received medical attention and returned to his gun section. ■

France. From left to right: PFC Henry "Dutch" Ira, PFC George "Cokie" Crim, and Cpl. Norman Deethardt of B Battery.

look out the second story of his barn for a short time. He would then leave the barn, and artillery fire would come in. The Dutch farmer was arrested and taken away by the Counter Intelligence Corps (CIC), and the shelling ceased.[8]

On another occasion a firing battery was emplaced in an apple orchard. A few hundred yards away, a girl would travel down the road, stop, and turn in a certain direction. Later in the evening that area would be shelled. This happened a few times, but then she disappeared and the shelling stopped. The rumor was that someone shot her.

> Division leaders knew from the beginning how easy it might be for the Germans to cut the [road] corridor, and what a disastrous effect such a stroke would have on the entire operation. It was obviously good German strategy to stop the flow of traffic somewhere near the base of the corridor and then deal at leisure with the Americans and British up north near Nijmegen or Arnhem. Nor was there an apparent defense against any strong German group that was determined to grab a section of the road. The division would not be strong everywhere; parts of the road were totally unguarded.[9]

It was under these conditions that artillery was needed, and needed often—not only for offensive fire missions, but also for defensive missions, such as covering infantry withdrawals. The 907th GFA would not arrive en masse until September and had to be ready to support the 501st PIR the next day with their sawed-off 105s. The 321st was the sole complete artillery unit representing the 101st until that welcomed glider lift arrived.

Outside Koevering on September 21, Lt. Eugene Brooks, Cpl. Charles R. Hunter of Springfield, Illinois, and the rest of their A Battery forward observer team were in the ditches alongside the road. They

Lieutenant Zeppenfield exiting L-4 pilots' quarters at Slijk-Ewijk.

Holland. A B-17 burned after a belly landing. WILLIAMS FAMILY

Holland. The interior of the burned B-17. WILLIAMS FAMILY

were with the 506th Paratroopers of the 1st Battalion to give artillery support. The Brits had entered the town with American-made Sherman tanks and were now returning after an engagement of about three hours. Hunter and the rest of the soldiers stayed in the ditches as the tanks rolled by. They noticed that tankers were wearing the traditional British tams. The hatches were open. Then, without warning, German potato mashers were thrown from the open hatches into the ditches lined with troopers. The friendly sight of Allied armor turned into something sinister. The Germans tossed as many grenades as possible before they were recognized for who they really were. Hunter was hit, receiving twenty-two fragments from the potato mashers, from his heels to the top of his head. None of his wounds were critical, but he spent the next three weeks in the hospital.

After being released, Hunter was again assigned to Brooks's team. Three days after his hospital release, a fragment from a mortar round ripped into

Holland. "Hells Highway." WILLIAMS FAMILY

Holland. "Hell's Highway," with civilians looking on. Captain Williams is in the foreground. WILLIAMS FAMILY

his throat, nicking his windpipe. He nearly drowned in his own blood, but survived once again.

The next day, September 22, the battalion was given the march order, which was completed in a record fifteen minutes. The 75mm pack howitzers were needed to support the 501st PIR southwest of Veghel. The Germans and their tanks were hitting hard in an attempt to cut the road aptly named "Hell's Highway." It was be a hectic day, with the battalion on the move for most of it. It was 1015 hours.

Reconnaissance officers went ahead, scouting for a new position so they could have a skeleton crew in place by 1405 hours. The rest of the battalion followed. German small-arms fire was intense. The artillerymen became infantry, setting up a local defense. This would not be the last time events triggered unusual tactics for an artillery battalion.

The guns were dug in; however, the enemy small-arms fire was incessant. The dangerous work of preparing the gun pits for the 75mms while under fire was completed. However, Colonel Carmichael opted for moving out. The entire battalion vacated its position for another only to discover, less than two hours later, that it was no better than the first. The events were so fluid that the battalion never recorded this last position for the batteries of the command post.

At 1610 hours, the entire battalion vacated the fields because of German fire. They took to the road. For the next hour or so, the guns of the 321st were set upon the road for direct fire missions. But this was another temporary firing position. Eighty rounds of M54 were put out by the 75mm pack howitzers from this area. The German fire dwindled during this short period.

Finally at 1730 hours, the battalion dug in one more time for the day. They were now just 100 yards behind the main line of resistance, northeast of Veghel. The survey crew had the guns registered in less than two and a half hours. German 88s shelled the

Holland. A 321st radio repair truck hidden in an orchard.

Holland. A 321st radio-equipped jeep under a discarded camouflage parachute. WILLIAMS FAMILY

Holland. From left to right: Capt. Frederic King, PFC Hugh Worthy, and 1st Sgt. Timothy Shea of B Battery having their first supper in Holland on September 19, 1944. SHEA FAMILY

dug-in positions shortly after. Forward observer parties located those the next morning, and the American gun batteries got their revenge in three volleys.

PFC Adams and his machine-gun crew of three others dug their foxhole. Pvt. Harold Hazelbaker, of Ripley, Ohio; Harry Conklin of Peekskill, New York; and Raymond Freddo of Sharpsville, Pennsylvania, were all inside the foxhole when a mortar barrage started. Adams started to count the incoming rounds, noticing that half of them were duds. As he was doing this, one of rounds hit inside their foxhole but didn't explode. Adams believed the Germans' slave laborers purposely made them defective, saving the crew. The rest of the men felt differently, complaining they now had to dig another hole because of the possibility the dud could explode at any time. Adams reminded them they should be thanking the good Lord that they were alive.

It was early morning on September 23 when both A Battery forward observer parties met. Second Lt. Henry Kowalczyk from Virnan, Pennsylvania, and Lt. Gene Brooks had a meeting. The second lieutenant was resting against a tree along with the rest of his men when Brooks walked up to him. Both officers wanted to get to work with their respective parties and freshly aimed 75mm pack howitzers, but only one team was requested by the infantry.

Each officer told the other, "I'll go and you stay here" and "I got it—it's ok." After a few minutes of wrangling, Kowalczyk, Cpl. Howard Rich from Cincinnati, Ohio, and the rest of their party took to the field. Lieutenant Brooks had reluctantly given in.

On April 1, 1944, the twenty-five-year-old Kowalczyk had written home to his wife, Margaret: "I'm just hoping the invasion starts real soon and I start with it, because, kid, I know that's the quickest way back to you." Colonel Carmichael decided otherwise and kept Kowalczyk and some others behind at their camp in England. The losses from the airborne invasion in Normandy were calculated to be high, and having a core of qualified replacements on hand was considered to be prudent. It is not known if Lieutenant Kowalczyk knew the reason for his being held

English £1 note good-luck charm, referred to as a "short snorter," signed by various 321st soldiers. Note the autograph of Jose Landeros, the classically trained violinist, "Always B Sharp." This item belonged to PFC Paul Miho (HQ Battery), who penned his autograph above the government official's signature.

Netherlands 1 gulden bank note invasion currency issued to PFC George Verbeke (A Battery) and signed by his gun section. The smeared ink was caused by the glider riders ditching in the English Channel. Second Lt. Sven Berg (glider pilot) and Lt. Ty Robinson (power pilot) also signed this good-luck charm.

PFC Robert Reeves's "short snorter." The front is signed by the glidermen who were going with him into Holland.

The back of Reeves's "short snorter." When he was captured, the Germans went through his wallet but missed this currency. While being held in a barn shortly after his capture, Reeves had others sign the back of this note. Note the signature of Sgt. Victor Truesdale, another 321st POW.

Former glider pilot Harold Axelson displaying a section of fabric he cut from the rear section on his Waco CG-4A on September 19, 1944. Note the holes made by machine-gun fire while his glider was descending to land.

Former farmhouse complex (now torn down) in the tiny hamlet of Heuvel, southeast of Veghel. While lying just outside the farmhouse and scanning for targets with their binoculars, Lt. Henry Kowalczyk and Cpl. Howard Rich were hit by a single mortar round. Kowalczyk was killed and Rich was wounded. The radioman and the tagalong glider pilot were inside the farmhouse basement and escaped injury.

Cardboard POW tag issued to PFC Robert Reeves. The Germans were overloaded with prisoners and ran out of square metal dog tags. After a guard tore up his tag in anger and threw it on the ground, Reeves was only able to locate three sections.

Observation post located at 16 Achterstraat Driel. The stairs lead down into the basement where a German sergeant started to descend but was fatally shot by several 101st soldiers.

An early 321st battalion crest. *Noli Me Tangere* is Latin for “Do not touch me,” a phrase taken from the Bible; Jesus says these words to Mary Magdalene shortly after the Resurrection. This early crest was manufactured by N. S. Meyer in New York, probably prior to World War II, and originally intended for use by the 82nd Infantry Division, which the 321st was a part of at the time. The deep red traditionally represents artillery. This crest was originally owned by PFC Elmer Wilkens (B Battery) and has a long pin and catch at the back. Another style made by Meyer has a threaded stud and nut at the rear of the crest, but this version is very rare.

German Fallschirmjäger (paratrooper) qualification badge taken as a souvenir by Sgt. Nelson Kopacka (B Battery) in Normandy. “Georg Schoppl, Frankreich,” is scratched on the back, most likely referring to the city in France where Schoppl received his jump training.

Lt. William Nugent’s (HQ Battery) 321st stenciled helmet. The painted tic is correctly at the 3 o’clock position on both sides of this steel pot.

Capt. George Dunkelberg’s (HQ Battery) Italian-made eagle patch. During his voyage home from Russia after his time as a POW, Dunkelberg’s ship pulled into an Italian port. Since he no longer had an eagle patch on his uniform, Dunkelberg had this one made to proudly show he was in the 101st Airborne Division.

Left: Studio portrait taken outside Camp Claiborne, Louisiana. From left to right: Pvt. Bill Plummer, an unknown soldier, and Cpl. Harvey Baker.

PFC Bob Reeves (A Battery) sent this SS overseas cap cutoff home, along with the soldier’s rifle, after leaving Normandy.

Sgt. Dick Moss's (A Battery) Ike jacket with an unauthorized combat leadership stripe, which is green and made out of a wool-like material. Artillerymen were not authorized to wear a Combat Infantry Badge; this stripe is the closest on-the-ground earned combat badge that could be worn.

Close-up of Moss's combat leadership stripe and British-made 1st Allied Airborne patch.

A 17th SS "Gotz von Berlichingen" *Soldbuch* brought home by PFC H. C. Warren, who picked up this souvenir in Normandy. Also included in the book were two cutoffs: the skull from the overseas cap and the eagle from the tunic sleeve.

T/5 Harmon Sites's (Headquarters) Ike jacket, along with an overseas cap adorned with another crest. His ribbons and glider badge were removed at the time of this photograph.

Close-up of Sites's early 321st crest and glider badge, commonly called glider wings, with one star denoting a combat glider landing. The badge is placed on an unauthorized oval.

Nugent's helmet displaying the "follow me" stripe on the back.

Lt. William Nugent's (HQ) Ike jacket with extremely rare 321st collar brass.

Nugent's *Mission Accomplished* battalion history with a rare jacket cover.

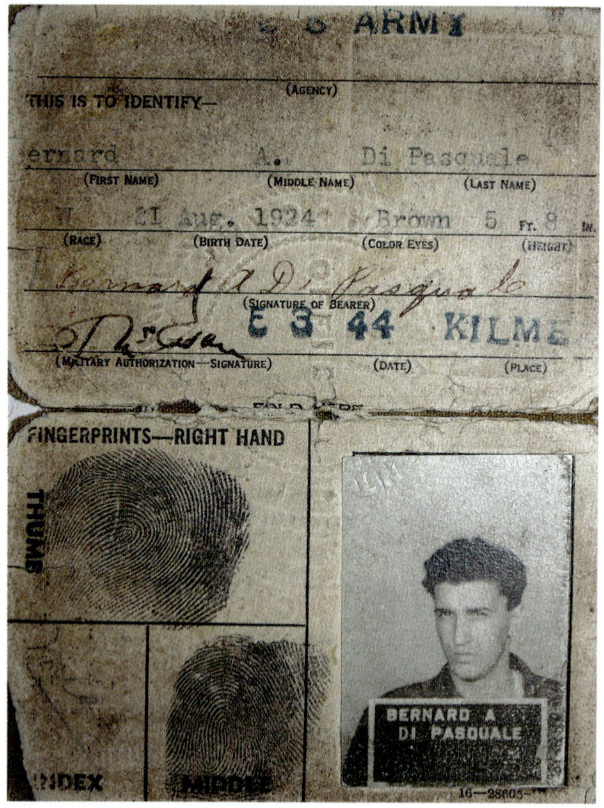

Opened Red Cross booklet belonging to medic Bernard DiPasquale.

Berchtesgaden souvenir brought back by T/3 Leo Corrigan. The area was a free-for-all hunt for souvenirs, and almost everything that wasn't nailed down was fair game. This is a handle for an overhead water tank flush-release valve, placed near the ceiling directly over a toilet.

Dog tag belonging to PFC Harry Sinkutch (HQ Battery). Sinkutch's pals were mostly 506th paratroopers, and he copied their ways. In this instance, he cut a piece of hose from a gas mask and wrapped it around his dog tags to keep them from clanging together and making an unwanted noise in combat.

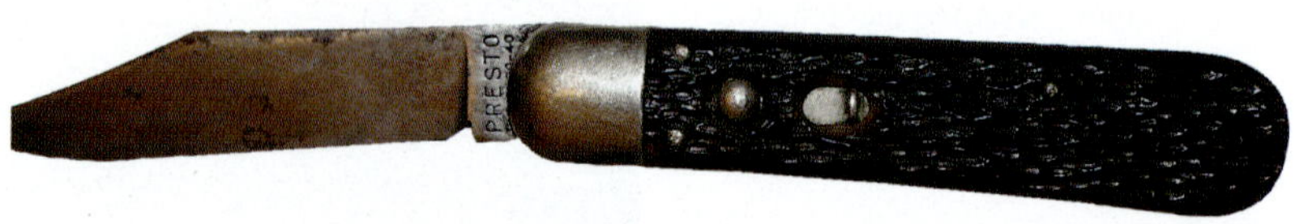

M2 Presto switchblade manufactured by Geo Schrade and carried by PFC William Buckingham of the B Battery Detail Section. These knives without the bale for cord attachment are believed to have been either an early model or made for civilian use, or perhaps both.

This hand-painted wooden plaque, albeit a touristy item, was sent home by T/3 Leo Corrigan (A Battery).

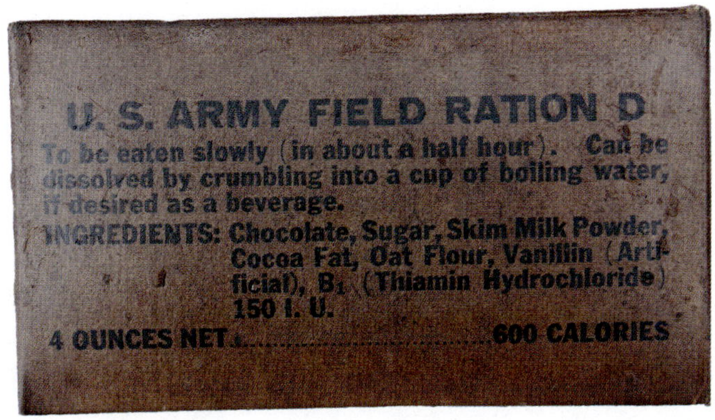

A much-appreciated "D bar," a chunk of chocolate about the size of a deck of playing cards.

The manufacturer of the D bar.

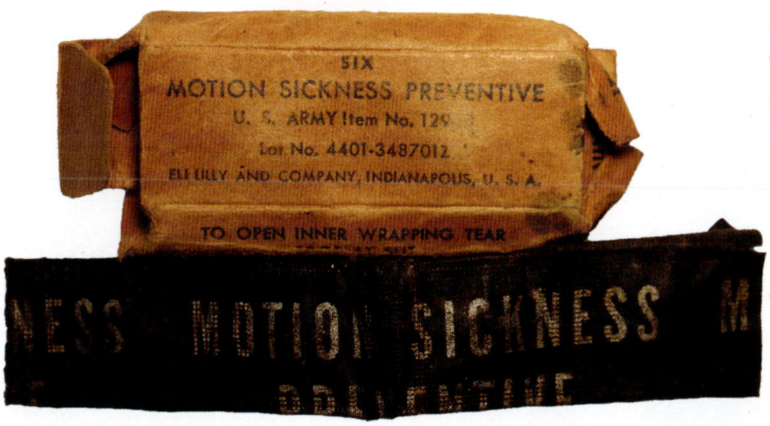

Issued packet of motion sickness pills. These were given out by officers just prior to takeoff to any glidermen who requested them.

M3 trench knife dug up from an orchard in Hemmen, Netherlands, by the homeowner. The 321st, along with other artillerymen, were dug in near the orchard. The blade is still razor-sharp, and the scabbard has two initials roughly scratched into it on both the front and back.

Propaganda leaflet dropped by German aircraft over the 321st area of Savy, Belgium, around December 21 and brought home by PFC George Adams (A Battery). Inset: The back of the propaganda leaflet.

One of two Berchtesgaden beer mugs sent home by Sgt. Mark Sullivan (B Battery).

A 907th helmet with proper stenciled markings applied. However, the other side is marked as belonging to the 321st, making it impossible to tell to which battalion it really belonged.

Left: A typical scrapbook filled during the course of the war. This example was kept by Merle, mother of Lt. James Nye, the executive officer of I Company, 3rd Battalion, 506th PIR, in Holland.

back, but he strenuously objected to his colonel's keeping him from the upcoming fight in France. It did him no good. He missed the first fight of the 321st, and there was nothing he could do about it.

The weather was cloudy on September 23, so much so that 321st air observer pilot Bernard Zeppenfield returned to base at Division Artillery in his L-4 Piper Cub airplane with his observer, Lt. Bernardo Knight, who volunteered regularly to fly with Zeppenfield. Low ceilings were the official cause for their quick return to the ground. The time was almost 0900 hours.

A little earlier, Kowalczyk had located a British tank and persuaded its crew to give his forward observer party a lift to the area of enemy activity. The lieutenant headed east to the tiny community of Heuvel, southeast of Veghel. Riding on the back of the tank, Corporal Rich thought to himself that being so exposed was a foolhardy thing to do. He kept those thoughts to himself. The Brits dropped off the hitchhikers short of their destination, and the men walked to a farmhouse complex some distance away.

Radio operator Walter Mitchell was part of the forward observer party. An unlikely participant for this mission was also along with them: a glider pilot who had asked Kowalczyk if he could accompany them and was given the OK. The glider pilot wanted to get into some ground combat to see the war up close and personal. The two men set up the radio in the main farmhouse's basement. It was a small, cramped area, its only window facing the spot where the team had positioned themselves approximately forty feet away with the communication wire strung out. This was the first taste of combat for Kowalczyk. They knew they were close to the Germans and most likely had received information on targets from the 506th PIR in that vicinity.

The artillerymen lay down on the ground under a stand of trees for concealment. They did not dig themselves in, but hurriedly began scanning the area with binoculars for enemy activity while lying in prone positions. It was 0900 hours.

Five minutes later, a single enemy shell burst above their heads into the trees, raining hot iron splinters upon them. A lone fragment pierced Kowalczyk's helmet and entered his head, killing him instantly. Another fragment tore into Rich's back, knocking him unconscious. When he awoke,

Holland. An L-4 piloted by a 101st air observer. WILLIAMS FAMILY

Rich tried to rouse his lieutenant by shaking him, then noticed a small trickle of blood alongside his head. He knew his lieutenant was dead. Rich discovered his leg was numb and assumed that was where he had been hit.

Rich never heard the explosion, nor did he have any idea where it came from. He put out two fire missions on unobserved infantry as his dead lieutenant lay next to him, then decided to get first aid. It was a painful mile-long walk before he came across an aid station. While there, a medic informed him that the shell fragments had lodged near his spine. He was evacuated back to England to a hospital in Oxford and recuperated there until December 1. When he was released, it didn't take long until he resumed his duties as a forward observer, this time in Bastogne.

Rich said years later, "They saw us before we saw them." What the party could not know at the time was that they were being observed by the Germans as they approached the farm complex. The Germans had set up an observation post in a windmill. Its window faced Veghel, where the party came from. The windmill was only 700 yards away from Kowalcyzk's position and provided a commanding view of the Dutch countryside. Additionally, a German mortar crew was positioned approximately 400 yards away and likely fired the deadly round.

Holland. The windmill observation post used by the German mortar crew and owned by miller Van den Heuvel. ERWIN JANSSEN

Left: Lt. Henry Kowalczyk with his wife, Margaret, and son, Sandy.

It would take another hour, but by 1000 hours, the enemy observation post was discovered. A different 321st forward observer team saw a German in the window of the windmill. A request for a volley of smoke from their batteries emplaced not more than two miles away was made to limit the enemy's visibility. The forward observers also requested tanks to blast down the windmill, but that didn't happen. Fire brought down the windmill the next day, September 24. The tar-papered wooden structure burned quickly, right down to its brick foundation.

Margaret Kowalcyzk was writing a letter to her husband on September 23 with her son, Sandy, on the floor near her. Suddenly, the nine-month-old boy did two things he had never done before: he stood up and walked, and said, "Daddy." Margaret tore up the letter as an eerie feeling came over her. She later learned via telegram that her husband had died on the same day her son so distinctively said "Daddy" for the first time.

Lieutenant Kowalczyk's last letter home to his wife was dated September 17, 1944. He wrote that England was taking off the blackout after five years; "kids have never seen what the towns look like with lights." To him, this might have been the first sign that the war was winding down. His footlocker and wallet containing $6.80 were sent home to his wife almost a year later. Missing were $2,000 in cash and his class ring, wristwatch, and glasses.

The men of A Battery had the highest respect for their lieutenant and knew of his strong desire to send his son to college. A collection was taken, headed by Sgt. Wayne F. Kuenzli of Marion, Ohio, and a $500 war bond was sent to the young lieutenant's widow for that express purpose. The glidermen didn't know that almost a year earlier, Kowalczyk had written home to Margaret and said, "We should get some kind of an endowment policy for Sandy so that he'll have money to go to school when he gets about 20 years old."

The reburial of Lt. Henry Kowalczyk on April 20, 1949. KOWALCZYK FAMILY

Austria. Sgt. Wayne F. Kuenzli (marked with arrow) with his A Battery gun section who initiated college fund donations for Kowalczyk's son, Sandy. KOWALCZYK FAMILY

Back in his hometown of Crucible, a coal-mining town in Pennsylvania, the lieutenant was a scoutmaster. His name was added to their honor roll. He was buried in Son, Holland, and later brought home to Greene County and reburied on April 20, 1949.

September 24 arrived with relatively good news. Seaborne elements led by CWO Edward Chaumont (HQ) arrived at 0630 hours at the battalion command post; with him were the 6x6 trucks, mail, and field kitchens. Two hours later, the battalion was on the move again.

The red-leggers dug in approximately two miles northeast of Veghel; for the next two days, they and the 506th PIR were cut off by the Germans. The enemy had cut the supply road. They were now isolated. If the Germans realized that the area was thinly held, a catastrophic loss could occur for the defenders. The Americans rallied. A total of 587 rounds from the pack howitzers was fired. "Artillerymen took over as machine gunners, bazooka teams and riflemen. The battalion proved again that it

Henry "Sandy" Kowalczyk, holding a brick taken from the farmhouse near where his father was killed. G. J. DETTORE COLLECTION

could operate efficiently under the most trying conditions and still deliver prompt and accurate artillery fire whenever called upon."[10]

The soldiers of the battalion were amazed how the British Army operated. There was a long column of vehicles traveling bumper-to-bumper on their way to Arnhem. However, at tea time, the entire column stopped and offered the artillerymen some tea and biscuits as they ate. The troopers enjoyed the Brits, but wondered how the Germans could let a target so great go unmolested. Not long after, the column was practically destroyed by enemy fire.

Again the battalion loaded up its equipment for another position, arriving at 1305 hours southwest of Uden. In the early morning, the battalion was alerted of a heavy counterattack. Most of the 321st troopers recall this day as one of the worst during their time with the battalion. September 25 had arrived, and it was going to be rough. A division liaison officer brought orders for the 506th PIR to move to Veghel and open the road south of the city where it had been cut again, reported the unit history.

The order of march was 3rd Battalion, 1st Battalion, Regiment Headquarters Company, and finally 2nd Battalion. The column arrived on the northeast side of Veghel at 0530 and waited for orders. Once again, the artillery would be needed for the sure-to-come counterattack by the 506th PIR. It was imperative to reopen the road.

The unit commanders received the order at 0130, and at 0300 the battalion was alerted. Five minutes later, the reconnaissance party departed. Its purpose was to locate a suitable command post and an effective firing position for the guns. At 0400 hours, the battalion was back on the road in complete darkness, traveling south toward Veghel. It was a forced march of 8 miles; jeeps towed 75mms and trailers filled with cloverleafs of 75mm ammunition, and kitchen and motor pool 6x6s trundled along, some piled with men and supplies. Other troopers had to do it the old-fashioned army way and hoof it. Almost 450 soldiers were in the column. After an hour and a half on the road, they arrived at their preplanned destination. It was 0530, and daybreak was about to occur.

The survey team was busy getting the aiming stakes in place to line up the howitzers. The field was abuzz in activity of all sorts. One of the artillerymen remarked that the building near them used to be Colonel Sinks's command post. Yet another commented that the Krauts had also used this place once. There were precise, deep slit trenches that the Germans had prepared in the hopes of dodging Allied airpower, bullets, and bombs. The Germans indeed knew this place well and were about to prove it.

The sun was just starting to appear on the horizon at 0610 hours. The guns had not yet been entirely emplaced when German 88s and mortars rained down in a nonstop concentration. The troopers of the 321st had never experienced anything so intense before in the entire campaign. The firing continued unabated for fifty-five minutes.

Cpl. Woodrow Stephens, an A Battery truck driver, jumped into his GMC 6x6 and moved it between two stone buildings for protection. He thought if the Germans did not see the truck, they wouldn't fire on it. Besides, it would take an expert to bring a round down between two buildings on a target they couldn't see. He dove from the truck just as a round exploded, hitting the gas tank and setting the truck ablaze.

T/4 Burdette Wilkinson (HQ) had told the men in his section just a few days earlier, "I hope I never see Veghel again." They were in Uden at the time. The liaison officer attached to the 506th was not at the command post when the battalion moved south and was not informed of the move. Consequently, the 321st was the only battalion at Uden by omission because the 506th had completely disappeared.

The liaison officer awoke. He had to walk over to notify the 321st commanding officer and report to Colonel Carmichael that the 506th had gone; naturally, all radios went with them on their move. The colonel decided to go south once again because he found out that was the direction the 506th had gone in; wherever they went, so did the battalion. The logical area of their location seemed to be the former 506th command post.

In a letter dated July 5, 1969, Wilkinson recalled, "If we did not know what was happening, the Germans did. The Panzers and mortars assumed we would go directly to the 501 CP, arriving at dawn. They were right, and they were ready, waiting for us." (Most likely no panzers were involved and the command post was actually the 506th's.)

PFC Elmo Smiley was assigned to B Battery's sixth gun as a jeep driver. His section's sergeant, Harvey Baker, alerted his gun section that they were leaving Uden with Veghel as their destination, a 5-mile journey. PFC Smiley remembers that night as the darkest he had ever seen. While on the road south with their howitzer in tow, he and his only passenger kept alert for enemy activity.

Sergeant Baker marched ahead of the jeep on foot in complete darkness. The only illumination came from his wristwatch hour hands that glowed with radium paint. He systematically raised his arm, exposing his watch to the rear, which enabled his jeep driver to stay aligned on the road directly behind him. Word spread throughout the battalion that any action encountered was to be fought to the very last man if necessary.

Darkness gave way to daybreak, and PFC Smiley was directed to a field off the main road to drop off the 75mm pack howitzer at its firing position. The rest of the gun crew had the responsibility of setting and emplacing the trail. The entire area was filled with the activity of the artillerymen.

Suddenly, the Germans poured their mortar fire precisely into the battalion's area. Smiley dove for cover in a shallow circular foxhole. His new entrenching shovel's handle created a problem; in Normandy he had cut his old one to a shorter length, but he had not done so yet in Holland. It wedged itself at a perpendicular angle, elevating his torso as he lay prone in the foxhole. While Smiley was attempting to rectify this problem, a shell fragment struck his helmet and sliced off a section of the netting. The concussion and the heat of the flying piece of iron that bounced off the front of his steel pot gave him the sensation that his body was on fire for an instant. He knew he was lucky to be still alive.

Sergeant Baker yelled to Smiley to go back into the field with the jeep and haul the howitzer back onto the road. A lull in firing lasted long enough to climb back into the jeep and head for the gun. Then the enemy mortars opened up again, and luck was once more with Smiley as the howitzer was hooked up and he pulled it back out of the field and onto the road without injury.

Smiley recalled that the position chosen for the guns was a poor one. He believed it was a former command post of the 502nd PIR. The terrain was low and depressed, making any targets for the battalion difficult to fire on. Obviously their location made an excellent view of fire for the Germans. A canal near the battalion offered no protection.

PFC Smiley later lost his dented helmet. He quickly found another lying in a field and put it on his head. This helmet, however, had a bullet hole near the front on the right side—a rather obvious hole, he thought—but this one would last him to the end of the war.

Third Gun Section Sgt. Norman Deethardt of B Battery got hit and went down. He thought to himself that this was it; he could feel a wetness oozing down his back. What a hole it must be. But he felt OK. A chunk of warm, whirling mud churned up by the artillery shelling was the cause, not a shell fragment.

Sgt. Larry Benninghoff from Headquarters Supply also became a casualty, wounded in the groin. He later returned to duty.

Cpl. Vernon Raker, cannoneer of A Battery's third gun, had just started to dig in their howitzer when the Germans opened up on them. They had passed a crossroads near a farmhouse, then went off the road approximately 300 yards into a field. The Germans were using time-delay rounds, sending shell fragments into the freshly dug emplacements. These pieces were ricocheting off the 75mm pack howitzers. To his dismay, while furiously digging, Raker looked around to see that the gun crew had dived for cover.

Raker quickly observed what he thought was the location of the enemy guns. About a quarter-mile away, a group of farm buildings off another main road provided concealment. He was just getting off his knees from digging when he observed an unlikely sight. Headquarters Capt. James Wicker from Sanford, North Carolina, and Colonel Carmichael had found themselves in the thick of it. At every shell burst, the colonel would hit the deck and Captain Wicker would turn in the direction of emanating fire and spit a stream of his chewing tobacco.

Things were not getting any better, so Corporal Raker made a dash across the field. Some fifty yards away, just past a barbed-wire fence, a slit trench was waiting. He dove in headfirst and landed on top of

Holland. B Battery motor pool Sgt. Willard Brown. TURKAL FAMILY

First Sergeant Davis of A Battery. The distinct sound of mortars leaving their tubes could be heard tearing up the area from the cluster of farm buildings.

Sgt. Willard Brown, one of four mechanics assigned to the B Battery motor pool, of Laconia, Indiana, ran for cover like the rest of the battalion. He and another red-legger jumped a garden fence near the farmhouse. They landed in an uncovered cesspool, up their waists. It would be days before they could clean themselves up.

In a letter home to his wife in Cleveland, Ohio, Sgt. Nelson Kopacka mentioned the day. Kopacka was in B Battery in charge of the machine-gun section and wrote that in all his days spent with the battalion, including Bastogne, he felt that September 25, 1944, would surely be his last. He didn't elaborate other than to say he felt the debacle was of Colonel Carmichael's making. It was a common but erroneous belief.

It was another lucky day for Cpl. Victor Sauerheber (HQ Battery) of Corydon, Indiana. While under the incoming exploding rounds, a piece of shrapnel sheared off the top of his aluminum canteen attached to his belt, leaving the plastic cap intact. He later found the handles of the knife and fork in his backpack also took a hit, keeping him injury-free. The other lucky day for him had been earlier on the nineteenth; his glider was just about to land when a well-aimed enemy mortar shell hit it broadside. It entered the glider at their backs, at eye level,

Camp Claiborne. Sgt. Nelson Kopacka with a .50-caliber machine gun.

Holland. An unidentified 321st artilleryman points to a dent in his helmet. LELONEK/DETTORE

between Sauerheber and the gliderman seated next to him. The round continued across the aisle between the heads of two glidermen seated opposite of them and out. No one was injured.

Perhaps the most amazing story of September 25 was what *didn't* happen: Not one of the battalion was killed. Three received much-needed medical attention, while many others declined it.

Nijmegen was the next destination for the battalion. By 1420 hours on October 2, the guns were emplaced and support was being given to the 82nd Airborne Division. It was here that the 321st fired the first 101st artillery round to fall on German soil. Enemy aircraft were bombing the area near the guns. By the next morning, the 321st was out of there and on the road again.

October 3 would be a busy day. At 0830 hours, a skeleton crew was sent ahead to pick the best spot to lay the guns. It was a field in the village of Hemmen. This rectangle of land was split by a small stream with a white-painted wooden structure in the

Holland. Cpl. Anthony Stempien (left) and PFC Edward Rymarczyk (right), wiremen for A Battery. LELONEK/DETTORE

Holland. An unidentified 321st gun section. LINZ FAMILY

center built to house racing pigeons. Tall trees were at the perimeter of the field, along with houses that faced it. A small cemetery was nearby. By 1045, the rest of the battalion was on the road there; some would march to it, while others rode in the backs of trucks and jeeps.

At 1230 hours, as the small convoy was on the move, a dogfight appeared overhead. Sgt. Paul Miho (HQ) along with Cpl. Frank Shellberg (HQ) of Moline, Illinois, and a group of others were riding in the back of a 6x6 truck. An American P-51 was flying behind a German fighter plane and firing away. All the soldiers jumped from the trucks and ran for cover. Shellberg dropped to the pavement, holding his leg in pain. A 20mm round fired from above had knocked him down. The German had spotted the trucks and was coming in for a run at them. The P-51 jumped the German and now was on the defensive. The fight continued with both aircraft taking evasive maneuvers across the sky and out of view. Shellberg, seriously wounded, was treated by the medics and sent on to the hospital. He did not return to the battalion and it was believed, at the time, that he would lose his leg.

Soldiers of the 321st recall October 5–8 as the busiest days of the war in terms of rounds expended. The battalion was in direct support of the 506th PIR in what became known as the battle of Opheusden in Holland. This small town was on an island formed by the Neder Rhine on the north and the Waal River on the south. Elements of the 101st Division were moving onto the island in order to relieve a British division. The German 363rd Volksgrenadier Division was east of Arnhem with orders to clear the island, forcing the Allies to retreat in confusion to the southeast. The island was generally a lower terrain and the Germans occupied territory with a higher elevation, giving them greater powers of observation.

The 321st relieved the British 147th Field Artillery Regiment near Zetten on October 3. The

Holland. T/4 Burdette Wilkinson in Nijmegen, September 1944. WILKINSON FAMILY

Brits informed the artillerymen that there was a "live and let live" understanding between them and the Jerries. The Brits wouldn't fire on the Germans if the Germans didn't shoot at the Brits. This area was relatively quiet until the 101st moved in and changed the rules dramatically.

The 321st was in direct support of the 1st and 3rd Battalions of the 506th PIR. They had 14,000 yards to cover with twelve guns, less than three miles from the main line of resistance. Forward observers spotted ferries loaded with reinforcing troops crossing the Neder Rhine to the island. The Germans were taking advantage of the lull, which was to be the last for quite some time. The 321st fired on them. According to the S-3 journal, the 75mm pack howitzers did their work "very effective[ly]." Over 2,700 rounds were fired that very first day, causing many an enemy to swim for his life. In two days, the Germans located the guns of the 321st at 0500 hours and hit back.

Information came back from the forward observers and the liaison officers at this new position. Because of limited observation due to dikes, ranging was limited to the nearest 400 yards. The forward observers didn't like those numbers and moved around, trying different observation posts. Ideally, a fire mission would fall within 100 yards of its target. Shrapnel would do the rest.

The 506th's 2nd Battalion had been badly mauled earlier, and another ferocious attack by the Germans

Holland. A knocked-out German tank. PERKINS FAMILY

was expected in the thinly manned area. Gen. Maxwell Taylor and Colonel Sink conferred at the 506th command post in a farmhouse. Adjacent to the house was a barn that housed a 321st liaison section commanded by Capt. Thomas White, including two others who sat on the floor, one of them White's radioman. The radio operator was trying to get through to the 321st FDC.

German artillery had been constantly dropping rounds in the area. One of them, from an 88, hit the barn, traveling through the wall and bouncing off the concrete floor. It ricocheted inside the barn, knocked out the radio, and, finally spent of energy, came to rest on a window ledge. The radioman was slightly wounded by flying debris, but the round was a dud.

Captain White exited the building covered completely in white concrete dust. His jeep driver, Byrnes, was outside the barn and had seen what happened. He remarked, "Captain White, you are white." The captain then went to the command post next door. General Taylor at first didn't recognize his former aide covered in concrete dust. White wiped his face, and the general exclaimed, "Jeez, Tom, you really are white!"

Sink then told White to take his team and go out as "far as he could" to set up that evening and be ready for the next morning. He would have at his disposal all available firepower, including the British artillery, to lay down a "curtain of fire." He was to call out the enemy coordinates at dawn, and that is what he did. For this action, Captain White later received the Silver Star. White recalled that in this rare instance, the planning and coordination worked perfectly, to the detriment of the Germans.

Another forward observer party led by Lt. Richard "Smitty" Smith (A Battery); his radio operator, T/5 Dwayne Wynkoop of Abingdon, Illinois; and another battalion soldier was assigned a different

Mourmelon. From left to right: Lt. James Davis, Lt. Richard Smith, Capt. Dr. David Davidson, and Capt. Thomas White.

Lt. Richard Smith, A Battery forward observer. SMITH FAMILY

T/5 Dwayne Wynkoop, A Battery. WYNKOOP FAMILY

area. They were sent north of the Waal River near Dodewaard, supporting I Company of the 506th led by Maj. Lloyd Patch. The line was long and thinly held.

The Germans attacked in force at the exact spot the party had established their observation post between the 1st and 3rd Battalions of the 506th. This sudden attack drove a wedge into the lines, causing the red-leggers to scatter. Under heavy mortar and small-arms fire, radio operator Wynkoop, all alone, put out continuous fire missions upon the enemy. The Germans advanced to within fifty yards of his position. They spotted him, forcing Wynkoop to change locations several times. Still alone, doing the work of three—spotting targets, plotting the coordinates, and radioing in fire missions—Wynkoop did not falter. That radio was the only communication link I Company had in operation. He successfully drove the German wedge back by pouring artillery fire into their ranks. By doing so, the outnumbered paratroopers were then able to restore their lines.

The forward observer party eventually reunited with Lieutenant Smith, now taking the lead. They moved their observation posts to various points along the front in order to maximize the killing firepower of the 321st howitzers. The enemy could be seen reorganizing for another assault, and Smith waited. When the Germans had gathered in sufficient numbers, Smith let loose with as many rounds as the battalion could put out.

Wynkoop received a Bronze Star for gallantry in action. Smith received a commendation.

The Germans attacked at 0600 on October 5, setting off trip flares placed by division engineers. The 3rd Battalion of the 506th was engaged first. The 321st positions were taking artillery fire for the first time since they had dug in, but suffered no casualties. Combined fires of the 506th PIR troopers and the

Col. Lloyd E. Patch, March 1955. He became the commanding officer of Headquarters, 1st Battalion, 506th, in March 1944, was promoted to major on June 9, and became the battalion's executive officer on July 31. On October 10, Patch was transferred to the 3rd Battalion of the 506th, where he took over as the commanding officer. He was promoted to lieutenant colonel in February 1945. PATCH FAMILY

321st held off the initial attack. Pvt. Wilson "Moon" Mullins of Verdunville, West Virginia, nicknamed after the comic strip character, was a member of Lieutenant Smith's A Battery forward observer team. They were under intense mortar and machine-gun fire, an attempt by the Germans to wipe out the team who had done some excellent work for the 321st. The communications wire was cut, and the walkie-talkies were not working anymore. Smith remarked that he wouldn't send a soul out into that hell of fire to fix the cut wire. Mullins simply volunteered, walking quickly toward the break and fixing it in full view of the Germans. Now it was their turn to let the enemy know they were back in the killing business. The enemy attacked two hours later at 0800, but was again repulsed. Throughout the day, while there were local withdrawals, the 506th always regained ground it had lost.

At one point on October 6, Lieutenant Smith's team was surrounded but continued to lay fire down on the enemy. He continued his work from his position, even though it was now behind the German lines. He stayed in position until the 506th brought its line back to the team.

Throughout the day, the 321st had nine forward observer teams calling in missions. From 0530 to 1350 hours, the guns of the 321st were firing almost continuously. More fire missions were sent back to the FDC than could be fired. Single batteries were given two targets to fire on.

Lt. Francis Canham, a forward observer for B Battery, was assigned to the 506th E Company and placed between two listening posts. A critical shortage of map overlay paper was noted by Lieutenant Canham. These overlays were drawings sketched on thin, transparent paper by forward observer teams and others showing coordinates and their positions in relation to landmarks and enemy strongpoints or targets.

At 1530 hours, the German onslaught stopped. A British infantry battalion was preparing for a counterattack, along with the 101st Engineers who would fight as infantry. A seldom-formulated fire mission by the 321st FDC was a rolling barrage. For forty-five minutes, this well-orchestrated, mathematically-advancing shoot tore through the enemy's lines, placing 1,200 rounds within their ranks. General Taylor phoned in his congratulations to the FDC of the 321st, saying it was the greatest shoot he had ever seen. When the numbers were tabulated, ammunition Sgt. Harold Dittmer dutifully logged in his book that 2,249 rounds were fired that day.

T/4 Wilkinson (HQ) wrote that between the counterbattery fire and the tremendous amount of outgoing rounds firing, burnt gunpowder permeated the air. It burned the nostrils of the cannoneers so they had to breathe through their mouths. Grit then formed on their teeth and throats. It gave the crews headaches and bellyaches as they fired continuously around the clock.

Holland. From left to right: PFC Harry Sinkutch, Pvt. Roy Davis, Sgt. Harold Dittmer, Sgt. Nugent, and Pvt. Samuel Lingenfelter.
DITTMER/DETTORE

Artillery was a determining factor in holding the lines amid the losses the Germans inflicted on the 506th. According to POW reports, nearly an entire regiment was wiped out. By 1700 hours, the battalion had only 100 rounds left, but the Germans didn't attack again that day. Many men of the battalion felt that October 6 was the very worst day of the war for them—ammunition nearly expended, short on sleep, and facing the dual threats of being overrun and counterbattery fire. Many of those interviewed stated that Bastogne was tame compared to the battle for Ophuseden.

The Germans had begun their counterbattery fire at 0500 hours, and it continued unabated until 1330 that afternoon. Wire sections were kept busy laying their much-needed communications wire up to forward observers. They had put down over 100 miles of the wire since the invasion of Holland, crawling over the Dutch countryside, much to the delight of the enemy observers.

The paratroopers withdrew from Ophuseden under the cover of darkness. By the end of the day, the 321st had put over 1,800 rounds of mostly M54s on the heads of the enemy, causing a casualty rate of more than 50 percent to elements of the German 363rd Volksgrenadier Division regiment. During the night, the enemy ferried over a fresh regiment. The 957th, 958th, and the 959th were all to have the same mission: to push the Americans southeast off the island. These Volksgrenadiers fared no better than the previous regiments. Committed piecemeal into a meat grinder, the Germans would not win the battle of Ophuseden.

The 321st also took casualties. In addition, an enlisted man from a wire section was seriously wounded and evacuated, and three others were

Holland. From left to right: PFC John Alicandro, PFC Anthony Stempien, PFC Albert Lelonek, and PFC Edward Rymarczyk. The DR-4 reels contain heavy wire, which was not used at the battery or battalion level. Lighter wire such as W-110 or W-130 was more commonly used by wiremen. LELONEK/DETTORE

Holland. Soldiers of the 321st with Dutch locals. STEARNS FAMILY

Holland. PFC Franklin E. Stearns (left) and unidentified soldiers of the B Battery wire crew.

wounded when their vehicle was damaged by German shellfire. Another trooper from the liaison section was wounded and his jeep damaged. A total of two jeeps were damaged, but within two hours both were repaired.

British tanks were on the road in Opheusden, and German tanks were waiting for them. Lt. Eugene Brooks (A Battery) was with his forward observer team, walking alongside some of the British tanks as they were moving down the road. The tanks stopped, but Brooks kept walking. He came to a building and noticed the barrel of a tank protruding through an opening in the wall. He went back to the British tanker; its commander was standing in the open hatch. Brooks pointed to the building just ahead, saying that a German tank was hidden inside and that the tank should fire a round into it. The tank commander didn't believe him, but Brooks insisted it was there and that he better shoot at it quickly. Upset that he was being told to fire on something he

Holland. A knocked-out German tank. LINZ FAMILY

believed wasn't there, the commander said, "I can't see the bloody bugger!" As Brooks started to walk away in disgust, a single round was fired from the German tank and hit the Sherman. The British tank caught fire and the crew bailed out.

Sgt. Earl Patchin had made his way to the 506th regimental command post outside of Opheusden, located in an apple orchard on a dairy farm. The liaison team was operating a forward switchboard set up in a nearby barn. They would receive fire commands from Patchin and T/5 Lawrence Wilkinson (HQ), who in turn forwarded the fire mission coordinates back to the 321st Battalion. Capt. Tom White was in charge of the forward observation party.

Patchin exited the barn with Captain White at his side early in the morning. Suddenly a German artillery barrage landed in the immediate area. One of the rounds exploded 6 feet in front of him, sending the sergeant 15 feet into the air. White was unscathed. The medics rushed to Patchin, providing first aid. His body was wrapped from his head down to the tops of his jump boots when they were finished. A Catholic chaplain tried to cheer him up by saying he would be home for Christmas. Patchin said later, "He was right, except it would take another fourteen months before it happened."

Doctors at the field hospital removed the large pieces of shrapnel from his face, arms, and leg. He was then shipped to England and arrived at the 61st General Hospital. Then he was sent to another hospital and placed on limited service to Tidworth near Salisbury. He ended up processing wounded air force personnel into the infantry because of the German breakthrough at Bastogne, Belgium. Patchin remembered them as being very unhappy soldiers.

The next transfer was to Namur, Belgium, to process high pointers back to the States. His records caught up with him here, so a formal presentation of the Bronze Star occurred, complete with a parade just for him. The commanding officer told Patchin, "It was a pleasure to award an earned one."

Two months later, he was sent home by a troopship for a November voyage across the Atlantic—a fifteen-day trip filled with seasickness. At one point, a wave rolled the ship 45 degrees, according to the ship's indicator. A crewman told him that at 47 degrees the ship would capsize.

Sailing into New York, the sight of the old lady, the Statue of Liberty, came into view. As the ship pulled into the docking area, a band was playing, which brought many of the men to tears. It was the happiest day of Patchin's life.

Sgt. Donald Roy of A Battery was just trying to take a break. Most of the time he was the leader of a forward observer team and rarely had an officer in charge. Under ideal circumstances, there were supposed to be an officer in charge, a sergeant, and an enlisted man. No matter—Sergeant Roy was quite comfortable to be on his own. He had been doing forward observer work since Normandy and had honed the skills needed in combat.

He was assigned to the 506th's 1st Battalion, which was pulled from the line the evening of October 6 and had arrived at an orchard to rest at dark. They dug in, feeling better that they were now behind their own lines just west of Hemmen.

Early in the morning of October 7, Roy decided to get out of his foxhole and stretch. He leisurely lay down on his side, his left hand propping his head up with his elbow on the ground. It was something he would never have done in combat. He daydreamed there for a moment until a shot rang out.

A German sniper apparently had been watching Roy and fired once, hoping for a head shot. Instead, the round hit Roy's helmet on the side and went into his left hand and out the back of the steel pot. The projectile continued on to the rear, striking a paratrooper nearby. Shouts of, "Medic! Medic!" could be heard. The shot signaled the start of the battle.

The Germans started to lob mortar rounds into the area, but their aim was so far off that the potentially lethal rounds fell harmlessly behind the Americans. Roy, although wounded, was bemused by their inability. He would see for himself the reasons for it at battle's end.

Roy got on a radio and called in a fire mission, giving the 321st FDC the map coordinates. He was refused; according to their overlay maps, that area was in friendly territory. Agitated, Roy explained German infantry was firing on them and said he could easily lay down artillery fire in their midst. No matter: artillery fire in that sector was forbidden by DivArty. Frustrated that he could do nothing to the targets that were extremely vulnerable to an artillery barrage, he could only watch the fight unfold. (Roy was refused artillery support on one other occasion, while he was in Holland, for the same reason. He later said he could only be effective if the battalion he was supporting had a knowledgeable officer leading it, one with a working sense of how to implement artillery support in his tactics.)

With Roy was a favorite radio operator, PFC Dwayne Wynkoop, who had a unique skill. The radioman could finesse the battery life out of a radio set like no other. Without radio communication, a forward observer team was practically useless.

Without hesitation, the paratroopers with Roy jumped up and formed into two groups. The Germans were in a wooded area that was supposed to be free of the enemy. At the time, it was believed that the Germans had followed the troopers during the night march, keeping out of contact until they could mount a surprise attack.

"At daybreak, all hell broke loose again. We were supposedly in back of our own lines but not 200 yards away must have been 400 Germans," recalled Sgt. Don Brininstool. "I heard a grenade explode. I jumped up, grabbed a machine gun and ran into a ditch and put the gun in action along with a couple other machine guns. Within minutes all you could see was white flags. The Germans said they had fought the men of the 101st before and didn't want any more of us. They also said they had heard us come in just before daybreak and thought we were their prisoners."[11]

When the battle started, Pvt. Robert Doyle of the A Battery forward observer team jumped up to be part of the infantry's assault. Doyle had a reputation as a soldier who tended to be in the action. It wasn't long before a group of German soldiers was being marched away with their hands up, now prisoners of the 506th. Roy watched them go and guessed there had to be at least 150; what struck him was that they were so young and apparently without combat experience.

Roy received medical attention at an aid station, then returned shortly to his team, refusing any stay at a hospital. He reasoned that forward observer teams routinely worked four to five days on, then had the same number of days off; he would use that off time to heal.

Holland. The first group of prisoners captured after a fight behind American lines near Opheusden. When the battle first started, the Germans thought they were very generous in offering to let the Americans surrender. NUGENT/DETTORE

Holland. A second group of German prisoners passes the gate to the orchard, which the 506th had entered at 4 A.M. after leaving Opheusden. The 506th troopers' only wish was for a long uninterrupted sleep, which lasted only one hour because of the Germans. Some of them were in the buildings. Here, the lieutenant is telling the POWs to get their hands up higher. NUGENT/DETTORE

Holland. The third and last group of prisoners is searched out in the field. The road is to the right and the orchard is in the background. NUGENT/DETTORE

Roy received his commission to second lieutenant in November 1944 and was transferred to the 326th Combat Engineers, but spent most of his time pressed into service as infantry.

Ammunition sergeant Harold Dittmer (HQ) needed transportation to convey the 75mm pack howitzer ammunition to the gun batteries. The Brits were in charge of the ammo dumps as long as they were under their control. There was always a shortage of jeeps and 6x6 trucks to pick up the shells. First he tried headquarters, then the motor pool, and lastly the firing batteries for the vehicles. It would most likely come down to a single jeep pulling three trailers. The trailers were always available; he could pack about fifty rounds per trailer. Pulling them was not a problem, but backing them up in an emergency was next to impossible. Nevertheless, in Holland, this was the procedure.

The town of Opheusden was now void of Allied troops since the withdrawal of the 506th 1st Battalion the day before due to heavy casualties and the fallback of its 3rd Battalion to consolidate its lines. At 0735 hours on October 7, British Typhoons swooped from the skies and started to unleash their rockets on German armor and infantry positions in and around the town.

Holland. A 321st ammo dump. LINZ FAMILY

Fire missions for the 321st started early, just a few minutes after midnight. A battalion forward observer spotted a ferry crossing the Neder Rhine loaded with enemy troops. Eighteen rounds alone were fired on this target, with good results.

At 0110 hours, the Germans launched an attack on the 506th and broke through their lines, coming within 1,000 yards of the 321st gun pits. The artillerymen were alerted that they may have to withdraw. Captured Russian 152mm guns were used against the firing 321st batteries with airburst to cull out the red-leggers. The artillerymen became infantrymen, grabbing bazookas and rifles. This was now the front line. Shell fragments bounced off the trails of the 75mm pack howitzers. It was confirmed that three German regiments of the 363rd Volksgrenadier Division were committed to this battle: the 957th, 958th, and 959th.

With a vengeance, the 321st responded. Nearly 2,700 rounds were fired into the German lines, targeting mortars, personnel, tanks, and observation posts. Effective fire was laid down less than 100 yards in front of the attacking 506th paratroopers as they pressed forward their assault, causing the enemy to fall back.

The Germans started to surrender to the 3rd Battalion but stopped when the rounds of the 321st started to thin out their ranks. A request was made to stop the fire in order to entice others to give up the fight. The firing stopped, and nearly ninety Germans came forward.

Most of the troopers knew that the rounds of the 75mms didn't have the velocity to punch a hole in the superior German armor. But knowing that didn't stop them from trying to knock out tanks anyway. The only hope was to hit a bogey wheel on an enemy tank to disable a track, rendering it unmaneuverable. A direct hit on armor manned by an inexperienced crew could also cause them to abandon the vehicle. The sound of the hit would be deafening for

Holland. Nugent in his covered slit trench a mile from the German border during the early part of the Holland trip. Cpl. Carl Espling is on the right. The trench was covered with pine branches and logs, 3.5 feet wide by 3.5 feet deep and 8 feet long, and had a sump hole in the corner and a sleeping bag. The raincoat covered the end of the trench to keep out the rain and cold. After three full hours of work to build the trench, he only used it one night. NUGENT/DETTORE

the crew, creating a psychological atmosphere of defeat or doubt that they would survive another direct hit. Two days before, it was reported that two German tanks were put out of commission by 321st howitzers.

The battalion did fire twenty rounds of high-explosive antitank (HEAT) ammunition. The Germans regrouped. A counterattack was expected by the 101st soldiers, a common tactic employed by the Wehrmacht. It began at 1850 hours, and by 1936 hours the fierce attack was broken by the deadly accurate fires of the 321st.

One hour later, as evening approached, startling POW reports began to come in to the S-2 section of the 321st. Capt. Joe Perkins learned that artillery fire was responsible for cutting down the enemy companies, leaving them with only sixty to eighty soldiers. Those left were shaking, crying, and totally useless as infantrymen. Most were fresh out of Germany; some had walked 90 miles and were sent directly into battle.

A captured German major who commanded the 958th Infantry Regiment of the 363rd Volksgrenadier Division stated flatly, "There are only three groups left in my battalion—those you have here [prisoners], those who are wounded, and those who are dead." His orders were to sweep the enemy back to the Nijmegen bridgehead, according to the maps found on his person.

Cpl. Vernon Raker (A Battery) manned the third gun. He recalled a conversation he had with forward observer Lt. Richard Smith soon after returning from their observation post. While they were sitting around their gun, Lieutenant Smith came by and joined them. "I really respected this man—he was absolutely fearless and treated us very well," Raker said. Smith told them matter of factly what had just occurred near his observation post. The timed-fire rounds were tearing up the Krauts, and in a short time the field was littered with them. He noticed two Germans come onto the field. One had a piece of white cloth on a stick, and the other was an officer.

Nijmegan, Holland. A Battery howitzer being loaded for a fire mission. LINZ FAMILY

All firing stopped as both groups met in an open field. Smith said the German carrying the flag did the talking, and the officer spoke through him. The German officer wanted a truce so that his wounded could be tended to and carried off the field. Raker asked Smith what he said. "I just glared at them and didn't say a damn word," Smith replied. The Krauts then turned around and went back, and so did Smith. Shortly after that the Kraut medics and stretcher-bearers came out to their wounded and started to work on them. Smith waited a little bit, then let them have it and "just got about all of them with time percussion fire."

Raker, stunned by such a brutal tactic, said, "Lieutenant Smith. I can't believe you could do such a thing—they called for a truce."

Smith, showing no emotion, told him that he hadn't agreed to anything. "War *is* hell," he said as he walked away.

During the heat of battle, one of the brass shell casings had wedged itself into an A Battery gun breech. The barrel (tube) became overheated due to the rapid firing of rounds. The crew had to forcibly knock out the casing with a rod, then wait for a time to start firing again.

Sgt. Gerald Shade of A Battery ordered PFC Lloyd Tomblin from his section to pour a bucket of water down the tube, noticing it was turning red from continuous firing. The gun's seasoned crew tried to stop him, but it was too late. The sudden cooldown caused it to crack, rendering it out of service. It was an embarrassment for the entire gun section to make such a rookie mistake, and a learning experience for the sergeant. Ordnance was notified for a tube replacement. The rest of A Battery continued to fire, launching 1,200 rounds in thirty minutes.

For a few days early in October, the 101st foothold in Holland was in danger, although the troopers themselves would not agree with that assessment. The report "Tactical Operation of the 321st," submitted to the commanding general of the 101st and dated November 17, 1944, reads in part: "D+21—Oct. 8, '44—Battalion fired in support of 327th Glider Infantry which relieved some of the 506th Prcht. Infantry on Opheusden front. Mortar and infantry targets were fired throughout the day. Harassing fires fired during the night. Battalion reverted back from the 327th to 506th in support of Neder Rijn sector."

The battalion fired 1,136 rounds by the end of the day on October 8. The forward observers of the battalion were hindered by fog in locating their targets. This also caused the Germans not to attack at first light as they did on previous days. The enemy didn't know that the battalion had shot nearly all the ammo available. The supply dump for the 75mm pack howitzer ammunition was nearly exhausted. One more German assault would cause the guns to go silent. Luckily, the Germans didn't try.

Forward observer 1st Sgt. James Dundon (A Battery) along with his team, had a clear view of Opheusden and was told the Germans might blow up a dike to flood the entire area. He was told to take an extra case of rations. Further instructions were troubling: if the Germans did blow the dikes, he would have an entire corps of artillery to fire on the town. He was warned that their observation post, a bar with a pool table near a picture window, was being watched by German snipers. The sniper waited for an unsuspecting soldier to pick up a cue stick and lean over the table, and then he fired. During their stay, a motorcycle also drove by and fired shots into the building but missed the team and escaped.

Ammunition for the 75mm pack howitzers needed to be replenished, so Cpl. Woodrow Stephens (HQ) jumped into his 6x6 GMC truck to complete the task. As he was returning to the battalion with a truckload of ammunition, he drove near the Nijmegen Bridge, not far from the emplaced guns. He spotted a lone German artillery round in the air and dropping fast, directly in front of him. The round hit the road just under the front bumper and exploded. It knocked out the oil pan, flattened eight of the nine tires on the truck, and blew up the gas tank. Stephens jumped out as the burst ripped through the floorboards and pushed the seats together into one jumbled mess. His M43 jacket and shirt were torn to shreds from his armpits down. When he got back to the battery, he was told to strip naked to see if he was hit somewhere, but he was not. During the course of the war, Stephens was known as the luckiest man in his battery: he would have three 6x6 trucks shot from under him without suffering a scratch.

In the late afternoon of October 8, the battalion forward observers registered the 75mm pack howitzers of the 377th PFA Battalion near Zetten. The guns of the 321st were close to theirs in a field nearby. Up to this point, the battalion had expended 11,208 rounds of 75mm ammunition during the Holland campaign.

Lt. Tony Linz was relaxing at an orchard close to the guns in the morning hours of October 9. As the A Battery executive officer, this didn't happen often. He had stripped to the waist, shaving and sunning himself at the same time. He barely noticed a group of men from the 377th standing under some trees across the field outside their C Battery command post.[12] The Germans must have noticed; they fired one round, scoring a direct hit. Linz instinctively crouched down. He could see body parts everywhere. It was mayhem, with everybody running in all directions and the unit finally leaving the area. He thought to himself they lacked an immediate transfer of control. Lt. John Sluzevich and S/Sgt. Peter Lutz were killed instantly. PFC Lawrence Davis was severely wounded and died the next day. They were all from C Battery. A number of others were wounded.

October 13 was another full day of fire missions and forward observer teams doing their work. The battalion fired 371 rounds, not including 10 rounds of smoke. At 1730 hours, Lieutenant Smith (A Battery) observed the enemy sending light signals in an effort to communicate. To disrupt this, he called for a fire mission using smoke rounds, thereby ending all possible signaling in this manner.

Holland. Cpl. Steve "Big" Stephens (left), a Headquarters Battery truck driver, and PFC Harry Sinkutch. SINKUTCH/DETTORE

Holland. A B Battery soldier with newly "acquired" headgear.

At approximately 2140 hours, Sgt. Leslie Sellers, from Silver Lake, Indiana, of the B Battery Detail Section reported to Lt. William Nugent (HQ) from Saugerties, New York, that two rounds of friendly fire fell short at coordinates 585751. Those rounds were thought to be slightly larger than 75mms.

On October 14, DivArty requested counterbattery fire from the battalion at the first light of dawn. At 1605 hours, the British requested volley after volley at or near those same coordinates. Another request was made by the Brits at 1845 hours. Liaison officer to the 327th GIR, Lt. Arthur Freeman from Geary, Oklahoma, called for fire missions in support of the Brits. Those requests came to the 327th GIR, then were relayed back to 321st. Another two volleys were by B Battery. Many of these rounds were an effort to silence the German artillery. "Despite the losses which they had already taken around Opheusden, the Germans were determined to break through, and from October 7th to the 14th, there were scarcely six hours when the 363rd [Volksgrenadier] Division did not launch some type of attack against the 327th."[13]

The final entry of the 321st S-2 journal for October 14 reads: "2025 Enemy attack accomplished nothing. Lost 3 or 4 tanks." The 321st expended 620 total rounds. This figure would turn out to be approximately 100 rounds over the average fired during each day of the Holland campaign.

The German 363rd Volksgrenadier Division tried different sectors and finally bled itself dry in its last assault on October 15. By then, the largest battle on the island had already been fought and lost by the enemy. The battalion had fired over 8,500 rounds of ammunition, and approximately 140 fire missions to date were completed. The artillerymen of the battalion later boasted that during the Holland campaign, not a single round fell short on its own men. When the infantry was given a choice, the 101st artillery was requested. It was believed that the British artillery had more of an interest in getting the rounds "out there" rather than on the coordinates called in.

Holland. Lt. William Nugent (front passenger seat) with his liaison section: jeep driver PFC Miller, Cpl. Carl Espling (left rear), and PFC Rudolph Falcon (right rear), who was killed in action October 7 near Zetten. NUGENT/DETTORE

The 321st excelled, both in its forward observers and its gunners, and was a favorite of Colonel Sink, the 506th commander.

Capt. Joe Perkins had an opportunity to visit the fields that the 363rd Volksgrenadier Division had attempted to cross just a short time earlier. It was a sight he would never forget. Bits of German uniforms and body parts dangled from tree branches throughout the area. Perkins recognized someone's intestines draped over a tree limb like fresh sausages—the work of artillery.

Lieutenant Smith and his team's performance was highly regarded by the paratroopers who worked with them. A letter of commendation was entered into Smith's file, originating in the 506th and signed by its commanding officer. (Colonel Carmichael of the 321st did not believe in rewarding those who exhibited extraordinary bravery on the battlefield, a fact known not only inside the battalion but outside as well.) Dated October 14, 1944, the commendation reads in part:

4th of October, to the 8th of October, 1944, Lt. Smith did perform his duties as forward artillery observer in such a manner as to set an example for all soldiers of his branch to follow. He did, during a determined enemy attack against Company "I" Kidnap Blue Prcht. Infantry's position, move his observation post to have complete observation on the enemy to our front at all times. He did cause to bring down numerous and great concentrations of friendly artillery fire upon large enemy troop concentrations which were deploying for an assault upon our position. Through his constant and untiring efforts during this period, he undoubtedly succeeded in breaking up the enemy's attack and created casualties among the enemy numbering in the hundreds. Furthermore, it is commonly believed by every man in this command that Lt. Smith's action against this superior enemy saved Company Item, Kidnap, from annihilation.

This commendation was written by 1st Lt. James Nye, executive officer of the 506th, and endorsed by Maj. Lloyd Patch, Colonel Sink, and Generals Taylor and McAuliffe.

There were two ways to transmit fire missions: by wire or by battery-powered radios. Wire was run from the FDC to the forward switchboard near a regimental headquarters. It could be then be strung out to the forward observers, who were assigned to the rifle companies. In combat, the wire was always left behind after a move. While in training, it was respooled for another day.

Wiremen were a different sort: they did dangerous duty all the time while out in the field, laying wire under German observation most of the time, many spools of it through miles of fields and over roads. If the line went dead, it had to be repaired no matter what was going on around them. Without it, communications could be compromised because radio transmissions put out over the airwaves could be intercepted by the enemy. Without wire, radios used precious batteries that were heavy and cumbersome and would have to be replaced. The forward observers and the firing batteries depended on them. The paratroopers were glad to see the wiremen and their wire because it was a sign that supporting artillery fire was on its way.

Wiremen spent much time at the front or going to it. Depending on the circumstances, it was either by jeep or more likely on foot. These men spent a lot of time with the paratroopers on the front lines and became friendly with them.

While completing their job of running wire to a forward observer's observation post in mid-October, PFC Albert Lelonek (A Battery) from Detroit, Michigan, noticed some 506th troopers butchering a cow. Another trooper became envious and was told

Holland. Standing (from left to right): Cpl. Vernon Raker, PFC Bernard Katz, and PFC Adolf D'Arcangelo. Reclining: Unknown soldier and Pvt. Normagene Holt with some Kraut ammo they found in the woods. RAKER FAMILY

by the officer that the Germans had shelled a farmer's field, killing the animal. It was forbidden to kill Dutch livestock, but not everyone respected that order. Adjacent to them was a field of grazing cows untouched by shellfire. The trooper opened the gates and moved the cattle into the field that was zeroed in by the Germans. It didn't take long for the enemy to drop in fire in that field, and now fresh meat was available for the paratroopers and their friends, the wiremen.

Journaling by the soldiers was a forbidden activity. Because of this, very few kept a written record of their daily lives in the service. Of those who did, only a few are known to still exist. The complete diary of Pvt. John P. Muscia (HQ Battery) from Auburn, New York, follows. Muscia's primary duty was that of a runner, carrying messages from the 321st headquarters to firing batteries and to the command posts of the supported infantry regiments in the 101st. He wrote twenty-nine entries.

Holland. PFC Frank Turano (left) and PFC Louis Kovacic of A Battery. H. C. WARREN FAMILY

Cpl. John Christener (HQ Motor Pool) was promoted to sergeant, taking over the job of his former boss, Sgt. Maxie Slayton of Indianapolis, Indiana, who was busted for drinking. The new motor sergeant did more than just supervise the men; he was a grease monkey (slang for mechanic) like the rest of them. Keeping the jeeps and trucks running for headquarters was a full-time job. The need to replace jeep wheel bearings was a common problem. At one time, five jeeps were out of commission because of the lack of spare parts; all of them needed fan belts. Yankee ingenuity came into play, and they were delivered by an air drop. ■

> Holland, Oct. 15—Nothing doing today. Our guns [75mm pack howitzers] stopped a Jerry counter-attack last night. Today the Jerries said they would use their secret weapon against us; nothing seen of it as yet.
>
> Oct. 17—Still in same position in Zetten which is between Nijmegan [*sic*] and Arnhem. A few Jerry shells came over during chow. Had steak for supper; it was tough. Nothing said of us being relieved yet. Jerries shelling Nijmegan at random and also the Nijmegan Bridge. The Jerries are fairly quiet here. Hear an occasional burst from Jerries machine guns or ours. . . . Not much messages to deliver. Am thankful the Jerries haven't used gas up to date. We were told to throw away our masks two weeks after we landed in Holland. It is very windy. Water is dripping in foxhole.
>
> Oct. 19—It rained intermittently during the day. Our foxhole (Pvt. Traskiewicz and I) is

caving in by the weight of the rain soaked dirt. A couple of airbursts landed closed to "A" Battery. Mud is three inches deep everywhere.

Oct. 20—Nothing happened today. Very dull.

Oct. 21—Got a chance to see a movie today, "Bathing Beauty" was on. It was very good. We got shelled by "screaming meemies" (rocket shells) while seeing movie—no one ran out.

Oct. 22—Fairly quiet.

Oct. 23—Four glider pilots and 130 others of our men were brought back from behind the enemy lines by 2 platoons of 506th Regt. Inf. They were held by the Dutch underground people. Jerries knew something was up. They immediately sent into our positions 2 salvos of rocket shells and many artillery shells. Two of them landed within 15 yards of my foxhole. Rocket shelling is unusually terrifying as the shells while in flight omit an unusually high piercing, screeching sound; the rocket shells are very big. One of the other outfit's command post was hit by a rocket shell and one man was killed and one injured. Our guns fired at the rocket pens and were supposedly knocked out. I doubt it myself.

Oct. 24—Am sending Sadie a German helmet. Made one run to Division Artillery today. A rumor is going around that we are going to be relieved, I hope.

Oct. 25—Had an interesting day today. I walked up to the front lines with Partin (medic) and Nelson (machine gun) and picked

Veghel, Holland. From left to right: Personnel Sgt. Hubert Jauquet, Supply Sgt. Charles Nugent, and colonel's orderly PFC Clarence Simmons at the headquarters area in September 1944, inspecting the results of the nightly "screaming meemies" attack.
PERKINS FAMILY

While in Holland (the exact location is uncertain), forward observer Lt. Eugene Brooks and his party were at the front with a battalion from the 101st Division. They stayed with the infantry for nearly three weeks, working hand in hand with a lieutenant who was most likely from the 502nd or 506th PIR. "If they wanted something done, I did it," Brooks said. The infantry suffered many casualties, but the lieutenant knew how to take advantage of the artillery at his disposal.

An enemy push was occurring, and the infantry lieutenant was ordered to hold. He confided to Brooks that he wasn't able to do so. "You take care of the short ones," Brooks told him. "I will take care of the long ones. . . . Let your HQs know that they will find us here in the morning, one way or another." His advice was taken, and the line held. The lieutenant was later promoted.

On the way back home to the States, the two officers were on the same ship. Brooks was now outranked by the former lieutenant, who came up and reminded him of the advice he had given in Holland, adding simply, "I thank you for that." ■

up souvenirs. A German belt, a bayonet, a Burp gun (hand machine gun) (I gave this to Sgt. Wiggins) and a canteen and cup. I saw some dead Jerries who were gruesomely bloated laying near a ruined home. I had to watch out for mines and booby traps which infest the area.

Oct. 26—Walked to the edge of booby trapped town and picked up a couple of belt buckles and a bayonet from dead German soldiers. 8PM Jerry shelling us. Have had shorts of English Arty land close to us and I always get out my prayer book when the Germans start shelling us.

Oct. 27—Quiet day today. We are going to move positions near to the 907th Glider Field Arty. Battalion.

Oct. 28—We are in our new position now. I dug a foxhole immediately upon arrival and got [shelled] an hour upon arriving. Sgt. Benninghoff jumped into my foxhole before I did and I jumped in on top of him. Cpl. Diso also tried to get in but only his head and shoulders fit as I dug a shallow slit trench. I was the only one in Headquarters Battery that had a slit trench dug. There were some abandoned English foxholes near which some of the boys used, they got all wet as there was about 2 feet of water in the bottom of the holes.

Oct. 30—Weather is getting very cold. Expect snow any day now.

Nov. 4—I was under another German shelling while at the 907th Glider Field Artillery Headquarters. A British soldier nearby was hurt and we brought him to a first aid station in our jeep.

Nov. 5—I went to the 907th Field Artillery Command Post again today to deliver messages and was under direct enemy observation, they must have seen me coming.

Nov. 8—I read a memorandum which I got at 101st Airborne Division HQ which stated that [we] were going to be relieved Nov. 10th.

Nov. 10—Sgt. Tesiams [possibly a paratrooper], Sgt. Orville Boggs [Headquarters, Baltimore, Maryland], Pvt. Roy Cale [Headquarters, Cleveland, Ohio] and Cpl. Eugene Wagner [Headquarters, Rochester, New York] got drunk on cognac and decided to go on patrol into the German lines. Sgt. Boggs gave me a few personal belongings to be sent to his fiancée in case he got killed. They started out and only got as far as the door of the barn we were staying in and came back. It's a good thing the Colonel didn't get wind of it or there would have been a lot of demotions.

Nov. 11—The Jerries shelled us again early in the morning. They landed close by, but no one got hurt.

Nov. 12—The Germans shelled us all day with heavy railroad guns. One of our boys [Pvt. Stanley Woods] was on guard in front of our Battalion Command post and a large shell landed 10 yards in front of him in a ditch. It blew out a hole as large as a truck but the concussion went up into the air. The soldier went to pieces and had to be sent to a hospital.

Nov. 13—We are still getting shelled. The Division Headquarters warned us to be ready to move out in 15 minutes in case the Germans blow up the dikes nearby and try to flood us out. I'm shell happy now. At night when I hear some of the guys snoring and wheezing in their sleep I think it is a shell coming in, as they sound similar to a certain extent. I feel like I'm going to break down myself if this shelling keeps up. I just sit around and sweat it out whenever we get shelled. 2100 hours the mail shed caught on fire and someone yelled "the Germans are coming." Boy was I scared. We all grabbed our carbines and rushed out expecting the worse. Clarence Simmons couldn't find his gun and ran out with his jackknife. It took us an hour to put the fire out. I'll never forget this night.

Nov. 14—No shelling today, thank the lord. Some Canadians troops moved in. I believe we are going to move out soon.

Nov. 15—The Germans shelled us again last night. Eleven out of seventeen of the shells were duds. One of "A" Battery's G.M.C. trucks

Southeast Opheusden, Holland. The 321st Headquarters' destroyed jeep with radio being inspected on October 6 by a 327th Headquarters gliderman, possibly in the vicinity of where Maj. Oliver Horton was killed. Note the numerous bullet holes at the left rear, including in the gas can. Private Falcon, Headquarters Liaison Section jeep driver, was killed in action on October 7 in this area, but it's unclear if this was his vehicle.

was hit and burned. Another shell went under a pile of ammunition of ours but didn't explode. If it had many of us would have been killed. The 506th Inf. Regt. Command post caught on fire and ammunition was popping off left and right. The English started a big drive 15 miles South East of Eindoven [*sic*]. The sound of shelling was awful, I couldn't sleep all night.

Nov. 16—We still haven't been relieved. We have been in combat 58 days so far without being relieved. The record of all wars is 63 days so we might beat that record yet. We got shelled again last night. The Germans are throwing time fire at us now which explodes in the air. I'm really worried now. I hope they don't (a couple just went off) shell us much more tonight, but I'm sure they will. I know I won't sleep tonight.

Nov. 17—The Germans are shelling us with delayed action shells again. When they go off in the ground the buildings shake. A few just landed.

Nov. 18—Jerry shelling came close this morning. I'm getting jumpy. We have been in combat 60 days so far.

Nov. 19—I went to Nijmegan today for 1 day's rest. I saw a couple of movies and took my second shower in two months. The Waal River is rising every day on account of the incessant rain. The water is up to the tops of the dikes. There is a rumor going around that we are going to be in combat for 101 days. God, I hope not. 2100 more delayed action shells just landed quite close.

Nov. 20—Hoffman [stayed] in Zettan [*sic*] all night with a girl. I was worried about [him] as the town is getting shelled always very bad. Patterson and Purvy [*sic*, Pervey] Robinson were killed when they went into Nijmegan for 1 day's rest. A German shell killed them. It just started to rain out very hard. The Waal River will surely overflow if this keeps up.

Nov. 21—A rumor is going around that we are going to be relieved on the 23rd. I hope so.

Nov. 24—Praise the lord. We are leaving for Reims, France tomorrow. We are being relieved by Canadian troops. Our Div. Arty moved positions because of the heavy German shellings. We are already sweating out another mission into Germany.

Dec. 3—When we moved from Holland the Germans blew up the dikes near our sections and flooded the surrounding area. Patrols were made from small boats by the Canadians.

The 321st S-2 journal entry for October 23 reads "0211 Lt. Canham and Brooks mission very satisfactory, returned with 138 British Airborne troops from enemy territory between Wageningen and Rinkum [*sic*, Renkum]." The entry fails to mention, most likely unintentionally, that six troopers of the 321st also crossed the Neder Rhine that night and participated in the rescue mission.

Colonel Sink of the 506th PIR called Lt. Gene Brooks (A Battery) and Lt. Francis Canham (B Battery) to his command post and was met by another 101st officer and a British officer named Colonel Dobey. The first question Sink asked Brooks was, "Can you swim?" Brooks replied, "Yes, sure I can swim. Why do you ask me that?" Sink told him, "Never mind that. Get a jeep." Capt. John Fuller, A Battery commander, of Cedar Falls, Iowa, told Brooks to grab his forward observer team and head up to division headquarters. When asked by his team what was happening, Brooks remained tight-lipped about the swimming bit and said, "I don't know what the hell is going on." Everyone was restricted to headquarters until the mission.

For the next hour, Colonel Dobey laid out the plan of rescue for the last remnants of the British 6th Airborne Division, which had evaded capture at Arnhem and were being hidden by various Dutch civilians. Among the few Americans in this group were downed fliers.

It was learned that Capt. Joe Perkins, S-2 of the 321st, was in charge of the artillery that might be needed in the extraction of the men. His job was to organize the firing batteries to provide a "box" of iron around the escaping soldiers if called for. The idea was that the Germans would not know what was happening until it was too late and the men were running down the corridor of falling friendly shells to the waiting boats. Approximately 100 guns were sighted on this small strip of enemy territory,

A Battery forward observer radio mounted on an M3A4 handcart for maneuvers in Tennessee on June 8, 1943.
U.S. ARMY SIGNAL CORPS

waiting for the code phrase, "Oh Susannah," from Captain Perkins to let loose.

The fourteen British assault boats, constructed from wood and fabric, left the banks of the Neder Rhine with 506th troopers and two 321st forward observer teams. Captain Fuller met Brooks on the riverbank to give last-minute instructions. One team was from A Battery and consisted of Lt. Brooks, radio operator Pvt. Bob Doyle, and Pvt. Don Falls. It was 1:00 A.M. Lieutenant Canham (B Battery) was assisted by Cpl. Paul Galant and Cpl. Elbert Douglas from Jellico, Tennessee. The teams were to maintain radio silence unless it was necessary to call in the fire mission.

It was a dark night, perfect for such a plan. The boats embarked to the relative safety of an orchard on the south side of the Neder Rhine in enemy-held territory. In minutes, everyone was across and the 101st troopers took their positions.

It was time to lay wire across a canal for a forward observer party of B Battery. PFC Hugh Worthy had been doing this job since Normandy; in Holland, it was mostly done at night.

He had made it up to a dike with his cart of wire spools in complete darkness when suddenly a huge thundering mass came running down the path at the top and knocked him down. He rolled down one side of the dike, and the cart rolled down the other into the river and disappeared. He later said he heard the animal, which may have been a horse, but never really saw it. The collision knocked him senseless. His mission was not completed.

The radio-equipped 321st parties fanned out, taking their positions as far as they would venture into German-occupied area, about 200 yards in. The gap between them was less than 600 yards.

In less than an hour, with the help of the Dutch Underground and 506th troopers, the 138 men were on their way back to friendly shores. All of this was done as quietly as possible. Lieutenant Brooks could hear the men being gathered but could not see them or the 321st observer across from him.

Back at the 321st FDC, Capt. Joe Perkins was on edge. He was 4,000–5,000 yards away from the river-crossing point. He had plenty of artillery training as a liaison officer at Fort Bragg and in Normandy. But this technique, a "box barrage," was a first. It should work in theory, but many lives were at stake if his theory failed. Perkins had only two days to put his plan together, coordinating all the guns and giving them specific points to fire on if necessary.

The forward observer teams noticed that the noise made by the escaping soldiers was diminishing and it was time to leave. Both teams were the last to leave the enemy shoreline; a second boat trip was made to pick them all up.

Whatcombe Farm. Cpl. Robert Doyle (A Battery).
REEVES FAMILY

In the excitement of the moment, a British engineer was paddling frantically, causing the boat to go in circles in the middle of the Neder Rhine. Fearing the Germans were going to catch on to what was happening, Lieutenant Brooks and Private Doyle grabbed the oar from the Brit's hands and took his place rowing toward the friendly shore. The men left the boats at the water's edge and climbed up the dike crossing the road.

At an observation post a few hundred yards away, Sgt. James "Jim" Dundon (A Battery) had heard a commotion on the road a few hours prior. He was alerted of a river crossing, but was not told of the scope or the intentions of those making it. He believed it was just another 506th night patrol. What he heard was the excitement of 138 men letting loose. Pvt. Don Falls remembered it as a "New Year's Eve party atmosphere." The metal horseshoe-type cleats on the British paratroopers' boots made quite a sound and carried well off into the night.

The Germans, sensing something, sent up flares and then lobbed in mortars that destroyed the empty boats on the riverbank. *Nebelwerfers*, or "screaming meemies," came over next, missing the crossing point and hitting the 321st battery area instead. The shelling lasted all night.

Sgt. Donald Marlarkey (E Company) of the 506th PIR took part in the rescue. "I brought the British paratroopers, one British tanker and one American, in my boat," he said. "The most interesting one was a sergeant from the British 7th Armored Division, who had escaped from a German prison camp. He said, 'Sarge, I'm all through. My wife has been a widow five times now, and she is not going to be again.' He was from the famed 'Rats of Tobruk' and been reported missing in action several times in Africa and for the last time on the continent."[14]

All 506th paratroopers who participated in the rescue were given a letter of commendation by Colonel Sink. None of the 321st troopers received such recognition for their participation. The next day, Brooks went to see Colonel Carmichael about this and was told to cool off and come back the next day. Brooks did and only got to say six words at the meeting: "Yes, Sir," three different times. He was ordered to be confined to Mourmelon when they got back. Major Tyler (HQ) said to take three days off.

On October 24, Lieutenant Canham (B Battery), approached Captain Perkins with news and a request. Canham had just returned from leading one of the two 321st parties that crossed the Neder Rhine. Less than twenty-four hours later, he wanted to return.

A Dutch civilian whom Canham had met recently had been at his town near Renkum, which was north of the Neder Rhine and occupied by the Germans. The Dutch "line crosser" stated that a lot of good targets could be had there and volunteered to go back and lead the way. Their destination was a two-story secondary schoolhouse that would make an excellent observation post for an aggressive trooper like Canham. It would be a one-day operation.

"I went direct to the Division G-2, as I didn't trust our wire net with this type of thing," Captain Perkins recalled. "He gave me the ok, so we set it up with the 506th to get Canham across and to pick him up 24 hours later. Nothing happened going over so we tuned in to this channel at dawn. By 1000 hours we had heard nothing, so I began to call him. Still nothing. It was a wreck of a day for me. The boat was sent back at the appointed time and he was waiting. His report was very complete on what he could see, but the controlled artillery fire was a washout."[15]

The forward observer party returned, and one of Canham's team members, Pvt. William "Jay" Stone, asked what had transpired on the other side of the river. Canham told him that they went into the building and up to the second floor, which was used as a chemistry lab. Before they could get any fire missions going, some Germans entered the building and stayed on the ground floor. The team could hear the enemy below them conversing. The troopers lined up along the wall next to the door of the second-story room, ready to grab the Germans if they ventured upstairs. The enemy stayed in the schoolhouse until dark and then left; the two troopers and their Dutch guide shortly followed. All three made it safely to the prearranged drop-off point and were ferried back to the American lines by 506th paratroopers. Lieutenant Canham never had a chance to use his radio for any contact whatsoever for fear of being heard by the Germans downstairs.

Holland. Lt. Carroll Holland at the 321st command post.
PERKINS FAMILY

The battalion moved in the late morning of October 28 to 500 yards northeast of Valburg. The move was done in the rain. The battalion remained in direct support of the 506th PIR, with one liaison officer assigned to regimental headquarters, one liaison officer with the 1st Battalion, and one forward observer team with each company of that battalion.

The guns of the battalion could not be registered due to enemy observation. During the evening, DivArty requested the 321st to fire on unobserved targets. Under cover of darkness, communication wire was laid down and completed. The Germans, occupying the high ground, had the advantage to observe any movements during the daylight.

The firing batteries were registered the next morning at 0925 hours. The weather turned cloudy and colder. It would be an unlucky day for some hungry German soldiers.

Holland. From left to right: an unidentified British soldier, an unidentified 321st soldier, and Sgt. Harry Stearns (B Battery). The sign reads "Military area under surveillance. No trespassing." STEARNS FAMILY

The forward observer team of Lieutenant Brooks (A Battery) had settled in for the day, getting acquainted with the terrain and gaining knowledge of the new sector. At 1915 hours, two German trucks pulled up and stopped at a crossroads (map coordinates 68227677). They parked directly on the registration base point where the battalion guns had zeroed in on earlier in the day. The German trucks were set up as kitchens—it was chow time for the enemy.

Brooks waited until the Germans came in from the adjoining areas and gathered around the trucks, forming into neat lines. The food was now being served to about forty to fifty enemy soldiers. He called the FDC and asked for "fire for effect" on the

Zetten, Holland. Two windows in the attic of a schoolhouse used as an observation post. The one on the right was later hit by a screaming missile, but the only casualty was a telephone. NUGENT/DETTORE

base point, an unusual request because it meant that no adjusting fire was necessary. A short explanation was given, and "on the way" was the reply. Six rounds came in and on target with excellent results. The forward observer team couldn't believe their luck on their very first fire mission at the new observation post.

Since the battalion had dug in near Valburg, it received constant counterbattery fire from the heavy artillery of the Germans. Although this had been going on since the 321st came onto the island, it was getting worse. Another constant indignity was that during a fire mission, the water around the guns would be blown back over the gun crew by the muzzle blasts. Each round fired created a horizontal spray that soaked the men.

The word came down from DivArty on October 29 to limit harassing fire missions to a battalion total of forty-eight rounds per twenty-four-hour period. The first harassing fire mission had occurred on October 5 at 2330 hours and the last during nightfall on November 21.

A vacant house was used by some of the soldiers from B Battery to sleep in; they stayed in the basement in case of enemy artillery fire. To keep from sleeping in water that was seeping into the basement, they brought in straw and laid it on the floor. By the time the battalion moved out of the area, the basement was nearly filled with straw.

At 1245 hours on October 30, the forward observer party had just put out a fire mission on German artillery. This was yet another new observation post for Lieutenant Canham and his men. They fired two rounds on coordinates 68.5-77.8 with good results. The enemy responded with both mortar and artillery fire. Cpl. Elbert Douglas (B Battery), the radioman for Canham's team, was wounded when a mortar round exploded near him. He was on the first floor of a Dutch house at the time of the blast, which sent fragments of the shell and the tiled roof into both him and the radio, demolishing it. He was sent home. Later, two 506th paratroopers were killed while in A Battery's area. There was also damage done to GMC trucks belonging to the battalion.

The challenge was in determining and pinpointing the locations of heavy artillery. The belief was that some of those artillery pieces were railway and self-propelled guns that changed positions constantly and tended to fire under cover of darkness, which meant they were safe from being spotted by the air observation pilots. (Air observers rarely flew at night, as it was extremely dangerous.) The Germans didn't want to lose some of their best artillery in the field.

> Near Sergeant Baker's B Battery gun pit, the crew of the sixth gun dug a large foxhole. A large-caliber German round came in and scored a direct hit—a blinding flash, then dirt and mud flying everywhere. The men checked themselves and then each other. No one was hurt; the incoming round was a delayed fuse and dug deep into the waterlogged soil before exploding.
>
> The next day, another German artillery round hit the same hole and exploded, but this time the foxhole was empty. The artillerymen had dug a fresh hole, not wanting to test their luck, and lucky they were indeed. ■

Most of the enemy artillery occurred at night for this reason, while the guns of the 321st fired any time suitable targets appeared. However, the fires of the battalion generally increased under cover of darkness. Many of the casualties in the battalion area were caused by unexpected daylight bombardments by the Germans.

Someone in the 321st came up with an idea to draw out the enemy guns at a particular time when both limited air observation and ground forward observers would be waiting and watching for muzzle flashes and sound, which could be used to detect the locations. This technique involved sending out two 75mm pack howitzers as roving guns, unhooking them, and firing, in the hope the enemy would take the bait and fire back.

A few hours prior to midnight on November 11, two 75mm pack howitzers towed by jeeps set out with skeleton crews. At a predetermined location, they were unhitched. Each gun fired six rounds then quickly vacated the area, staying in both north and east sectors. This routine was rotated between A and

Passierschein

(GULTIG FÜR EINEN ODER MEHRERE ÜBERBRINGER)

Der deutsche Soldat, der diesen Passierschein vorzeigt, benutzt ihn als Zeichen seines ehrlichen Willens, sich zu ergeben. Er ist zu entwaffnen. Er muß gut behandelt werden. Er hat Anspruch auf Verpflegung und, wenn nötig, ärztliche Behandlung. Er wird so bald wie möglich aus der Gefahrenzone entfernt.

DWIGHT D. EISENHOWER
Oberbefehlshaber
der Alliierten Streitkräfte

Englische Übersetzung nachstehend. Sie dient als Anweisung an die alliierten Vorposten.

SAFE CONDUCT

(VALID FOR ONE OR SEVERAL BEARERS)

The German soldier who carries this safe conduct is using it as a sign of his genuine wish to give himself up. He is to be disarmed, to be well looked after, to receive food and medical attention as required, and to be removed from the danger zone as soon as possible.

DWIGHT D. EISENHOWER
Supreme Commander,
Allied Expeditionary Force

One of the surrender leaflets dropped on the Germans.
G. J. DETTORE COLLECTION

B Batteries, keeping the dangerous mission from falling on one single battery or gun section. During the night, two locations were used to accomplish this task in the course of one hour. Then both 75mm howitzers and their partial crews returned to the gun pits they had left just a few hours prior. The Germans took the bait, firing back and exposing their location.

This unorthodox method lasted for six continuous nights and yielded excellent results.

The word spread. Prior to the 321st moving off the island to head for base camp, the British replacement artillery took notice. Not only did they place dummy guns in bogus artillery potions, they also used two roving guns of their own, copying the Yanks.

About this time, PFC Thomas Morrison sent a letter home, telling his family not to worry about him. He added, "Every night while on guard duty is a regular 4th of July, as there are plenty of . . . ack ack, strange flares of all colors and rockets plus a lot more, and German planes." He continued, "I picked up an Allied surrender leaflet from Eisenhower. You know or heard of them I guess, for the Germans to come to our lines safely, but it looked like they didn't pick many up—a mistake indeed."

Serving as a jeep driver for liaison officer Capt. Samuel Williams of Drewry, Alabama, was a dangerous job with unique perks. T/5 Frederic Sheppard of New York City was a fast learner and an excellent driver. He was assigned to Captain Williams, as it turned out, for the duration of the war.

The code for Williams was "Lucky One," which aptly applied to many of the close calls that nearly ended Sheppard's days in the 101st. He spent most of the time delivering forward observer teams to their positions; dropping off batteries, rations, and radios; and visiting infantry command posts with fresh map overlays. These overlays were the lifeblood for both the infantry and the 321st command posts and apprised the firing batteries of the ever-changing positions of both friendly and enemy troops. Sometimes, Sheppard dropped off the overlays and learned of changes that necessitated return trips to the front and back. Then he would get word to do it all over again, not knowing if the Germans by now had the roads he was about to travel zeroed in for a few quick rounds. He traveled mostly alone, trying to stay off the beaten paths and roads, knowing he was possibly under the eyes of German observers. Despite the danger, Sheppard could enjoy the perks: he had transportation practically at will, as well as mobility both on and off the battlefield.

Near the end of October, during the Holland campaign, Sheppard and three 2nd Battalion troopers of the 506th hatched a plan while eating leftover British rations for their evening meal. The paratroopers needed quick transportation, and Sheppard could provide that. Under the cover of darkness, the only time it was possible to travel safely on the open road, the group headed for Elst, a small farming community situated approximately two miles northeast of

Valburg where the guns of the 321st were dug in. Their destination was a deserted jam factory, a brick building rumored to have a large amount of cash in its safe, located on the second floor.

Sheppard drove past the outpost, unaware that the soldiers in the outpost called the jeep's ID number and information in to the 506th command post. It was a quiet, moonlit night—"too quiet"—as far as shells exploding and small-arms fire, Sheppard wrote.

When they arrived at the building, the four men went up the outside steel staircase. One suggested that Sheppard keep an eye out, so he went back down the stairs to the jeep.

Suddenly, there was "a real loud bang and things lit up for a split second." One of the paratroopers was carrying a bazooka and a bag of rockets. They'd seen those same rockets knock out German tanks—surely a safe would be no problem. The bazooka rocket did its job. The safe was blown apart and a canvas bag was stuffed with paper money. Running down the steps to the waiting jeep, they clamored in with bazooka and additional rockets in hand. The single blast had reverberated through the area, alerting all within earshot.

Even though the band of safecrackers drove over fields and down forgotten paths, they ended up at the same manned outpost, whose guards again wrote down all pertinent vehicle information before waving them on.

Arriving back at their sleeping quarters, located in a shed, they opened the bag to divide the loot. German marks! They had hundreds of thousands of worthless enemy currency. Sheppard wrote:

> We decided to bed down. That lasted only a few moments when a runner from the [506th] CP found me and I was advised that Capt. Williams wanted to see me at the battalion CP. He was waiting for me outside. He told me about the OP informing the CP of our trip, the explosion, etc. "I want to hear the truth," he said. I told him and asked if I could get the other three to come with me to confess to the Colonel [Sink]. They agreed and the four of us went in with Capt. Williams. We confessed. We received [a] "royal reaming" along with being busted to privates.

It wasn't long before the group was branded the "Dalton Gang" and took copious amounts of verbal abuse from their buddies. They had risked being sent to Leavenworth prison for German marks? For those not involved, it was a hilarious scenario.

Driving alone again in his assigned jeep some time later, the now Private Sheppard discovered an empty Nazi administration building. This time, all the property was German and it was to be fair game: spoils of war, he thought. It was common knowledge that Germans were famous for producing some high-end items, among them cameras, automobiles, and typewriters.

Scouring the offices for anything he could sell for quick cash in hopes of developing a bankroll, it hit him: all the offices had typewriters that were left behind and very available. Typewriters, one of the marvels of the day, were too expensive to purchase for the average Joe, but here they were for the taking.

Sheppard grabbed as many as he could carry and loaded them into his jeep. He eventually made enough trips into the building to tally somewhere between twelve and fifteen of those costly machines. Now it was time to make some easy money. He pulled up to a group of soldiers, made a quick sales pitch, and threw aside the canvas tarp to expose the liberated typewriters. "Sure, they look good, but do they type in English?" was one of the first questions asked. Duped again, he couldn't sell a single typewriter—he couldn't even give them away. Sheppard eventually had to discard his goods on a farmer's front steps when it was time for the 321st to move out.

After those two incidents, nobody wanted to be seen with Sheppard and kept their distance. Refining his store of goods eventually proved to be a moneymaker as the war progressed, once the private narrowed his wares to war trophies. If someone wanted to buy a German pistol, rifle, or belt buckle, he was their man—a rolling warehouse of Nazi militaria.

On November 12, Lt. Eugene Brooks (A Battery) led his forward observer team consisting of PFC Don Falls and Cpl. Joseph Karasevic to a stone farmhouse approximately a half mile south of the Neder Rhine. It had been used as an observation post by the British, who had moved out earlier.

Savy. Cpl. Frederic Sheppard (left) and PFC Deveraux (right) inspect supplies destined for a forward observer party. WILLIAMS FAMILY

Ochten, Holland. A Battery forward observer party at their observation post (from left to right): PFC Louis Kovacic, Cpl. Everett Nichols, and 1st Sgt. James Dundon. Note everyone has a bottle, even the toddler. The building was a café run by the Meeuwes family, who also operated a dairy farm during the war. The café was demolished in 2011 and a new house built in its place. From this post, the 321st party could see another observation post in Druten across the Waal River, manned by the Princess Irene Brigade, the only Dutch Army unit in existence fighting in Holland. NICHOLS FAMILY

It had been six days, and it was time to rotate the forward observation party from the observation post located on the front lines. The team would have to locate it in daylight. The most important items they carried to facilitate their duties were the fresh batteries for their radio. Without contact with the firing batteries, their presence at the front was inconsequential to the paratroopers whom they were there to support.

The team followed the road's drainage ditches, which provided both cover and concealment from the ever-watchful eyes of the enemy. At one point in their journey up to the front, the ditch split into a Y. Brooks was unsure if the post was to the left or right. He sent Karasevic down one side of the ditch for about 150 yards and Falls down the other in hopes of making contact with the other 321st forward observer team.

Falls had made it down the ditch about 100 yards or so when he discovered that the Germans had used a portion of it for a latrine. Human waste partially filled the ditch, along with German newspapers and letters used as toilet paper. Falls had not reached his destination, so he had to crawl on all fours and carefully straddle the bottom of the ditch to keep from being exposed along the top. He was glad to make it past this spot and traveled about another 50 yards without making contact. Now it was time to take the same route back to his lieutenant and give him the news.

In reaching the makeshift German latrine, he again raised himself up, only to find the enemy had spotted him and opened fire. Falls instinctively plopped down on his stomach and started to crawl through the narrow river of excrement and urine, keeping his head above the mess. He would travel a few yards, gag, raise himself up a bit to take a breath, and continue. It was a 30-foot experience he would never forget. Falls later said it was the worst thing he ever had to do while in the service.

Private Karasevic had located the observation post. For the next six days, Falls had no choice but to wear the soiled uniform. He tried to find ways to clean it and himself, but in their secluded position it was a difficult task. In retrospect, Falls was thankful for those Dutch ditches that, in the end, saved his life.

Holland. From left to right: PFC Don Falls, PFC Charles Hunter, and PFC Joe Karasevic of A Battery after coming back from the front for a rest. FALLS FAMILY

Word was the Germans had captured a couple of Brits earlier and had taken them back to their lines. It was obvious the enemy knew what the buildings were being used for. To see over the dike, the Americans used the second floor of the house (which still stands at 16 Achterstraat Driel) as the observation post. The artillery registration point was a destroyed bridge 1,000 yards away that led to Arnhem.

Darkness fell. Paratroopers of the 1st Battalion of the 506th, two forward observer teams from the 321st, and 1st Sgt. James Dundon (A Battery), leader of another forward observer team, were in the farmhouse. On guard was one of the 506th troopers who were using the buildings for their command post. The newest member of Dundon's team was T/5 Everett Nichols (A Battery) of New Meadows, Idaho, and he was bored. Nichols, a member of a gun section, had been granted permission to get into front-line action as a forward observer.

The steps leading to the basement of the house were wooden. The building was dry and safe from enemy shellfire, but it could easily turn into a bad situation if the Germans got the drop on them. There were about ten 101st troopers, in addition to the others, in the basement, which was divided into two rooms by a thick wall. The basement floor was strewn with mattresses of various types.

First Sergeant Dundon went down to the pitch-black basement to lie down. He used his helmet as a pillow. Next to him was Lieutenant Brooks. Both men were at the foot of the steps. They went to sleep lying on the concrete floor. It was a short rest.

Dundon heard a sound that grew louder by the second. It was the noise made by a German flashlight. This type of flashlight had a lever that had to be pushed rapidly to create the electricity that powered the small lightbulb, creating a unique high-pitched whine. The flashlight was cradled in the hand of a German who took a couple of steps down into the basement and yelled, "Hands *Hock*!" Lieutenant Brooks, a sound sleeper, didn't hear a thing at first.

It was a mistake for the German soldier to use his noisy generator-style flashlight. It only illuminated a very narrow area about fifteen feet deep, and the bulb that glowed bright white added to his impending problem. He could barely see Brooks and Dundon at the bottom of the stairs, and certainly not make out the others who were patiently waiting for the right moment to make their presence known.

More importantly, he could not see that Dundon had his .45-caliber semiautomatic pistol out of the holster at his side. Dundon always slept that way while at the front. He raised his pistol just off the basement floor and fired several times (his shots caused Lieutenant Brooks to later lose hearing in his right ear). Others followed suit, and the work was done. The enemy soldier tumbled down the steps and was dead before he hit the bottom. He was a staff sergeant from a Fortress battalion, but some said he was from the SS.

Hearing the commotion inside the building, the other Germans waiting outside started to remove the

Germany. From top to bottom: T/5 Everett Nichols, 1st Sgt. Marlin Davis, and PFC Woodrow Kinnear. WARREN FAMILY

bricks that were piled against the small basement window. Fearing what was going to happen next, Lieutenant Brooks yelled for someone to block the window opening with one of the mattresses that were lying on the floor. One of the paratroopers yelled back, "You do it, lieutenant, it's your idea." At this moment, PFC Joe Karasevic (A Battery), part of Brooks's forward observer party, grabbed a mattress and raced to the open window. He just made it before a thrown potato masher grenade bounced off the mattress and exploded outside, causing the Germans to retreat back to their lines. Karasevic's action helped to maintain the situation.

Explosions could be heard coming from outside the building from more exploding German potato mashers and the firing of German machine pistols. One of the enemy patrols was captured. Paratrooper Cpl. Hank Gogola (B Company, 506th) was slightly wounded by a bullet that grazed his head. He too fired at the Germans with his captured P-38 pistol, three shots at close range standing just feet away at the basement door.

Holland. From left to right: 1st Sergeant Dundon, PFC Victor Zuccarelli, Sgt. Lawrence Weinberg, and PFC Louis Kovacic of an A Battery forward observer party. DUNDON/DETTORE

Lt. William Nugent and his gang at the entrance to their quarters, an air-raid shelter for a bombed factory in Uden, Holland. Kneeling: Harry Miller (left), his driver, and Nugent. Standing: Rudolph Falcon (killed in action October 7, 1944), acting radio corporal (left); and Cpl. Carl Espling, acting sergeant. They had two kinds of tommy guns and a carbine—a lot of protection. NUGENT/DETTORE

First Sergeant Dundon was taken aback due to the fact he never got a chance to take any of the medals the German was wearing; the other 101st boys did. Lieutenant Brooks picked up the handheld generator flashlight and kept it for years. T/5 Nichols returned to his gun section the next day, wanting no more part of a forward observer team. It would take a few days before he calmed down from the incident. The German sergeant was eventually buried in the apple orchard behind the farmhouse.[16]

Lieutenant Brooks didn't learn who fired the shots next to him that caused his later hearing loss until the summer of 2000. Likewise, First Sgt. Dundon hadn't known who was sleeping next to him on the basement floor that night. Both were being interviewed by the author at Brooks's home in Richmond, Virginia. They hadn't seen each other since the end of the war, but now lived only minutes apart. Brooks yelled to his wife, "This is *that* damn fool that made me deaf in my right ear!"

The 321st S-2 entry for November 12, 1944, recorded that a fifteen-man enemy patrol surrounded 1st Platoon, B Company Headquarters. "Apparently

Near the end of the campaign, 1st Sgt. James Dundon (A Battery) and his forward observer party were at their observation post when they spotted a white flag being waved from the second story of a building in enemy territory (coordinates 706.751). General Taylor heard about it over the radio at his command post and decided to take a look for himself. Dundon, who had a habit of not wearing a helmet, pointed to the building where the white flag was still visible. Taylor took a studious look with his own higher-magnification pair of binoculars and told Dundon it was just white curtains flapping in an open window. He lowered his binoculars and said to Dundon, "You might lose your fine head." He also reminded him that a soldier not wearing a helmet was subject to a $50 fine if caught. Dundon put his helmet on, and the general left the observation post. ■

A chow line in Holland. LINZ FAMILY

Holland. PFC Robert West (left) from Painesville, Ohio, and PFC Alton Westrick (right) from Leipsic, Ohio, both of the 321st. Note Westrick is wearing a folding-stock carbine scabbard on his belt. WESTRICK FAMILY

this was part of a coordinated effort to gather prisoners and information during this night. . . . plans were found on a dead German [who] was part of a recon patrol; another member was taken prisoner. These plans were to find location of forward positions, take prisoners if possible, [and] find strength and equipment." The S-2 journal entry also noted that the dead soldier was from 11th Company, 21st Regiment, 41st Fortress Battalion, and carried an automatic weapon, hand grenades, and a flare pistol.

The next night, the observation post was shelled. Thirteen days later, the 321st would be relieved by the Brits.

At 0645 hours on November 12 a heavy German counterbattery barrage landed in the A Battery area. It wounded several men and hit a building; casualties were light because rounds exploded deep in the muddy soil. General McAuliffe was in the area to observe the damage when another barrage came in. He jumped into a hole filled with water and mud. Lt. James Wicker, A Battery commander, accidentally fell on top of him. Both stayed put for about ten minutes. Wicker apologized profusely to McAuliffe, who was soaked with mud. McAuliffe said, "Please, I don't want to hear anything about it—just glad you were on top of me."

One of the slightly injured was PFC Harry Sinkutch (HQ). When the battalion first moved into the area at the end of October, he was approached by several Dutchmen. He thought they wanted to barter smokes for digging a foxhole. It seemed unusual, but he went with the flow and allowed them to dig. It was quite a large hole by Sinkutch's standards. Small logs were scavenged and placed on top when they were done. He then understood the task completed was out of gratitude for their liberation, not for cigarettes. The foxhole was to be his home for the next two weeks.

When the Germans started shelling on the twelfth, he jumped in along with Sgt. Harold Stockwell (HQ) from Pine Bluff, Arkansas. There was plenty of room. They could hear the iron splinters of exploding

An unidentified bombed-out town in Holland.

shells that tore into the logs placed overhead. It was coming in heavy. Stockwell and Sinkutch were both nervous. Stockwell said loudly, "Pray for us to be saved." Sinkutch replied, "Get off my back. I'm having problems myself." Fifteen minutes later, the shelling stopped and Sinkutch climbed out of his hole. He sat down next to a tree, trying to calm himself. One more shell came in and exploded. He looked up and realized he was flying in the air and everything was upside down. Not knowing what had happened, he asked, "Am I hit?" Somebody was calling for a medic, but the only wound he had was a slight cut underneath his chin. Waving off medical attention, Sinkutch climbed back into the hole and demanded to be left alone.

For the next couple days he was a nervous wreck, scared of his own shadow and jittery about everything. "In combat some days it was like a Sunday walk and other days you were about to jump out of your skin, you're just a bundle of nerves," he said. As it turned out, that last shell wasn't German after all. It was a British short shell caused by a wet powder charge.

Each battery had its own kitchens. Enemy fire started to land and scored a direct hit on A Battery's kitchen. One of the cooks was slightly injured and later received a Purple Heart. Pvt. Alfred Stumpo, along with the rest of the "chow hounds," ran for cover, finding what looked like a foxhole. He dove into a "slop hole," the spot where the cooks got rid of the mess kit rinse water and garbage. Another red-legger jumped on top of him. Afterward quite a few of the boys in the battery got a good laugh out of it. Stumpo said, "It will wash off."

On November 18, 1st Sgt. Timothy Shea gave the okay for three soldiers to go to the showers, which had been set up in Nijmegen in the back of some trailers by the division engineers. The routine was simple: shower, get their clothes dry-cleaned, have a meal, see a movie, and get back to the battalion.

PFC Pervey Robinson, the B Battery barber, from Sylacauga, Alabama; PFC John Patterson (B Battery) from Anderson, South Carolina; and PFC Frank Kanspik (B Battery) from Chicago, Illinois, were heading back from the showers when a German 88 round came in and exploded in front of their jeep. All were instantly killed by shell fragments to the head.

The next day, division got the dog tags and started to call various units in order to determine which one the soldiers had belonged to. Just before the battalion departed for Holland, a telegram came from the Red Cross for Robinson: his wife had just delivered twin boys. A small party was held for the father.

Lt. Bernard Zeppenfield flew an L-4 for the 101st Division and was assigned to provide air observation for the 321st, adjusting fire and looking for targets of opportunity. The first week of November was clear, perfect for flying and spotting targets from the air. Zeppenfield and his observer Lt. Joseph Yourie's normal routine was to fly at 1,500 feet right up to

Nijmegen, Holland, near the bridge. Buildings used to stand in the foreground. One of the typical churches can be seen just beyond the half-track. NUGENT/DETTORE

the main line of resistance and then drop back a half mile. From this point, they would call in fire missions or adjust fire as needed.

Once, Zeppenfield flew a pattern of figure eights, continuing to turn at a certain spot. The Germans caught on to this routine and fired an 88 round. It hit the bottom of the fabric-covered L-4 airplane between the pilot and his observer and went out the cockpit roof. Zeppenfield said when it hit, it sounded like "a bass drum." The round continued, bursting 1,000 feet above them, perforating their airplane with iron fragments. The pilot and observer didn't even get a scratch.

On November 20, he searched for a particular target. This was the third attempt in six days of flying into darkness and clouds with occasional rain in a desperate search for a German railway gun. It was a request from General McAuliffe of division artillery to locate and get the coordinates of the gun for the artillery and knock it out. It had been harassing the 101st and other areas, causing casualties and fraying nerves. Its rounds had been landing in the 321st area.

The problem with locating the big gun was that it only fired around 7:00 P.M. when observation was nonexistent. The Germans were being cautious with this artillery piece. The only air observation pilot with night-flying qualification was Lieutenant Zeppenfield. He volunteered for the mission along with his trusted observer Lieutenant Yourie, of Bronx, New York, from the 321st.

The plan was simple. If the Germans fired their railway gun, the crew was to plot its location. The method was crude but had been successful in the past during complete darkness. The flash of the gun gave the approximate area, and then Yourie was to count the seconds until he heard its report. Then he would formulate the coordinates while seated behind the pilot, operating the SCR-610 radio. This was their third try—on the first two, the gun had stayed silent—and both men felt comfortable with each other's ability.

The Germans, unaware that they were being stalked by this L-4, fired the railway gun. The hunt was on. The air crew was at 1,500 feet in total darkness. For the men of this Piper Cub, the third time was the charm.

Computations of the flash and sound showed that the gun, so large it was placed on a flatcar, appeared

PFC Walter Mitchell in Mourmelon, back from the front, removing his combat clothing for cleaning. WILKENS FAMILY

PFC Burton Carpenter of the 321st in Mourmelon.

to be approximately six miles north of Arnhem. Lieutenant Yourie radioed in on the SCR-610's B channel to Div Arty FDC. Due to the target's location, it was outside the range of the 101st artillery and therefore was a British target. The crew was switched over to the British artillery, and the target type was given with its coordinates.

The air observers expected to adjust the fire of the British guns and called, "Fire for effect. Will adjust." What they got was totally unexpected. The entire British Corps artillery opened up on the target. Ninety guns of all types and calibers let loose with a magnitude that awed the crew of the L-4. The rounds traveled overhead and fell on the target from such height that it resembled a carpet bombing by Allied bombers. The entire area, about a half-mile square, was vaporized into dust. The gun and its surroundings ceased to exist. Zeppenfield stated, "We were expecting the usual round then adjusting. We were speechless." No more harassing fire came from that gun.

The division occupied an area lower than the Neder Rhine. It was obvious that with all the rain, flooding could occur either naturally or from the Germans blowing holes in the dikes. It wouldn't be a sudden wall of water, but most likely a continuous, gradual flooding that pushed men and materiel out of their dug-in positions and up onto the road and left the island underwater. What were the Krauts waiting for?

Starting on November 14, 2nd Lt. Arthur Freeman (HQ), assistant communications officer, was given the task of recording the depth of the river and reporting it to division headquarters. It was up to 11.38 meters that day; it rose to 11.6 meters less than twelve hours later.

On November 18, a top-secret brief for Operation Noah was distributed to selected men and officers of the 321st. Preparations for Noah had been completed a week earlier on November 11. Three possible phases of evacuation were given: water wings, spring tide, and deluge. The latter was the most serious. It called for immediate withdrawal of vehicles to prearranged rendezvous points and for foot elements to follow each battery, taking one side of the road each and moving out. The vicinity of the Nijmegen Bridge was the destination area to which Major Henderson would lead the foot element. The vehicles would leave under the direction of Major Tyler.

This plan was never put in effect during the 321st's days on the island, as they left on November 25. Pvt. John Muscia logged in his diary that on December 3 the Germans blew the dikes near the former gun emplacements of the 321st, flooding the area completely.

On November 19, radio traffic to the battalion forward observers was a bit different. An excitement not related to targets was in the air. Lieutenant Brooks received word that a garbled radio message was heard by Corporal Karasevic. The A Battery stated that its firing batteries were getting ready to fire 30,000 rounds. He couldn't believe what he heard; looking through his binoculars, he spotted no massive targets. He said out loud to his men that he doubted 30,000 rounds were available to the entire 101st Division. Brooks asked the FDC for a repeat of the message and learned that at 1107 hours the battalion was to fire the 30,000th round since landing in Holland. Press reporters were even on hand for the occasion. It had been just a short time ago, on October 2 that the 321st fired the first round to fall on German soil from a 101st gun.

On November 25 at 0345 hours, the Brits relieved the 321st. The Germans must have noticed that the kitchen trucks and staff left the evening prior, just four hours after the battalion was alerted of the move.

At 0700 hours, the enemy unleashed an artillery attack on the positions of the 321st. It was believed to be a parting reminder of their German counterparts and is labeled in the 321st journal as a "hate barrage." Sixteen and a half hours later, all of the 321st would be at their base camp in Mourmelon, France.

As the 101st was leaving Holland and the soggy fields behind, a soldier took off his rubber galoshes and threw them to the side of the road. It didn't take long before the sides of the roads were littered with thousands of the protective rubber boots. In a few months, they would be a sought-after commodity in Bastogne.

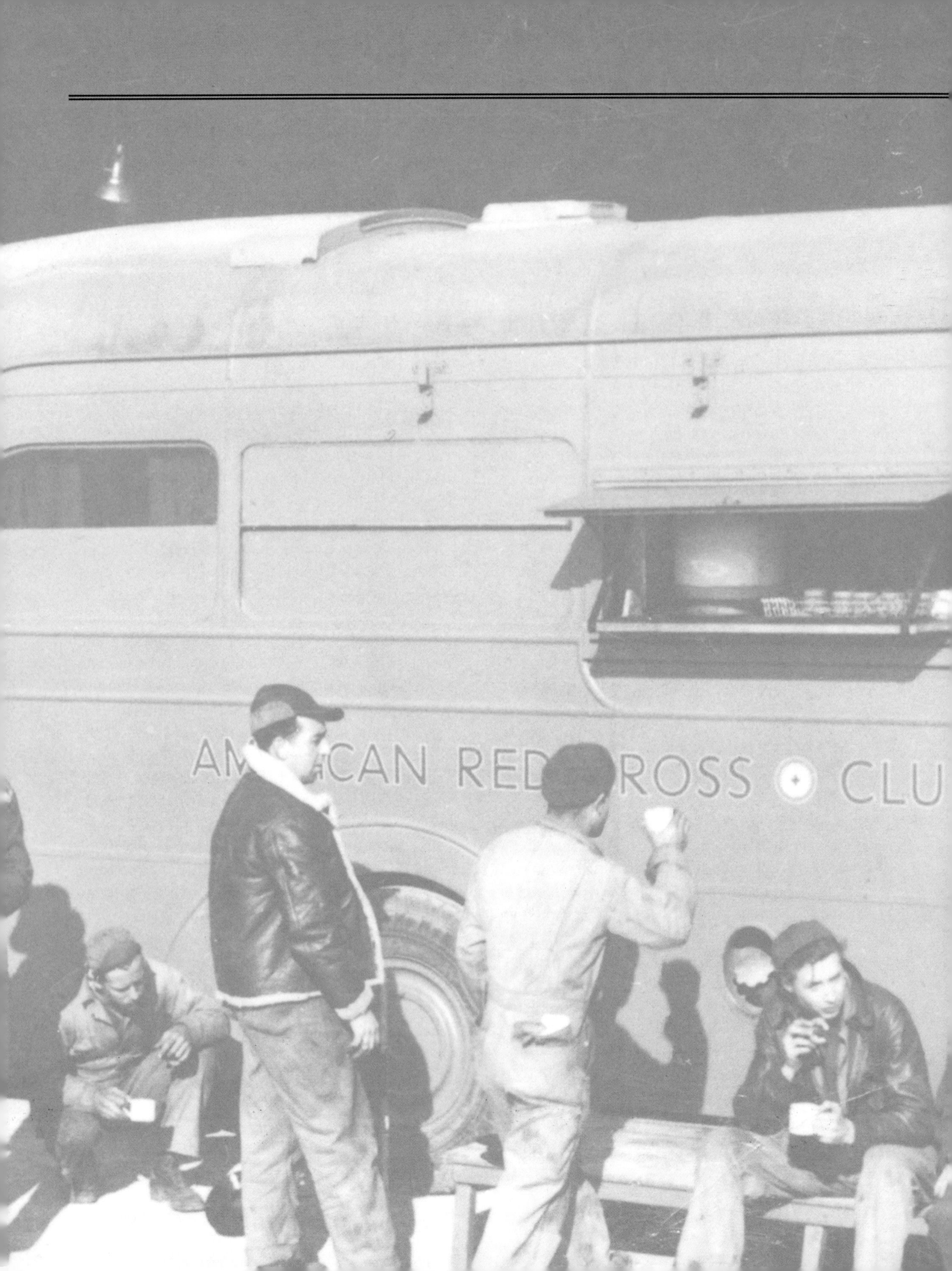

CHAPTER 5

Back to France

IT WAS GOOD NEWS INDEED. November 25 was an uneventful day of traveling, with the majority of the 321st being transported to their new base camp. The word was out that the mobile Red Cross doughnut trucks were dead ahead at Bourg-Leopold, Belgium. This was the halfway mark to the camp, and approximately eight to ten Red Cross trucks were indeed waiting for the convoy and its ranks filled with hungry, war-weary occupants. The trucks were parked at the edge of a huge open field; music was playing, and a number of women dressed in their Red Cross uniforms were ready to serve the onslaught of 101st boys.

In military precision, the troopers formed a line that seemed to stretch back to Valburg in the Netherlands. Happiness soon turned into indignation. It wasn't the long lines that caused problems; it was that they were being charged money! Coffee, doughnuts, and razor blades were some of the items normally handed out for free—but not today. The price was paid grudgingly, as the wait in line wasn't going to be wasted. The bitterness toward the Red Cross stayed with many 321st soldiers throughout their entire lives.

The battalion arrived at their destination of Mourmelon at 0130 hours. They were safe at last.

A Red Cross Clubmobile.

Gun section members at Mourmelon. Top row (from left to right): PFC Robert Palm, PFC Larry Boudreaux, PFC Roby Williams, PFC Billy Wilkens, PFC Stan Strapakas, PFC B. L. Witcher, and Pvt. William Mullins. Bottom row (from left to right): PFC Gilbert Quinn, Sergeant Gerald Braden, and PFC Louis Palusak. WITCHER/DETTORE

A Red Cross Clubmobile coffee and doughnut line in Belgium. TURKAL FAMILY

Mourmelon-le-Petit, France, formerly housed a French artillery garrison and then served as a tank depot for the Germans when they occupied France. The 321st stayed in ill-kept stone buildings on site.

Reims was 20 miles away. It was a city filled with culture, thirteenth-century architecture, and the famed Cathedral of Reims. But to most of the troopers, it meant cheap champagne! Affordable, never-ending champagne. They were, after all, in the Champagne region of France. For those who partook in the bubbly, it was heaven. However, most of the men soon found out that an all-night drinking fest of champagne was not to be topped off with a drink of water in the morning. That would re-create the drunken state of the evening prior, now with the unenviable task of standing roll call.

A few days after arriving, pinned on the bulletin board was a notice that a USO show was going to open that evening. The lines of 101st troopers went on for blocks and blocks. It was going to be a packed house. However, entertainment this was not. A middle-aged lady from the States ran the show, which turned out to be light opera with a string accompaniment. According to Pvt. Don Falls (A Battery), "This was certainly not what the guys expected to get." The next USO show followed a few days later with entertainment much more to the soldiers' liking. It included dancing girls and was a huge success, much more appreciated than the last.

At Mourmelon, the 82nd and the 101st Divisions were not allowed into town at the same time. The troopers were constantly fighting with each other, and the cheap champagne didn't help matters. Cpl. Anthony Tabone (A Battery) and several of his buddies decided to break that rule. Since they were close to town, it looked like it would be worth the walk. A jeep with military police stopped them and said the 101st was on alert. Thinking it was a ploy, Tabone said, "Yeah, right, we knew that," and pretended to walk back in the other direction. Taking an alternate route, the group started back to where the fun was. Again they were spotted. It was the same military police. This time the group took off running. All the boys were chased down, placed in the jeep, and taken directly to camp. It was only then that Tabone believed what he was told. It was now 0200 hours, December 18, and Mourmelon would have to wait.

While at camp in Mourmelon, a soldier from A Battery came to see the executive officer, Lieutenant Linz. The private had just a small problem, and Linz was trying to settle everybody in. He explained to the soldier that this was not the time to discuss his issue—everybody had a problem of some sort or another. Not getting the message, the soldier went on and on about his minor complaint. Finally, Linz said exasperatedly, "Go tell it to the chaplain." This retort was a well-known phrase used by soldiers and aimed at those who complained about the most minor things. Usually upon hearing that phrase, the complainer would shrug and walk away. But not this time. The soldier took his complaint to the chaplain, who also didn't appreciate the pettiness of the complaint taking up his time and the manner in which it came his way. The chaplain contacted Colonel Carmichael, informing him about a minor gripe his executive officer had failed to address. Carmichael brought Linz into his office and chewed him out severely. Linz never uttered that phrase to another soldier for the rest of the war. ■

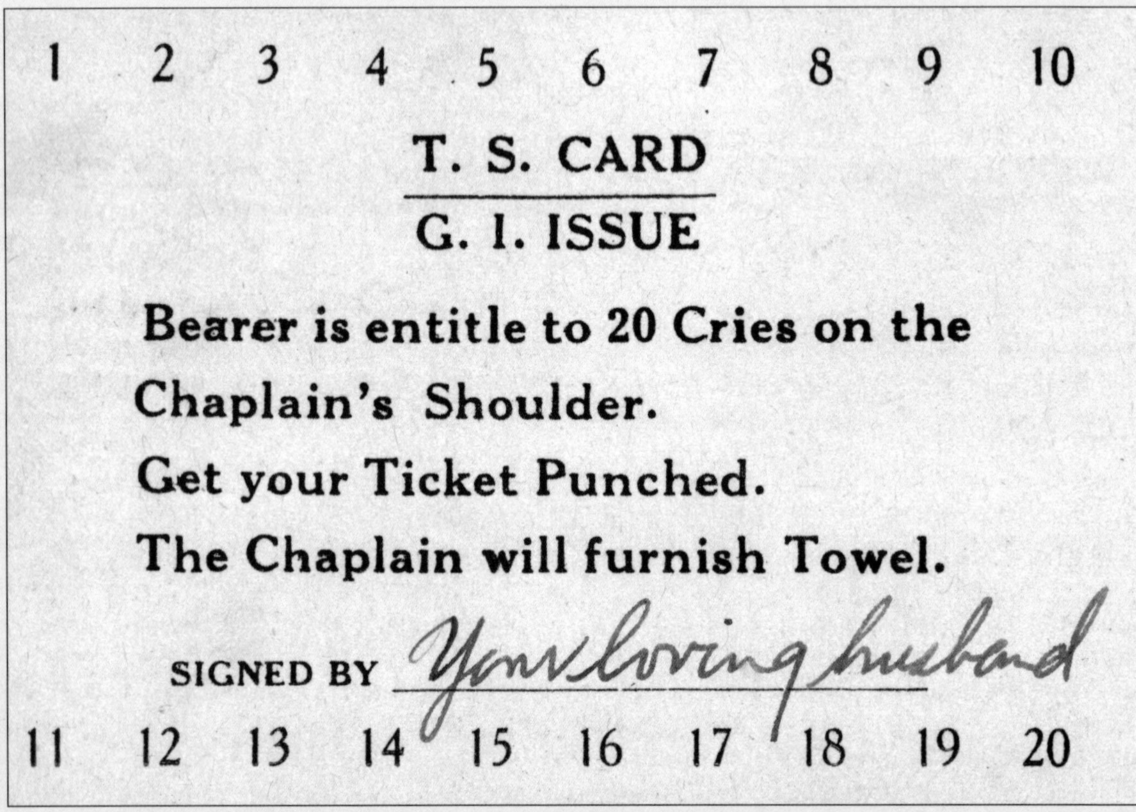
1 2 3 4 5 6 7 8 9 10

T. S. CARD

G. I. ISSUE

Bearer is entitle to 20 Cries on the Chaplain's Shoulder.

Get your Ticket Punched.

The Chaplain will furnish Towel.

SIGNED BY Your loving husband

11 12 13 14 15 16 17 18 19 20

A "Tough Shit" (TS) card given to soldiers complaining about minor things. G. J. DETTORE COLLECTION

In early December a party for the officers was thrown in one of the buildings on base and attended mostly by 321st officers who brought plenty of champagne and liquor. It was the first time many of these officers had been together all in one place since the start of the Holland campaign. It was loud—they had a lot of catching up to do and stories that needed to be told while the booze flowed freely.

Colonel Carmichael walked in, a most unwelcome guest. He attempted to walk through the celebration but was stopped by a question. Captain White asked, "Colonel Carmichael, why was it that you never showed your face while we were on the island?" The colonel ignored the question and walked out. The festivities continued until the next morning. Sometime later, White was notified that the colonel ordered him restricted to his quarters.

A knock on White's door woke him; he was to report to General Taylor right away. White wondered if Carmichael had blown the whistle on him. But he knew that would take guts, and everyone knew what he said was true. Instead, Taylor asked if he wanted to go back to the States with him. A conference in Washington, D.C., was going to be held, and Taylor could bring one officer with him. White asked when they would leave, and Taylor's reply was "As soon as you can pack your bag."

It was December 4. General Taylor and Captain White met General McAuliffe at the airfield just as he exited the C-47. McAuliffe was returning from a short stay in the United Kingdom. After a short chat on the runway, Taylor and White boarded the same aircraft, taxied down the runway, and departed. Thus began the first leg of their journey back to Washington, D.C.

Colonel Carmichael sent someone to check on White to ensure he was confined to his quarters, only to discover he was gone. He then learned that not only was White not in his room, he was on his way to the States. That pleased the 321st officers immensely.

The colonel complained to acting commander General McAuliffe that White had disobeyed his direct order and was gone. Another 321st officer heard the conversation and later told White about it. McAuliffe asked, "What did you ground him for?" Carmichael replied, "They had a big booze party, and everyone was too loud and White was the ranking officer." McAuliffe replied, "What the hell do you expect them to do after more than two months on the front lines?" That was the end of the conversation.

Back in the States, after learning on what was happening in the Ardennes, General Taylor cut his airborne conference short at the Pentagon to return to his surrounded division. White wrote, "On the 24th of December I was sitting in the Statler-Hilton [New York City] having a scotch and water. . . . On the 26th I was in a cold wet cellar in Bastogne getting bombed by the Jerries!"

CHAPTER 6

The Bulge

THE ARDENNES OFFENSIVE WAS HITLER'S IDEA. His forces were to strike en masse over difficult terrain in a region called the Ardennes, which encompassed parts of Belgium and Luxembourg. Bastogne itself is approximately twenty miles from the German–Luxembourg border. The area consists of the Ardennes plateau south of the Meuse–Sambre trough, the central lowland, and the coastal plain in the northwest area. The terrain slopes toward the northwest, cut by deep ravines with narrow streams. The central lowland (Bastogne) area is gently rolling and continues to decrease in elevation toward the northwest. The lowlands are farmed and forested with beech and pine trees.

Hitler believed the Allies had overextended their supply lines and that a major counteroffensive would certainly break those lines and force the Americans to retreat back to the shores of the Atlantic, repeating the Dunkirk debacle. The Allies would then have no choice but to sue for peace, allowing Germany to rebuild. This part of Europe was chosen by Hitler so that it would have the greatest destructive consequence for the Allies. Chief of Operations Staff General Alfred Jodl and a few other trusted aides knew of the plan. Jodl stated after the war in a *Life* magazine article that "even if we succeeded in destroying thirty divisions [in Russia] it would have made no difference. On the other hand, if we destroyed thirty divisions in the West, it would amount to more than one third of the whole invasion army."

The German invasion route through the Ardennes would be the same as the one in 1914 and 1940. Therefore, the German war machine was quite familiar with that territory, since its armies had recently spent four years there until September 1944. The intended target was the Allied supply port of Antwerp, Belgium. The Germans had 25 divisions of approximately 300,000 men, 1,900 pieces of artillery, and 970 tanks and armored guns.

Seven roads radiate out of the town of Bastogne, good routes for moving the men and materiel of war. Defended, it could be a major roadblock to the port of Antwerp. The race was on.

It was cool but dry while at Camp Mourmelon-le-Grand, and the troopers of the 321st were thinking of Christmas on December 17, 1944. They had been at their base camp for only three weeks after spending over two months on the line in Holland. All equipment was turned in for reworking and refitting. Combat gear and clothing were worn-out and slowly being replaced by new supplies. The mud and rain of Holland had taken a serious toll on all the equipment needed in making war. The only good news was that they were no longer under the command of Field Marshal Montgomery.

All the ammunition for the 75mm pack howitzers was turned in, as most of it was waterlogged and unusable. The howitzers themselves were sent to ordnance due to cracked tubes (barrels); those that weren't still needed major overhaul.

The men of B Battery expected a lengthy stay and started to set up NCO clubs and recreation facilities, gathering champagne and cognac from this famous region. As they did in England at Whatcombe Farm, the 321st planned a big Christmas party for the children in the surrounding area. In true airborne fashion, it seemed that half the 101st Division was in the stockade for minor infractions while in the rest area. These were festive days, but that was to change.

The battalion was alerted at 9:30 P.M. on December 17 that it was to move out the next day at 4:00 P.M. It all started when the first sergeants came into the sleeping quarters blowing whistles. The men glanced at their watches. It certainly was too early for roll call. The destination was unknown and only the location of an assembly area was given, with orders for a full combat load. Their mode of entry into combat was not by glider nor by sea, but via

Mourmelon. Some 75mm pack howitzers being inspected.

trucks. It would be a 110-mile ride to their final destination, which only a few knew at the time.

Mission Accomplished recorded the following:

> The gravity of the situation was so much mist to most of the men until the following morning. True, the rumor flashed out like lightning when the alert came down, but well, rumors are rumors, however interesting or charged with dynamite they may be, and they are usually treated with reserve until substantiated by somewhat official sources.
>
> Although we knew of the counterattack, it did not seem likely to us that the 101st would be committed. Our optimism was quickly dispelled at the morning formation. "This is it, men! And make it fast!" Tension was high, and the comments at breakfast were varied. No one could visualize anything worse than an excursion lasting a few days. How little we knew!
>
> We had become used to the confusion and disorder of moving, but this was truly the acme of perfection in a messy sort of a way. The first consideration was, of course, the section equipment. Not a man could be found who was not dashing about like a fugitive from your favorite home for the mentally deficient. No doubt, to the casual observer the scene was one that forbade nothing but disaster for the entire operation.
>
> Somehow the equipment was loaded in its proper place and tied down in preparation for the journey. Surely no one would say from appearances that there was any semblance of system in the complete chaos that reigned there that morning. And yet, all those painful months of training and practical experience behind had made their mark. Everyone knew what to do and performed the necessary task without realizing that he was an essential cog in a smoothly operating machine. It was not until much later, that a realization of the excellence of the performance came sifting through the maze of reminiscences.[1]

Sgt. Nelson Kopacka of a B Battery machine-gun section remembers it this way:

> At about 2:00 A.M. [December 18] the call of March order came. Pack your field packs, leave everything else and fall out. Carbines, rifles, and ammo were in a pile. Grab one, load your pockets with ammo; each man was reasonable. Gun Chiefs sent men to ordnance to get their 75mm howitzers. Many of the guns had to be reassembled, cracked tubes and all. . . . The gates of the stockade were thrown open and the guys told to report back to their units on the double, and they did—all of them.
>
> I had to see that the 75 ammo was loaded, the same waterlogged stuff we brought out of Holland, and that the machine gun section was in order. This was all done in less than an hour, and suddenly there were those long Quartermaster low-bed cattle trucks all over the place and we loaded into them.
>
> Some of the men didn't even have overcoats or galoshes as they had to be turned in, expecting new issue. One thing that made the enlisted men feel good . . . was [that] the officers were in the same boat as us.

Kopacka started his journey to the unknown with the boys of his machine-gun section on December 18 at 2:00 A.M. They were in a 6x6 truck, and it started to drizzle as they headed out of Mourmelon-le-Grand. The trucks would slow down, causing them to bunch up, then speed up again and try to catch up with the others, resembling an accordion. Kopacka's truck skidded off the roadway across a wooden bridge and went through the railing. This bridge was over a 35-foot-deep ravine, and the speed of the 6x6 propelled it to the other side, knocking over a 4-foot concrete wall and landing on its side. A 1-ton trailer was still attached to the truck and dangled over the edge of the ravine. One man was seriously hurt; the rest reloaded onto the back of the low-bed cattle cars. They became soaked, not by the drizzling rain but by the condensation that built up on the underside of the tarps stretched over the trucks. The troopers couldn't stand up when the tarp was pulled over them. What surprised them most was that the headlights were on; this convoy would be an easy target for the Germans. Luckily, the enemy was looking somewhere else.

The after-action battle report for January 26, 1945, reported that the convoy started out at 1600 on December 18 and arrived at the designated division assembly area at 0730 on the nineteenth, with one man injured in a truck accident en route.

> Immediately on arrival at assembly area, the Battalion Commander and party went on reconnaissance for gun positions in vicinity of SAVY (P5449), one kilometer west of BASTOGNE (P5558), to support the 506th Parachute Infantry Regiment. At 1330 the Battalion was in position and ready to fire. At 1530 all wire communications were complete. There was a total of 1,342 rounds of ammunition on hand in the battalion, including all types. Very little firing was done during the day.
>
> On the morning of the 20th the enemy attacked and cut off the First Battalion 506th Parachute Infantry and was the first contact with the enemy in strength. 816 rounds of our small supply were expended during this attack [at the town of Noville]. The battalion sent out three ammunition trucks to the rear in the morning for resupply and succeeded in getting back to the unit during the night with 1,040 rounds. This was the only ammunition that came [through] for division artillery until the 23rd when the first air resupply mission was flown. During the night all roads leading into BASTOGNE were cut off by the enemy. One Forward Observer with First Battalion killed by enemy shell fire.
>
> On the 21st, gun positions were moved into the open where they could fire any direction, and anti-tank positions were established. Ammunition very low and smoke shells fired with H.E. expenditures were held to a minimum on important targets.
>
> On the 23rd the battalion received 2,190 rounds from air resupply. From this point on the battalion had an average of 400 rounds per day available for missions. The artillery was used in general support of any sector of the perimeter where the enemy attacked, coordinated by Division Artillery, and in direct support of the 506th Parachute Infantry the entire operation. The battalion C.P. was bombed and strafed by P-47s accidentally on the 23rd but fortunately no casualties resulted. The Battalion area was shelled intermittently the entire time, which resulted in a few casualties. Gun positions could not be changed due to [the] small size of area occupied. All installations were well dug in and proved to be suitable protection from enemy shell fire.
>
> Contact was made with the 4th Armored Division on [the] evening of 26 December and supplies started coming in by truck from 27th on to end of campaign. From the 27th of December until 1 January enemy artillery and air forces were quite active.

Lt. Eugene Brooks, an A Battery forward observer, was in the last jeep in the column heading toward Bastogne. While en route, his job was to keep the vehicles moving. At times this was a frustrating mission. Many of the vehicles were operated by the 397th Quartermaster Truck Company, or "Red Ball Express," primarily made up of black soldiers. The column moved along at a maximum speed of about 20 mph and sometimes didn't move at all. On numerous occasions, Brooks, "sweeping the road," had his driver pull alongside a stopped truck. He would get out, wake the driver and assistant driver, and tell them to get them back into the column. When they stopped, the vehicles behind them would go around, thinking a mechanical failure had occurred. On one occasion, an air raid siren went off and all vehicles stopped. A few explosions could be heard in the distance.

Brooks vividly recalled when the cattle trucks, used for transporting the infantry, finally emptied their troopers. One group debarked on the right side of the road and another on the left. After this, the cattle trucks made a quick U-turn and briskly accelerated toward the south. By the time he was released from the rear of the column and arrived in Savy, the 321st had several of its guns emplaced.

The entire 101st Division was on the road. Few knew where they were or where they were supposed to end up. The 321st mingled with the convoy, riding in jeeps, 6x6 trucks, and cattle trailers. Lt. Anthony Linz (A Battery), executive officer, was somewhere

Savy. Artillery moving to a new position in December 1944. TURKAL FAMILY

at the front of the convoy, intentionally placed on the road with the 506th PIR. He had one 75mm pack howitzer with his group. His assignment was to arrive in Bastogne prior to the firing batteries and get orders for where to emplace the remainder of the battalion.

That job was extremely important, not only to the battalion, but also to the troopers who would need their artillery support. With his single howitzer, Linz and a handful of soldiers peeled away from the column after arriving in Bastogne and headed to the area of Savy as ordered. Linz described the whole situation as "one horrible mess."

On December 18, Colonel Sink of the 506th had orders to base his regiment's position on contact with the enemy that the 501st encountered. It wasn't until 1700 hours that Sink gave Linz the approximate placement of the battalion guns: 1,500 yards west of Bastogne.

The 321st would be in direct support of the 506th PIR, so its twelve 75mm pack howitzers had to be able to send out accurate rounds on target anywhere the regiment needed artillery fire. Those targets would be chosen mainly by the company commanders of the 506th and the forward observers of the 321st assigned to them. Ideally each of the three regiments would have a liaison officer in each of their respective headquarters, who in turn would have at least one forward observer team in the field working under him.

Linz picked the open fields down the hill from the village of Savy on the farm Grandes Fontaine. He placed the single howitzer at 1700 hours and planned to dig in the other five from A Battery when they arrived. Because the front lines of the 506th were fluid, he was unable to register the gun.

While at Savy, the battalion was under constant enemy artillery fire. Occasionally they were bombed by German aircraft at night and strafed by fighters. A fair number of enemy artillery rounds were duds; because of that, many lives were spared. However, the Germans' aim was still quite good, so living another day was always a gamble.

Linz could do nothing more than wait for the other guns to arrive, not knowing when the rest of the battalion would arrive or if orders would be

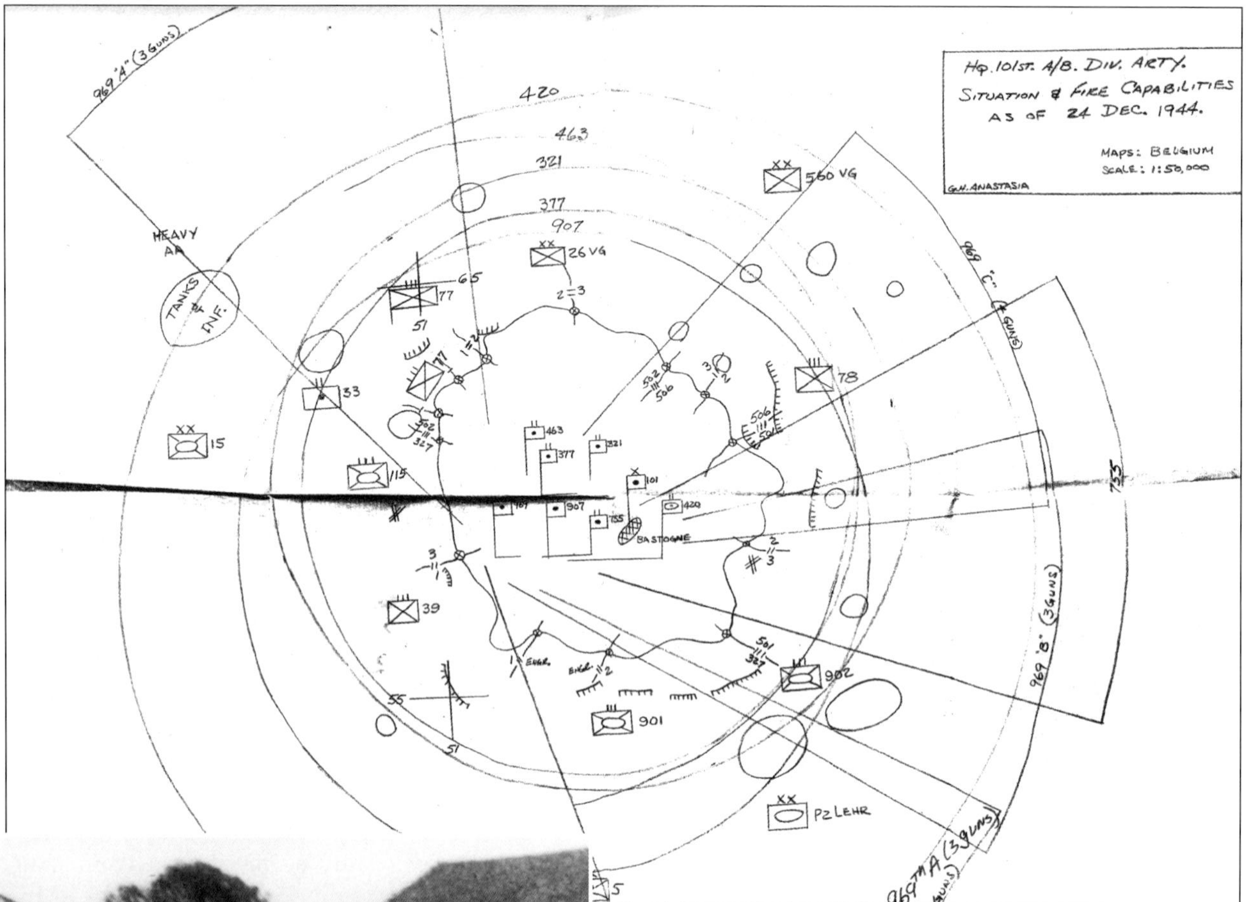

A Bastogne overlay indicating the location of all artillery units under 101st Division artillery. This clearly defines the maximum range of all artillery units, coinciding with the front lines of the various 101st infantry regiments. This overlay is quite possibly the inspiration for the commonly used phrase at the time, "We are the hole in the donut." BANDO COLLECTION

Left: A female farmer with PFC William Buckingham (B Battery) in Savy. WARREN FAMILY

Savy area.

An A Battery sergeant learning to lay the guns. LINZ FAMILY

changed to move to another location. He thought of the disarray on the road coming into Bastogne, of all the soldiers going in the opposite direction. Many were without weapons or separated from their assigned units, and they looked so strange without helmets on their heads. The few artillery soldiers Linz had with him for his security detail were nervously posted as guards near the gun. Later, Colonel Carmichael—and not Lieutenant Linz—would receive the Silver Star for the quick emplacement of his single howitzer at Savy.

The 3rd Gun Crew had dug in their piece, enabling it to fire in 180 degrees, and they were just about to open their K rations when Linz reappeared. They were to enlarge the pit to enable them to fire 360 degrees, a full circle. Cpl. Vernon Raker (A Battery) and his crew were exhausted already. He said to Linz that if he wanted it that way, he should dig the damn thing himself. Linz dropped his head; it appeared he was dead tired as well. He said, "Corporal, I'm merely handing down orders from my superior. Now do as I instructed." It didn't take long before that gun, along with the others, were firing from different positions in their individual gun pits, necessitating a full-circle gun emplacement.

In his memoir, Raker recalled that the next day, Lieutenant Linz came back to check on the ammunition at the gun sections. Raker said, "Lieutenant, I owe you an apology for what I said yesterday. Any other officer would have court-martialed my ass, and I would have deserved it. I'm very sorry."

Linz replied: "Corporal, it takes a man to apologize in front of his crew. You've just proven your manhood to me, and I'm very happy to accept your apology. We're all overwrought and tired—this damn war makes men do strange things."

The rest of the battalion departed Mourmelon on the eighteenth at 1700 hours. After traveling all night in the 101st convoy, they arrived at a rendezvous point outside Bastogne at 0815 hours on the nineteenth.

At 1035 hours, the battalion proceeded from the rendezvous location to the fields Lieutenant Linz had chosen, arriving there at 1220 hours. Only one hour later, all the pack howitzers were dug in. A and B Batteries were initially separated by a stand of pine trees.

By 1510 hours, all the communication wire was laid and the radios were set up. The news came in that the Germans were wearing American uniforms, were armed with American weapons, and driving captured American vehicles. This put the soldiers on edge. Guards were doubled and passwords were now the norm. Tanks were reported to be in the vicinity, but whether they were friendly or not was the bigger question.

Newly promoted to first lieutenant, Francis Canham was a twenty-three-year-old from the apple orchard area of New York. He had been with the 321st for five months and was admired by everyone he met, both on and off the battlefield. He was in charge of one of the two B Battery forward observer parties and the only one with the 506th at this time. The other two in Canham's party were Sgt. Bill Plummer, the former chief of the section for the B Battery third gun, and Pvt. William "Jay" Stone, a radioman.

Normally, Cpl. Paul Galant would be with this group, but he was assigned to a quartering party for the 321st B Battery. Plummer took his place. The jeep driver was Pvt. Wendell Byrnes, who provided the transportation and equipment because it was up to the firing batteries to get their men to the front.

The forward observer party was ordered to the S-3 of the 506th PIR on December 18 and was told that the 321st was to be in direct support of the 506th. Furthermore, they were to get in the column leaving Mourmelon with the 506th. They arrived at the assembly area outside Bastogne during the night and waited until daylight to find out their destination.

Daylight found the party at Mande-Saint-Étienne, the bivouac area of the 506th headquarters. They waited for assignment while Colonel Ewell's 501st PIR made the initial probe east toward Neffe.

The 1st Battalion of the 506th was traveling north on road N15 on December 19. The remnants of the 28th Infantry Division passed them, moving south away from the Germans. Many were without weapons or equipment, sometimes moving in twos and threes. The men of the 28th Infantry were amazed that this group of soldiers was heading for

Noville and couldn't help but notice the shoulder patches on their jackets: screaming eagles. It was the 101st, looking for action. The troopers would be face to face with the Germans only 7 kilometers farther up the road.

This group was part of Team Desobry, named after Maj. William Desobry, their commander. Combat Command B (CCB) of the 10th Armored Division was also part of this group, whose mission was to occupy Noville and keep the enemy out. This would buy time for the defenders of Bastogne to set up their defense and solidify their lines.

Canham's forward observer party had learned the Germans were using captured American tanks from the 9th Armored Division, which made things more difficult. It was brought to the 321st boys' attention that the paratroopers had no ammunition for their carbines; artillerymen normally carried the folding-stock carbine. Without hesitation, this was remedied by sharing the .30-caliber ammo with the men who were without. That scene was replayed many times over with the 506th and the troopers of the 321st at Bastogne.

For a short time, Canham's party dropped back to Foy. On December 20, it was back to Noville to work with the 1st Battalion of the 506th. They were to find A Company, which would have work for them to do. Early in the morning, the Germans were trying the town, attacking east and northeast without much success. It was thought it could be bypassed to the north and south. No American troops were north of Noville, which made the work of the only forward observer party with the 506th extremely important by bringing down artillery of the 321st.

Radioman William Stone wrote:

> At this time, Noville was taking a beating. The Germans were pounding the village and us with everything they had. The piercing whistle of incoming projectiles followed by the sounds of their explosions assaulted our ears. Their blasts buffeted our bodies. The sharp, bitter smell of the exploded powder invaded our nostrils. Buildings were severely damaged. Wounded were walking or being carried to the battalion aid station. If the enemy could take the village quickly, he would have the freedom to continue his advance to the west, where he was ordered to seize the crossings over the Meuse River, or a straight road into Bastogne provided he could break through the other battalions of the 506th.

Lieutenant Canham chose a two-story stone barn for his observation post, which was northeast of Noville. Fog was a problem; it would come and go, obscuring targets and then suddenly exposing them. The forward observer party was just behind A Company lines. It was 0830 hours, and they were set up. The fog lifted and Canham could now see a few hundred yards out the window, crouching underneath it and then peering out for any enemy activity. It was a prime observation post. A seasoned trooper, he understood that the Germans also were now able to see. They would keep a keen eye out for activity from such a location.

The terrain sloped down from the barn and rose to one of several ridges that dominated this field of fire. There were woods on top of the ridge, with tanks of the Panzer-Lehr and its infantrymen coming out of it.

The range of the 75mm pack howitzers was at its limit, as they were dug in at Savy some six miles away. The 321st fired nearly 800 rounds of M54 that day.

The expectations of this forward observer party were the same as in any other engagement: observe from an area, which gave a commanding view of enemy activity, and bring down accurate fire from artillery upon both men and equipment. If the party was to be successful, it had to be concealed and have cover. In combat, this was not always possible. In Canham's case he had both, but it didn't make any difference.

In setting up the observation post, the preferred method on that particular day was to have a battery-powered telephone with 60 feet of line running between both phones, with Sergeant Plummer at one end and Private Stone on the other. Plummer, stationed with Canham, could relay fire directions and corrections from his lieutenant to Stone, who was set up in a farmhouse across an alley from the barn. Stone, using a 321st frequency on his battery-packed radio, would relay the information from

Savy. An unidentified 321st gun section.

Plummer to the 321st FDC. Stone had to listen intensely to both his radio and his phone, each having a completely different function, to differentiate between the voices. The noises of battle made this job even more difficult.

Lieutenant Canham peered out the small, frameless barn window, looking for targets to inflict the most harm on with the 75mm rounds of the 321st. The fog lifted like a giant curtain, exposing the Germans assembling their tanks and infantry. He called for a fire mission: "Kansas 12, this is Kansas 68. Fire mission. Over."

The fire missions were all going through the FDC at the battalion level of the 321st. This radio was the only link the men of Noville fighting for survival had to the relative safety of the troops in Foy. All communications were cut, except for this single SCR-610 radio.

"Kansas 68, this is Kansas 12. Over," came the response.

Canham gave the location of the German buildup: "Coordinates 69462968. Enemy infantry and tanks moving out from woods across open field. Fuze VT, will adjust. Over." Battalion FDC repeated the coordinates, plotted the target, and sent two rounds over. Canham observed where they landed and adjusted the fire accordingly. This had to be timed just right to keep his presence hidden at the window. He only looked out when the shells burst or to catch a quick glance to locate the targets moving on Noville. Plummer also looked out the window to identify hits.

The corrections were made until the rounds fell within 100 yards of the target. Canham calmly said, "Tell them let's have it," over the telephone.

Stone relayed, "Fire for effect." Two minutes later, the radio operator for the gunners transmitted, "On the way." The message was relayed to Plummer, who then looked through his binoculars to see how the battle was going: "End of mission. Fifteen infantry casualties. Tanks forced to button up."

This scenario was repeated for an hour, causing destruction to the Germans and confusion by forcing the tank commanders to keep their hatches closed while under bombardment. This slowed the German offensive because it limited the commanders' 360-degree vision required to keep an all-out assault effective.

The battle still raged outside of Noville; tanks were moving to the west, slowing pushing in. The enemy was encircling the town and the 1st Battalion of the 506th. Not knowing any of this, Stone became aware of the silence. The phone line was quiet. It was now 0945 hours, and Sergeant Plummer's voice crackled over the 60-foot phone line. "Hey, Jay! Come over here quick. I think Canham is dead." Stone ran down the alley to an aid station, found a medic, and both ran up the stairs of the barn. The corpsman confirmed that the bravest man Stone had ever known was dead.

A German tank had spotted movement in the barn's window and fired a round when Canham looked out to adjust fire. The high-explosive projectile hit the right side of the stone windowsill, driving shell fragments and stone shards into the young lieutenant's head. His body was left where it fell because it was time to leave and set up somewhere else. The attack had not diminished, but instead intensified, and the Germans had located their observation post.

The body of Lieutenant Canham was later buried in a small village cemetery miles away from where he died. Who buried him is still a mystery. His remains are now interred at the American cemetery in Hamm, Luxembourg, Plot B, Row 8, Grave 179. When his body was disinterred from the initial burial, it showed signs of having been burned. Most likely the barn used as the observation post caught fire during the battles for Noville while his corpse lay inside. In a letter to the American Graves Registration Command in Europe, dated January 9, 1948, Canham's father wrote: "I have talked this over with Francis' mother, two brothers and sister, and none of us can see any use of disturbing Francis' remains to bring them back. Please let them remain in peace [in Luxembourg]."

The 321st FDC was informed of the death of its forward observer party's leader. Somehow the

B Battery gun section in Savy in contact with the FDC. WITCHER/DETTORE

Cpl. William Stone, a forward observer radioman for B Battery, in Bastogne.
CARPENTER/DETTORE

message was garbled, and the S-2 believed Canham was only wounded. It wasn't recorded until 1755 hours that he died of his wounds.

As the remainder of the party—with Plummer in charge—looked for another observation post, they were told not to leave Noville and to continue the fire missions. Both men were taken aback because their only intention was to stay and kill Germans. While dodging enemy fire, they spotted a column of men on the edge of town moving into Noville. Plummer carried a M1 rifle, which he preferred to the folding-stock carbine. He snapped the rifle to his shoulder and was ready to fire when he realized that the file of men were Americans.

PFC Victor Sauerheber (HQ Battery) of Corydon, Indiana, came into Bastogne via a 6x6 truck. He was assigned to Lt. William Nugent as his radio operator, part of the liaison section. Nugent came down with pneumonia, leaving Sauerheber alone at Sink's 506th PIR command post as his radio operator. After the first few hours, Sink's paratroopers were in position at the main line of resistance.

That night, Colonel Carmichael believed his position was being infiltrated by the Germans and requested a platoon of paratroopers to guard the command post. Sauerheber made a disparaging remark to Sink about the colonel's request. Sink admonished the private for feeling that way, saying that if sending men would satisfy him and the artillery fire came when requested, then so be it. Sink told Sauerheber to go to the line, get the men, and lead them back to the 321st area and to the command post. On foot, he traveled about a mile and a half to get the troopers and then back to Savy.

Sauerheber then returned back to Sink's command post to find Sink operating the radio himself. Sauerheber took over the radio again. For the next three days and nights he stayed with the radio, without sleep. Sink wasn't feeling well and sat in an overstuffed chair wrapped in a blanket. Finally, another radio operator arrived and sent Sauerheber back to the 321st battalion's command post. Once there, he was ordered to yet again man the radio. While relaying information on a firing order, his voice became garbled, and no one on the other end

PFC Victor Sauerheber of Headquarters Battery.
SAUERHEBER FAMILY

could understand what he was saying. His colonel was nearby and heard the conversation, saying, "Soldier get the shit out of your mouth!" Sauerheber became angry, but before he could utter another word, he passed out. After a few hours' sleep, it was back to work.

On the nineteenth, near Savy around 0800 hours, Brooks's forward observer team was still with A Battery because nobody knew where the no-fire lines were. Lt. James Wicker, the battery commander, approached Brooks and told him to grab a rocket launcher and some rockets. The order was to assemble his team and hunt down the German tanks moving in from the north. The group headed out without finding any enemy armor. It didn't bother them a bit to come up empty on this mission. What they didn't know at the time was that it was not German tanks but American tank destroyers that were spotted.

Without communications to the firing batteries, the howitzers were pieces of useless iron. Running wire, miles and miles of it, was a never-ending job. If Holland could be called bad for wiremen, Bastogne was even worse. The cold and snow upped the ante. PFC Albert Lelonek (A Battery) and another wireman, PFC John Alicandro (A Battery) from Edge Hill, Pennsylvania, worked well together. If the forward observers needed supplies, they went and delivered them; if someone needed relief, they provided it themselves. Their mindset was that of the forward observers: fearless.

On one occasion, Lelonek and Alicandro went out to find a break in the wire and repair it. By now, the wire had been damaged so many times that new wire was run alongside the old. This time when they went out into the field, ten to twelve separate lines had been laid down. One of them was bad, but which was anyone's guess. They constantly had to tap into the line to find out if it was bad and if it was going out to the infantry or in to the battery. If there was no clear cut, the wiremen had to take their gloves off and run the line between their fingers to feel for a nick in the wire. Their fingers would become numb from the cold and they would have to switch hands. Once the correct line was found, it couldn't be dropped for fear it would become jumbled up again with the rest in the snow. Wires stretched over roads, under fences, across flat stretches of fields, and even in the trees. If they found a dead German, it was considered acceptable to elevate one of the corpse's hands and run the wire between his fingers. The enemy soldier was now of service to them.

It was getting dark when Lelonek and Alicandro wandered into a company of paratroopers where a guard was posted. Not knowing who it was, the guard issued a password challenge. Alicandro yelled the password, but the wind was blowing so hard in

A hidden American tank in Bastogne. WILLIAMS FAMILY

PFC Sam Lingenfelter (HQ) in Savy. SINKUTCH/DETTORE

the other direction the guard didn't hear it. The wiremen watched as the guard took the safety off his rifle and raised it to fire. Alicandro yelled again. This time the wind stopped and the guard heard his response. He lowered his rifle.

The Germans spotted the wiremen walking across an open field, looking for the wire break, and fired an 88mm gun. As the wiremen ran, another 88 was fired and missed. The round went over their heads, exploding in the distance. The Germans' habit in Bastogne was to fire two rounds; if they didn't score a hit, the firing stopped.

Lelonek and Alicandro found the break, made the repair, and returned to the battery.

The 321st command post was a two-story stone building that had formerly been a girls' school. The schoolhouse belonged to Lochman Feron, who had a wife and four-year-old daughter. The battalion officers became friendly with the family and learned

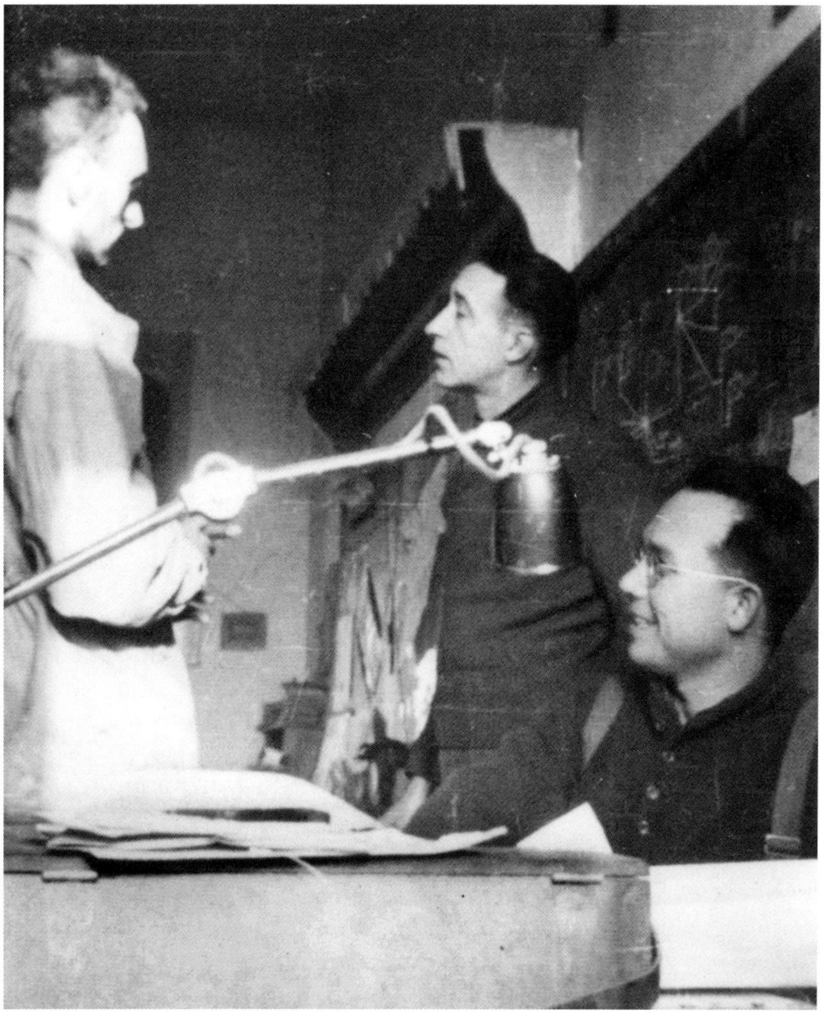

Inside the 321st schoolhouse command post at Savy. From left to right: Captain King, Colonel Carmichael, and Major Henderson. PERKINS FAMILY

that Feron was a sniper for the Belgian Underground. He stayed with them long enough to kill two German paratroopers at the beginning of the siege. Since the Americans were in his home, he felt it was safe to leave and permanently rejoin his group. He did not return while the 321st was in Savy.

Besides the shortage of ammunition for the battalion, food had run out for those in the command post. Feron's wife went to the basement with a shovel and dug up plenty of canned pork and cabbage preserved in mason jars and fed the new occupants. When food supplies did arrive by air and by trucks, the Feron family home became packed with foodstuffs. All the food was donated, courtesy of the men who were fed by the Belgian family. Their generosity was repaid many times over, and the Headquarters staff of the 321st were more than happy to do so.

Just outside the schoolhouse was a stone shed used to house the radio operators. A single German 88 round hit nearby, the shrapnel just missing Pvt. Neal Batchelor (HQ) as he was coming around the corner of the building. Another fragment of the exploding round struck the second-story wall and entered the bedroom where Colonel Carmichael slept. A little later, the colonel came out of the command post and, spotting Batchelor, motioned for him to come inside. When they got to the bedroom, Carmichael pointed out the headboard on his bed. There was a chunk missing. "If I was sleeping there," he said, "it might have killed me!" Batchelor replied, "Yes, sir, you're right," and walked back to his unheated stone shed. It was the first and last time he was ever invited into the warm building, which was off-limits for enlisted men.

S-2 Captain Perkins photographs himself on the second floor of the schoolhouse command post at Savy. PERKINS FAMILY

Pvt. Wendell Byrnes (B Battery) was in the Detail Section; his duties included driving the forward observer teams and their supplies toward the front lines. As a jeep driver, Byrnes had to be cognizant of not only the paratroopers' positions but also those of the Germans. Many times he would travel along on unfamiliar back roads, driving around a sector of contested terrain. He would not know for sure who held the road he was on at that moment. Constantly shifting the gears of his jeep, working the clutch to rev the working four-cylinder engine up and down, was like music to him. The sound it created was Byrnes's only American companion.

Prior to Normandy, it was Byrnes's conviction that he was going to earn the Medal of Honor. He felt that it was his destiny to be so recognized. In Normandy, he had learned what the cost of such an honor might be, and now, in Belgium, his priority was simple: do his duty and stay alive.

In the first days of the Bastogne battle, the fight raged around Noville and Foy. The forward observer team of Lieutenant Canham, Sergeant Plummer, and Private Stone was directing fire for the 506th, and they were the only working 321st forward observers in the field calling out for fire missions. It was time for them to be resupplied.

Byrnes loaded his jeep with extra batteries, ammunition, and food for this team. He knew where they were approximately, but the front lines were fluid and nothing was certain except that the Germans were making a major assault in this area. Checking his map, he knew he was getting close. He heard the roar of all types and calibers of guns. The usual routine involved parking somewhere off the road and then asking any trooper he saw for the location of a specific company. He jumped from the jeep when he spotted two paratroopers and asked for the whereabouts of A Company of the 506th 1st Battalion. They responded that the only thing known for sure was that help was needed up the road, and that was where they were headed. At that instant, Germans came onto the road with tanks and infantrymen; they turned toward the group and opened fire.

The rate and scope of fire was so intense that all three ran across the road in the hope of reaching the ditch that ran alongside. Byrnes looked back as he jumped into the ditch. He saw both troopers, who had been running on each side of him, shoulder to shoulder, fall backward. Both had been felled by a single shot to the forehead. He was unscathed and scrambled back toward the woods where the jeep was parked. The forward observer team was not able to get their supplies that day. Byrnes reported back to the 321st and told Captain King (HQ) what had happened.

Byrnes knew from the early days of Bastogne that things were going to be quite different from Holland.

A group of 321st soldiers and female farmers from Grandes Fontaine farm, Savy.

Captain King (left) and Major Henderson (right) at the Savy schoolhouse command post. Note the gun emplacements marked on the blackboard. PERKINS FAMILY

The schoolhouse exterior with camouflaged vehicles alongside. PERKINS FAMILY

Every time he loaded the jeep with supplies for the forward observers or was sent somewhere, he could count on having an unpleasant experience. Nearly one-third of the battalion's jeeps were damaged by shell fragments during the Bastogne battle.

A few days into the Bastogne cauldron, Captain King told Byrnes to use his jeep and drop off badly needed supplies up the road. It was a cold, very dark night; the only light was what squinted through the slits of the headlight blackout covers. As usual, Byrnes was working alone.

After driving a short distance, he heard firing up the road. Moving slowly, he observed a half-dozen or so GIs walking away from the direction of the gunfire. They seemed neither in a hurry nor concerned—an odd reaction to have. Sensing something wasn't right, the seasoned trooper pulled to the side of the road, grabbed his carbine from alongside his seat, and slid into the adjoining ditch. If he was overreacting, everybody would get a good laugh at

Another shot of the schoolhouse. PERKINS FAMILY

his expense, but Byrnes knew he could live with that. He stayed hidden, carbine at the ready, as the group spotted the jeep. They ran toward it, yelling like schoolboys on the playground—in German! They were so excited that they never checked the ditch. They laughed at their good fortune, piled in, and sped off into the darkness.

Byrnes walked back, deep in thought; he needed to come up with a story for Captain King. The Germans had stolen King's personal jeep, and it couldn't be easily replaced. The airborne division was short of everything, especially transportation with fuel. Telling King that his jeep was gone wouldn't sit well with the battery commander. Keeping his lie simple, Byrnes said that German artillery hit it and that he barely escaped with his life.

Less than a week later, Captain King scrounged up another jeep and sent Byrnes on another trip through the Belgian countryside. This time it was daylight, which caused another set of problems. It was known that the enemy had certain road intersections under observation, with the coordinates already plotted by German firing batteries. Whether or not a German forward observer would call in fire on a single vehicle was anyone's guess. Private Byrnes hoped he was not going to be a target of opportunity for some bored enemy observer. He traveled as fast, or faster, than the conditions allowed. Every artilleryman knew that a moving target was much more difficult to hit. But then again, this place was so different.

German 88s started to explode on the road in front of him. The rounds were not just on the road, but on both sides. Even worse, the Germans were "walking" their artillery up the road toward him at a fast pace, a World War I move the British called a rolling barrage. Byrnes was always frightened beyond words of enemy artillery fire, especially the famed 88s. These high-velocity rounds would explode on their target before anyone heard the report of the shell being fired, a trait unique to the German 88s. This peculiarity made the 88s both envied and feared.

Byrnes had just a few seconds to formulate his plan. He slowed down and jumped from the jeep, rolling into a ditch. He watched his driverless vehicle continue down the road, impervious to exploding German shells. As quickly as the barrage had rained down, it lifted, but fearing a second shelling, he stayed put.

A group of excited Germans appeared from the woods and spotted an intact, running American jeep directly in front of them. The 4x4 had come to rest against a tree, bumper to bark, still in gear with its wheels spinning in the soil. Within seconds, the lucky group jumped in and sped off in the very direction that Byrnes was originally headed.

What would Captain King say this time? Byrnes decided that since the first excuse for the loss of a jeep had worked so well, it should work again. He hoofed it back to the 321st command post and sought out his captain, who was standing next to B Battery's 1st Sgt. Timothy J. Shea. This worried Byrnes because he knew Shea was the smartest noncom in the battery. Nothing got past him.

Byrnes told his story factually up to the part when the Germans jumped into the jeep and drove off, then stated that the rolling barrage had blown up the vehicle just after he jumped out. King replied, "You gotta be shitting me. Both of those jeeps were mine." Byrnes replied, "But Captain, if that's not the God's honest truth, I wouldn't be standing here right now. I would be spread all over the road with that damn jeep." King couldn't argue with that logic and bellowed at Byrnes, "If you ever lose another one of *my* jeeps again, I will personally kick your ass from here to Mourmelon!"

Captain King disappeared into the command post. Sergeant Shea looked at Byrnes and asked what really happened. Byrnes confessed, "The Krauts stole it." Shea pondered the response, then quietly stated, "Don't worry about it. These things happen—but don't tell the captain." Nothing more was ever said of the incident by Shea.

At 0805 hours on December 20, enemy tanks were reported moving from the north. That put B Battery at a disadvantage because it could not fire over the treeline in a northern direction. They moved into the same field as A Battery, which took them forty minutes to accomplish. Hand grenades were used to accelerate the digging. Sgt. Mark Sullivan was in charge of B Battery's 2nd Gun Section and had no time to waste. He dug a small hole, pulled

A P-47 mistakenly bombed and strafed the 321st staff buildings and vehicles in Savy. PERKINS FAMILY

Capt. Fred King, B Battery commander, in Savy. WILLIAMS FAMILY

American armor at Savy. FULTON FAMILY

An unidentified B Battery gun crew at Savy. CRIM FAMILY

PFC Gilbert Quinn (kneeling) of B Battery uses a blanket piece for warmth in Savy. WITCHER/DETTORE

the pin from the grenade, and dropped it in. The explosion loosened the surface of the frozen ground, enabling the gun crews to quickly excavate a pit for their 75mm pack howitzer with picks and shovels. In anticipation of the unique request for artillery support, all the howitzers were dug in to fire in a 360-degree radius, the first time this was done by the entire battalion.

When enemy counterbattery fire started to land near A Battery's location, B Battery must have wondered if it hadn't been safer in its prior location. It was 1120 hours, and German counterbattery fire would not be out of the ordinary in this farmer's field for the rest of the time in Savy.

Division artillery was notified of the shortage of 75mm rounds and instructed all artillery battalions to share ammo for their guns and to conserve what was left. The battalion put in wire to the 969th Field Artillery and registered their 155mm guns at 1154 hours. The small supply of 75mm ammo was nearly expended supporting the 1st Battalion of the 506th; a total of 816 rounds was fired that morning.

It was necessary to locate the 506th PIR command post. Forward observer Lieutenant Brooks (A Battery) and his party were told it was at a farmhouse nearby. Arriving at the building and standing alongside it, they observed a Sherman tank and thought they now had it made. Instead, it fired one round at them, hitting a chicken coop and sending white feathers everywhere. It looked like a snowstorm. Everybody piled out of the house. The tank fired a second round, striking a tree and wounding a paratrooper. The Germans had captured a Sherman. Everybody took off including the FO party.

Brooks continued to search for the 3rd Battalion of the 506th and its commanding officer, Maj. Lloyd E. Patch. He ran into the executive officer of the battalion and asked him, "Where do I take these people?" The officer pointed to another area and told him Patch was over there. Again, the forward observer party searched but couldn't find him. They started to dig in anyway, but someone told Brooks not to dig there because a machine gun was set up to fire over that section of ground. They moved, and later in the afternoon the 3rd Battalion jumped off. The forward observer team was unable to put out a single fire mission due to the confusion at the front.

As the ammunition sergeant of the 321st, Harold Dittmer (HQ) had the job of making sure the 75mm pack howitzers were properly supplied. After unloading the initial ammo brought from Mourmelon and dispersing it to the firing batteries of the 321st, it was time to check on the supply situation. Dittmer discovered the army supply dump didn't have any ammunition for the 75mm pack howitzers because it was set up long before the current crisis. They had only M2 ammo, which was a much longer shell for the tanks, and no M1 rounds designated exclusively for the 75mm pack howitzer. Without additional ammo, the 321st would be ineffective in a very short time. On December 19, the battalion had a total of 1,342 rounds, or approximately 100 per gun. Most of

By December 20, the battalion was down to fewer than ten rounds of 75mm ammunition per howitzer in Savy.

A Battery soldiers at Savy stayed in the tree line for protection when not at their guns. LINZ FAMILY

these rounds had been brought back to France from Holland, only to be reissued. On a busy day in Holland, that would only last one day.

Sergeant Dittmer knew the dire consequences of this situation. The 506th PIR would be without support from its artillery. One of the lessons learned in Normandy was that paratroopers without adequate artillery support suffered heavy casualties. Something had to be done quickly.

It was decided that it was time to leave. Dittmer gathered some drivers and two GMC 2.5-ton 6x6 trucks. The A Battery drivers—Pvt. Emerald McCoy (HQ) from Humboldt, Tennessee; Cpl. Samuel Lingenfelter (HQ) from Amsterdam, Ohio; and Pvt. Woodrow Stephens—were part of this airborne caravan headed out of Bastogne back to Mourmelon. The group of men would be on the move for over twenty-four hours straight, hoping to find an ammo dump that wasn't depleted at their base camp.

Adding to the gravity of the situation, but unbeknownst to this group of troopers on the road, on the morning of December 20 the Germans attacked the 1st Battalion of the 506th. The 321st expended 816 rounds of 75mm ammunition in that action. Fewer than forty rounds per gun remained, most of which were smoke (white phosphorus) and high-explosive antitank (HEAT), unsuitable against infantry. Air resupply was not possible due to the weather conditions.

The troopers' plan was to travel back to Mourmelon the same way they had come, but retracing the route was made even more difficult because it had started to rain, making the roads all the more hazardous. As they pulled out of Bastogne, equipment littered the roadsides; overturned jeeps, GI coats, rifles, and helmets were left behind to make the retreating Americans' loads a bit lighter. They traveled as fast as they could with their 6x6 trucks, trying not to slide off the road on the steep downgrades. The danger and need to shift gears kept all the men wide awake despite their exhaustion. They had left at 1600 hours the day before and pulled into Mourmelon around 0700 hours on the twentieth. It was time to load up and get it done fast.

The 75mm rounds at the ammo dump were stored in cardboard tubes, one round per tube. A metal packaging device shaped like a cloverleaf was on each end of the tubes; this allowed three rounds to be handled at once, minimizing stacking problems and decreasing the time it took to load. The weight of this bundling system was approximately 54 pounds per set.

Sergeant Dittmer stacked the rounds on the truck. He could barely keep up with Corporal Lingenfelter, who had worked as a coal miner before the war and was tossing the rounds like they weighed nothing at all. The truck canvas was rolled forward, exposing all possible room for the valuable cargo. Each truck was to carry over 8 tons of ammunition, 1,040 rounds each, which made the vehicles grossly overloaded. One well-placed shot would obliterate all traces of the men and their trucks.

In the remaining space, the crew threw the battalion's four bags of Christmas mail on top of the canvas that now covered the stacked rounds. It would be the only mail in weeks that any 321st boy would receive from back home.

Heading back to Bastogne was easy initially. The troopers approached the town of Neufchâteau in the dark, using the blacked-out headlights referred to as "cat eyes." A roadblock was directly ahead, and the three 6x6 trucks were waved to a stop by military police. One of them told Dittmer, "I can't allow you to go any further; the Krauts cut the road."

It was approximately 2230 hours and they were 75 miles out of Bastogne. The group was not about to be deterred from their mission. Dittmer thought fast and yelled to the police, "Go get your officer. I want to talk to him." The soldiers turned around and started toward a small house near the road. Dittmer yelled to his driver, "Go, go!" The other trucks followed, and they never looked back.

Things certainly had changed since they had traveled the road earlier. An American weapons carrier headed southwest sideswiped the first truck, its outboard machine gun making contact. It might have been loaded with Germans in a captured American vehicle, probing the road. The overladen truck with its 8 tons of ammunition never quivered.

The trucks arrived at the battalion command post early the next morning at 0140 hours. It was December 21, and the men were beat. That same morning, S-4 Lt. Roe Wilkins (HQ) of Leesburg, Florida, decided to make another ammunition run using the same southwest road. He reasoned that several Sherman tanks and armored cars were escorting trucks back to Mourmelon, and this way, they had a chance of getting there in force. Some of the 321st crew was changed, and Pvt. Harry Sinkutch (HQ) decided to go along.

They inserted three trucks between the armored vehicles with the permission of the tank commander: one tank, then a truck, then another tank, and so on. This enabled them to have some protection. Sergeant Dittmer was again in the lead 6x6 truck. The convoy traveled in the dark and had to stop at times because German tanks were crossing the roads in front and to the rear. The two groups infiltrated each other and a firefight could have erupted at any moment, but none did. Later, it was learned that the Germans were from the Panzer-Lehr Division and that the tanks were part of a reconnaissance assignment. Their mission was to reach a checkpoint and not be bogged down in a prolonged fight prior to reaching their objective.

This assorted group of GIs was headed for Neufchâteau. The situation deteriorated rapidly when the convoy came under attack from all sides. The tanks were drawing fire and would not get through. The road was now sealed. Dittmer yelled to his driver, "Let's get the hell out of here!" The trucks of the 321st followed his lead. They all turned around and headed back to Bastogne. Private Sinkutch was sitting in the back of one of the trucks, with the canvas cover pulled over the bed. He heard, but could not see, the attack taking place. One of the troopers poked his head out of the back of the truck and said, "I see Germans all along the side of the road in foxholes." Miraculously, not a single 321st man was hit, and all returned to the battalion command post at Savy. It was now daylight on December 22.

The officers of the battalion recommended Sgt. Harold Dittmer for the Silver Star. Colonel Carmichael declined to endorse the paperwork, saying that Dittmer was only doing his job.

A Battery was preparing to dig in their guns when word was sent down that they indeed would be staying there. The Germans were advancing and nobody was leaving. A truck driver from the "Red Ball Express" (397th Quartermaster Truck Company) was agitatedly throwing duffel bags over the side of his 6x6 truck. He said he knew this was going to happen because the last time he transported the 101st was in Holland, and they had been surrounded there too. He finished unloading, dug a deep foxhole and parked his truck over it, then crawled inside. Sometime later, a P-47 mistakenly dropped a 500-pound bomb into the bed of the truck. Unknowingly, the driver had dug his own grave.

Casualties started to mount for the battalion. Just over an hour earlier, a 3/4-ton Dodge truck carrying a 321st Headquarters wire crew was hit by shrapnel from a German 88. They were laying wire to the 2nd

Sergeant Dittmer on the banks of the Rhine River, near Dusseldorf, Germany.

Harold Riley (HQ).

Battalion of the 506th, who were in reserve approximately three miles south of Foy near Luzery. Pvt. Samuel Reidman from Suffolk, Virginia, was killed when the 88 round exploded on the road in front of them. Splinters from the explosion tore apart the front of the truck, flew toward its passengers, and struck Reidman's head. He died instantly. The other linemen survived. Cpl. George Turkal was wounded in the neck by a piece of the exploding round. Cpl. James Parker, also from Suffolk, Virginia, was seriously wounded. Both Turkal and Parker eventually returned to the battalion.

At 0600 hours on December 21, the battalion was firing on the enemy with ammunition again running low. What little remained to fire was mixed in with smoke rounds, about 30 to 50 percent. The Germans

This unidentified 506th paratrooper in Bastogne was killed by a German mortar round moments after this picture was taken. CARPENTER/DETTORE

PFC Burton Carpenter (B Battery), from Chicago, Illinois, in Bastogne.
CARPENTER/DETTORE

believed the division had such a store of ammunition that they were just wasting it by using smoke. This gave a psychological advantage to the artillerymen. Division artillery expected a breakthrough by evening; with it would come the ammunition needed. But that did not happen.

The S-2 journal states: "1110 hrs. Ammo very low. Positions chosen for defense against enemy tank attack using HEAT [high-explosive antitank] when other ammo is expended."

It was a bad day for Lt. Brooks's A Battery forward observer team. After having found the front lines too fluid to bring down artillery fire upon the heads of the Germans the day before, Brooks and Privates Doyle, Falls, and Karasevic now found themselves east of Foy in the foggy midmorning.

The fog lifted and they spotted a German tank approximately eight hundred yards distant up on a hill across a road and in the tree line with a commanding view. The men knew that if they could see the tank, it probably was aware of their presence too. It fired a round across the open field between them, which exploded just ahead of the group of artillerymen and knocked Brooks down, sending iron splinters into his legs. He couldn't walk and ordered his men to leave him behind; they were to head for the woods, Bois Jacques. They refused to leave him. Doyle helped Brooks up, and they slowly limped toward the safety of the woods. The tank fired a second round, knocking Brooks down again along with Doyle and Karasevic and destroying the radios. Falls was the only member of the forward observer team unscathed. It was 1015 hours. It appeared Doyle was wounded in the upper thigh, but he still could walk. Karasevic's wounds were considered minor. Brooks again told his team to leave him behind, but Doyle said, "Lieutenant, between the both of us we have two good legs." However, it didn't take long for them to realize Doyle had sustained the greatest wound, to the upper inner thigh. Brooks told Falls to

France. Kneeling (from left to right): PFC Karasevic, PFC Falls, and Cpl. Charles Hunter. Standing (from left to right): unidentified staff sergeant, Sgt. Howard Rich, PFC Carl Wilson, and PFC H. C. Warren of A Battery.

get Doyle to an aid station, and the team of injured split up. Karasevic assisted Brooks, taking another route to an aid station.

Brooks and Doyle spent the remainder of their time at Bastogne in separate hospitals. Both Falls and Karasevic returned to the 321st Battalion headquarters after leaving the aid station.

As it turned out Brooks's wounds were more serious, and because of that the two men were split up. When the siege was broken, Brooks was evacuated to Sedan, France. One afternoon, the nurse told Brooks that he had someone who wanted to see him. He was at a loss trying to figure out who could it be. It was Doyle. After his visit, they were again separated and didn't see each other again until they returned to the battalion in Germany. Brooks said of his Bastogne experience, "All I did was take up space. I didn't get a chance to place a single artillery round on the enemy."

While in the hospital in England, Brooks was approached by a female newspaper reporter who wanted to know about his experiences in Bastogne and, especially, in Holland. She took notes and a few days later showed him the typed-up article. She wanted him to sign off on it for both accuracy and any necessary censoring.

Brooks read it and refused to sign off on it, appalled at the inaccuracies. He told the writer that what she wrote was fiction and that if any of his superiors read it, they would court-martial him—and rightly so. Part of the story had him falling back 50 miles. "Lady, you're crazy as hell," he said. "The whole damn place, crossing north to south [or] east to west, wasn't 25 miles."

The reporter changed the article, which was published but still full of grandiose statements. A copy was sent to Brooks's parents, courtesy of the reporter.

Germany. From left to right: Sergeant Rich, Lt. Donald Roy, Cpl. Louis Ivers, and Cpl. Robert Doyle. ROY FAMILY

Austria. Front: PFC Dennis. From left to right: Cpl. Charles Hunter, PFC Clemmons, and PFC John Alicandro. WARREN FAMILY

It was 0600 hours on December 22. Without having been resupplied, defensive positions were set up. The artillerymen prepared themselves to be overrun. This was the darkest day for the 321st since coming into combat. Rifle ammo had been given away earlier to the infantry, leaving just ten bullets per rifle for the artillerymen. Rockets for the bazookas had also been given away to needy paratroopers, leaving only a few per weapon at the firing batteries. The battery commanders—Lt. James Wicker (A Battery) and Capt. Fred King (B Battery)—came down to talk to their men at the batteries. They attempted to lift spirits by saying that General Patton and ammunition were to arrive soon.

In truth, artillery ammunition was in a critical shortage. Col. Thomas Sherburne, acting commanding officer of DivArty, skillfully lied to all but a few about the shortages. The reality was that some battalions had only 200 rounds available, and others fewer. General McAuliffe's only real worry was that the artillery battalions would run out of ammunition. The Germans had not been able to coordinate their attacks effectively in any one area due to the firing batteries' massive firepower. McAuliffe told his batteries to hold their fire "until you see the whites of their eyes." Both McAuliffe and Sherburne were of the opinion that as long as the artillery ammunition held, so would Bastogne.

It was here that Capt. Samuel "Bennie" Skinner, performing forward observer work, did the extraordinary. He and his party observed a battery of German artillery directly in front of them that arrived and started to emplace their guns. Skinner, aware of McAuliffe's orders, called Colonel Carmichael twice on the wired radio, saying, "I can see the whites of their eyes." Both times he was denied the shoot because of lack of ammunition.

Skinner did not call Carmichael a third time; instead, he called General McAuliffe directly and told him an entire German battery was lining up directly in front of him. He said their guns were pointed toward Bastogne and not a finer target could be had, even if artillery had only a few rounds left. McAuliffe gave the okay for two shots from each 75mm pack howitzer of one battery: a total of just twelve rounds for the fire mission.

Skinner gave the coordinates to the FDC, telling them to fire only one round and that he would adjust from that. When it hit, the Germans ran for cover. Knowing that a single round would be interpreted as a random shot, Skinner waited. The Germans returned to their guns a half hour later to complete the emplacement. In the meantime, Skinner was mentally making adjustments and forwarding them

PFC Rosario DeSantis of B Battery in Savy. CRIM FAMILY

Lt. Richard Smith, A Battery forward observer, in Savy, proudly displaying his much-desired winter boots. SMITH FAMILY

Right: Savy. Lieutenant Smith (right) mentored 1st Sgt. James Dundon (left), who in a few weeks on February 16, 1945, would receive the only battlefield commission in the 321st during the war, to second lieutenant. He received the news from WO (jg) Samuel Meyers while in his foxhole and accepted the promotion with the understanding that he would stay in his present position. No second lieutenant bars were available at the time. DUNDON FAMILY

Late in the evening, away from their guns and settled in a 4-feet-deep trench alongside a haystack, PFC George Shepard (A Battery) from Plano, Texas, and Cpl. Vernon Raker (A Battery) pondered what tomorrow might bring. Normally the two friends would take their boots off at night and use them as pillows, but on this evening they slept with them on, fearing the enemy would overrun the trench.

Shepard began a conversation, saying it might be an "every man for himself" type of morning. He went on to remark, "By the time those Krauts get to us, they're going to be dog-tired. I'm going to be nice and warm, with warm tootsies, and there ain't no way they will be able to catch me. Beside slippin' in the snow, they're also gonna be slippin' in my shit. Come on stove, *get hot*!" Shepard then wrapped his 6-foot body around his pal, sharing what little warmth was available. They went to sleep with their carbines near. ■

to the FDC with orders to wait. He finally gave the order: "Fire for effect!" All eleven rounds landed within the ranks of the enemy. It was a massacre. German ambulances arrived to take away the dead and the dying. The enemy and their guns pulled out. Skinner would suffer from nightmares for the rest of his life about this single fire mission.

Samuel "Bennie" Skinner was recommended twice for the Silver Star for his work during Bastogne, but Colonel Carmichael declined to approve the write-ups and forward them up the chain of command.

The much-anticipated resupply arrived by parachute drop at 1115 hours on December 23, along with air cover for the first time. Another resupply came at 1530 hours. The battalion's guns fired all night, until 0330 hours the next morning, responding to an enemy attack from the south.

During the drop, soldiers climbed out of their gun pits and foxholes or left their tree lines and command posts throughout the entire area. They looked up and cheered. PFC Hubert Warren (A Battery) remembered the cheering came from all compass points and reverberated throughout the area.

The drop supplies floated in with different colored parachutes denoting their contents. The artillerymen of the 321st were happy to see their color: red, meaning ammunition. In the midst of blues, reds, greens, and yellows, a few tiny white chutes floated down. These were of special interest to the soldiers.

The younger men in the battalion were chosen to pick up the dropped supplies in the field. Jeeps were assigned and trailers were hooked up. If they landed close by, the packages were dragged to a safer location. The Germans still had the fields covered with their mortars, and artillery was at the ready. As an incentive to go out into the open fields, the officers told the men they could keep one chute for themselves; these were used as blankets in their foxholes. Small-arms fire curtailed a complete recovery. What could be quickly picked up was then sped back to safer territory. A fair percentage of the supplies landed on the enemy, which was expected in a parachute resupply.

The tiny white chutes recovered with packages attached created much curiosity. PFC Bernard Simmons (B Battery) opened one of the packages. Inside was a carton of cigarettes and a note that said, "Keep it up." Pvt. Don Falls (A Battery) opened his and found a fruitcake with a message that said, "Merry Christmas from the guys of the Happy Goose." PFC Raymond Nagell (B Battery) from Minneapolis, Minnesota, retrieved one of the small white parachutes; his prize was also a fruitcake. These packages meant the soldiers were not on a forgotten battlefield, and that thought felt good.

Capt. John Fuller had become the A Battery commander after Normandy and stayed in that position until Bastogne, when he was transferred to division headquarters as a liaison officer. Fuller was tall and well-built with a quiet demeanor; he exuded confidence. His walk was unmistakable. The mere presence of this soldier could calm jittery nerves. Every man in the battalion either knew him or knew of him. Fuller was a most respected man, a born leader.

On December 23, while sleeping in a former barracks that until recently had housed the DivArty

Part of the B Battery crew with their pea shooter in Savy on Christmas 1944. Note the poison-gas detection brassard worn by the soldier on the left. The brassards would change color depending on the type of poison gas they came in contact with. Since the Germans didn't use gas as they did in World War I, it is unusual to see someone wearing a gas brassard at this late date and shows the height of some artillerymen's fear. TRUE FAMILY

headquarters command post, Fuller was killed by an exploding 88 artillery shell. The command post had moved to a more secure location in a nearby basement. The explosion was felt by the officers in the basement. That move had undoubtedly saved some of their lives.

The 88 round crashed through the roof before exploding. The explosion was so great that the shrapnel became embedded in the walls of the room from floor to ceiling. They were so numerous, there was not a hand's distance between any of the fragments except in one small area: the bottom of the wall just above the floor, where Capt. John Fuller was sleeping, absorbing the iron splinters. He was identified by his dog tags. A few others lying in bunks perished there also.

John "Jack" Fuller's brother, Murrey, wrote to his parents describing the death of their son. Capt. Murrey Fuller was in an engineer outfit tasked with demining the German-held area. In the letter, dated May 25, 1945, he told them that the cemetery where Jack was buried was on a hill overlooking beautiful farming country in France.

> The grave registration says he died from a shrapnel wound in the head. Now for the story the men of the 101st told me. Jack was killed the night of Dec. 23, the third night they were in Bastogne. The town was entirely surrounded, and according to Maj. Tyler, the Germans were in range with every piece of artillery they owned. Jack and some others were asleep in the basement and the shell was either a delay action or nearly a dud, because it went through the roof, 2 floors and 3 walls before exploding. They said Jack didn't regain

An empty 321st gun pit in Savy with a newly acquired parachute concealing a dugout. The howitzer was possibly pulled out temporarily for an antitank position.

A parachute resupply at Savy. PERKINS FAMILY

A C-47 crashed and burned in the distance near Savy after being hit by German ground fire. PERKINS FAMILY

C-47s dropping supplies at Savy. PERKINS FAMILY

The 321st soldiers in Savy hear the resupply C-47s for the first time on December 23. (Restored photograph.)
CORRIGAN/DETTORE

PFC Raymond Nagell (left) and an unidentified 321st soldier with a shot-down C-47 Stardust in the Bastogne area, near Sibret.

Left: Camp Claiborne. Capt. John "Jack" Fuller.
N. PERRY JACOBS COLLECTION

consciousness before he died. I believe I told you the colonel said that the way the men fought after seeing Jack and a few others go, the whole darn German army wasn't big enough to take that town away from them. There is one IF to the whole thing that didn't happen. Jack and Maj. Tyler were in England while the division was in a rest area. They got word that they were moving into Bastogne, and grabbed a plane for the continent and a train and truck to Bastogne. Had they missed one connection, as one other officer did, they would never have made it. That's about all to tell, except that Maj. Tyler has a diary of Jack's views on the jump at Nimigen [*sic*], and I got a picture from the division headquarters taken in Bastogne that shows the cemetery where he was buried first. He's in good company, Mom. A [private first class] is buried on his left and a corporal on his right, and they are by no means alone on that hill.

The Fullers received the official word via telegram on January 14, 1945, that John was killed in Belgium on December 23. His last letter home, dated December 7, 1944, was to his folks in Cedar Falls, Iowa, responding to a letter his mother wrote. She thought that her contribution to the war effort as a riveter was minimal and wanted to do more. "I'll tell you how we feel about the whole thing," he responded. "I've crawled along hedgerows so close to the Krauts that you could hear them scream when my concentration hit. I'm not bragging because that's what we're supposed to be doing. So let those who can get mixed up in this thing and the rest of you 'old ladies' (where did you get that idea anyway?) keep those home fires burning. Build 'em so hot we can feel 'em over here and don't worry—you'll be doing your part plenty. 'Nuff said. Love, Jack.

A few weeks later, in mid-January while at Hilbesheim, France, Lt. Tony Linz, executive officer of A Battery, entered his sleeping quarters. Just as he sat down, the door opened. He saw a ghost: his best

Jack Fuller and his brother Murrey (left) at their Iowa home. N. PERRY JACOBS COLLECTION

friend, Jack Fuller. In the silence, a calm, deliberate voice said, "I'm looking for my brother, Captain Jack Fuller. He's a battery commander." Linz had to give him the news that his brother was dead. Capt. Murrey Fuller looked just like his brother Jack in the low light.

On December 24 or 25 (the exact date is unknown), Cpl. Harry Sinkutch (HQ) was ordered by Lt. Roe Wilkins (HQ) to find three 6x6 trucks and recover parachutes from the fields. The chutes were going to be used as blankets at the hospital in Bastogne. There had to be hundreds of them all over the place. He located three drivers and helpers for the mission.

They went into the fields slowly because of the fog. The men would spot something, grab it, and move on. The pickings were slim. The driver, while on foot, heard a motor running. The fog was about two feet off the ground, obscuring the source, but the sound came from something big. He dropped down and looked under the fog, as if peeking underneath a curtain. It was a German tank 150 feet away, bogey wheels in clear view. He grabbed Sinkutch and dropped down as before, pointing. Sinkutch followed suit and made a quick decision: "Let's get the hell out of here." He quickly gathered the other men and they made a dash for their trucks. The few chutes they had located could fit in a single jeep.

The chutes were taken to the church hospital in Bastogne. There was barely enough room to walk between the aisles of the wounded. On Christmas Eve, a report came in to the 321st that an aid station was hit in Bastogne, with forty killed.

At 0805 hours on December 25, enemy tanks were reported in the vicinity and a 321st security team took up antitank positions. Forty minutes later, five enemy tanks were knocked out approximately a thousand yards to the rear.

Some of the Germans gave up after their tanks were made useless, raised their hands, and became POWs. Others were shot by a hail of bullets fired from every direction when they jumped out. A group of the fortunate ones came through the 321st area and were loaded in 6x6 trucks. Lt. Charles LePors (HQ) from Olympia, Washington, was asked for food by one of the POWs.

Bastogne church, Christmas Day 1944. WILKINSON FAMILY

A group of soldiers were going through the POWs' pockets before loading the prisoners into the trucks. One German kept pushing a soldier's hands away. The soldier opened up the tunic to expose breasts; it was a woman!

A headquarters man told an older POW to get moving and climb in the truck. The German said in halting English, "I wheel not took anuder step." The 321st PFC replied, "That's fine with me, pal," and shot him several times in the chest with his M1 rifle. The remaining Germans moved quickly to the back of truck and jumped in.

Unidentified B Battery soldiers in Savy warming up their mess kits, keeping smoke at a minimum. CRIM FAMILY

B Battery soldiers in Savy preparing to eat. CRIM FAMILY

One of the Savy houses in the background was where the Jerry tank was knocked out. WITCHER/DETTORE

In the large barn at the Grandes Fontaine farm, a Christmas mass was held for the 321st by Catholic priest Father (Captain) McGettigan. Whenever a mass was to take place in the area, Lt. Tony Linz (A Battery) would notify Cpl. Vernon Raker (A Battery). This happened for the duration of the war. At this mass, Linz served as the altar boy. German artillery rounds came whistling in, and the priest quietly said to Linz, "If I'm hit, would you dispose of the Host for me?" Linz nodded. Explosions were heard throughout the area, but the soldiers seemed at ease. No one moved. Their heads remained bowed until services were completed.

At 0850 hours, 1st Sgt. James Dundon (A Battery) and his forward observer team were near their jeep, getting ready to leave for the 506th PIR area. An American P-51 fighter came in from behind and fired twin .50-caliber machine guns at them. The rounds hit both sides of the jeep but missed everyone. There was a white hospital blanket in the back of the jeep. Dundon had one soldier on each

An unidentified 321st soldier in Savy communicating with the FDC. CRIM FAMILY

B Battery 4th Gun Section in Savy. WITCHER/DETTORE

B Battery 4th Gun Section in Savy. Front (from left to right): PFC Gilbert Quinn (holding carbine), PFC B. L. Witcher (cigarette in mouth), and PFC William Mullins (holding crackers). WITCHER/DETTORE

Americans on the move in the Bastogne area. WILLIAMS FAMILY

end help him hold it up in front of the jeep. Dundon stepped in front of the blanket, which highlighted him as the airplane came in from the side for another run. Frantically waving both arms, he hoped the pilot would get the message that it was his own troops he was shooting at. The pilot didn't fire but wiggled the wings instead in a gesture of acknowledgement and veered away. It was Dundon's error—all American vehicles were supposed to have colored identification panels draped on them, and his did not.

Ten CG-4A gliders landed without mishap in the 377th PFA area on December 26. One of the gliders, loaded with medical supplies, contained two surgeons and two enlisted men from the 12th Evacuation Hospital. They arrived in the afternoon following the thirty-minute glider ride from the airfield at Verdun, France. All the gliders that participated in the resupply had seen prior service and were missing seat belts, which were most likely removed by farmers while the gliders sat in their fields after being abandoned by their crews on prior missions.

Lt. Charles LePors, Headquarters communications officer. LEPORS FAMILY

Lt. Carroll Holland, assistant S-3, leading captured Germans through the 321st area in Savy. Note the snow on Holland's uniform from when he initially lay in the snow for concealment after spotting the enemy. CORRIGAN/DETTORE

An American tank in the 321st area in Savy. WILKINSON FAMILY

Lieutenant Smith at the Grandes Fontaine farm complex in Savy. LINZ FAMILY

None of the gliders were recoverable from the fields of Bastogne. A second parachute resupply drop occurred just before the gliders came in.

At 1215 hours, air liaison pilot Richard Fort was the first to report what he believed were friendly tanks on the road heading for Bastogne. He was about a half mile away in the air when he noticed the tanks; they were covered with 6 inches of snow, but their profiles were unmistakable. This was the lead element—a handful of Shermans from the 4th Armored Division had stopped, occupying 200 yards of road. They were being cautious. Twenty-four hours later they would roll into the lines of the 101st.

As the skies cleared, Lt. Bernard Zeppenfield climbed into his L-4 with his regular spotter, Lt. Joseph Yourie. They flew over Houffalize and Marvie, directing Typhoons to their targets. The towns were leveled when the mission was over.

A C-47 tug was hit just as it released its glider, part of the resupply mission on the afternoon of December 27. The tug, *Ain't Misbehavin*, was piloted by Capt. Ernie Turner and copilot Lt. Keistutis Narbutas, both from the 94th TCS/439th TCG. They had a crew of two enlisted men. As the plane came down with one of its engines on fire, the nylon towrope had not been released and was swinging from side to side. The end of the 350-foot rope was whipping about and making a *vvvvvhh, vvvvhh* sound. It was loud enough that some of the 321st men heard it from their gun pits.

The descending aircraft came in for a belly-landing over a road, startling a 6x6 truck driver when it flew over and nearly hit the vehicle. The panicked driver hit the brakes, causing a 180-degree turn that now had him heading in the opposite direction, but he did not slow down.

Lieutenant Turner had placed flak jackets on the floor of the cockpit for protection from ground fire. They had become doormats coated with dried mud. This created another problem when the craft took on antiaircraft fire from underneath the cockpit: the flak

Capt. Sam Williams, liaison officer, in the Bastogne area. WILLIAMS FAMILY

The B Battery forward observer party receives civilian assistance in the Bastogne area. CARPENTER/DETTORE

jackets caused a minor dust storm when hit, so intense that the pilots couldn't see anything, including the gauges needed for flying.

The towrope snapped off the tops of trees as it wrapped around them. The aircraft just cleared the road and headed for a stand of trees. The towrope twisted around a power pole, which now acted as an anchor. The aircraft was sliding up a snow-covered incline toward a line of trees when the rope pulled taut, slowing down the aircraft. The wooden pole snapped in half 8 feet above the ground but caused the aircraft to slow enough to turn slightly away from the trees as it came to a stop. A disastrous crash was averted. The hot engines sizzled as they lay in the snow plowed up around them.

Turner's head hit the dashboard, temporarily knocking him out. He was treated by the battalion surgeon, Capt. David Davidson, and sent on with the rest of his crew to division headquarters in Bastogne.

Resupply gliders coming in to Savy. PERKINS FAMILY

A C-47 crashed near Savy. PERKINS FAMILY

A resupply CG-4A in the Savy area.

From left to right: Colonel Carmichael, Major Henderson, and unidentified battalion staff officers stand outside their command post at Savy to watch resupply gliders coming in.

PFC Woodrow Bowser (B Battery) and PFC "Pappy" Deskins blew this foxhole in Savy with three grenades. WILKENS FAMILY

It didn't take long for a 321st soldier to claim the prize: a fuel-laden C-47. The gasoline was drained from its wing tanks, and the radio guys from communications cannibalized the radios for replacement tubes. Sgt. Harold Dittmer removed the compass and sent it home. Everything was fair game.

Along with General Patton's 4th Armored Column came highly sophisticated radar-operated 90mm antiaircraft guns. Three of these were placed near PFC George Wilson (A Battery), an ammo handler from Duncan, Oklahoma, on December 28 and mounted on a tractor-trailer. In talking with the crews, Wilson learned that the guns' operating mode was a secret. These weapons could only be used when enemy aircraft were leaving the area, not when they were flying directly overhead. It was the latest antiaircraft technology on the battlefield.

"It [the gun] had a screen on it and you could tell if the projectile hit the plane or not," Wilson wrote. "I went out to talk to the gunners and while I was there . . . came two German planes, and I got to watch them in action. According to the radar screen, they got one kill and one cripple."[2]

On the twenty-ninth, General McAuliffe wrote home to his wife:

> The 101st Airborne was released by the censors today. So the newspapermen are really starting over again on the siege of Bastogne. My reply of "Nuts" to the Germans naturally has caught their fancy and this, [along] with many colorful incidents, is making 101st good copy. I had a gallant team here, one which a commander couldn't miss. I never doubted the outcome. There is still plenty going on, but the Krauts around Bastogne are licked. I'm fine. Fondest love to you and Patty.

It was much more difficult to be a machine gunner for the battalion during this time frame than in the past. The enemy might come from any direction at any time here in the fields outside Savy. The three

C-47 *Ain't Misbehavin* in front of the 321st gun pits, which are across the road in the background. PERKINS FAMILY

C-47 *Ain't Misbehavin* in Savy. Note the shrapnel in the pilot's windshield in the bottom photo.

Another shot of *Ain't Misbehavin*, seen on December 26, 1944, in Savy. FULTON FAMILY

An unidentified 321st gun section in Savy.

An American half-track in the Savy area. CRIM FAMILY

An American tank in the Savy area.

teams from each battery of machine gunners had to depend on each other. Their sections were placed approximately 350 yards in front of the guns of their respective battery and 300 yards from each other.

Looking for some relief, PFC George Adams noticed some tank crewmembers who had lost their tank in battle. They were in back with the firing battery, and he asked them if they would help out. They could give a couple of the men at the machine gun a break by taking their place for a bit. Adams was surprised at their answer: according to their way of thinking, since they had no tank, their job was done.

A 506th paratrooper walked off the field with two German prisoners around 0700 hours on December 30. He stopped for a short chat with Adams, saying, "Boy, I hope to get a hot cup of coffee in Bastogne." A bomb was dropped from an enemy aircraft as he walked away, about 400 yards from Adams. It killed the 506th soldier and the two Germans. Another dropped bomb hit outside a B Battery machine-gun hole, burying the crew of six, but none were seriously injured.

Colonel Carmichael with unidentified Savy children.
PERKINS FAMILY

Gen. Maxwell Taylor returned from the Washington, D.C., conference on December 31, Capt. Thomas White (HQ) with him. White, the general's former aide-de-camp, went right back to his liaison job alongside the 506th PIR; forward observer work was what he liked most. White was known for his unparalleled vision. He had the ability to see targets that the rest of his party could not. After a successful fire mission, he would say in a boisterous tone, "Well done, fair Harvard!" His men respected his intelligence and common sense. He was a man who treated those who were less in rank as equals on the battlefield.

Capt. David Davidson, a battalion surgeon, dreamed of opening a small practice back home. He was barely out of medical school when he was drafted. He made his way into the 321st and put that dream on hold. The protocol for officers was to request a jeep driver if they needed to be somewhere that required motorized transportation; they were not supposed to drive themselves anywhere. When Davidson went to the local English pubs in town, he always invited the driver in and insisted he sit at the same table.

Somewhere in the vicinity of Bastogne, he was captured by the Germans and taken to a high-ranking officer who was terribly sick. He suffered from some type of respiratory congestion and was bedridden. A deal was made that if Davidson could successfully treat the German, he would be taken back to his lines and released. During his time in captivity, his quarters were a chicken coop. Days later, the German officer recuperated, and the doctor was taken back to his lines and released. He told his family later that all he did for his patient was give him penicillin.

The A Battery wire section had a problem to fix. It was daylight on January 2, 1945, and one of their forward observer teams reported that there was a break in their communication wire. The team was set up approximately a quarter mile outside Foy, and the 506th was about to make a push forward.

Cpl. Charles Grauel (HQ) from Logansport, Indiana; Cpl. James Parker (HQ) from Suffolk, Virginia; and PFC Albert Lelonek (A Battery) from Detroit,

B Battery 2nd Gun Section in Savy, holding up a newspaper. PFC Ray Nagel is in the foreground. SULLIVAN FAMILY

A Bastogne farmer's outhouse. WILLIAMS FAMILY

Michigan, jumped into a jeep and headed to the problem area. The forward observer team believed the break in the wire was in a commercial tree forest, most likely in a firebreak that separated the rows upon rows of trees. The wiremen checked their map and stopped. They exited the jeep and made it to the firebreak just before a single German 88 artillery round exploded near them. Parker was hit in the elbow by shrapnel and taken back to the medics.

The wiremen informed Sgt. James Bennett (HQ) from Charleston, West Virginia, of what had happened. He told them to return and fix the wire. They did return, but parked their jeep a far distance away this time. They walked through the woods and found the damaged wire not far from the blood-soaked area of snow they had left earlier. They repaired the break and left. This time the Germans did not see them. Parker, although seriously wounded, would later return to the 321st.

German artillery was hidden somewhere in the fields near Savy. The enemy had the map coordinates of the 321st firing batteries, specifically the ones for B Battery. A shell would land and explode every twenty minutes January 4–8 in the battalion's gun sections area. The explosion (or report) was less than what they had experienced in the past, but it was still a deadly business. This type of counterbattery fire went on for days, and the artillerymen wanted it stopped.

One of the 88 rounds exploded just above the trees. Even though he was in a foxhole, PFC Herbert Turner (A Battery) of Biggers, Arkansas, was hit. A piece of iron came down and lodged itself near his spine. The medics couldn't help him—there was no place to evacuate him to. Turner stayed in his hole until he regained his mobility. Much later, when medical staff arrived, they determined surgery was too dangerous. The fragment would have to remain and was never removed.

Lt. Richard Smith photographed on February 2, 1945, in Harthausen, Germany. DUNDON FAMILY

Right: Lixheim, France. 1st Sgt. James Dundon (right) and Sgt. Lawrence Weinberg in February 1945. DUNDON FAMILY

C-47s dropping supplies to the 321st soldiers in a tree line in Savy. CARPENTER/DETTORE

In order to get the exact location of the German guns, they needed to be observed. Certain soldiers in the battalion were trained how to determine the location of enemy artillery by its sound when fired. The battalion fired back, which unfortunately did not deter the enemies' guns. But they knew they had to be close to getting on target.

PFC Louis Palusak, an ammunition man for B Battery, had an idea: an air liaison pilot could possibly help them locate the German guns when the weather improved. The plan was to fire four 75mm pack howitzers into the area the Germans were believed to have set up their guns, and then wait for counterbattery fire. The pilot already had an idea of where they might be and would pinpoint the location when the Germans fired back. It was a job the L-4 pilots were accustomed to and very good at.

The plan was put into action. Four 75mm pack howitzers fired into the area believed to be gun pits for the enemy. The air liaison pilot flew above and waited for the Germans to retaliate with their artillery. The Germans responded. The coordinates of their guns were radioed to the battalion by the pilot. A fire mission was put out, and the enemy guns were finally silenced. The battalion ceased to receive counterbattery fire on January 8.

Assistant S-2 officer Lt. John Jordan was a 1941 graduate of the Virginia Military Institute. He became a liaison officer to the 506th Headquarters and took over Capt. Sam Williams's position in the early morning of January 9, 1945.

Approximately one and a half miles southwest of Noville, PFC Hugh Worthy (B Battery) of Brookhaven, Georgia, found himself in the thick of things. He was on a hill in a patch of pine trees. He had volunteered to go up to the front lines with Jordan, not in his normal role as a wireman but instead to help carry part of the radio and assist Jordan's team in any way necessary. His wire section sergeant, Harry Stearns from Wellington, Ohio, gave the okay for him to go. This was Worthy's first time as a forward observer. It was time to rotate a 321st soldier from the front lines back to the battalion for a rest. This type of rotation was done with the forward observers and liaison teams, about every four days if at all possible.

Liaison officer Jordan headed his party as L-1. They were referred to on the radio as "Lucky 1." His radioman was S/Sgt. Raymond Ruhling from Painesville, Ohio. It was a traditional three-man team acting more as forward observers—which were needed at the time—than as liaisons.

On the way up, the team spotted a group of about six or more Germans dressed in white from head to toe. The enemy soldiers appeared to be coming from Noville. The Americans dropped to the ground; they were outnumbered, but more importantly, their mission was to bring in artillery fire for the 506th. The snow helped to hide the forward observers, even though they were dressed in olive-drab. The enemy simply walked by them as they lay in the snow. They made it to their destination, locating the 506th in a patch of woods.

A gun section at Savy. Note the fresh straw being used.

B Battery 4th Gun Section at Savy (from left to right): PFC Gilbert Quinn, PFC Robert Saracinco, and PFC B. L. Witcher.

WITCHER/DETTORE

The Germans were firing mortars and tank rounds into that patch of woods, causing heavy casualties for the 506th. Worthy was hit in the left shoulder late in the evening. The other two team members escaped injury. Worthy crawled out of the foxhole and took cover near a tank parked near the road. Eventually he was picked up by a jeep and taken to Bastogne. He was operated on the next day at 0200 hours to remove a piece of metal from his shoulder. This took Worthy out of the war. He would have to wait until he reached England to get the wounds closed. His arm was taped up over his head, and the bandages were wrapped all the way down to his navel. In rehab, he couldn't even grasp a magazine with his left hand. It eventually got better with therapy.

It was now up to Lieutenant Jordan and Sergeant Ruhling to continue their work. Luckily, the radio was still intact. Jordan called into the 321st headquarters at about 0100 hours and told them he was signing off for the night. Just as he did, a captured Russian 190mm artillery round exploded at the edge of their foxhole. The concussion sent both men into the air. Ruhling was mortally wounded, and Jordan's left arm and leg received shrapnel. The shrapnel had pierced Jordan's arm and traveled through it and on into Ruhlings's chest. Both soldiers landed in a 6-foot-deep crater created by the exploded round. Ruhling landed on top of Jordan and died in his arms a short time later. Jordan suffered a partial paralysis in his left arm, which also put him out of the war. Numerous pieces of German iron remained in his leg for the rest of his life.

While doing forward observer work on January 10, Pvt. Clyde True (B Battery) of Louisville, Kentucky, was seriously wounded. An enemy artillery shell burst above the trees. The shrapnel destroyed the radio and tore into his arm. He would have to be evacuated to an aid station.

True, along with Lt. Donald Groff from Durham, North Carolina, had attended forward observer school at XVIII Corps, Ogbourne St. George, England, since December 9, missing the early part

An American tank in the Bastogne area. Note the barrel wrapped with white sheets. WILLIAMS FAMILY

Bastogne area. The 321st leaving Savy. WILLIAMS FAMILY

of the battle. Both had just returned to the battalion on January 10 to apply their new skills when True was hit, having been a forward observer for only a matter of hours. Three days later, he was transferred to the hospital. True would recover from his injuries, coming back to the battalion near the end of the war. By this time the 321st was at Berchtesgaden, Germany.

On January 13, the entire battalion was scheduled to move out of their positions. But before they could, the Germans sent them a parting reminder that they were still under observation. An uncharacteristically heavy shelling replete with timed fire landed in A Battery.

Among those hit was Pvt. Percy Nason of Westbrook, Maine; shrapnel from an 88 struck him in the head, chest, and arm. He went down on his back in the snow. His buddy, PFC Herbert Turner, was the first soldier to get to Nason, who was now gurgling in his own blood. He was flipped over, and when the medics arrived, they placed him on the litter. Turner watched as the jeep drove off to the aid station; he had thought Nason was dead. Much to his surprise, Nason returned, meeting Turner at Mourmelon ready for duty.

On January 16, Lt. James Wicker, A Battery commander, notified the 3rd Gun Section that they were to leave for a new area. The skeleton crew went ahead with a jeep, aiming sticks, shovels, and a few rounds of ammunition. They pulled the howitzer to a new location and dug in, a routine they were familiar with.

They had traveled no more than 50 feet when a German round came in and exploded. It sounded like the round had hit near the gun pit. The jeep halted, and they jumped out and ran back to the dugout. They found the remaining crew inside, where a heated argument was taking place between PFC Bernard Tutas and Pvt. Donald Rogers from Dunbar, Pennsylvania. Tutas was berating Rogers for not wearing a helmet. Rogers emphatically said he *was* wearing it, but not seeing it on his head gave Tutas the high ground in the argument. PFC Lloyd Tomblin, the jeep driver, spotted a helmet lying outside the dugout. It had a large, triangular gash on the

A water supply tank in Savy. CRIM FAMILY

—Journal Staff by Robert J. Doyle

More precious than gold is Milwaukee beer which found its way to England by way of India. Sergt. Bob Wessel (left), Cincinnati, Ohio, of an air borne artillery unit, received the cans of beer from his brother, who is stationed in India. Staff Sergt. Arnold Bucholtz (center), New London, Wis., shows how the sight affects him as Sergt. Jesse Loop, Crivitz, Wis., tries to r[illegible]train him. All three took part in the fighting [illegible] France.

A hometown newspaper clipping from Whatcombe Farm, England. LOOP FAMILY

The 321st in the Bastogne area, moving to Lorraine, France. Capt. Sam Skinner, liaison officer, wears long johns as a scarf. WILLIAMS FAMILY

Left: Newly promoted Lieutenant General McAuliffe leaving the 321st command post at Savy after saying his farewells to Colonel Carmichael and the battery commanders on or around January 15, 1945. Captain Perkins, S-2, asked McAuliffe if he could take his picture and told the general he would send him a copy, which he later did. McAuliffe was to take over command of the 103rd Infantry Division. Note the waiting jeep and driver in the background. McAuliffe has not yet affixed his second star to his helmet. PERKINS FAMILY

B Battery Sgt. Nelson Kopacka proudly wearing a procured women's white fur coat in Bastogne. Note the German POWs in the background. STEARNS/DETTORE

top; obviously a piece of shrapnel had knocked it off Rogers's head. Had he not been wearing it, he would have killed.

One crewmember from an A Battery gun section located farther away from the blast, Pvt. Eldon Rushing from Corinth, Mississippi, was lightly wounded by fragments.

T/4 Jesse Loop (A Battery) from Crivitz, Wisconsin; Pvt. Charles Hunter (A Battery) from Springfield, Illinois; and Cpl. Lyle Wood (A Battery) from Kingsville, Ohio, spent the night of January 16 in a sturdy stone barn that had served them in the past as their observation post. This forward observer team sought some protection from both the elements and enemy fire. Loop led the team, with Wood assisting him. Hunter was the radioman.

Early in the morning, as the group exited the barn doorway for the last time, a single German 88 artillery round came through the roof and exploded. The concussion of the blast traveled through the well-made building and exited via the path of least resistance—the door. Everybody was thrown from the blast.

Loop, who was closing the door, was hit full force in the chest by numerous pieces of shrapnel. Several lodged so close to his heart that not all of them could be safely removed later. Wood was struck in the right temple. His helmet, worn cocked to the right as was his habit, saved his life. Hunter was the least seriously wounded. He stared at Wood, who asked him, "What are you looking at?" The radioman looked at the hole in his corporal's helmet and wondered if the wound would soon be fatal. Wood realized that his helmet was pierced and felt for the hole in the steel pot and the wound underneath it. When he removed his hand, it was covered in blood; he fainted at the sight. The cylindrical piece of German iron would be removed later by a surgeon; it was approximately 3/4 inch by 1/4 inch. For years Wood kept it as a memento of his good fortune. The only lasting result was a small scar.

This group had the unenviable distinction of being the last hit during the Bastogne offensive.

The 321st left Savy for the Corps Reserve at 1000 hours on January 18. The entire battalion arrived at the rear area on January 19 at 1215 hours. They were on the road to a new area the next day at 1245 hours. Their next mission would be to reinforce the fires of the 35th Division, Seventh Army.

On January 18, a ceremony was held in the town center of Bastogne. Gen. Troy Middleton, the VIII Corps commander, presented three Silver Stars. Among the 500 men in attendance representing the 101st was PFC Virgil Teaford (B Battery) from Syracuse, Ohio. It struck him as odd that a German soldier on a motorcycle sped unopposed into town and back out carrying a white flag.

The battalion had been relieved on the nineteenth, but it was short-lived. After a few days at Bercheaux,

A Battery kitchen trailer in Haguenau, France, January 1945. BUSCH/DETTORE

Unidentified 321st soldiers in France.

France. A jeep belonging to Headquarters medic Bernard DiPasquale. DIPASQUALE/DETTORE

Haguenau, France, February 1945. A B Battery forward observer party placed a fire mission on this German armored vehicle, unaware that A Battery wireman Cpl. George Turkal was nearby. He wanted to take a picture of the German vehicle, but wasn't aware it was about to be fired on. Turkal somehow managed to keep taking the photographs and survived without injury. TURKAL FAMILY

More of Turkal's photos of the armored vehicle at Haguenau, France. TURKAL FAMILY

Belgium, it was off to Hilbesheim, France. The battalion made the journey by motor in open cattle cars. Some remember it as a trip on icy roads and colder than their time in Savy.

On January 24 at 1215 hours, the 321st guns were dug in near the small village of Meisenthal, France. This was the Vosges mountain area, and the plan was to support the 35th Division. But there was more to it. The guns were placed on the side of a mountain, and to get them there they all had to be disassembled. Twelve 75mm pack howitzers were broken down, carried up the mountain by the soldiers, and reassembled. They were now looking down on the enemy, so close that a single bag powder charge put the 75mm round to the rear of the German lines. It was a dry run; about two hours later, it was time to pack up the guns and go back down the mountain. They were returning to Hilbesheim.

By the time the artillerymen pulled into Hilbesheim late in the evening that same day, they were cold and exhausted. Lt. Tony Linz, executive officer of A Battery, made sure his first responsibility was taking care of his men. He was the last man in his battery to make it to his sleeping quarters.

The after-action report for February 1945 said the period "opened with the 321st Glider FA Bn still in direct support of the 506th PIR. The supported infantry was disposed along a line generally east and west along Roer River north of Hagenau [*sic*, Haguenau]. The Battalion Command Post and gun positions at Dauendorf [coordinates 93402592]."

During February 1–5, 1945, enemy activity was "very light" and the battalion's missions were mostly against scattered groups of enemy, counterbattery, and mortar, with "a good number of harassing missions fired."

On February 4, the 506th Combat Team received orders to relieve the 313th Infantry Regiment of the 79th Infantry Division in and around Haguenau. Reconnaissance was begun at 0800 on the fifth, and by 1200 on the same day both batteries were registered in their new positions. The command post was at Harthausen (coordinates 996202), A Battery was

A group of 321st vehicles at Harthausen, February 1945.

Harthausen, Germany. From left to right: PFC Wills, PFC Sidney Vaucher, PFC Alois Sucharski, and an unidentified soldier.
WILKINSON FAMILY

PFC Vincent Walsh (left) and T/5 Merle Fulton in France. FULTON FAMILY

Unidentified soldiers in France. Note the large 321st stenciling on their helmets.

France. Back row (from left to right): PFC Marshall Burnett, PFC Mike Knezevic, T/5 Fulton, and PFC Francis Madden. Front row (from left to right): T/5 Paul Miho, PFC Walsh, PFC Neal Batchelor, PFC Ralph Miller, and PFC Charles Rocco. FULTON FAMILY

Classically trained violinist PFC Jose Landeros from New York City playing a tune in Harthausen while PFC Clarence Simmons performs a "hillbilly jig." TURKAL FAMILY

While overseas, Landeros kept his violin at the ready, eager to entertain if the circumstances allowed it. On numerous occasions, the officers at the FDC would have him play and piped the music over the phone system to the firing batteries. It was a guaranteed morale booster. TURKAL FAMILY

Some 40/8 cars in Germany loaded with 321st soldiers. WILKINSON FAMILY

PFC Joseph Weidle was killed on his way to procure hospital supplies when shrapnel from a German artillery round struck him under the chin. RAKER FAMILY

Helmets being freshened up in Mourmelon with new 321st stencils.
WILKENS FAMILY

Chow time at the camp in Mourmelon.

PFC Ralph Rose (left) and PFC Robert Miller, B Battery cooks, in Mourmelon.
WILKENS FAMILY

From left to right: Sgt. Harvey Baker, PFC Lemuel Slayter, and PFC B. L. Witcher in Namur, Belgium. WILKENS FAMILY

PFC Burton Carpenter (cigarette in mouth) in Bastogne. CARPENTER/DETTORE

Mourmelon. From left to right: B Battery soldiers PFC Walter Mitchell, PFC William Buckingham, PFC Paul Galant, PFC Carpenter, and PFC Louis Palusak. WILKENS FAMILY

Howitzers in for servicing at Mourmelon.
CRIM FAMILY

Building the base camp at Mourmelon. DAVIS FAMILY

Mourmelon. From left to right: B Battery Sgt. Mike Sullivan, PFC Pervey Robinson, PFC Ernest Booten, PFC Raymond Nagell, and PFC Franklin E. Stearns. Robinson, a skilled barber, was killed in Holland, the father of twin boys born just three months before. SULLIVAN FAMILY

From left to right: Sgt. Burdette Wilkinson, Cpl. George Turkal, Sgt. Paul Miho, and PFC Salvatore Campisi in a French tent city in Mourmelon after a retreat parade.

Left: Sgt. Paul Miho (center) of Headquarters Battery in Mourmelon receiving his glider qualification badge.
TURKAL FAMILY

at coordinates 999225, and B Battery was at 996225. The infantry completed their move at 2200 on February 5.

The mission of the 506th Combat Team throughout the remainder of the period was of a defensive nature with extensive patrolling. Targets fired by the 321st GFA Battalion were mostly those of opportunity, patrol, support, some counterbattery and mortar, and nightly harassing missions. While in Haguenau, infantry outposts were "very successful" in adjusting artillery fire, working through the liaison officer. Reinforcing the fires of the 321st in the Harthausen position were the 242nd Field Artillery Battalion, February 5–12, 1945, and the 499th Field Artillery Battalion, February 12–17.

Observation posts in Haguenau were located in buildings overlooking all the enemy positions in the 506th Combat Team's sector. On one occasion the observation post in the middle of town received enemy fire, while it was manned by S/Sgt. Leslie Sellers, map coordinates 35043993. It took direct hits by 150mm shells with no casualties, and continued to be used.

During the evening of February 20, B Battery received counterbattery fire and moved to its alternate position, coordinates 002208. Retrograde positions were selected and surveyed in February.

On February 22, 1945, operations were begun in preparation for the 133rd Field Artillery Battalion of the 36th Division to relieve the 321st in its sector. The 321st departed the Harthausen position on February 24 and moved by truck to the vicinity of Saverne, France, and from there moved by organic vehicles and train the next day to Mourmelon. A base camp was set up there on February 26.

Fire missions continued to support the 506th. Cpl. Albert Lelonek (A Battery), part of a forward observer team along with Pvt. Edward Rymarczyk, (A Battery) of Buffalo, New York, spotted a good observation post: a church steeple in the town of Hagueanu. They were just getting set up when a German 88mm round hit the steeple as they were climbing the stairs. It did not explode and kept going. They had been spotted and quickly extricated themselves. Though the war was almost over, Lelonek wondered if he was going to make it.

The battalion left Haguenau, France, on February 23 and headed back to their camp. They boarded 40/8 (forty men or eight horses) railroad cars for the journey. The men decided to pull up the wooden planks of the cars and make a fire to keep warm. More wood was needed, so more and more planks were torn up as the journey progressed. A fire in one car burned a hole in the floor and fell through onto the tracks below. Sparks were seen flying in all directions. The center portion of the railroad car was gone by the end of the trip; the soldiers left only a small walkway on each side. It was too dangerous to move around for fear of falling off the walkway and under the moving railroad cars.

They arrived back at their camp in Mourmelon after a three-day journey. This time, they were living in tents instead of barracks. They spent their time fixing up the camp and training during their stay.

At Reims, all of the battery commanders went to see the officer in charge of DivArty at headquarters: General McAuliffe had been promoted, and Col. William Gillmore took his place. They requested that either they or Carmichael be transferred out. Gillmore told them that he couldn't do that because Carmichael's rating was listed as "superior," and he had no just cause to do so. Gillmore remarked, "He's the best we got." It was no use and just another reason why the men hoped the war would be over soon.

On March 15, the battalion walked 8 miles to the parade grounds to receive their Presidential Unit Citation from General Eisenhower. It was a spit-and-polish ceremony that the men complained about as being a waste of time, held just to put on a show for some generals. However, when they arrived at their destination and saw everyone who was there to honor them, the men reveled in it. They said that it made them feel special.

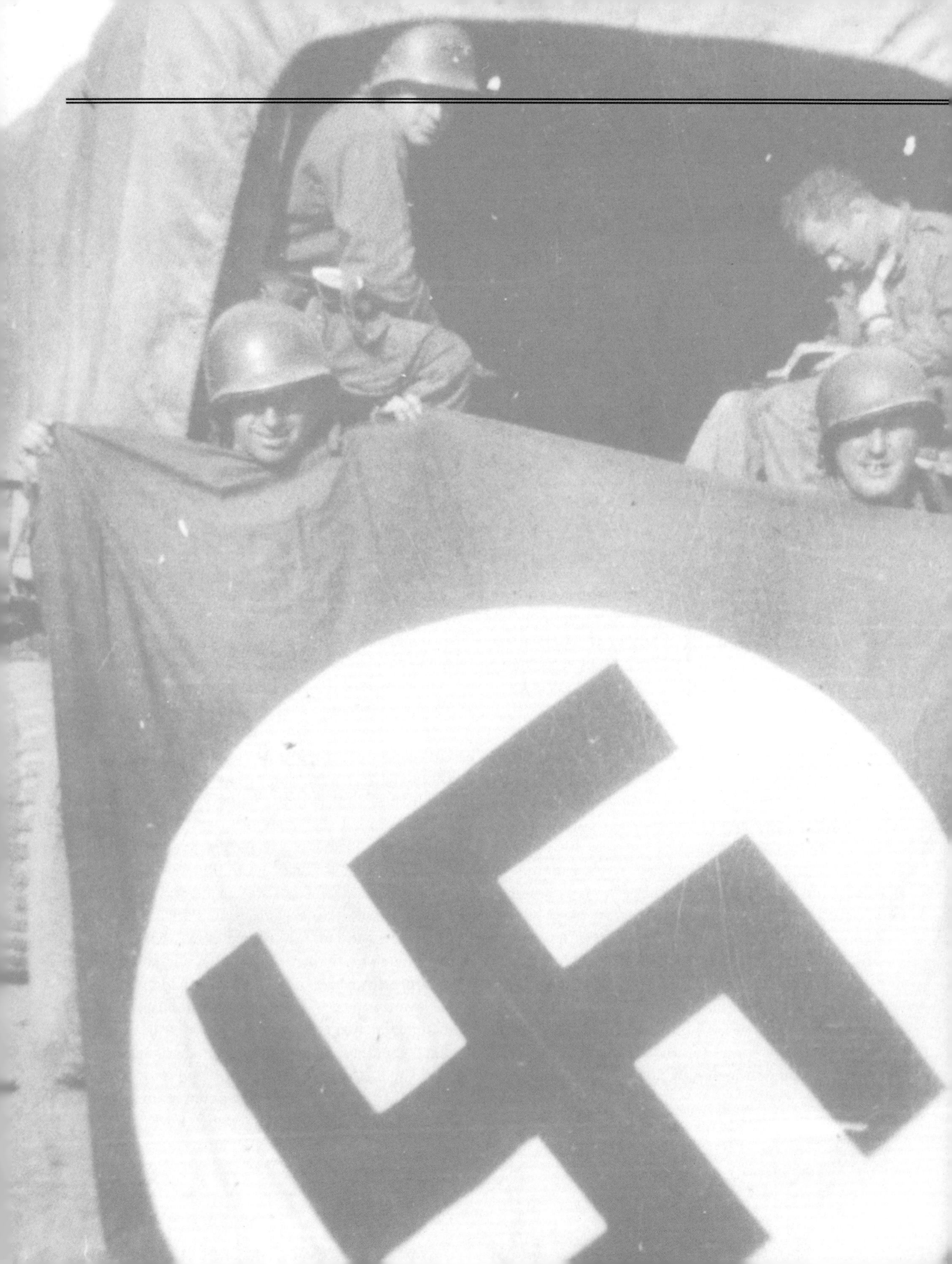

CHAPTER 7

Germany

ON APRIL 6, 1945, Lt. Richard Fort, liaison pilot for the 321st, sent a letter home to his sister. "As you probably noticed at the top of this letter, I'm now in Germany, and that makes me happy to be in the home stretch of winning this war," he wrote. "From now on we'll be blowing their homes and property up instead of the French & Belgians. Believe me, we are wrecking everything. I'll tell you all about it when I get home."

The battalion departed Mourmelon on April 3, traveling by motor vehicles to Nievenheim, Germany. It arrived there on the fourth, and Lt. Marvin Mikles (B Battery) from Magazine, Arkansas, registered both firing batteries.

While here, the Germans employed a new technique. At 1030 hours on April 16, three civilians near the A Battery guns were observed lighting a pot filled with a flammable liquid; it emitted thick black smoke that could be easily seen from a distance. It was an attempt to mark the gun pits of A Battery. A group of soldiers from that battery captured two of the civilians; the third escaped on horseback. It was believed that these Germans were soldiers posing as civilians.

Later that same afternoon, at 1730 hours, it happened again. This time one civilian, an eleven-year-old boy, was marking A Battery with a smoke pot and was quickly caught. He was put in a jeep and taken to the battalion command post. The idea was to scare him and then release the lad. Colonel Carmichael was to "put the fear of God into him," but the Hitler Youth had done their job well; the boy was not remorseful and showed contempt not only for the Americans but also for the colonel. He called Carmichael a pig. The colonel had enough and slapped the boy hard across the face. The jeep driver was ordered to take the boy to

A train ride from Neinhawsen to Schwarzhausen, Germany.
WILKINSON FAMILY

Right: A 321st A Battery machine-gun section at the Ruhr Pocket in Germany.
LELONEK/DETTORE

A forward observer party dug in at the Ruhr Pocket. PERKINS FAMILY

From left to right: PFC Bernard Tutas, PFC George Wilson, and PFC Dick Moss of A Battery posing with their howitzer in the Ruhr Pocket. Note the name, *Battered Bastards of Bastogne*, written in white chalk on the gun. WILSON FAMILY

Germany. Sgt. Bernard DiPasquale, a medic. Note the rubber raft on top of his assigned jeep. DIPASQUALE/DETTORE

Emulating General Patton's famous gesture of March 24, 321st Headquarters soldiers urinate in the Rhine River. FULTON FAMILY

An unidentified 321st gun pit at the Ruhr Pocket. PERKINS FAMILY

the 506th Headquarters for further interrogation. The little Nazi would join the other two civilians captured earlier in the day.

In April, Lt. Richard Smith (A Battery) asked around for volunteers from his battery to take a pack howitzer and have it repaired. The destination was Dusseldorf. Cpl. Anthony Tabone said he would do it, and he was to pick someone to assist him. As he did every other time, Tabone volunteered his buddy, PFC Alfred Stumpo, for the mission.

With gun in tow, the pair was about to cross the Rhine River on a floating Bailey pontoon bridge when a dogfight occurred overhead. The road to the bridge was clogged with horses and wagons filled with civilians on the move. "I don't know how Tabone got past those horses and wagons because he was watching the planes more than the road," Stumpo recalled.

The soldiers made it across the one-lane floating bridge and were stopped by a captain of the Engineers. He told them about the number of men who

A pontoon bridge in Germany, courtesy of American Combat Engineers. STEARNES/DETTORE

Germany, Ruhr Pocket. The day after this picture was taken, two shells landed about eight feet from the gun. WITCHER/DETTORE

A bridge constructed in Germany by A Company, 298th Engineer Combat Battalion. WILLIAM A. WILTSIE SR. FAMILY

were killed building the bridge. The captain turned to Tabone and, pointing his rifle at him, said, "If you don't stay with the speed limit going back, I will shoot your ass."

The pack howitzer was dropped off at a maintenance depot, and for their effort Lieutenant Smith arranged for the two to sleep in the officers' quarters for the night. "Things were a little quieter going back and Tabone took it slow," Stumpo wrote.

On April 26, the battalion executed a two-echelon move, one part arriving at Schwabhausen, Germany, by train, and the other by motor transport. Along the way, Privates Edward Weir (B Battery) from Webster Groves, Missouri, and Marlin Foster (B Battery) from Springville, Mississippi, were accidentally left behind. This wasn't discovered until the next day, and a jeep was sent back to find and bring them back to the battalion.

While at Schwabhausen, at 0930 hours two rifle shots rang out from a patch of woods. The intended target was Colonel Carmichael. A group of 321st men were gathered to scour the woods. Someone from town came forward and said that there were four SS troops in the area and that they were probably the guilty ones.

As the 321st soldiers were considering their plan of action, Carmichael noticed that one of them was drunk. The A Battery soldier insisted that he wasn't drunk, but the infuriated colonel snapped, "Don't lie to me—I'll stomp you into the ground." Capt. James Wicker—who had taken over as battery commander when Captain Fuller was transferred to Division Headquarters at Bastogne—was standing with the group and said, "Colonel, I won't have you talking to my men like that." Wicker then ordered the inebriated soldier back to his section, away from the assault group and the colonel.

The price for interceding was steep. Captain Wicker's beloved battery was taken away from him. Taking his place was Capt. James Davis from Lake Okeechobee, Florida, the Headquarters motor officer at the time. Wicker was reassigned to the battalion staff as a liaison officer.

PFC Albert Lelonek (A Battery) had also been standing with the group and was surprised that so much fuss was made over a soldier that had

From left to right: 2nd Lt. James Dundon, PFC Victor Zuccarelli, Sgt. Lawrence Weinberg, and PFC Louis Kovacic of an A Battery forward observer party at the Ruhr Pocket. DUNDON/DETTORE

been drinking. It wasn't uncommon; he observed it many times while laying wire at the front to the paratroopers.

On April 28, the battalion was headed for Holzhausen, where it was to be billeted. One of the two assigned liaison pilots for the battalion, Lt. Richard Fort, was up in the air when he spotted what appeared to be a prison camp, about a mile and a half east in the town of Landsberg.

The artillerymen could smell something foul when they approached. It was a concentration camp. The stench was understood when the magnitude of its cause was seen with their own eyes. A field outside the camp was filled with executed inmates

A wire crew on their howitzer at the Ruhr Pocket, April 1945. From left to right: PFC Anthony Stempien (holding phone), PFC Edward Rymarczyk (with 75mm round), and PFC Al Lelonek (without helmet). LELONEK/DETTORE

PFC Anthony Stempien (left) and PFC Lelonek at the Ruhr Pocket.
LELONEK/DETTORE

PFC Stempien at the Ruhr Pocket. LELONEK/DETTORE

wearing striped uniforms. The executioners had fled prior to the arrival of the Americans. Inside the camp, the SS had locked the doors of the wooden huts and set them afire. The 506th along with the 321st tried to put out the fires. The inmates were from Eastern Europe; most were civilians, but there were some soldiers too. It was a work camp where living standards were below the bare minimum. Piles of corpses littered the grounds like pieces of scrap paper. Battle-hardened soldiers vomited; some turned away in horror, and others wanted to take revenge on the Germans. Not a man who saw this ever felt the same about the enemy he was fighting.

On the outskirts of the camp was a large German army hospital. Executive Officer Lieutenant Linz

(A Battery) visited it and made a quick decision. All ambulatory patients were to be evacuated; to where was not his concern. The beds were emptied and filled with survivors from the camp. Catholic nuns assisted by bathing the former inmates and placing them in the beds of their former enemies. A local priest, about seventy years old, was taken to the camp. He broke down in tears when he entered. The next day was a Sunday. He told his parishioners to gather blankets, sheets, pillows, and food and to bring the supplies to the hospital. Their country had done this, and everyone was responsible.

PFC Albert Lelonek at the Ruhr Pocket. WILKINSON FAMILY

Civilians under 321st guard in Landsberg. DITTMER FAMILY

Concentration camp inmates outside the camp. PERKINS FAMILY

A young German, a medical sergeant from the hospital, refused to go to the camp and assist in the transportation of the sick and ailing. His reasoning was that the Geneva Convention excluded him from that type of chore. One of the nuns, Sister Rosa Bauman, spoke English and became the interpreter. Linz ordered the sister to tell the sergeant that two trains were leaving Landsberg: one for England and the other for Russia. Which train did he want to be on? It was a bold-faced lie, but the German didn't know it was a bluff. There were no more problems with him while the battalion was there.

A burial detail was needed. Linz spotted Corporal Raker with a German soldier who could speak English. The soldier was told to recruit some of his comrades to start digging graves. Shovels had

Corpses outside the camp. PERKINS FAMILY

Outside the camp. Note the snapped makeshift crutch lying next to an executed inmate. PERKINS FAMILY

Inside the camp grounds. PERKINS FAMILY

Landsberg. From left to right: Maj. Tom Henderson, Capt. Roe Wilkins, Capt. Joseph Perkins, CWO Edward Chaumont (without helmet), and Capt. Sam Skinner. Center foreground: Col. Edward Carmichael. Far rear: Lt. William Nugent.

Germany. 321st soldiers, from left to right: Sgt. Larry Benninghoff, Sgt. Nelson Kopacka, and PFC Elmer Wilkens.
WILKENS FAMILY

already been located and were stacked nearby. Both entered the German Army hospital mess hall while a meal was being served. Raker pointed to some of the able-bodied soldiers and told the interpreter to have them come along with him. One of the Germans responded with a "don't bother me" gesture. When asked what the man said, the interpreter replied, "He will accompany you after he finishes his meal." Enraged by his response, Raker pulled out his German P-38 pistol and stuck it in the ear of the man eating. He told the interpreter, "You tell these men I want them now!" The chosen group dropped their eating utensils as fast as they could and left the table to follow Raker. Raker pointed to a spot, and the soldiers started to dig graves on the hospital grounds. Civilians from the town were also put to work digging and were placed under guard while they accomplished the task. Linz noticed the civilians were digging a mass grave. He made them fill it in and dig single ones: a grave for each inmate. It put a smile on every soldier's face when they heard what Linz had made the locals do.

Pvt. John Voytek (A Battery), who had not been in the camp, was guarding the soldiers digging on the hospital grounds. He sat down against a tree, his carbine across his lap, not taking much notice of his prisoners' progress. They had it easy, chatting, smoking, and leaning on the shovels more than digging with them. Then Voytek was relieved of guard duty and told to take a ride to the camp and to have a look around. When he returned, Voytek approached the group, unslung his carbine, and racked in a round. "Dig, you sons of bitches, *dig*!" he yelled. The words might not have been understood, but his body language was.

PFC Robert Bunyard (A Battery jeep driver) of Meridian, Mississippi, was captured in Holland after his glider came down in enemy territory. He became a POW, one of the lucky ones. He spent most of his time away from the prison camp working as a farm laborer. The farmer's wife would sew on a patch whenever he wore out a section of his field jacket. Soon the jacket looked more like a quilt than a military-produced garment. He was at *Stalag* VII-A, north of Moosburg, when it was liberated by the 14th Armored Division on April 30. He could have been processed and sent home as a released POW, but Bunyard chose a different route. He discovered where the 101st was and went to rejoin them, taking whatever he needed along the way. He had learned enough of the German language to facilitate that task. He came across an occupied German command car and ordered the driver and officer out by convincing them that the war was over and that he had won. He made it to Holzhausen, Germany, by May 2, driving the command car.

A 321st patrol spotted an enemy command car that looked fit for a general parked in front of a house. They entered the building cautiously and

Berchtesgaden, Germany. From right to left: PFC John Voytek, PFC Raymond Freddo, and PFC Robert Bunyard. One of Bunyard's friends said he could see a little difference in him after his time as a POW. H. C. WARREN FAMILY

Ludwigshauen, Germany. From left to right: PFC Fred Miller, PFC Elwood Rothe, Cpl. Max Raglin, T/5 Merle Fulton, and PFC Carl Espling, April 1945. FULTON FAMILY

An SS officer's estate outside Landsberg, Germany. WILKENS/DETTORE

Unidentified soldier, Sgt. Norman Deethardt, Cpl. Dick Moss, and another unidentified soldier in Germany. Note Deethardt's pistol holster, adorned with SS Death's Head metal insignia. DEETHARDT/DETTORE

heard moaning coming from an upstairs room. They just knew it was a big-shot general and called up the stairs. A male voice yelled back down; they recognized it as Bunyard's. They asked themselves, how could that be possible—wasn't he a POW?

Bunyard had stopped for a break and made friends with a German woman, but he was now ready to leave with his buddies. One of his comrades asked him where he got the fancy command car. Bunyard said, "I took it from some Krauts." He was also wearing a German officer's boots.

The battalion pulled into Sternberg, Germany, for the night and looked for a place to sleep. One of the homes taken over was quite nice, with a large piano in one room and glass display cases showing expensive fine tools in another. The woman owner complained to Capt. Fred King, the B Battery commander, that the soldiers were bringing mud into her house and playing her piano. Prior to Landsberg, homeowners had been given two hours to vacate their homes when they were seized for billeting. This was changed to ten minutes following the concentration camp liberation.

One of the men found a high-ranking SS uniform inside a closet and showed it to King. The woman's voice grew louder with indignation. The soldiers were going through her closets! She didn't know that these men had just left a concentration camp. Discovering an SS uniform in her closet was the clincher. King's temper boiled over when he saw the uniform. He told the men if that woman said one more goddamned word, they should shoot her. The woman, understanding English, made for the door as someone pounded on the piano keys with all his might.

Those in the house wanted to clear it of any valuables but shied away from outright looting. PFC Elmer Wilkens couldn't help himself. He was at the concentration camp and felt like making the homeowners pay. He removed a small windup travel clock from the master bedroom and placed it in his pocket.

A 321st gun crew in Sternberg, Germany.

A French-manned American tank in Berchtesgaden.

A Battery .50-caliber machine gun at the Ruhr Pocket. LELONEK/DETTORE

Cpl. George Turkal (left) and T/4 Merle Fulton in Berchtesgaden, May 1945. Note the camouflaged guardhouse. TURKAL FAMILY

V-E Day in Berchtesgaden, Germany. WILKINSON FAMILY

A roadblock set up by U.S. soldiers at the entrance to the grounds at Hitler's place in Berchtesgaden, May 6, 1945. Note the French officers conferring with U.S. soldiers. TURKAL FAMILY

Some 321st soldiers with French officers at Berchtesgaden, May 5, 1945. PERKINS FAMILY

U.S. vehicles on a road in Berchtesgaden.

Berchtesgaden, Germany. From left to right: T/5 Merle Fulton, Cpl. Francis Madden, and PFC Irving John. MIHO/DETTORE

A mine detector being tested in Germany. TURKAL FAMILY

He found stamp corners, used by collectors to hold individual stamps in a book, in another room. Someone must have hidden the collection away.

Cpl. William Stone also stole something, a first for him: he ran bathwater and took a luxurious warm bath in the master bedroom's bathroom.

The 3rd Gun Section and their acting sergeant, Corporal Raker, along with forward observer Lt. James Dundon and his party, detached from A Battery and attached to the 3rd Battalion of the 506th PIR. Their mission was to determine enemy strength east and south of Chiemsee Lake. They needed to take and secure the town of Berchtesgaden.

Damage done by British warplanes in Berchtesgaden.
LELONEK/DETTORE

A French tank crew in the center of Berchtesgaden.
TURKAL FAMILY

This force was stopped on May 4 at 1430 hours by artillery and small-arms fire that was covering a blown bridge outside of the town of Inzell. Three rounds of white phosphorous were fired at the 88mm gun, which neutralized it at 1800 hours. By 1530 hours the next day, the bridge was repaired. The combat team was on the move and arrived in Berchtesgaden, capturing the town at 2030 hours on May 5. Those three rounds were the last fired in combat by the 101st Division in Europe during World War II.

On May 5, T/4 Merle Fulton (HQ Battery) wrote home to his wife: "I guess you have heard many times of the war being over and all about it. We have

George Turkal snapped this photo of the bus A Battery rode in the day they left Berchtesgaden, May 10, 1945.
TURKAL FAMILY

A Battery gun section in Germany. LELONEK/DETTORE

A civilian removes a Berchtesgaden street sign now considered offensive. TURKAL FAMILY

Lt. Don Roy visiting former A Battery forward observer comrades in Holzhausen. Roy was transferred to the 326th Engineers prior to Bastogne after receiving his commission. LELONEK/DETTORE

waited a long time for that day. But since it is here and passed it doesn't seem so important. I guess it is because of the other one we still have to win. Anyway we are still glad that this one is over. I'm still in Germany."

On May 7, PFC Dallas Stratton (A Battery) was shot by a sniper while guarding prisoners, the last 321st soldier wounded by enemy fire in World War II. The bullet was fired from an elevated position, entering his left buttocks and lodging behind his right knee. While at the hospital, he was visited by men in his gun section, who told him the sniper was found and killed.

Just prior to being wounded, he watched as a German armored vehicle loaded with soldiers traveled underneath a concrete bridge. The driver and its passengers, oblivious to the bridge's low height, partially wedged the vehicle underneath. Seven of the crew died instantly from the massive head trauma of striking the concrete. Stratton said he felt bad for the enemy soldiers, who were probably heading home after having survived a war that was almost over.

Stratton was operated on for his injuries several times after the war and received a 10 percent disability. Veterans Affairs told him that if he filled out more forms, his payment would increase. He refused, saying that life had passed.

The A Battery had just returned from their special mission supporting the 3rd Battalion of the 506th, spending two days with the paratroopers on the front lines near Berchtesgaden. They were now in Miesbach, Austria. It was May 8, 1945.

The batteries of the 321st were united again. It was only one day away from the official V-E Day, but for now the war was still going on in the eyes of some Germans and combat-hardened red-leggers.

Enemy activity was light at this time, but the area was unsecured. It was filled with Germans surrendering in such great numbers that they were just pointed in a direction and told to keep moving. Trooper Don Falls (A Battery), who worked with forward observer teams along with Charles Hunter, would watch these masses of uniformed enemy soldiers pass by. When SS soldiers—identified by the black cuff bands with unit identification on the left sleeve of the tunic and the SS runes on the uniform collar—were observed in a group, Falls would motion for them to stop and come over. Falls would rip the cuff bands off the uniform and inform them that they could not pass. He would make them march in the opposite direction. Falls warned they would be shot on the spot if they tried to pass him again. The cuff bands were kept as souvenirs.

Cpl. Vernice Hilst (B Battery), seen here at the battalion command post in Holland. WILLIAMS FAMILY

PFC Henry Ira (left) and PFC George Crim perform a mock burial of Hitler in Berchtesgaden. While they were posing for the camera, a German civilian stopped and spat. At first, the two soldiers thought they had raised the ire of the German woman for their comical pose. Then the woman said, "Hitler *kaput*!" in a disgusted tone and continued on her way. CRIM FAMILY

Cpl. George Turkal in Holzhausen using a 2-franc coin as a monocle, mimicking a German officer. TURKAL FAMILY

Some of the retreating Germans mingled with the local civilian population. They set booby traps and sniped at 101st soldiers, along with other acts of sabotage. They left booby-trapped weapons behind such as pistols and in one instance a potato masher grenade. When a 321st soldier, PFC Vernise Hilst, picked it up for inspection, it exploded, wounding him severely.

It was time to find sleeping quarters for Headquarters Battery. A house was eventually chosen and the homeowners kicked out. Men squabbled for the best rooms or the biggest bed, a routine that played out each time a new location was chosen. Anything was better than sleeping in a foxhole. One of the soldiers, PFC Robert Devereaux, picked his bed for the

Mourmelon, France. PFC Robert Devereaux (Headquarters Battery) with his dog that was killed by a booby trap. TURKAL FAMILY

night. His dog—one of many strays that the soldiers of the battalion found and kept—followed him into the room. The soldier pointed to the bed and the dog dutifully jumped on it. The bed exploded, killing the dog. It had been rigged with explosives that blew up the mattress. No other injuries were incurred.

For a short time, Pvt. Bernard Simmons (B Battery) was a rich man. Hitler's house was being looted by the paratroopers, and he followed the crowd. He noticed that a group of them were jumping over each other to get into a room in the basement. Someone yelled, "Diamonds!" Hearing that, Simmons elbowed his way to a bunch of narrow wooden drawers that might have been made to hold

Cpl. George Turkal (left) and PFC Victor Sauerheber sitting in front of a "guest hotel" in Berchtesgaden with a wastebasket taken from Hitler's Berghof in May 1945. FULTON FAMILY

Some 321st vehicles parked near their lodgings in Germany.

maps. He yanked open one of them, which was lined with felt, and was dazzled by large diamonds. They were scooped up by the handfuls and put in the pockets of his M43 trousers. There were more to take, but the scene had turned into a brawl, with fists flying. It was as hard getting out of that room as it was getting in.

When no one was around outside, he surveyed his loot. Some of the stones he gave away to friends in his battery. The very next day an announcement was made that anyone who took any jewels from the basement had to return them. If they did, there would be no repercussions and no names would be recorded, but if they didn't return the jewels, court-martials would be convened. The end result for the guilty would guarantee that going home was not going to happen.

At the appointed time and place, Simmons walked up to the tables and found officers seated in chairs. A line formed and the precious stones were turned in. Simmons had heard that his diamonds were industrial and were not worth much, so it wasn't much of a dilemma for him. He gave back a handful, all he had left in his possession.

When his troopship was en route to New York, he heard that a number of soldiers took a chance and kept their looted stones without a problem. One of the 321st boys said he would sell his for $2 each but had no takers. Others said that the officers never turned in the stones they got back from the troopers.

While in New York, Simmons bumped into one of the men whom he gave a diamond to. The soldier thanked him profusely for the gift; he had pawned it and with the money was going to buy a car. It turned

Capt. Joseph Perkins on Hitler's Berghof balcony. Note the loot he has accumulated. PERKINS FAMILY

out the diamond was worth $800—not industrial after all.

During the course of the war, Lt. Tony Linz (A Battery) had some close calls. The last one was the most disturbing because the war in Europe was essentially done. He was scrounging for liquor at Hitler's home in Berchtesgaden. He noticed some French soldiers milling about, but that was unimportant compared to his task at hand. In a cabinet he found eight bottles of cognac. He left with his find, carrying a few bottles and stuffing the rest into his pockets. As he was heading out of the house, the Frenchmen blew a safe open. The concussion knocked him out the window he was walking by. Shaken but uninjured, he couldn't but laugh upon seeing that not one of the bottles was broken.

Sgt. Norman Deethardt (B Battery) and a number of men from the battery looted enough champagne from the Platterhof Hotel's basement to keep them drunk for days. Contests were held to see who could knock out a hanging lightbulb with a cork when opening a bottle of bubbly.

Lt. Richard Smith (A Battery), a forward observer and recon officer, had a reputation as a fearless, competent leader who always got the job done. Wounded twice in battle with the 321st, he was all business and his men knew it.

Smith received orders on May 8 to pick eighteen men, procure six jeeps, and head to a small town called Markt Pongau, where he was to put down a riot between a camp of Allied POWs and the civilians. This camp was called *Stalag* XVIII-C, or 317 South Camp, by the Germans.

The information came from a British medical officer, Capt. D. R. Holden, who had been a POW at *Stalag* XVIII-C.[1]

He made the northerly 25-mile trip from the camp and headed straight for Salzburg, Austria, knowing the Americans had occupied the area since May 5. A Swiss Red Cross official had entered the camp on May 6 to ensure the Germans would be held accountable for any atrocities committed by defeated and retreating soldiers.[2]

The last recorded inspection by the IRC had been on February 22, 1945, by E. Mayer.

The camp was a transfer-point *Stalag* and not meant to hold more than 4,000–5,000 prisoners. Because the Allied forces were approaching the

Cpl. David Englander and Sgt. Harold Dittmer located this dark-maroon vehicle in Goering's garage in Berchtesgaden. Keys were in the ignition, but the vehicle was empty of gas. That inconvenience was quickly remedied. Englander then located some paint and brushed a large white star on each door. He had it for a few days until a 101st officer took it for his own. WILKENS/DETTORE

POW camps, other *Stalags* were emptied and the men were forced into death marches. Most POWs were not healthy enough to keep up and fell by the wayside, where they were shot on the spot. POWs from other camps were glad to leave their former *Stalags* and were fed well by local farmers while on the roads to Markt Pongau.

The camp had swelled to nearly 13,000 prisoners by the end of April 1945, and its ability to house and feed them adequately was overwhelmed. Standard medical care was not possible; sick men lying on the floor in every corner of the hospital was a common scene.

The camp was divided into a south section for Allied prisoners and a north section for the Russians. The Russians had it the worst; since Russia was not a signatory of the Geneva Convention, Stalin had no interest in their fate. The Germans had no problem interpreting that fact. Approximately 3,700 Russians died during the camp's existence, from March 1941 until liberation. The slightest infraction meant execution. The townspeople of Markt Pongau witnessed that policy routinely.

A curious mix of 1,000 Poles who fought against the Germans during the Warsaw Ghetto Uprising existed in the north camp. Many were not part of a

Berchtesgaden, Germany. PFC Lelonek assists in the liberation of the hidden Platterhof Hotel wine cellar. Note his flashlight. LELONEK/DETTORE

Berchtesgaden, Germany. PFC Hubert Warren (foreground) and PFC Albert Lelonek (sitting on right side of truck) with a 6x6 load of the Platterhof Hotel's wine, champagne, and silverware being loaded up for later distribution. Note the Platterhof container.
H. C. WARREN FAMILY

standing army but were given rights as a legitimate military army of Poland and treated as such if they would surrender. SS General Von dem Bach, who was eventually called in to wipe out the Poles, recognized their tenacity and brokered this deal to guarantee an orderly surrender in a timely manner, much to the surprise of his superiors.

The German guards had the good sense to withdraw from the camp on May 2 even though fighting was occurring in the vicinity. The POWs were now responsible for controlling themselves. There were not enough Red Cross food parcels on hand to feed this large mass of men, and the situation deteriorated.

About 200 POWs broke out of their camp on May 6, looted a nearby German supply train, and fought with some of the town's civilians. Some of the prisoners—among them a few American airmen—had spent many years in camps, having been captured in Dunkirk, North Africa, or Holland. The situation was brought back under control for the time being by the Allied POW camp officers. They feared another incident could get completely out of control. The Russians prisoners were a special concern for the Allied camp commanders; they were fearful of another escalation of violence against the Germans nearby. The Russians wanted revenge at any cost.

This situation was made even more explosive by a German Army division that was retreating from Italy. This nearby group totaled somewhere between 12,000 and 15,000 armed soldiers who had intervened in the riot.

Lieutenant Smith and his small convoy of eighteen glider riders, plus a mixture of 321st and 327th glider infantry troopers, were racing into this situation. This was a dangerous mix of 30,000 anxious soldiers from both sides of the war and the frightened townspeople. Anger, fear, and revenge were in the air.

Around 1300 hours on May 8, PFC Elmo Smiley was pulled from a group of B Battery comrades who had just been told that the war was over. To his surprise, Smiley was told to get his jeep and be ready to travel for a mission. He was to be Smith's driver. Mounted outside the front passenger seat was a .30-caliber machine gun. The entire scenario was odd, since he had just been informed that the war was over. They had a small convoy ready for battle and headed into unknown territory.

The group traveled through the mountain passes to the POW camp and arrived late in the afternoon. The German general and his troops stood by and watched the small band approach. The general approached the jeep and gave Smith a crisp salute. He surrendered his command and the camp into American hands. The 321st Unit Journal entry for May 1–10, 1945, reported that 13,000 Allied prisoners of war were "now officially liberated and went most wild with joy."[3] Smith and his party were placed on special duty with the XV Corps until relieved.

The German general stood by the driver's side. Seeing this as an opportune moment, Smiley reached over and removed the luger from his holster, never getting out of his jeep. The general did not react negatively to this bold move; Smiley said he almost appeared to expect it. Smiley kept this war trophy and brought it home.

In the interim, Smith and his men took over enforcing discipline within the camp. The only way to get out was with a pass. By May 9, a convoy arrived loaded with parcels for the newly liberated prisoners. Smith was relieved by a British colonel and he and Smiley headed back to their prior position near Berchtesgaden via the long way, a scenic ride through the Brenner Pass to the Italian border.

Running low on gasoline, it was time for a fill-up courtesy of the German Army. Long lines of Germans walked and clogged the roads at intervals. Interspersed with these soldiers were slow-moving vehicles. Smiley spotted a large truck loaded with men and jerricans of gasoline strapped down alongside. He exited his jeep and untied the containers of fuel under the eyes of the Germans, poured the contents into his vehicle, and sped off. Not a word was said by anyone. Much later, Smiley would reflect that his actions were more bold than wise. The jeep ran poorly for the rest of the trip.

The prisoners of war believed their liberators were paratroopers, not glidermen, and hold this view even today. One of the reasons for this slight misunderstanding was the stenciling on the jeep

The Platterhof kitchen. TURKAL FAMILY

A Markt Pongau postcard.

Stalag XVIII-C at Markt Pongau, Austria.

SS barracks at Berchtesgaden, May 3, 1945. VERBEKE/DETTORE

bumpers, which designated the unit as 101st; therefore they must be paratroopers. Division artillery had deemed it unnecessary to hide the vehicle unit designations on April 4—that way the Germans would know whom they were dealing with.

Stalag XVIII-C would stay in existence a little bit longer as a British Intelligence detention center for ex-Nazis. (Among the infamous Nazi prisoners held at the camp were SS *Obersturmbanführer* Rudolf Hoess, the first commandant of Auschwitz, and *Obersturmführer* Franz von Bodman, the camp physician at Auschwitz, Majdanek, and other concentration camps.) The camp then became a home for displaced persons (DPs) until 1947. The town would go back to its prior name, St. Johann im Pongau.

It became official; May 9 was V-E Day. Upon hearing the news, the battalion was subdued as they took it all in. A number of 321st men said they never heard singing as beautiful as that of German prisoners after their surrender in celebration of surviving the war. However, the war with Japan was still

Some 321st officers toasting V-E Day in Berchtesgaden. PERKINS FAMILY

Berchtesgaden, Germany.

Field Marshal Hermann Goering's house in Berchtesgaden. MORRISON FAMILY

Berchtesgaden, Germany. Standing: PFC Harold Turner (left) and PFC Henry Ira (right). Sitting: PFC Raymond Nagell (left) and PFC Schofield (right). This flag was brought back by a B Battery soldier and now is in the possession of his family. WILKENS FAMILY

German troops walking to holding areas in Austria to surrender. They were not allowed on the roads when the Americans were using them. VERBEKE/DETTORE

ongoing, and they knew it would be their next combat mission.

The battalion arrived at Grossgmain, Austria, on May 23 and stayed until July 8. While here, an updated M1 carbine was issued, the M2. This weapon was selective-fire, capable of firing in full automatic mode or single shot. A range was established, and the artillerymen were trained in its function and use. The war in Europe was over, but the Japanese were still willing to die for their emperor.

While at Grossgmain, Sgt. Charles Nugent (HQ) was given a mission to take all the battalion's 6x6 trucks and proceed to a small German air base at Zell am zee. They were to pick up a large group of Russian POWs and forced laborers and transport them to a DP camp. While at the airfield, a German pilot landed a Henkel airplane; the payload was his entire family. He made sure to surrender to the Americans.

In a letter home dated May 26, glider rider Sgt. Clience Sutherland of the 327 GIR wrote to his wife, Pearl, and described the prevalent feelings of soldiers in the division. "The Germans are allowed to pick up scraps [of food] and cigarette butts after us. It is alright—the 101st are sure breaking the Germans in RIGHT. Well, after all they asked for it. The 101st still hasn't forgotten the friends of ours they killed."

T/4 Merle Fulton (HQ Battery) wrote home to his wife: "Yesterday [June 6] was a holiday so we had the day off. Guess we will have our arrowhead in the next couple of days to wear on our ETO pin. Too bad it doesn't give us five more points. We got parachute boots just after we came back from Normandy. Our Glider pay stops at the first of this month unless we take a glider ride. Back at Mourmelon last March we took two rides in less than 30 minutes so we would get the extra pay until now. But I don't think they are going to give us that extra money since they don't have any use for us right now."

Three days later he sent another letter home. "We are now in Austria. We took two glider rides this morning so we can draw extra pay until January 1st. We have to only take at least 4 flights a year to get the pay. We were only in the air for about 5 minutes each trip. So we made 200 dollars in 10 minutes. There is nothing to it when you land on an air strip. I don't like a glider as much as I did before we went into Holland."

Fulton's actual monthly pay since July 1944 was as follows: base pay for the rank of T/4, $78; another $20 for overseas pay; glider pay, $46.80 or 20 percent of his base pay; and service pay, $8.90. His total pay was $153.70 per month.

Of all the veteran interviews conducted by the author, one story about Colonel Carmichael created more bad feelings than any other against their commanding officer. An article entitled "Hoofing It Across the Atlantic" was published on the front page of the September 16, 1945, issue of the *Stars and Stripes* newspaper (European Theater edition). The article reported that while the battalion was billeted in the town of Grossgmain, Austria, it had access to

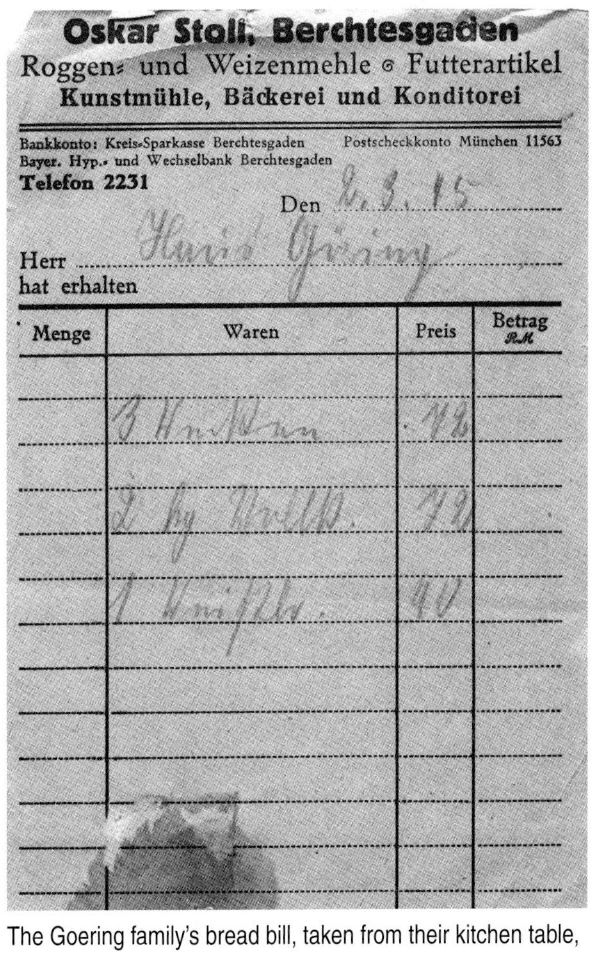
Oskar Stoll, Berchtesgaden
Roggen- und Weizenmehle ◎ Futterartikel
Kunstmühle, Bäckerei und Konditorei

Bankkonto: Kreis-Sparkasse Berchtesgaden Postscheckkonto München 11563
Bayer. Hyp.- und Wechselbank Berchtesgaden
Telefon 2231

Den

Herr
hat erhalten

Menge	Waren	Preis	Betrag RM

The Goering family's bread bill, taken from their kitchen table, dated March 2, 1945. G. J. DETTORE COLLECTION

A group of 321st B Battery soldiers training on their new M2 carbines in Grossgmain, Austria. DAVIS FAMILY

riding stables, which had been built by the Germans and housed horses for the officers' enjoyment. The stables had been maintained by a small contingent of Wehrmacht personnel, but now that the war was over, the only riders were Americans. The former German soldiers kept their positions for the time being—they fed, watered, and groomed the horses, and kept the stalls clean for their new masters. Many a 321st soldier would grab a horse, with or without tack, and go riding with his buddies.

Colonel Carmichael had a small, rented former horse farm back home in Hudson, Wisconsin. He fancied himself an expert on horse flesh, and now hoped to get the pick of the litter and send a horse back home. He didn't take one horse—he took two. Nobody really cared, but those qualified to go home were told space on board the ships was limited. These high-pointer men had done their service but couldn't get passage home. Someone in the battalion got this information to *Stars and Stripes* reporter Thom Yates, hoping to get their colonel in trouble.

Carmichael stated in the article that he paid the equivalent of one dollar for each horse in Munich (to whom he paid the money is not mentioned). The colonel also paid for the freight, which cost him $120 per horse. The horses were two year olds, and Carmichael bragged to the press that he might race or sell them for a nice profit.

Sgt. Ernest White (B Battery) of the 321st, who was known for his ability with horses, was detailed to take care of them on the voyage back to the States aboard the cargo ship *Santa Marta*.

The article caused quite a stir throughout the European Theater, and newspaper reporters from all over were waiting on Carmichael's front porch when he got home. They wanted to know the story of the horses. The colonel lost his cool and shot back that everything was paid for, so what was the big problem? The two horses, one of which he named Tammy, were not anything special and were used only for riding. However, they were worth more than one dollar.

Austria. B Battery sergeants (from left to right): 1st Sgt. Timothy Shea, Sgt. Harry Stearns (radio sergeant), Sgt. Bill Plummer (forward observer), Sgt. Norman Deethardt (chief of 1st Gun Section), Sgt. Mark Sullivan (chief of 2nd Gun Section), Sgt. Ted Thibodeaux (chief of 3rd Gun Section, staff), Sgt. Gerald Braden (chief of 4th Gun Section), Sgt. Haig Pauley (chief of 5th Gun Section), Sgt. Harvey Baker (chief of 6th Gun Section), Sgt. Ill Roberson (machine-gun section), Sgt. Nelson Kopacka (ammunition), Sgt. Raymond Riddle (supply), Sgt. James Steffen (mess), Sgt. Willard Brown (motor), and Sgt. Ernest White (recon).

A Battery soldiers at a billeted house in Grossgmain, May 10, 1945.

A B Battery detail section in Grossgmain (from left to right): Cpl. William Stone, PFC William Buckingham, and Cpl. Walter Mitchell.

Right: An assortment of the items PFC Hubert Warren picked up around Grossgmain. This photo shows only two of his pistols—"not a bad collection."
H. C. WARREN FAMILY

The jeep PFC Bernard DiPasquale drove in Germany. DIPASQUALE/DETTORE

Bad Reichenhall, Germany, where everything was up for grabs, May 20, 1945. FULTON FAMILY

T/3 Leo Corrigan (HQ Battery) in Austria.

Colonel Carmichael was officially relieved from his command on July 3, 1945, and made his way home to Hudson, Wisconsin. The new commanding officer of the 321st was Col. Paul Oswald.

In mid-July, a one-year anniversary parade commemorating the liberation of Brussels, Belgium, occurred. The 101st sent representatives from all its units. The 321st sent one soldier from each battery, a total of three. PFC Elmo Smiley (B Battery) was one of them. The city's inhabitants crowded the streets. It was a massive parade and noisy. Smiley recalls that it was difficult to keep cadence while marching down the streets. It was a spit-and-polish affair. Nothing was said to him about his helmet, which had a bullet hole in the right side near the front. He had lost his original helmet in Holland and picked up his current one off the ground. To him, a helmet was a helmet.

The 321st went home piecemeal in September 1945, attached to other units on paper for the ship ride back to the States. Lt. Richard Smith and Lt. Tony Linz, both of A Battery, found themselves on

Sgt. George Wiggins supposedly wearing Hitler's uniform in Berchtesgaden, May 1945. TURKAL FAMILY

Glidermen of the 321st earning their qualification rating for glider pay in Grossgmain. TURKAL FAMILY

Right: The interior of a CG-4A in flight over Grossgmain. PERKINS FAMILY

A kitchen at Sens, France, October 1945. George Turkal said their kitchen was the best in the division. TURKAL FAMILY

Grossgmain. Note the 101st eagle drawn on the canteen cup. MORRISON FAMILY

Belongings being inspected prior to soldiers boarding a ship for the trip home. TURKAL FAMILY

the same ship. Just about all the returning soldiers had six months' pay with them. It was one continuous card and dice game for the duration of the voyage. So much money was changing hands that the big winners paid the most feared men as their own personal twenty-four-hour bodyguards.

At the height of this gambling frenzy, dollar bills were pulled from the games and thrown overboard—they slowed down the game. As the ship was pulling into New York harbor, the pots grew immense, so large that winning one could be a life-changing event. Lieutenant Smith had a full house in the very last card game. It took every cent he had to stay in the game. All the others dropped out. His single opponent laid down his cards: a straight flush. Linz had to lend Smith money so he could get home.

A victory parade was held on January 12, 1946, in New York City, consisting of 13,000 airborne troopers. It was led by Gen. James Gavin of the 82nd Airborne Division along with 8,800 of his own men. The others came from the 101st, 17th, and 13th Divisions. Forty-five C-47s participated by towing gliders, along with 100 P-47 Thunderbolts, tanks, and other military hardware. The crowd was estimated at 3.5 million.

Epilogue

ON OCTOBER 2, 1987, three war buddies met in Lancaster, South Carolina. They had not seen each other since the war and spent a few days together reminiscing. A newspaper reporter heard about this small gathering and interviewed the old soldiers: Victor Truesdale, Merle Fulton, and Burdette Wilkinson. In my interviews with these airborne veterans, a common theme developed when they spoke of their comrades and life after the war. What Wilkinson said in 1987 to the reporter summed up what I was told many times by other 321st boys: "Some people keep war memories with them in their daily life. I wanted to forget the whole thing and get on with my life. The only memories I really kept were of my close friends—these two."

In a letter to his sister, dated June 22, 1949, Capt. Joseph Perkins, the battalion S-2, described the process of compiling the unit history, *Mission Accomplished.*

> We had moved to the town of Grossgmain, Austria [June 1945] to take over a section of Austria for patrolling and hunting for VIPS [very important POWs]. In their travel, many of the fellows had picked up cameras, and one group brought in a complete darkroom truck loaded with German photo supplies. We set up a darkroom and held classes in photography for those interested. It didn't take long before the demand for prints was more than could be supplied.

A 321st reunion at Fort Bragg, where James Dundon (left) and Joseph Perkins met for the first time since 1945.
SMITH FAMILY

Right: A Boston newspaper article dated February 9, 1945.

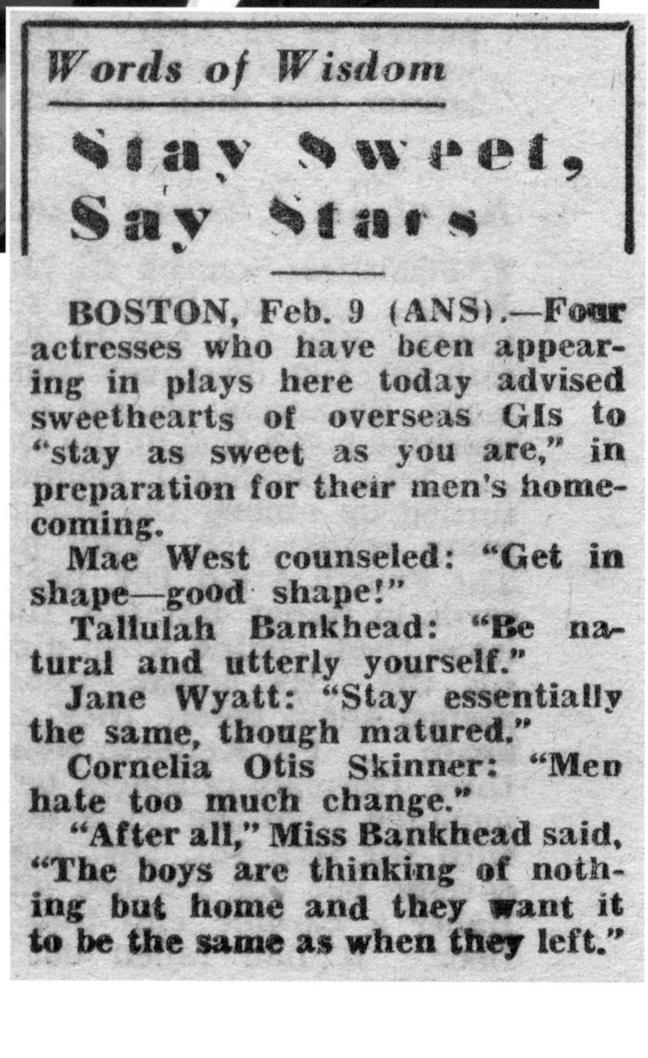

Words of Wisdom

Stay Sweet, Say Stars

BOSTON, Feb. 9 (ANS).—Four actresses who have been appearing in plays here today advised sweethearts of overseas GIs to "stay as sweet as you are," in preparation for their men's homecoming.

Mae West counseled: "Get in shape—good shape!"

Tallulah Bankhead: "Be natural and utterly yourself."

Jane Wyatt: "Stay essentially the same, though matured."

Cornelia Otis Skinner: "Men hate too much change."

"After all," Miss Bankhead said, "The boys are thinking of nothing but home and they want it to be the same as when they left."

In fact the Colonel knew that I had been taking pictures throughout the war and wanted a complete set—750 or more. The only way I could keep everybody happy, that I could see, would be to put the best pictures in a printed book of some kind. When this idea was advanced to the Colonel in June, he said "Good idea, but you better get started."

To get the ball rolling, I got a pass to go anywhere and be gone for any length of time, then took off for the nearest town of any size, Salsburg [*sic*]. This is the Music Center of Europe, the birthplace of Mozart, and the site of the famous Musical Festival.

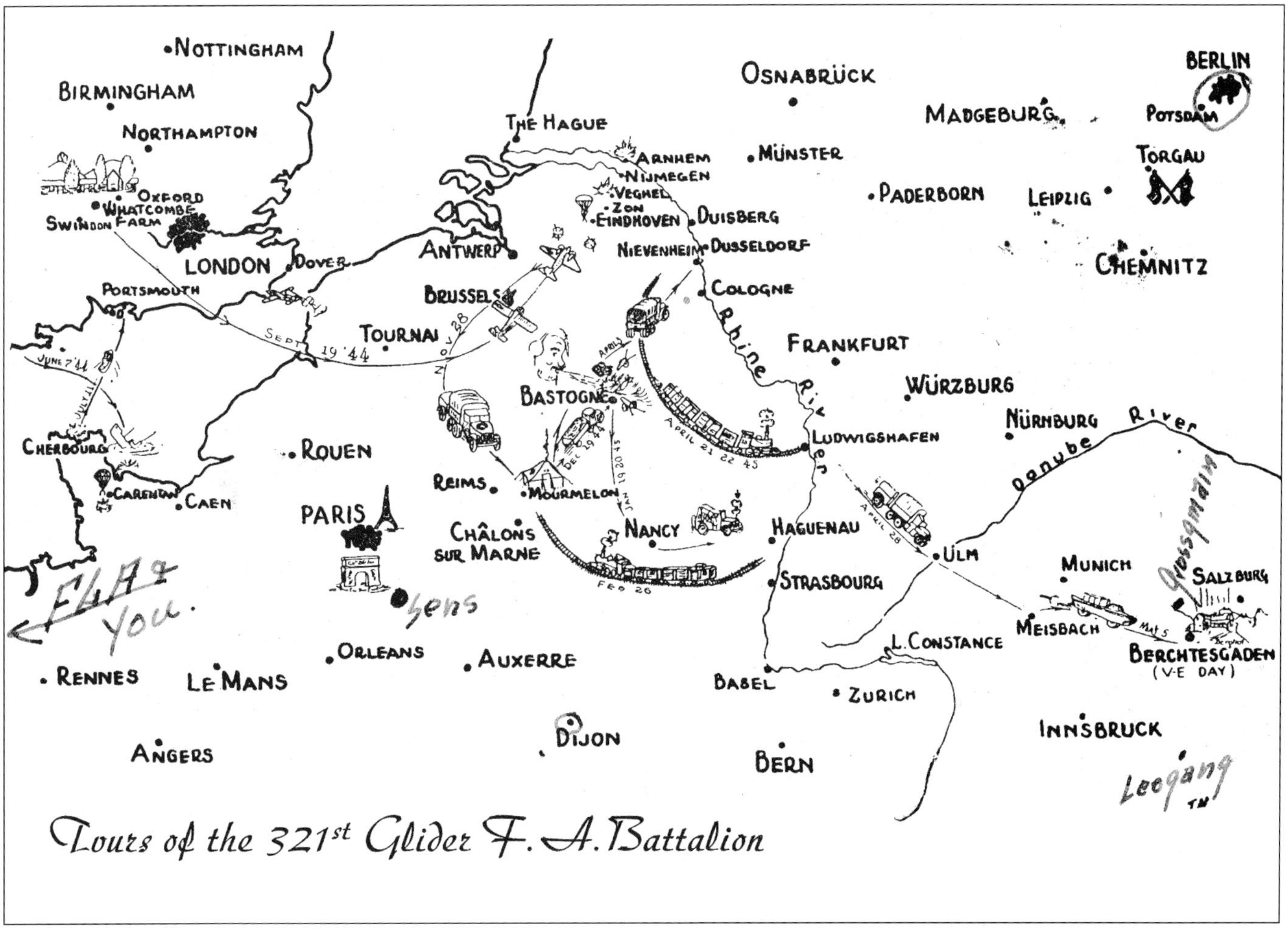

A 321st tour postcard drawn by PFC Tom Morrison (HQ Battery) in 1945.

I found a good publishing company, but their engraving department was still in a cave to protect it. The local Military Government allowed me to contract a newspaper to make the plates. Subscriptions at $5.00 each were taken from the men in the unit interested in the book and 750 were sold. This was too much, as I found out, so $3.50 had to be returned to each fellow who had subscribed for the book.

Some descriptive matter would be nice in the book, so I asked each Battery Commander to send me two men whom they knew, from censoring letters, had a flair for writing. Depending upon when they came to us and which campaign they had been in, they were assigned a section of the history to write. However, a bad thing happened: before [the] script could be corrected for factual and grammatical errors, most of them were shipped home on points, and the first of July, rather than correct it myself or have it done by someone else really qualified, I decided to print it just as it was written, keeping the style, and the heck with the errors.

The following write-up for Col. Edward Carmichael's Silver Star citation was also written by Captain Perkins, who was ordered to do so by Colonel Carmichael.

While serving with the Army of the United States, [Carmichael] distinguished himself by

> The death of the glider did not come quickly, but with the advent of the helicopter, its demise was inevitable. Gliders were last used for resupply and rescue missions from New Guinea to the Arctic. By the mid-1950s, helicopters were becoming dependable, due in part to the Korean War. By 1958, the 10th Rescue Squadron was no more. Its six gliders, based at Ladd Air Force Base in Fairbanks, Alaska, had been stricken from its rolls. ■

> gallantry in action. On 18 December 1944, in the vicinity of Bastogne, Belgium, when enemy infantry and tanks infiltrated through the front lines and threatened his gun positions, Colonel Carmichael rapidly organized strong security detachments from the gun crews of his battalion and prepared to halt the enemy threats, one of which was stopped just short of his battalion gun positions. Despite the critical situation, Colonel Carmichael continued, by use of the remaining howitzers of his battalion, to maintain artillery support necessary for the front line infantry. During the entire siege of Bastogne, Colonel Carmichael's gallant example was an inspiration assuredly to his men. The marked success of his battalion in accomplishing its mission depended largely on his courageous and energetic leadership. His actions were in accordance with the highest standards of the military service. Entered military service from Wisconsin.

It's interesting to note that on December 18 the battalion was not emplaced; it was at an assembly area chosen by Colonel Sink of the 506th PIR, near Savy, Belgium. Lt. Anthony Linz (A Battery executive officer) took one gun to Savy ahead of the battalion and waited for further orders (see page XXX). It wasn't until the nineteenth at 1220 hours that the battalion positions were established and ready to fire.

On December 21 at 1045 hours, the 321st received erroneous information that the Germans were in the town of Bastogne. The firing batteries had only chosen positions in case of an enemy tank breakthrough. It's possible Captain Perkins knew that these contradictions to Colonel Carmichael's Silver Star write-up would come to light, either by those who were there or by future historians.

Carmichael's Silver Star was formally presented at the end of the war. During its presentation, with the battalion in attendance, many of the soldiers showed their displeasure. Cpl. Thomas Morrison (HQ Battery) stated that the battalion "damn near fainted when Carmichael received the Silver Star at Bad Reichenhall." After the war, Carmichael was eventually promoted to the rank of brigadier general of the 84th Infantry Division, a training division based at Fort McCoy, Wisconsin. He retired in 1964.

The second of the two Silver Stars awarded to the 321st GFA was given to Capt. Thomas White of A Battery.

Captain Thomas White's Silver Star Citation

> While serving with the Army of the United States, [White] distinguished himself by gallantry in action. On 4th of October 1944 in the vicinity of Opheusden, Holland, he was assigned to duties of a liaison officer with a parachute infantry regiment when the enemy launched a strong attack on friendly positions. By Captain White's careful direction of effective artillery fire, the attack was repulsed in efficient time to enable reinforcements to enter and secure the sector. When the enemy launched a stronger, more determined attack, Captain White, located at a forward battalion command post, efficiently coordinated the artillery fire of two battalions on the enemy. Operating under the most hazardous conditions of enemy fire which destroyed his vehicle, two radio sets and the buildings which he occupied, he directed such destructive artillery fire that the advance of the enemy was repulsed at every point. When the battle had reached a climax, Captain White brought upon

> the enemy the fire on one hundred and twenty guns which prevented the enemy from making any further attempts to penetrate the area. His actions were in accordance with the highest standards of the military service. Entered military service from Massachusetts.

During World War II, the 321st had approximately 775 soldiers, including officers, in its ranks. Broken down, the numbers were approximately 175 artillerymen for each firing battery. Headquarters had fewer men, about 115. The Medical Section had 12 medics. The other 425 soldiers came and went for myriad reasons.

The lowest turnover rate was in headquarters, with 28 total soldiers; A Battery had 180 and B Battery had 205. The turnover rate was higher in A and B Batteries because the men did not stay with their respective battery for reasons such as transfer to other units, injuries while in training, hardships at home, medical ailments, or being wounded in action. All the numbers are rough estimates.

APPENDIX 1

75mm Ammunition Fired

Training ammunition fired in England	6,610
Normandy	11,496 + 615 smoke (white phosphorous)
Holland	31,357 + 488 smoke
Bastogne	12,714 + 500 smoke
Haguenau	6,767 + 237 smoke
Germany	2,233 + 101 smoke

The majority fired was the M54 timed super quick ammo, followed by M48 (high-explosive, not used until the Holland campaign), HEAT (high-explosive antitank), and smoke.

APPENDIX 2

321st Prisoners of War Captured during Market Garden

PFC ROBERT REEVES, an A Battery machine gunner, traveled the 5 miles from Whatcombe Farm to the departure air base at Aldermaston. He would go into Holland with five other 321st glidermen—Pvt. William Cox of Springfield, Illinois; Pvt. Robert Bunyard of Meridian, Mississippi; Ross Davis from Lincoln, Nebraska; glider pilot F/O Elmo Tibbetts from Victorville, California; and copilot PFC Francis Watson from High Point, North Carolina.

The glider load consisted of a trailer packed with a .50-caliber machine gun and its ammunition. Under the taut canvas cover of the trailer was other essential equipment, such as Reeves's 1-gallon can of fruit cocktail that some cook back in England was most likely searching for.

At 1230 hours, the glider was airborne after leaving Aldermaston. Halfway over the English Channel, the trouble began: fog. It became so thick the other tugs and gliders disappeared; shortly thereafter, even their own tug vanished. Without warning, the towrope became limp. All the other glider riders thought the C-47 had already released. The pilot, Elmo Tibbetts, ordered his riders to get ready to inflate their Mae West floatation vests. They were going to ditch in the channel, having already dropped to within 25 feet of the water. Suddenly the fog cleared, and they discovered they were still attached to the C-47. The power pilot had engine trouble and lost altitude, but now he had full power back and on to Holland they went. As it turned out, that was the best part of the flight.

The lone tug and its glider circled for quite some time until other pairs appeared out of the fog. Being last in their flight path provided a great view of what was up ahead, which was nothing these troopers wanted to see. The C-47s were being knocked down from the sky, along with some of the CG-4As. The 88s and anything else the Germans had were zeroed in to the altitude, speed, and direction of the waves of incoming flights. Being last in this group was no comfort, only terror.

Now it was their turn. The German fire poured into the C-47, causing one of its engines to catch fire. The plane started to lose altitude again. Tibbetts hoped the tug could hold on just a bit longer to get to Landing Zone W. To cut loose from the tug now would mean landing in enemy territory—they'd become POWs for sure. He hesitated, hoping for a better choice, but it didn't come.

Tibbetts held on as the fire from the Germans perforated the glider. Severed control cables made a *twang* sound when the tension released from the twisted steel. Bullets found their way into the welded steel-tube airframe, making sounds like popcorn popping each time the thin fabric covering was punctured. The wings and tail were also hit. The trailer had numerous 5-gallon gas cans sitting inside, but no one wanted to think about that now.

Tibbetts later said he should have cut loose before then. The controls were gone, the altitude was bad, and there was not another tug or glider in sight. He released the towrope. They were going down all by themselves; it was a lonely descent. Small-arms fire came from a wooded area just underneath them. They needed a clear field and some cover when they landed. The ground was coming up fast.

The Waco plunged to the earth, creating a deep furrow in the soft ground. It skidded along and stopped. Their training enabled them to react as if on cue. They jumped out of the glider, circling it to defend its cargo and themselves. They spotted a jeep approaching them from across the field and their hope soared. It was short lived. The occupants of the jeep jumped out, ran into the ditch, and opened fire. Damn, they were Krauts.

The group of Americans was in an open field between two wooded areas, one occupied with the enemy for sure, and the other an unknown. What to do? They took a vote. It was decided to surrender. But each man had one more thing to do before capture.

Their rifles were quickly rendered useless—the removed parts were pushed into the soft Holland soil. Private Reeves knew from training that any German souvenirs he had on him would anger the capturing Germans. Rough treatment would be sure to follow. He had only minutes to rid himself of insignia cut from the uniforms of dead SS while fighting in Normandy. He opened his wallet, snatched out the jagged pieces of cloth, and jammed them deep into the soil, burying them along with a way of life he was not to experience for quite some time.

Nobody had anything on them that was white. How could they surrender without a white flag? Cautiously, one of the glider riders stood up and waved. The Germans fired a few more shots but missed. They approached the group slowly. The German soldier in charge was young and agitated. He got close to the Americans and waved his pistol around, yelling something at everyone. The prisoners had no idea what he was saying, and it made them nervous. At this time, another group of Germans appeared from the woods the glidermen had previously thought about making a run for. It seemed surrendering was the smartest thing to do under the circumstances.

The captors entered the crashed glider and exited with Reeves's gallon of fruit cocktail. That was the last time he saw the prized can. Other Germans decided to search the former glider riders, taking various items for themselves. Reeves lost his wallet, fountain pen, and watch. He hadn't realized until now that he had been hit by ground fire. His right ankle was bleeding and filled his boot with blood. Luckily, in a few days it healed itself.

The captured group was marched to a big barn that held approximately 200 men from the 101st. They were close to Tilburg, behind German lines. It was time for interrogation. The German interrogator spoke perfect English; he wanted to know what outfit the captives were from, where they were going, and other such details. Reeves gave only his name, rank, and serial number. The courteous German said he would answer all of his own questions, as he already knew the answers anyway. All he had to do was look at the trailer in the glider, which was stenciled in white paint with "101 A/B 321 GF."

The interrogator must have been amused by this game because he gave Reeves a plug of American chewing tobacco. Reeves, a nonsmoker, gave the tobacco to his friend, Pvt. Milton Moore of Jackson, Tennessee, who had been in the same glider. Moore stretched the tobacco by mixing it with leaves found during their forced march to captivity. The seeds would pop and flare into the air when lit, causing some badly needed comic relief.

As the 200 or so captured Americans were marched through the Dutch villages, the local inhabitants gave them things to eat, such as apples and other fruit. Some Dutch civilians would ask for the oilcloth American flag brassards worn on the right sleeves of the marching GIs. Originally, the invasion planners thought these flags would help to identify them as liberators and keep misidentification between soldiers to a minimum. Some cut the brassard down to the size of a small American flag and had sewn that to the sleeve of their jacket. Most opted for the "as issued" form, a safety pin that secured the two wrapped ends together. Other 101st troopers were asked for their eagle patches. The Germans allowed this interaction to continue, as it

Whatcombe Farm, England. PFC Robert Reeves of the A Battery machine-gun section. REEVES FAMILY

eased the responsibility of feeding these men. Private Reeves declined to remove his insignia, wanting to let everyone know he was proud to be airborne.

This march lasted for days until they reached the town of Utrecht, Holland. It was time for a train ride into Germany. Reeves wrote:

> Our first stop of any length in Germany came on October 1 when we reached Stalag XII-A near Limburg, where the famous cheese was made. We were served rations of the cheese at times, but as hungry as I was, I couldn't force myself to eat the foul-smelling stuff. This location seemed to be a POW distribution center, since the American GIs were being shipped to other camps from here. The facilities were ghastly, with terrible soup to eat and floors simply covered with straw for sleeping. While we were being processed at Limburg, the Germans stenciled a large white triangle on the back of our jackets and on the back of each pant leg in the area of the thigh. We were told this was a target for a guard to shoot at in case we tried to escape. This provided us with a good incentive to stay put!

Standing on the left side of the road was a German soldier watching the troopers march past. He watched Reeves go by and in a startled tone yelled, "Carentan! Carentan!" Seeing the eagle patch apparently brought back bad memories of Normandy. Reeves continued to march down the road with eyes forward, not missing a step.

Reeves continued:

> It was at Stalag XII-A that I had my billfold returned, but never saw my watch or fountain pen again. As expected, all my invasion money [Dutch notes] was missing from my billfold, but thankfully, all the pictures were still intact. That I still had my pictures from home was good for my morale as I spent many hours looking at them in times to come. I was also given a deck of cards that hadn't been mine,

but which I gladly received. That deck of cards would also prove to be very beneficial to me later.

Ten days later, Reeves, Private Moore, and others left Limburg by train to another camp. They traveled mostly at night, supposedly as a safety measure to keep the train from being strafed by Allied airplanes.

"We were given nothing but bread and water (and very little of that) while we were on the train. We had to relieve ourselves in old coffee cans, and then empty them out the high window slots that were covered with barbed wire," Reeves wrote. "We were, incidentally, supposed to detrain in Frankfurt for much needed food and rest, but our German train commander was from Frankfurt and when he saw how U.S. bombers had devastated his home town, he ordered us to be kept locked in the foul boxcars straight through to our destination."

Around this time, Reeves's mother received a letter that she had sent her son, postmarked October 5, 1944. One word written on the outside of the returned envelope caused a wave of grief through the farmhouse in Gridley, Illinois: "Deceased." Underneath that word was the signature of an officer of the 321st. No explanation was given. The officer, Lt. Samuel Meyers, from Columbus, Georgia, was new to the outfit and most likely had taken over for the regular censor of the 321st, Capt. George Dunkelberg, who also became a POW during the Holland invasion. Mrs. Ida Reeves would not learn the truth of her son's capture for some time.

Reeves and his fellow glider rider, Private Moore, an A Battery cook, managed to stay together. Both of them finally reached their new home: *Stalag* VII-A, located 40 miles north of Munich near the town of Moosburg, Germany. It was the middle of October and raining as the new arrivals were indoctrinated at the camp. The prisoners were lined up smartly in rows of five and forced to stand in the pouring rain for hours. They could see the camp buildings, but were still outside its gates.

Tired and hungry, Reeves kept his hands in his pockets to keep them warm. He slouched a bit. A German guard approached Reeves from the rear. He silently removed his bayonet from the scabbard attached to his belt. The guard gripped the handle of the bayonet and struck the 321st soldier without warning across the back several times, knocking him to the ground. The guard was bellowing something in German, which was not understood by the muddied and sore trooper. Only later did he find out that he was being punished for bad posture and having his hands in his pockets. Reeves and the others would play jokes on these same brutal guards in the months to come, but there would be no laughter among the captives on this day.

When POWs were processed, they were asked by their captors about their job classification. The Germans liked to keep the men who had the same job classifications together. Private Moore was a cook. Reeves was a machine-gunner. In order to stay together, they devised a plan that they would both be cooks, Reeves, getting some quick lessons on kitchen cuisine from Moore in case he was quizzed. No questions were asked. Later, Reeves would rethink that early decision.

The camp would grow to house over 110,000 Allied prisoners of war. It was a system of buildings so great that they were divided by "streets"—one of them even named Main Street. Reeves and Moore were assigned to the north side of the Main Street barracks.

Living quarters were a series of bunk beds three high placed on rough-hewn boards. The mattresses were filled with straw, which compacted quickly and became infested with vermin. Electricity, heat, and water were luxuries and not included for the 250 men who lived there. The wood stove was of little use since there was nothing to cook, and there was a severe shortage of anything that would fire the two burners.

The source of water was an outside tap centrally located and used by many barracks. The only hot water available was the concoction the Germans called coffee. It was usually warm, and the POWs used it to shave. Men in need a haircut visited the camp barber, who had the strictly forbidden scissors and hand-operated clippers. A haircut would cost between one and five smokes: free enterprise at work.

One afternoon, Reeves decided not to use the latrine, a building that consisted of broken drain tiles made of crockery placed in a vertical position.

Those were the toilet seats placed over a pit that overflowed if not pumped out regularly. Overflow was a common occurrence.

To his surprise, a German guard with his Doberman pinscher observed him urinating outside the building instead of inside. The dog was let loose. He jumped on Reeves and knocked him down. As Reeves rolled on the ground to protect himself, the dog jumped on his chest, snarling and snapping. The teeth of the guard dog were just inches from his face. The animal lunged, but did not get any flesh as the guard pulled the leash back every time.

As the war dragged on, the guards who originally ran the camp were needed by their Führer to replace soldiers killed in the onslaught of the Allied offensives. Older, less indoctrinated men who were pressed into service as camp guards replaced them. Some even felt sorry for their captives. Unfortunately, Reeves would receive one more beating from a guard who was not a front-line soldier.

Reeves wrote:

> Our daily rations were neither generous nor nutritious. Breakfast consisted of a cup of the ersatz coffee that was more suitable for shaving than drinking. Supper was an inch-thick piece of hard, brown bread and an un-skinned boiled potato. For noontime, we always had the concoction they called soup. It was usually a very watery potato soup with an occasional green bean. Once a week, we got a ration of meat: a one-inch thick slice of bologna about two inches in diameter. . . . Most other food I got had to be begged, bartered or stolen from the Germans, or received from the International Red Cross.

He continued:

> I sent many letters home to Gridley during my imprisonment and it appears that most of them arrived. I was sent letters and packages from home, but received none of them. Letters had been returned to the senders and if the packages arrived in Germany at all, it's certain that they were confiscated and the contents used by the Germans. My mother was surprised by a number of letters and postcards from residents of the East Coast of the United States. These good Samaritans were passing along shortwave radio messages they had received that I was in good health and hoped to be home soon. I have no idea of the source of these radio broadcasts. Perhaps the Germans were in the custom of sending them to the U.S. as propaganda.

It was announced that all the cooks were to assemble. It seemed an inordinate number of American POWs claimed to have this classification. A German officer who spoke perfect English got up and stated to the group, "I don't expect you to make food out of shit, but I want to see what you can do." He continued, "If any of you are not cooks, just leave this room now." Knowing the truth would come out, Reeves got up promptly and left the room.

Reeves was now forced to plant potatoes outside the prison gates. The pieces of potatoes were placed in straw-filled troughs and covered with more straw and soil; this was the supply for the camp that supplemented their meager rations. It was an opportunity to get some extra nutrients, so he stuffed his pockets. Most likely, the prison guards anticipated such a deed and observed the actions of the hungry POW. Reeves wrote:

> He [the guard] delivered a severe thrashing to me with the bayonet scabbard hanging from his belt. . . . After the beating, the man demanded to see my metallic prison identification tag that should have been issued to me back in October. By the time I received my ID number though, the Germans ran out of the metal tags, and I was issued one printed on cardboard. Not knowing that some of us had cardboard IDs, the guard angrily tore mine up and threw it on the ground. I was able to find three out of four pieces of the ID card and I still have those three pieces that contain my German ID number: 075718.

At times, the POWs would approach a guard, being careful that he didn't understand English. The GIs would say, "me American," speaking slowly and pointing to themselves; then, pointing to the guard, he would say "you German." The guard would parrot the words in English, pointing to himself, saying "German," then pointing to his captives, saying "you Americana." The punch line was then put forward: "We nice guys, you asshole." The German, believing his English lesson was continuing, would say, "You nice guys, me asshole." Smiling, the Eaglemen would say, "You got that right, brother," and walk away.

As the war dragged on, the POWs increased, overflowing the already-crowded barracks. These new prisoners were segregated from the current ones, who were displaced by the fresh arrivals. This controlled the flow of new information from the outside world. Morale was low, and the Germans wanted to keep it that way. Every evening, an American barracks leader was given news from the captors at *Stalag* VII-A to relay back to the men living in the barracks. The news was always the same—grim.

The mighty German army and Luftwaffe were gaining on all fronts. At first, it was viewed as pure propaganda because most of the Americans, prior to capture, believed the war was almost over. However, as weeks turned into months and the camp overflowed daily with new POWs, doubts about the invincibility of the Allied victory settled into their thoughts. Maybe it was true the Allies were losing badly after all. Then, in April, a German guard offered a local newspaper as proof-positive; the headline boldly proclaimed the latest news. It stated that FDR was dead and that he had committed suicide due to the war going so badly. After hearing only negative news of failed Allied offensives for seven months, this seemed plausible. The war was being lost.

The forced labor of Reeves and Moore, along with the other men in their barracks, increased. They were now working on repairing the railroad tracks outside Munich six to seven days a week. Extra-good rations were given out to these crews. It was a welcome relief to be able to get out of the filth and boredom of barracks life.

The routine was nearly the same. Roll call was at 5:00 A.M., and the men were lined up in rows of five. If a soldier was missing, chaos would follow. The guards and their dogs searched the area; the men sometimes waited hours until the "count" was correct. More often than not, the problem was with the Germans, who made an incorrect count.

At 7:00 A.M., fifty POWs were crammed into a boxcar with five armed German guards. These guards sat on a bench that faced the prisoners. Both doors of the boxcar were slid open and secured. Conditions were so crowded the prisoners stood because there was no room to sit. The destination could be hours away. When a soldier needed to urinate, he requested permission from his captors to step forward to the open door. He would grab the doorframe with one hand to keep himself from falling out of the rolling, jerking train while he relieved himself.

Reeves wrote:

> One day in Munich, we were working on the railroad tracks outside a machine shop. During our lunch break, a German worker wearing a greasy, leather apron came out of the shop and asked me, in broken English, if we were Americans? When I told him we were, he said he had something to show me. Out of his apron, he pulled a dirty, many-times-handled letter. He said it was from his son who was in a POW camp in Georgia in the States. His son wrote that he always had fresh fruit to eat and slept in a bed with sheets on it. The machinist wanted to know if this was the truth, or was the son just telling him this to make dad feel better. I told him that it was all true, and that the United States treated all POWs that well, or better. The German citizen said he felt badly that we had to work so hard and were given such poor food, but that was all his country had at the present. He wanted to know if there was anything he could personally do for me to show his appreciation for how my country was treating his son. Thinking quickly about a make-shift lamp I had already fabricated from a tin can and a wick-controlled element (stolen from a railroad signal lantern), I told the man I could surely use some fuel oil to burn in my little lamp. He left and returned with three soda pop bottles of fuel. After bribing the guard (I don't remember how many cigarettes

I lost in that one), I got to keep the bottles, which I put under my belt and covered with my thin coat. Unfortunately, on the train ride back to camp, one of the bottles broke, filling my pants with glass shards and fuel oil. I warned everyone around me not to light any cigarettes, or I might go up like a torch.

Reeves continued:

Milt Moore and I then parlayed my lamp and the deck of cards that I had received back at the distribution camp in Limburg into a source of revenue for us. After our official barracks lights went out, we threw a blanket on a table and ran a poker game. Naturally, cigarettes were used for money in this gambling venture. Neither Milt nor I played in the game, but we dragged one "house" cigarette from every pot. And from that day on, Milt and I always had cigarettes to trade, and he always had as many as he wanted to smoke. This arrangement lasted for many months, providing a great deal of recreation for our buddies, and kept Milt and me "in the chips."

Incidentally, our patrolling guards knew this clandestine game was going on. About once a week, a guard and his dog would come into the barracks, lay his hat bedside the table, and scoop that pot of cigarettes into the hat. That was his cut for allowing the game. The guard was happy, Milt and I were happy; it was only the players who complained when it was their cigarettes in the confiscated pot! Milt, by the way, contributed to our little casino one day when he managed to steal a bottle of wine while working in the basement of a Munich hospital. He rationed that alcohol out to us at the rate of a bottle-cap-full every night until it was gone.[1]

Overcrowding in the trains caused consternation for Reeves and Moore. They were assigned to boxcars during the night and slept at a siding in Munich. There was danger of being bombed by Allied airplanes; many times during the night the POWs were herded into bomb shelters.

One night about 10:00 P.M., the guards came past our cars, unlocked them, opened all the doors, and then disappeared. We all got out and scurried to the nearby air raid shelter, where we bolted and secured the door from the inside, not opening it for anyone unless he could speak good English and identify himself to our satisfaction. We had no desire to admit an angry German soldier with a gun who might shoot all of us. This was the first time we had ever been left alone and didn't know what the enemy had planned for us, if anything. We could hear that there was no firing or bombing taking place, which was as frightening to us as if there had been an air raid, because this sudden change might be bringing some kind of disaster.

We stayed put and speculated on these new circumstances all night and carefully emerged at dawn. We could hear heavy vehicle movement, but couldn't see the source. Finally, as we slowly spread out from our shelter, some of us topped a ridge to discover a long-awaited sight. There, rumbling along the road were American tanks, topped with our GIs casually leaning against the turrets, smoking cigarettes. Munich had fallen to the United States military! You can imagine our jubilation to see our troops again—armed, battle ready, and flying the American flag.

We were liberated that day, April 30, 1945, by the 42nd Rainbow Division of the United States Army. We surely must have been a sorry-looking bunch of humanity. We were all in filthy clothing that had, in many cases, been given to us to replace our worn-out GI clothes.

The freed Americans had made socks from thin, worn-out blankets back at the camp. Underwear had simply disintegrated and the soldiers had to do without. But all of that was behind them now; it was time to live like humans again. They were free and now knew they were the victors after all.

When these former POWs were debriefed in Munich, they would occasionally come across a former civilian railroad boss. These bosses wore a unique uniform of a black hat, jacket, and trousers—a conspicuous sight. The POWs reviled them more than the German guards because they were crueler and far more demanding. Sometimes while walking through Munich, the newly freed captives would spot one of these railroad bosses and ask him for the time. That would be the last time he would see his watch. It was time for retribution and intimidation, specifically against the hated railroad bosses. A watch, a cap, maybe even a belt was demanded. It wasn't so much about the item as the idea that now the Americans were in charge, even of the railroads.

Prior to gliders' takeoff, a change was made and PFC Harry Sinkutch (HQ) switched places with communications Sgt. Victor Truesdale (HQ). Sinkutch climbed out of communications officer Capt. George Dunkelberg's glider; instead, Sinkutch would now be flying into Holland with Maj. John Tyler (HQ) from Nashville, Tennessee. He sat down, fastened his seat belt, and began to pray. Before he knew it, they were airborne. This glider load consisted of twelve personnel, including the glider pilot. Most of the other gliders carried far fewer soldiers and much more equipment. This overloaded glider carried only an additional forty-two rounds of 75mm ammunition.

Captain Dunkelberg was another Camp Claiborne "original." He came into the 321st as a first lieutenant, as part of the 82nd Infantry Division, in March 1942. He was assigned to Headquarters Battery as a communication officer. Traveling with him in the glider were fellow battery members Sergeant Truesdale of Westville, South Carolina, and jeep driver Pvt. Louis Swidzinski of Butler, Pennsylvania. A fourth 321st trooper from another battery also was assigned to the group. In the belly of their glider was a jeep with its gas tank filled right up to the fuel cap and an extra 5-gallon gas can. Their glider was chalk number 2.

The men triple-checked the lashings of the jeep, making sure it was secured to the plywood flooring of the Waco CG-4A. Heavier loads tended to shift during landings and sometimes broke loose from their moorings, flinging cargo at the glider riders. The trip into Holland was not going to be a routine glider ride, if there was such a thing. The landing and all its complications would never be forgotten by its occupants.

Captain Dunkelberg was the copilot that day; Sergeant Truesdale sat in the passenger seat of the jeep and Private Swidzinski was in the driver's spot. The other 321st soldier, in the jump seat along the fuselage of the glider, was the only one with the benefit of a seat belt. This particular Waco had an intercom with its tug, an unusual feature. Most intercoms tended to fail during air turbulence, which caused the telephone wire to snap because it was taped to the outside of the stretching nylon towrope.

As the group of gliders and their tugs approached enemy-held Holland and made the approach down "Flak Alley," all hell broke loose. The Germans had brought every available mounted gun to this area in hopes of decimating the invasion while it was still in the air. With every additional wave of gliders, the flak got worse. Dunkelberg's group was hit severely, but its C-47 tug caught the brunt; the right engine was on fire. This caused the tug to break formation, pulling its heavily loaded glider downward. The flak punctured the fabric-covered Waco from all directions. The trooper seated in the jump seat was struck in the chest. The intercom crackled with the dreaded words that the glider pilot must release his glider: the flames from the descending C-47 tug were threatening the fabric-covered CG-4A. The pilot released.

Capt. Joe Perkins (HQ Battery) looked out the window of his glider, which was flying to the right of Dunkelberg's. He watched in horror as a glider and its tug took an immense amount of flak. He thought it was Dunkelberg's glider, but hoped he was wrong. Another burst of flak struck the right wing of the falling tug, which caused its wingtip of about 8 feet to fold up as if it was hinged. It suddenly sheared off and sliced through the air backward. "Oh, God," muttered Perkins. The tug and its glider separated, both going down in different directions. The piece of wing was deadlier than any German ground fire. It was not losing altitude, and the remainder of the 321st gliders were in its path.

Pvt. Bernard Simmons (B Battery) had decided to stretch his legs. He unbuckled his seat belt to take a look out the clear, plastic windshield in the nose of the Waco. He felt comfortable in a glider, so much so that he often signed in as another trooper to take the required glider rides for those who would rather stay on the ground or who succumbed to air sickness prior to leaving the ground and got "sick just looking at a glider."

Simmons looked out the windshield and saw sights that were never observed during training flights. C-47s and CG-4As were lined up as far as he could see. He wondered how they kept from colliding. The tugs and their tows would rise suddenly, then drop as if they were in an elevator suffering from a snapped cable. Dangerous as this flight was, it still had a beautifully orchestrated look to it all.

All of those thoughts came to a halt as a shiny object appeared in their flight path. It was a chunk of wing detached from its airplane. The deadly piece of aluminum was gliding effortlessly through the air currents and never deviated from its path. Gliders and tugs were not going to change flight paths to avoid a collision with this object; that radical move could cause a dangerous chain reaction in the air.

Private Simmons and the rest of the men in his glider never saw Captain Dunkelberg's tug take any flak and were unaware of what had happened ahead of them. Those troopers had no reason to believe that something *friendly*, something made in America, might just knock them out of the air. They observed this object headed straight toward them. Would it cut the towrope? Or slice off a wing of their glider? It only took seconds to get an answer: it was going to penetrate the glider's nose. This would certainly cause a fatal crash by killing the pilot and copilot. The glidermen cringed and ducked, as if this would somehow save them. At the last possible moment, the wing section changed its course, tilted a few degrees, and passed over them along the fuselage, causing no harm.

It was time to pick a landing spot for Captain Dunkelberg's glider. The pilot worked hard—all the terrain below was unfamiliar. It had to be enemy territory, as there was not a landed glider in sight. Sergeant Truesdale had a perfect line of sight, sitting in the jeep looking over the heads of the pilot and copilot. He saw a farmer's field. A farmhouse jumped into view—the glider was going to hit it.

The glider riders' flight had turned silent: no tug and no flak. The only sounds were made by the wind under the wings, which also caused a slight rustle of the fabric that stretched over the steel-tube welded airframe of the Waco. A deceptive peacefulness was felt by the occupants during the last moments of descent. The glider met its impromptu landing zone with a fury, plowing a furrow through the field and knocking off the landing wheels. The dirt pelted and ground into the skin of the CG-4A, creating not only an overpowering sound but also a vibration throughout the craft. The steel landing skids created heat by friction of the earth as the glider slid forward.

Enough speed allowed the pilot to maneuver just to the left of the farmhouse, but this put him on a collision course with a stand of trees. Somehow the glider pilot pulled out anther trick that surely only a talented F/O could manage. To the amazement of the Eaglemen, the glider skidded between two trees, knocking off both wings simultaneously. This created such a bang that anyone in the area who may have missed seeing the landing certainly was aware of it now. The last of the inertia brought a few more feet of travel, causing the heavy load to dig deeper than before. It created a mound of dirt that buried the nose and put the tail up in the air, making it difficult to move around. That turned out to be the smallest problem.

Rifle fire started to rip through the broken glider, sending all of the occupants to the floor. Volley after volley perforated the skin of the Waco. The bullets pierced the gas tank of the jeep, sending a stream of raw gas toward the angled-down cockpit. In the back of the jeep were seven 5-gallon jerricans of gasoline. The men were trapped. One spark would ignite the fuel vapor into an explosion.

The Germans were close, but the only way they could be seen and counted was if someone stood up and looked out a side door window. Amid the rifle fire, Sgt. Victor Truesdale did just that. He saw plenty of the enemy and nowhere to run. Captain Dunkelberg asked how many were out there. Truesdale yelled forward, "A whole mess of them!" The firing continued, striking the jeep again and again. Dunkelberg asked Truesdale if he had anything white to wave at them. This seemed an odd question, since nothing the glidermen wore was white, not even their underwear. The gas continued to pour from the fuel tank and soaked into every crevice below the wooden floor of the glider. The floor was slippery and flammable. Truesdale was soaked from lying flat in the raw gas. He made the only decision one could make. He knew that the gas vapors contained in their craft were far more dangerous than its liquid form. He opened the latch of the emergency exit and stepped out into the Dutch countryside. He waved his arms furiously. To his surprise, the Germans had made their way to within a few feet of the wingless glider. The enemy stopped firing their rifles and yelled, "Hands *Hock*, hands *Hock*!"

The rest of the glider riders started to cautiously step out. Pvt. Charles Spagnola, from Chicago, Illinois, although having suffered a chest wound, walked out under his own power. The Germans searched the Americans and took their weapons. They also took Truesdale's chocolate D-bar and the trench knife attached to his right ankle. The troopers retained all their personal valuables.

This group, along with other newly captured Eaglemen, were ordered to march—and march they did. While being herded into a barn that evening, the men noticed another bunch of 321st glidermen. It was Pvt. Robert Reeves and the rest of his men. All gathered around and signed Reeves's "short snorter," a piece of paper currency signed by a soldier's comrades for good luck prior to a division-wide mission. They all knew that's certainly what they needed now.

During the subsequent roadside march, various Dutch Underground members would converse with the Allied POWs at opportune moments to tell them of the sabotaged rail lines. The Dutchmen continually told Captain Dunkelberg that the Germans couldn't transport them out of Holland. Sergeant Truesdale approached his captain, telling him he wanted to make a run for it. The enemy had too many prisoners, and the Dutch were friendly to the captured liberators. He knew he could get away, but his captain was against it, so he stayed in line.

All the men, excluding the wounded, were put into boxcars. They spent the next six days traveling to Germany. True to their word, the Dutch Underground struck, attempting to stall or stop this mass movement of men. The railroad spikes were removed during the night, causing the train to derail. Unfortunately, at sunrise a P-51 strafed the locomotive, knowing it contained Allied human cargo. The men were ordered off the train and walked past the hissing, bullet-ridden locomotive. They learned that the engineer was killed when the boiler exploded. They were forced to march until transportation by rail could be arranged again. The group finally arrived in Frankfurt, Germany, at a transit camp, and the POWs were separated by rank for shipment to other camps throughout the shrinking Nazi empire. Truesdale traded his class ring for two loaves of bread and his watch for a can of tuna. Hunger was to be a constant companion.

One more week passed before the captured NCOs were again placed in boxcars en route to their final camp: *Stalag* III-C. It took seven full days of riding the rails before they reached their destination, the town of Alt Drewitz, Germany, approximately fifty miles from the Polish border. The soldiers were relieved they could vacate the cramped, stench-filled wooden boxcars. However, they had to march one more time. The prisoners were lined up, and their captors had them march right through the heart of town. The children of Alt Drewitz stopped what they were doing to stand by the side of the road and stare at the ragged but proud group. These children did not stay motionless for long; they spat on the prisoners as they went by. The Hitler Youth had done its job well.

Camp life was life at a minimum. Soup with worms and body lice were the norm. During nearly four months in captivity, Truesdale had one delousing and one bath. No soap or even toilet paper was given out. Once, Truesdale had temporary use of a single bar of soap to wash his hands. Afterward, he was forced to give it back to the attentive German guard who had lent it. Truesdale had earned the soap for performing a chore prisoners were ordered to do on a routine basis. The outhouse was about a hundred yards from the barracks and could be visited anytime, day or night. The pit quickly filled up with accumulated human waste and needed to be emptied. A wagon containing tubs of sorts to carry out the waste would arrive in camp. This "honey wagon" was manned by a civilian. The pit would be emptied by using a cedar pole with an American helmet attached to it to scoop out the waste. Surely the designers never envisioned this use of the steel-pot helmet. Truesdale wondered how the GI helmet had made its way into this place, when one of the first things the Germans did was order their prisoners to discard their steel helmets. It was after this messy detail that Truesdale got his hands on the bar of soap.

Winter weather was fierce, dropping snow throughout the area. Near the end of January 1945, distant artillery could be heard, but whose was it? A buddy of Truesdale's, German-speaking Sergeant Smitz, learned from a German guard that the Russians were near. A movement of the camp's inhabitants was being planned by the commandant. A couple hundred or so POWs decided on a course of action to stall the forced march, hoping to give the Russians time to get to the camp and liberate them. But how far could they push the enemy?

Stalag III-C was a primitive POW camp even by German standards, but what made it unusual was a hidden radio. Access was limited because most prisoners didn't know where it was or who had it. Information gleaned from this source was passed through to the men. What was known for sure was that the Germans were losing the war and the Russians were rolling through them.

Some of the POWs decided to pull up the wooden floor of their barracks and dig pits. The sandy soil was carried out under their jackets and dumped while on the way to the latrine. These were not to be tunnels, but hiding places. The soldiers would jump into these holes if the Russians neared and the Germans ordered the camp to be emptied. Once in the hole, the flooring would be pulled back over their heads to its original position.

The sound of guns drew nearer, and anxiety showed on the faces of the enemy guards as to what was about to happen. They knew the Russians rarely took prisoners. Most of the guards were older men and had been placed in a noncombatant role because of their age.

There were 2,000 Americans plus a few British placed in huts or barracks in *Stalag* III-C. There were approximately twenty huts, each containing about 100 soldiers. A barbed-wire fence separated them from another compound that held 1,000 Russian POWs. Nearly all of the huts were given an order to march toward Berlin. Some of the men refused. Some stayed in their huts while others milled around outside. Extra guards were called in to intimidate the Americans.

About twenty men from Hut 3 refused to move, and Truesdale was one of the main instigators. They sat determinedly outside their barracks in the snow. Other huts had already emptied and the soldiers were standing in formation. They were marched outside the barbed-wire fence, where they stood watching. Waiting for their comrades, they wondered how this event would turn out. The commandant approached with armed guards. A German interpreter relayed his words to the men in English. The German colonel said if the men did not get in line to march out of the camp, he would leave them all dead in the snow. The men did not move. The colonel had the guards face the seated Americans. His barked-out orders were translated into English. The guards snapped to attention, rifles held across their chests. The bolt actions charged a bullet into the chamber. The men still stayed put.

The colonel was not backing down. He shouted another command. The guards brought their weapons to their shoulders and leaned into their targets, pulling the rifles tightly in anticipation of the kick. The Americans had taken this as far as possible. They stood up and fell in line. The revolt held up the move for two hours. They were now going to march.

As they left camp, the men had no idea when their odyssey would end. The march was on a road covered with 18 inches of snow. They had gone about eight miles when they approached a fork in the road. Three Russian tanks, part of a recon element, appeared from the other direction intersecting the POWs. Thinking they were Germans, the Russians opened up on the group, killing many Americans. A lull occurred; everyone except the Russians was lying flat in the snow. One of the prisoners, known only as "Whitey," jumped up and ran to the tanks. A German guard fired a shot that killed him.

Truesdale looked around. He saw a German guard near him and he thought of jumping him, but he decided to wait. There was more firing, then another lull. It was time to make a move. Truesdale and ten to twelve others jumped up. They yelled at the Russians, "Americans, Americans!" hoping the machine guns wouldn't open up on them once again. A Russian holding a PPSH, a handheld machine gun, stood on the tank; another stood on the ground near it and watched the group run toward them. Both held their fire.

The Americans did not see that a German guard had also run up to the tanks with them. He wanted to surrender to the Russians. They looked at him with disgust and pushed him backward so forcibly that it knocked his helmet off his head. It landed in the snow. The Russian standing on the tank opened fire, killing the German, who fell into the snow next to his helmet. The remainder of the men joined the Russians. It was January 31, 1945. The camp commandant was last seen riding his bicycle across the snow-covered fields. It is not known if the Russians ever found him.

A friend of Truesdale, Sgt. K. D. Martin of the 45th Infantry Division, was in the last hut to leave the camp. As his group approached the road junction, most of the shooting was over. The Russians, who appeared drunk, rounded up all the German guards they could find. They shot them and piled them up in a mass about four feet high.

Sergeant Martin watched as a German guard was told to step up on the pile. The guard said nothing. A Russian fired one shot from his rifle at point-blank range into the German's forehead. He was added to the mound. Another was brought to the pile. However, this time the armed Russian noticed the Americans. He motioned with his eyes over to the side of the road where two young German girls were being held. Eye contact was the only communication—a glint, a stare, then a quick jerk of the head; not a word was spoken. The obvious meaning was horrendous. The Russian wanted to know if Martin and his small group wanted the two German girls to walk up the pile.

The two young girls who had happened to be walking down the road were now facing the ultimate brutality of war. This was Russian retribution for what the Germans did to their people, and the Russians loved it. The group of Americans wanted to leave this sight and take no part in what they were witnessing. However, they couldn't just walk away because they had been asked a question. Not to acknowledge the Russian could be seen as an insult, and these American soldiers were unarmed; could the Americans be next to walk up to that pile? The shoddily clothed, nearly starving bunch of weaponless GIs who had been ill-treated by their captors did the only thing they could do. They shook their heads in the universal gesture for no. The Russian, without hesitation, motioned for the girls to walk back home. The American witnesses quickly left as the Russians continued to add to their pile of corpses.

The soldiers of *Stalag* III-C who were liberated decided to break off into small groups and head for Russia. The war was raging, and they certainly didn't want to return to Germany. The Polish border was near, so they would go that way.

Truesdale's group walked a few miles until they came to a dairy farm of eighty Holstein cows. This was heaven for the men. The Russians had refused to feed the newly liberated group, advising them to do what they did: take whatever was needed from the German people. Take they did. The group slaughtered a cow and a hog and fried them up in the farmer's house. The occupants were kicked out and the soldiers slept in their beds—almost. During the night, the Russians appeared. Waving their guns around, they told the former POWs to sleep on the floor.

Continuing their trek, they encountered a Russian officer who told the group it would be wise to make some small American flags to wear on their shoulder and to head for the Russian headquarters at Landsberg Warthe, Germany (now Gorzow Wielkopolski, Poland). They were able to hitch a ride on an American Studebaker truck carrying Russian supplies and went into Poland by crossing a river boundary. They were now back on foot.

The men soon discovered that since the Polish population was under German occupation, all the signs were in German. It was Hitler's idea that Germany needed this land to perpetuate the idealized agrarian way of life of old. The recently transplanted farmers were German. The language spoken was German. The Polish children's first language that was being taught in school was German. While in Poland, the American POWs who had learned German in the camp or at home had an advantage. While traveling across Europe, they learned something else rather quickly. If a town in Poland was under Soviet control, speaking German was a bad idea. The Russian military treated them as potential spies. It became a case-by-case gamble on what tongue to speak.

Truesdale's group, consisting of five men, was struck by the kindness of the Polish people they encountered. The Germans had taken everything from the farmers, but they willingly gave sustenance to the POWs in the form of soup.

It had been decided early on that small groups could traverse the countryside without alarming the Russians or the locals. Plus, it was easier to find food for a handful of soldiers than it was for a large group. These men remained unarmed throughout their journey.

On one occasion, a Polish farmer who could speak English understood what the men had gone through and knew their plight was far from over. He helped out in his own meager way. The elderly man, in order to make room in his small farmhouse for all the men, dismantled his bed and laid down wheat straw for them to sleep on.

The band of Americans walked through most of Poland and back into Russia, heading southeast toward the port of Odessa. The final week of travel was done by rail, with the luxury of heated boxcars. Since their escape from the enemy, the American soldiers had traveled approximately 900 miles.

Arriving at Odessa on the Black Sea, they found other POWs who had escaped in various ways and were awaiting their fate. The Russians were allowing the GIs—sparingly—transport via an Australian ship named *Moreton Bay*, which was anchored in the harbor. The ship was to leave as soon as they were done unloading supplies and a few thousand Russian POWs repatriated from the west. It was here that Sergeant Truesdale met his captain once again. George Dunkelberg had also escaped his captors and found his way to Odessa. They had parted under German gunpoint in September 1944 and now were ready to ship out toward home in March 1945. They greeted each other with a handshake and told each other their exploits.

The first thing the Germans had done was remove Dunkelberg from the group of POWs and place him in solitary confinement for five days. His only contact was with German interrogators at the camp called Frankfurt am Main. One of the enemy officers asked him what he expected to do after the war. He replied he would return to his prewar occupation, and asked the German what he was going to do after the war. The German officer replied, "Germany is finished. It may rise again, but I don't want to rise with it. If there is any place in the world where a German can go after the war and be decent, I want to go there." Dunkelberg was uncertain if the art of propaganda was being plied here or not.

After being moved several times from one temporary camp to another, he reached his final destination on November 13, 1944: *Oflag* 64 at Szubin near Bydgoszcz, Poland. This *Stalag* was the former POW camp for Brits after Dunkirk and the largest the Germans had for American army officers, numbering around 1,400. It was halfway between Warsaw and Berlin, positioned just outside a German troop concentration center for the Eastern Front. A major Russian offensive was to start on January 12, 1945, which put this camp directly in its path, with Berlin the final objective. But none of the Americans were aware of this upcoming drive.

Captain Dunkelberg, captured on September 19, was listed as MIA. His wife, Dorothy, and three young sons were notified of this via a Western Union telegram dated October 10, 1944. It read in part, "If further details or other information are received you will be promptly notified." Confirmation that he was alive as a POW came on November 10 via a telegram that originated from Washington, D.C.

At *Oflag* 64, the officers-only camp had some interesting activities. Besides the usual sports teams, a camp newspaper was published once a month. It was named *Freedom and Whitebread* (a popular 1920s Nazi party slogan was "Freedom and Bread"). Other reading material included a 2,000-volume library supplied by the YMCA. Classes were given, ranging from plain geometry to agriculture taught by Professor Dunkelberg, who before the war had taught at Clemson College in South Carolina. Musical instruments enabled the soldiers to form a swing band.

The POWs received Red Cross packages that supplemented their daily diet of one-sixth loaf of bread, two bowls of sugar beet soup, and a cup of ersatz coffee. The German diet for their American prisoners was kept at a starvation level of 1,300 daily calories; the universally accepted minimum was 1,800, even for those bedridden. Sudden movements such as standing up caused many to black out, especially at the roll calls done twice a day.

Dunkelberg's wife sent both food and clothing parcels at his request. The first request was for the following items: 2 pounds of Kraft cheese, 1 Kraft dinner, 12 ounces of Nescafé, 1 pound of rice, some compressed oats (three minutes), a small can of cinnamon, 1 pound of raisins or other dried fruit, some bouillon cubes, about a pound of Hershey bars and the same amount of solid candy, 1 pound of cocoa, 1 pound of dried peas or beans, tea, pancake flour or dried soup, and ten razor blades. Twenty-two letters and parcels were sent to Dunkelberg, but not one was received. All were returned to Fort Sill, Oklahoma; the reason was never known. The wool socks and dried fruit along with all the other items languished there for the rest of the war.

On January 20, the German guards gave the prisoners twenty-four hours' advance warning of a move. The entire camp was to be marched toward Berlin in compliance with the requirements of the Geneva Convention. Approximately 1,400 POWs would leave, but all the wounded were to remain. The reason was clear: the Russians were advancing. On the twenty-first, the camp was nearly emptied as they all marched west. The telephone lines sagged with the weight of ice, and the road was deep in snow. Along with Dunkelberg was Capt. James Coles of the 15th Infantry's L Company. Coles had been captured in France and received seven wounds while fighting with his unit.

On the third day of the march, three of the officers decided death from starvation would come soon if they didn't somehow escape. It was agreed that as soon as things looked right, all three of them would go. The large group of POWs was being marched west by 250 less-than-enthusiastic German guards. A few stated they would not shoot at escapees, but their comrades would. Some of the guards dumped their helmets and packs along the route. Stragglers were slowing the movement considerably, putting pressure on the enemy guards, who were afraid of running into the Russian onslaught. Germans who went to Poland to "resettle" it were now crowding the roads as refugees, heading for Germany. Many would yell at the Americans, "It's all your fault!" from their overloaded wagons. After four days of marching, still in Poland but nearing the German border, two Americans left the column to hide (the third officer stayed with the column). One hid in a Polish farmhouse, the other in a Polish field.

The Germans had a deadly routine when it was believed prisoners had escaped and hid in a farmer's fields. It was intended to instill a fear of dying by being wounded and left behind when the column moved out. Camp guards would go to the likely hiding spots, such as stacks of hay or barn stalls filled with straw or other crops. They would then either affix bayonets to their rifles and plunge them deep and hard into the hiding spot or fire an MP40 machine pistol into them, sometimes finding their target and leaving the men there to die.

The men of *Oflag* 64 knew these risks but took them anyway out of desperation. To some, it was either escape or starve, if the harsh winter elements didn't kill them first. Approximately 600 men would die on the march.

Captain Dunkelberg found a shock of wheat and stayed inside it. Coles located another suitable hiding spot nearby. Their guards noticed they were missing and started a search, but could not spend much time pursuing them. It was time for the column to move on. For five days, the two escaped soldiers hid with the Polish farmers until they heard tanks. The noise they made was familiar, but they didn't sound German. When the rumbling stopped, the men cautiously looked out and discovered a row of M4 American Sherman tanks operated by Russians. Their destination was Berlin. A decision was made that the former captives would fight with these Russian soldiers as riflemen. At least they would be armed.

For one week, they fought alongside their liberators. What they saw both amazed and repulsed this tiny American army. The drinking seemed constant. Women served alongside the men as equals; the only way of knowing was when their long hair fell from underneath the winter caps. The women even carried machine guns and drove tanks.

Captain Coles stated, "Many a time I have seen commanders point to a town and cry 'tuda,' meaning 'there,' and advance until they drew fire, then start shooting and moving forward. Their losses were terrible, but they seemed not to mind and kept going until somebody got there, and the town didn't amount to much when they were through with it. As far as I could see they paid little attention to tactics."

Communication was difficult. The only method that seemed to work was the "point and grunt" system. The men hoped the Russians would give the Americans documents that would allow them ease of travel to Moscow—or at least transportation of some sort in that direction. Allies or not, if they were to leave it was to be an "on your own" process, was the standard Russian response. The former POWs hit the road.

The Americans were stopped constantly and detained for days at a time. They were always asked the same question: "Where are your documents?" Of course they had none. Then they would be released, traveling to the next town either by foot, wagon, or truck, only to have the entire process repeated. One evening, they hitched a ride on a Russian truck carrying empty oil drums near the town of Katnow. The driver hit a shell crater in the road, sending the GIs up in the air. They landed spread-eagled on their backs on top of the oil drums. The injuries kept them stiff and sore for days. Captain Coles would suffer the rest of his life from injuries sustained that night.

Finally, the hungry and cold duo backtracked far south to Kiev and managed to board a train for Odessa, Russia. They had made it.

On the way back to the States, their ship pulled into an Italian port. Captain Dunkelberg heard about a seamstress at a particular shop who was an expert and could make anything. He located the place and drew the eagle shoulder patch of the 101st Division. He presented the drawing to her and asked if she could make one. His original was long gone, and it was time to replace it. She communicated in hand gestures that she would make the shoulder patch. Dunkelberg was quite satisfied with the finished product. There were no more questions regarding the division he was from because that patch said it all.

Capt. George Dunkelberg returned to his beloved Clemson College as a professor. Later, he successfully became mayor of the town, its first Republican mayor since Reconstruction.

Author's Note

MY GRANDFATHER, John L. Boycott, was an immigrant from Chester, England, and became a Canadian citizen in 1907. Wanting to show loyalty to their new country, his parents encouraged him to enlist and fight. They signed a waiver that allowed their underage son to join the Canadian Army. He was later assigned to the 1st Field Company Engineers of the 1st Canadian Division as a sapper. His time in France was spent on the Western Front. In 1917, he was wounded in the ankle by a German bullet; he recovered and was sent back to the front. Emotionally, the scars of war lasted a lifetime. In one of his letters sent from the front to his mother, he prophetically wrote, "I'm quite certain that this war will not end all wars."

Later in life, when he stayed with my family in Detroit, Michigan, I would hear him scream and moan at night. I learned later that after the war he underwent electric shock treatments to rid himself of those wartime nightmares.

In 1971, when I was fresh out of high school, my grandfather took me to Europe to walk the battlefields of his youth. He located them all from memory. But his deeper quest was to pay respect to his fallen comrades. He had attended graveside services for two of them in particular in 1916: Lt. Roland Walter Lines and Sapper Andrew Myllymaki were both killed by a German sniper on the same day at different locations. We did locate their graves at Albert Communal Cemetery, Somme, France. It was an enlightening experience that I never forgot.

Afterward, we talked of my chronicling his movements during the Great War and someday writing a book. I failed to do either one. In some small way, I sincerely hope that this book makes up for my earlier shortcomings.

Notes

CHAPTER 1

1. Joseph K. Perkins, *Mission Accomplished: A Story of the 321st Glider Field Artillery Battalion in WWII* (Salzburg, Austria: 1945), 16.
2. Ibid., 18.
3. Ibid., 19.
4. Just a few weeks earlier in March, a battle was being raged between the old army and the new, with Gen. George C. Marshall initiating changes for modern warfare and its doctrine. It was in this new army that Stephens and every other soldier were about to be enlisted. Maj. Gen. Robert Danford, chief of field artillery, wrote to General Marshall and argued for the continuation of horse-drawn artillery over the anticipated motor-drawn vehicles, reasoning that "horses could feed off the land and motor trucks could not."
5. More accurately, a P-51 airplane cost $51,000, a P-40 cost $45,000, and an early CG-4A cost $30,000. Once Ford Motor Company got its production up and running, the cost for a glider dropped to $18,500. For comparison, Ford dealerships sold their 1941 six-passenger station wagons for $950.
6. Glider secrecy was extremely important at this early stage of the war. The Germans were years ahead in this evolving field in terms of construction and tactics. However, the enemy did not have a glider capable of bringing in artillery. The British and the Americans would have that advantage shortly. The sight of a howitzer coming into battle by glider would be a first, and the 75mm pack howitzer would earn its keep.
7. In another version of the story, Matycich and Gring get credit for retrieving the major's body, but this was hotly disputed by Horner.

CHAPTER 2

1. Leonard Rapport and Arthur Northwood, *Rendezvous With Destiny* (Sweetwater, TN: 101st Airborne Division Association, 1948), 33.
2. In 2001, the author received a phone call from a BBC reporter, Claire, who had heard about my association with the 321st. She went on to say that an older lady was cleaning out her deceased mother's house and came across a suitcase. In it were handfuls of unopened letters sent to her during the war from Private Januskevitz, her former fiancé.
3. Joseph K. Perkins, *Mission Accomplished: A Story of the 321st Glider Field Artillery Battalion in WWII* (Salzburg, Austria: 1945), 46.
4. PFC Sidney Vaucher of Overland, Missouri, also attended the naval school, but it is unknown where he carried out his mission.

CHAPTER 3

1. Leonard Rapport and Arthur Northwood, *Rendezvous With Destiny* (Sweetwater, TN: 101st Airborne Division Association, 1948), 55.
2. *Rendezvous with Destiny*. On page 151, the text erroneously states that the *Susan B. Anthony* sank on June 6. This error caused quite a few 321st soldiers to question themselves on their memory.
3. Underwater photography has recently proven that two mines sunk the *Susan B. Anthony*. The Germans had developed underwater mines that allowed numerous ship contacts to occur without exploding, but whether or not this type of mine was responsible for the sinking is unknown.
4. Vernon Raker, untitled postwar narrative, 50.
5. RESTRICTED Headquarters Company, 327th Glider Infantry, APO #472, New York, NY, "History of Combat in France" (National Archives, College Park, MD: 1957), Box 1.
6. Joseph K. Perkins, *Mission Accomplished: A Story of the 321st Glider Field Artillery Battalion in WWII* (Salzburg, Austria: 1945), 49–50.

CHAPTER 4

1. Joseph K. Perkins, *Mission Accomplished: A Story of the 321st Glider Field Artillery Battalion in WWII* (Salzburg, Austria: 1945), 50.
2. Leonard Rapport and Arthur Northwood, *Rendezvous With Destiny* (Sweetwater, TN: 101st Airborne Division Association, 1948), 313.
3. Power pilot washout rate was 60 percent of the class.
4. Perkins, *Mission Accomplished*, 53–57.
5. Kiley "was killed by a sniper in the Woensel church tower. Someone got off a bazooka round, hit the tower and silenced the sniper." Rapport and Northwood, *Rendezvous with Destiny*, 302.
6. Hans den Brock.
7. Ibid., 256–57.
8. The CIC placed one officer and five enlisted men in each division. In 1939, the CIC had 16 men; as of December 6, 1941, it had grown to 513 men. "Counter Intelligence Corps: History and Mission in World War II," Carlisle Barracks, PA.
9. Rapport and Northwood, *Rendezvous With Destiny*, 352.
10. Perkins, *Mission Accomplished*, 59.
11. George Koskimaki, *Hells' Highway: A Chronicle of the 101st Airborne in the Holland Campaign, September–November 1944* (Sweetwater, TN: 101st Airborne Division Association, 1989), 393.
12. CONFIDENTIAL 321st Glider Journal, 2100 7 Oct 44, Serial number 135 (NARA: College Park, MD), 9.
13. Rapport and Northwood, *Rendezvous With Destiny*, 393.
14. Koskimaki, *Hell's Highway*, 423.
15. Ibid., 416.
16. For another account of this incident, see Koskimaki's *Hell's Highway*, 430–32.

CHAPTER 6

1. Joseph K. Perkins, *Mission Accomplished: A Story of the 321st Glider Field Artillery Battalion in WWII* (Salzburg, Austria: 1945), 67–68.
2. George E. Wilson, *This Is My Story* (Oklahoma: private printing, 2007), 36.

CHAPTER 7

1. Ian Brown, "The Final Days," Prisoners of War, www.stalag18a.org.uk/frameset.html (accessed December 26, 2012).
2. Ibid.
3. Headquarters, SECRET Unit Journal, 321st Glider Field Artillery Battalion, Period 1–10 May 1945 (College Park, MD: Department of the Army, June 13, 1945), 8.

APPENDIX 2

1. Excerpted from Jack Canfield, Mark Victor Hansen, and Sidney A. Slager, *Chicken Soup for the Veteran's Soul* (Deerfield Beach, FL: Health Communications, 2001), 133–34.

Bibliography

Bando, Mark A. *101st Airborne—The Screaming Eagles in WWII*. St. Paul, MN: Zenith Books, 2007.

———. *Avenging Eagles—Forbidden tales of the 101st Airborne Division in World War II*. Detroit, MI: Mark Bando Publishing, 2006.

Boycott, John L. *Universal Peace Through Religion*. Livonia, MI: Ekland Book Publishing Co., 1978.

Brok, Hans den. *Battle of Burp Gun Corner*. New Orleans: Walka Books, 2015.

———. *Wings of Freedom*. San Francisco: Blurb Publishing Co., 2010.

Brown, Ian. "The Final Days." Prisoners of War. www.stalag18a.org.uk/frameset.html. Accessed December 26, 2012.

Canfield, Jack, Mark Victor Hansen, and Sidney A. Slager. *Chicken Soup for the Veteran's Soul*. Deerfield Beach, FL: Health Communications, Inc., 2001.

Day, Charles L. *Silent Ones: WWII Invasion Glider Tests & Experiment, Clinton County Army Air Field*. Wilmington, OH: private publication, 2001.

Headquarters. SECRET Unit Journal, 321st Glider Field Artillery Battalion, Period 1–10 May 1945. College Park, MD: Department of the Army, June 13, 1945.

Henderson, Maj. Thomas D. "Normandy SECRET S-3 Report No. 1." 321st GFA Battalion. College Park, MD: June 19, 1944.

Koskimaki, George E. *Hell's Highway*. Sweetwater, TN: 101st Airborne Division Association, 1989.

MacKenzie, Fred. *The Men of Bastogne*. New York: David McKay Company, Inc., 1968.

Minick, Bob. *Kilogram: The Story of the 907th Glider Field Artillery Battalion*. Hobart, IN: private publication, 1979.

Perkins, Joseph K. *Mission Accomplished: A Story of the 321st Glider Field Artillery Battalion in WWII*. Salzburg, Austria, 1945.

Raker, Vernon. Untitled postwar narrative. Madera, CA, 1966.

Rapport, Leonard, and Arthur Northwood. *Rendezvous With Destiny*. Sweetwater, TN: 101st Airborne Division Association, 1948.

RESTRICTED Headquarters Company, 327th Glider Infantry, APO #472, New York, NY, "History of Combat in France." National Archives, College Park, MD: 1957.

Wilson, George E. *This Is My Story*. Oklahoma: private printing, 2007.

Acknowledgments

OVER THE TWENTY YEARS of conducting interviews and chasing down leads for this book, my twin daughters, Cassandra and Anthea, have been part of my research team. They were dragged across this country during our "family vacations." Despite spending hours on end waiting as I interviewed 321st boys, my girls did not complain.

We traveled through Europe hoping to get glimpses of former 321st gun emplacements. They never asked how long this book research was going to last.

Without my lovely bride, Helen, computer-savvy and even-keeled editor, this work would still be in lockdown on my ancient word processor. Whenever I became flustered, she calmed the waters and gave me encouragement. How lucky I am and continue to be.

Mentor, friend, and fellow policeman Mark A. Bando gave me the lead on this group of cannoneers in 1995. He walked me through many a problem. His unfaltering assistance and wealth of knowledge on the intricacies of the 101st Airborne Division were endless. Without him, this book would not have been written.

Others—most importantly 321st veterans themselves and their families—also contributed immensely to this work: Christine Wilkinson, Fred King, the Richard Fort family, Marilyn Smith, the Vaucher family, Tom Henderson, Greg Baker of Baker Graphics, Ricky Long, Sandy "Priya" McDivitt, Jean Mosbrook, Hans den Brok, Don Doubek, Charles Day, Brian Siddall, Cardon Thierry, Lee Rich, June Hollis, Jake Powers, DeAnn Vinson, Kathey Wilson, Ken McAuliffe, Tom Timmermans, Sandy Kowalczyk, Guert van Rinsum, Tom Cooper, and so many others.